Understanding, Diagnosing, and Treating AD/HD in Children and Adolescents

THE HANDBOOK
OF
INFANT, CHILD,
AND
ADOLESCENT
PSYCHOTHERAPY

A Series of Books from the

Reiss-Davis Child Study Center

ॐ

The Handbook of Infant, Child,
and Adolescent Psychotherapy:
A Guide to Diagnosis and Treatment
Volume 1

Bonnie S. Mark and James A. Incorvaia, editors

The Handbook of Infant, Child,
and Adolescent Psychotherapy:
New Directions in Integrative Treatment
Volume 2

Bonnie S. Mark and James A. Incorvaia, editors

Understanding, Diagnosing, and Treating
AD/HD in Children and Adolescents:
An Integrative Approach
Volume 3

*James A. Incorvaia, Bonnie S. Mark-Goldstein,
and Donald Tessmer, editors*

Understanding, Diagnosing, and Treating AD/HD in Children and Adolescents

AN INTEGRATIVE APPROACH
REISS-DAVIS CHILD STUDY CENTER
VOLUME 3

edited by
James A. Incorvaia, Ph.D.
Bonnie S. Mark-Goldstein, Ph.D.
Donald Tessmer, Ph.D.

JASON ARONSON INC.
Northvale, New Jersey
London

Production Editor: Elaine Lindenblatt

This book was set in 10 pt. Garamond and printed and bound by Book-mart Press, Inc. of North Bergen, New Jersey.

Library of Congress Cataloging-in-Publication Data

Understanding, diagnosing, and treating AD/HD in children and
    adolescents: an integrative approach/edited by James A. Incorvaia,
    Bonnie S. Mark, Donald Tessmer.
        p.   cm.
    Includes bibliographical references and index.
    ISBN 0-7657-0184-7
    1. Attention-deficit hyperactivity disorder. 2. Attention-deficit
-disordered youth. 3. Attention-deficit-disordered children.
    I. Incorvaia, James A. II. Mark, Bonnie S. III. Tessmer, Donald.
    RJ506.H9U54   1999
    618.92'8589—dc21   98–42746

Printed in the United States of America on acid-free paper. For information and catalog write to Jason Aronson Inc., 230 Livingston Street, Northvale, New Jersey 07647-1726. Or visit our website: www.aronson.com

Contents

PART III:
TREATMENT OF AD/HD
IN CHILDREN AND ADOLESCENTS

PART IV:
TREATING COMORBID LEARNING
DISABILITY SYMPTOMS IN AD/HD CHILDREN
AND ADOLESCENTS

PART V:
FUTURE TRENDS IN THE DIAGNOSIS AND TREATMENT OF AD/HD IN CHILDREN AND ADOLESCENTS

Preface

This book is devoted to a clinical area of child/adolescent work that is especially meaningful to me. Shortly after beginning my postdoctoral work at the Reiss-Davis Child Study Center in Los Angeles during the early 1970s, I also took a position, not far from there, at the Marianne Frostig Center for Educational Therapy as clinical director. While there, I had the privilege of working with Drs. Marianne Frostig, executive director, emeritus, and Mario Pascale, executive director, two leading professionals in the area of learning disabilities who played important parts in shaping my interest in and knowledge of the learning-disabled child. During the ten years that I spent at the Frostig Center, I also enjoyed working with the many learning-disabled children, their parents and their devoted teachers, and educational therapists. Though I also learned many different things from each of the people with whom I came in contact while I was working there, I especially grew to appreciate the immensity of the problems facing learning-disabled children and their families. I also grew to appreciate the extraordinary potential of these young people, if given the appropriate environment to grow and the appropriate services to remediate their learning and/or emotional problems.

While at Frostig, I first became aware of another important problem facing a number of the learning disabled children and adolescents at the school and center—something that was then called minimal brain dysfunction (MBD). This dysfunction caused some of these learning-disabled young people to have difficulty controlling their levels of activity and/or their ability to attend and concentrate. Though I did not know it then, that diagnostic category would grow, change its name, and by the mid-1990s become the most frequent psychiatric diagnosis given to children in our country—attention deficit/hyperactivity disorder (AD/HD).

When the Frostig Center moved to Altadena toward the end of the 1970s, I became concerned about the void in services to the learning-disabled and MBD child on the Westside due to its departure. Feeling the need to fill the void, I applied for and received a grant from the Parsons Foundation to develop the Psycho-Educational Diagnostic Service (PEDS) program at the Reiss-Davis Child Study Center in order to offer diagnostic evaluations for learning disabilities and its comorbid dysfunctions to young people on the Westside area of Los Angeles. As the program grew, services were expanded to include both educational and psychoeducational psychotherapy (see my article in Volume 2 of the *Handbook of Infant, Child, and Adolescent Psychotherapy*). We later developed a training component of our PEDS program for pre- and postdoctoral psychology and educational psychology students to receive specialized training in the assessment and treatment of learning disabilities and, more recently, of AD/HD.

By the late 1980s, I was aware that the AD/HD diagnosis was being given to an inordinate number of young people, and that the psychopharmacological treatment of choice, Ritalin, was being dispensed to children and adolescents like no other medication. Troubled by the inordinate use of this medication, concerned that the diagnosis was being overused, and fearing that children were being misdiagnosed as having AD/HD in place of other psychological problems, I wanted us at Reiss-Davis to start researching this phenomenon called attention deficit disorder.

At that time, together with Don Tessmer, the director of our PEDS Learning Disabilities Clinic, and Van DeGollia, the medical director, we developed an AD/HD clinic to study, diagnose, and treat those whom we found to have AD/HD. Because of the high incidence of the comorbidity of learning disabilities and AD/HD, starting in the early 1990s all children and adolescents being assessed for learning disabilities at Reiss-Davis were also evaluated through our AD/HD clinic. As a result we have seen hundreds of AD/HD children at the Center, and we have come to comprehend not only the reality of this psychiatric condition, but also the impact it has on those children and adolescents properly diagnosed with this disorder.

As we began to diagnose and treat these young people with AD/HD, it also became apparent to us that there had to be more than one subtype of dysfunction in this diagnostic category, for we were seeing not only the more popularized hyperactive-impulsive type but also the "quiet" inattentive type, and occasionally another, more overfocused, type of AD/HD child. In fact, as demonstrated in this volume, some researchers in the field are suggesting that there are as many as five or more subtypes of this dysfunction, and, more importantly, that different methods of psychopharmacological and other interventions appear to be needed for the most effective treatment of each subtype. As a result, more than ever before, to determine whether or not a child/adolescent has AD/HD, and if so, which subtype, necessitates a comprehensive diagnostic assessment, something that has always been an integral part of our Reiss-Davis program.

Through our work in the AD/HD clinic, we began to appreciate that AD/HD is a much more complex disorder than is represented in the popular literature, and that Ritalin may not always be the best or only way to treat this disorder. Our work also raised many questions about the state of knowledge and current practices in the field. This book, resulting from the search for answers to those questions, addresses the complexity of this dysfunction called AD/HD by focusing on the areas of diagnosis and treatment of the disorder and its comorbid dysfunctions, through assembling significant articles from a number of authors who have been concerned about the state of AD/HD and how our knowledge and clinical practices impact on children, adolescents, and their families.

James A. Incorvaia, Ph.D.
Director, Reiss-Davis Child Study Center

Acknowledgments

To compile a series of articles into an integrative approach to attention deficit hyperactivity disorder takes many people working together. The editors want to thank, first and foremost, the many authors who contributed their articles to this endeavor. Their special knowledge of AD/HD and their unique perspectives on how to better understand, diagnose, and treat this complex disorder have made it possible for us to assemble these wonderful articles under one cover. Without their contributions, this book could not have been written.

In addition to the authors, many others have given of their time and expertise to make this book a reality. We want to especially thank Grayce Stratton, Lynda Winkler, Lee Freehling, Jan Goldstein, Ariel Mark, and Marion and Matthew Solomon, for their assistance in seeing this project through.

We also want to thank the staff, fellows, and consultants of the Reiss-Davis Child Study Center for their encouragement as this book was being formed, and the many children and adolescents who taught us a great deal about AD/HD.

Finally, a note of gratitude to all those at Jason Aronson Inc., including acquisitions editor Cindy Hyden for her advice in developing this book, and also Jason Aronson, Michael Moskowitz, and Norma Pomerantz for their support. And a special thanks to Elaine Lindenblatt for guiding us through the editing of *Understanding, Diagnosing, and Treating AD/HD in Children and Adolescents: An Integrative Approach.*

Contributors

Daniel G. Amen, M.D., Director, Amen Clinic for Behavioral Medicine, Inc., Fairfield, CA.

Russell A. Barkley, Ph.D., Director of Psychology and Professor of Psychiatry and Neurology, Department of Psychiatry, University of Massachusetts Medical Center, Worcerster, MA.

Anne Hatcher Berenberg, Ph.D., Director of Psychology, Josselyn Center for Mental Health, Northfield, IL.

Deborah Berger-Reiss, Psy.D., Psychotherapist in private practice, Los Angeles, CA.

Thomas M. Brod, M.D., Assistant Clinical Professor, Department of Psychiatry, UCLA; private practice, Los Angeles, CA.

Dennis P. Cantwell, M.D., Joseph Campbell Professor of Child Psychiatry, UCLA Neuropsychiatric Institute (NPI), Department of Biobehavioral Sciences, Los Angeles, CA.

Persila Conversano, Psy.D., Associate Professor, California Graduate Institute; Consultant, Reiss-Davis Child Study Center; private practice, Beverly Hills, CA.

Leah Ellenberg, Ph.D., Associate Clinical Professor of Pediatrics and

Psychology, University of Southern California School of Medicine; Diplomate in clinical neuropsychology; private practice specializing in neuropsychological evaluations, Malibu and Beverly Hills, CA.

Michael J. Goldberg, M.D., Staff: UCLA, Cedars-Sinai, Regional Medical Center of Encino; Director of the Neuro-Immune Dysfunction Syndromes, medical advisory board and research institute; private practice, Tarzana, CA.

Lawrence Greenberg, M.D., Professor Emeritus of Child and Adolescent Psychiatry, University of Minnesota; Director of Research and author of the T.O.V.A., St. Paul, MN.

James A. Incorvaia, Ph.D., Director, Reiss-Davis Child Study Center; former Director of Clinical Services, Marianne Frostig Center; Assistant Clinical Professor, Department of Child Psychiatry, UCLA NPI; private practice, Brentwood, CA.

David A. Kaiser, Ph.D., Cognitive neuroscientist at EEG Spectrum, Encino, CA.

Marcel Kinsbourne, M.D., Professor of Neurology, Eunice Kennedy Shriver Center, Waltham, MA; Harvard Medical School, Boston, MA; private practice, New York City.

Judith Kushnet, M.F.C.C., Co founder and Director of Advancement, Center For Counseling and Training; Supervisor, Maple Counseling Center; former consultant, Reiss-Davis Child Study Center and Pacific Hills High School; private practice, Beverly Hills, CA.

Dani Levine, Ph.D., Consultant, Reiss-Davis Child Study Center; psychologist, Westmark School; Adjunct Professor, California Graduate Institute and Ryokan College; private practice, Tarzana, CA.

Bonnie S. Mark-Goldstein, Ph.D., Supervisor, Maple Counseling Center; instructor, UCLA extension; private practice, Los Angeles, CA.

Siegfried Othmer, Ph.D., previous Cornell University physicist; Chief Scientist, EEG Spectrum, a clinical service delivery organization and network of EEG biofeedback clinicians, Encino, CA.

Susan F. Othmer, B.A., Biofeedback Certification Institute of America-Certified (BCIAC), previous postgraduate work in physics and neurophysiology at Cornell and Brain Research Institute at UCLA; Clinical Director, EEG Spectrum, Encino, CA.

Joseph Palombo, L.C.S.W., Founding Dean of the Institute for Clinical Social Work, Chicago Institute of Psychoanalysis; research associate, Department of Pediatrics, Rush-Presbyterian-St. Luke's Medical Center; private practice, Chicago, IL.

Sebastiano Santostefano, Ph.D., Director, Institute for Child and Adolescent Development; former Director, Department of Child and Adolescent Psychology and Psychoeducation, Hall-Mercer Children's Center of McLean Hospital; Associate Professor of Psychology, Department of Psychiatry, Harvard Medical School; private practice, Wellesley, MA.

Terri L. Shelton, Ph.D., University of Massachusetts Medical Center; Assumption College, Worcester, MA.

Dana Levin Shrager, Psy.D., Consultant and psychoeducational therapist, Reiss-Davis Child Study Center; clinical and educational therapist, private practice, Beverly Hills, CA.

Lance Steinberg, M.D., Clinical instructor, UCLA, Cedars Sinai; private practice, Encino, Calabassas, and Beverly Hills, CA.

Donald Tessmer, Ph.D., Director of Educational Services, Center for Early Education; former Director of the PEDS Learning Disability Clinic, Reiss-Davis Child Study Center; private practice, Los Angeles, CA.

Introduction

Attention deficit/hyperactivity disorder (AD/HD) is the most diagnosed psychiatric disorder of childhood and adolescence. Estimates of AD/HD range from 3.5 million to 17 million children and adults, with all researchers agreeing that boys are likely to be diagnosed with this disorder six times as often as girls. At least 1.3 million of the children in the United States are treated for AD/HD with a drug called methylphenidate, selling under the brand name Ritalin, while the rest of the world uses only about 20 percent of the rate used in our country. It is no wonder, then, that there are a large number of books published each year on this subject.

But why another book, you may ask? First, it should be noted that most of the books on AD/HD are written from one perspective. The author has a point of view to present, related to this disorder, one with which he hopes the reader will agree and possibly embrace. Unfortunately, because of the plethora of material currently available to the professional and lay public alike, there are many viewpoints, each purporting to have the "answer." This book differs in that it presents a number of viewpoints in three areas that the editors feel are important to consider in working with AD/HD children and adolescents: methods of diagnosing the disorder, approaches to treatment, and the consideration of techniques to use for one particular comorbid disorder—learning disabilities—that affects a large number of those with AD/HD.

Second, from the experiences many of those contributing to this book have encountered in diagnosing and treating this disorder, and its attendant comorbid dysfunction of learning disabilities, in children and adolescents, a number of issues have been raised, a number of observations have been noted, and a number of ideas have been developed. It is the hope of the editors of this book that presenting these issues, observations, and ideas, with only one overriding theme—the wish that the reader be open to considering multiple approaches and techniques in working with this complex disorder—will ultimately lead clinicians in this field to move toward an integrative approach to the understanding, diagnosing, and treating of AD/HD in children and adolescents.

This book, a journey into this complex disorder of childhood AD/HD, is divided into five sections. In Part I, the late Dr. Dennis P. Cantwell, a pioneer in the field of AD/HD, begins the journey into the understanding, diagnosis, and treatment of this disorder by presenting an overview of the state of attention-deficit disorder from 1986 to 1996.

Between the first chapter, where Dr. Cantwell reviews the state of AD/HD over the last ten years, and the last chapter, which focuses on Dr. Michael Goldberg's look at future trends in the field, there is a wide array of important articles on the diagnosis and treatment of AD/HD and its comorbid disorder—learning disabilities. Because it is our view that without the proper diagnosis the treatment of AD/HD can be no more than left to chance, in Part II diagnostic issues are addressed from a variety of perspectives. Once the proper diagnosis is made, one is ready to deal with the appropriate treatment modality. Part III is devoted to various treatment approaches, not only the more traditional method of psychopharmacological intervention, but also the other modalities and adjunctive services that can be used to help the AD/HD child or adolescent.

In Part IV, one particular comorbid dysfunction, one that affects many AD/HD children and adolescents—learning disabilities—is discussed from a number of perspectives. Finally, as noted above, in Part V, Dr. Goldberg, beginning where Dr. Cantwell's initial article ended, takes us on the final leg of our journey, as he suggests current as well as future trends in the diagnosis and treatment of AD/HD as we approach the new millennium.

It is our hope that the reader will find this a very informative and stimulating journey into the complex world of child and adolescent attention deficit/hyperactivity disorder. It is also our hope that the reader will take many of these varying views of current thought and practice in the field and use them to develop a more integrated, comprehensive model for diagnosing and remediating AD/HD in young people.

PART I

Introduction to the Field of AD/HD

INTRODUCTION TO PART I

No book on AD/HD would be complete without at least some reference to the pioneering work of the late Dennis P. Cantwell, M.D., a UCLA child psychiatrist internationally known for his research on attention deficit/hyperactivity disorder. His death on April 15, 1997, at age 58, was a tremendous loss to the field.

Dr. Cantwell was the Joseph Campbell Professor of Child Psychiatry at UCLA and was the recipient of numerous awards, including the Agnes Purcell McGavin Award and the APA Award for Research in Psychiatry from the American Psychiatric Association, the J. Franklin Robinson Award for Research in Child Psychiatry, the Blanche Ittleson Prize for Research in Child Psychiatry, the Norbert Reiger Award, the Elaine Schlosser Lewis Awards from the American Academy of Child and Adolescent Psychiatry, the Edward A.

Strecker Award, the Rosenberry Award, the C. Charles Burlingame Award from the Institute of the Living, the Lifetime Achievement Award from the Southern California Psychiatric Society, the William D. Reynolds Award and the Emil T. Hofman Award from the University of Notre Dame, and the Lifetime Achievement Award from the Washington University School of Medicine.

Dennis Cantwell received his undergraduate degree from Notre Dame University and graduated from Washington University School of Medicine, where he also did his residency training. He joined UCLA in 1970 and was appointed Joseph Campbell Professor in 1980. From 1972 to 1991 he was also the director of residency training in child psychiatry. Dr. Cantwell, who had an international reputation in the areas of child psychiatric research, training, and practice, was admired by students and professionals alike, here in Los Angeles, for his encyclopedic knowledge and extraordinary grasp of children and their families, all conveyed in a sensitive yet humorous style.

There is no question that Dr. Cantwell's research has contributed significantly to many important changes in the diagnosis and treatment of child and adolescent mental health problems. During his career, he authored or co-edited five books and over 200 research articles and chapters in the area of child mental health.

While Dr. Cantwell believed firmly in the use of medication in the treatment of AD/HD, he was open to exploring other avenues of treatment as well. In fact, just before his untimely death, he was about to embark on some new and vital research at UCLA into an alternative form of intervention, electro encephalograph (EEG) biofeedback with two leaders in that field, Sue and Siegfried Othmer. His breadth of knowledge and many contributions to the field of AD/HD in children and adolescents as well as his continued interest in furthering the understanding and treatment of AD/HD is an inspiration to all of us who work in the field of child and adolescent mental health. For these reasons, and because he so well represents the integrative approach on which this book is based, we have chosen to honor him by dedicating this book to his memory.

Chapter 1 presents one of Dr. Cantwell's last articles, which summarizes his unique view of the condition of AD/HD over the span of 1986 to 1996. His article begins our journey into the better understanding of this complex and often misunderstood disorder.

1

Attention Deficit Disorder: A Review of the Past Ten Years

Dennis P. Cantwell

Attention deficit disorder (ADD) is one of the most important disorders that child and adolescent psychiatrists treat. It is important because it is highly prevalent, making up as much as 50 percent of child psychiatry clinical populations. It is a persistent problem that may change its manifestation with development from preschool through adult life. In interferes with many areas of normal development and functioning in a child's life. Untreated, it predisposes a child to psychiatric and social pathology in later life. More importantly, it can be successfully treated.

This chapter first appeared in the *Journal of the American Academy of Child and Adolescent Psychiatry*, vol. 35, no. 8, pp. 978–987, copyright © 1996 by Waverly, Baltimore, MD, and is reprinted by permission.

EPIDEMIOLOGY

The figure usually given for prevalence of ADD in the general population is approximately 3 to 5 percent of school-age children. This figure does not take into account preschool, adolescent, and adult populations. Prevalence rates, however, vary according to the population that is sampled, the diagnostic criteria, and diagnostic instruments that are used. More recent data suggest higher figures in school-age children.

Wolraich and colleagues (1996) and Baumgaertel and colleagues (1995) have recently completed two epidemiological studies using *DSM-IV* criteria (American Psychiatric Association 1994). One was conducted in Tennessee and one in Germany. Teacher information was the sole source of data in both studies. The prevalence rates for the primarily inattentive, primarily hyperactive, and combined subtypes of *DSM-IV* ADD in the Tennessee sample were 4.7, 3.4, and 4.4 percent, respectively. In the German sample the rates for the same subtypes were 9.0, 3.9, and 4.8 percent respectively.

Both in clinical and epidemiological samples the condition is much more common in males—9 to 1 in clinical samples, and 4 to 1 in epidemiological samples. This suggests selective referral bias, since girls may have primarily inattentive and cognitive problems and less of the aggressive/impulsive conduct symptomatology that leads to earlier referral (Baumgaertel et al. 1995, Cantwell 1994b, Wolraich et al. 1996).

ETIOLOGY

The etiology of ADD is unknown. It is unlikely that one etiological factor leads to all cases of what we call the clinical syndrome of ADD. Most likely there is an interplay of both psychosocial and biological factors that leads to a final common pathway of the syndrome of ADD. Thus, there are some known conditions such as fragile X syndrome, fetal alcohol syndrome, very low birth weight children, and a very rare, genetically transmitted thyroid disorder that can present behaviorally with symptoms of ADD. However, these cases make up only a small portion of the total population of children with the diagnosis (Arnold and Jensen 1995, Cantwell 1994b).

Early ideas were that this condition was some type of brain damage. This idea was derived from the early studies of children who had suffered encephalitis in the encephalitis epidemic of 1917 and 1918. More recent studies of brain morphology involve modern and much more sophisticated measures. Hynd and colleagues (1990) produced magnetic resonance imaging findings suggesting that children with ADD had normal plana temporal, but abnormal frontal lobes.

Giedd and colleagues (1994) demonstrated reduced volume in the rostrum and rostral body of the corpus callosum. This has been interpreted as being consistent with an alteration of functioning of the prefrontal and anterior cingulate cortices of the brain in addition to altered premotor function (Steere and Arnsten 1995).

Pathophysiology of ADD has also been investigated using other imaging techniques including single photon emission computed tomography (SPECT) and positron emission tomography (PET) (Lou et al. 1989, Zametkin et al. 1990). SPECT studies revealed focal cerebral hypofusion of striatum and hyperfusion in sensory and sensorimotor areas. The PET study by Zametkin and colleagues was of adults with ADD who had a child with ADD. Compared with normal adults, the adults with ADD had lower cerebral glucose metabolism in the promotor cortex and in the superior prefrontal cortex. These brain areas are involved in the control of motor activity and attention. The same authors used PET to study adolescents with ADD. The results were not as strong. Adolescent females with ADD did have reduced glucose metabolism globally compared with normal control females and males, and compared with males with ADD (Cantwell 1994b, Zametkin 1993).

The results might be explained on the basis of the adults having a "familial" and a persistent subtype of ADD. All adults in the Zametkin study continued to manifest the syndrome from childhood on and had a child with ADD. It may be that the adolescents did not all have a familial subtype and/or that their ADD will not persist into adult life.

There is general agreement that psychophysiological studies have not revealed global autonomic underactivity in children with ADD. However, a more specific pattern of underreactivity to stimulation has been suggested by studies showing more rapid heart rate deceleration and smaller orienting responses on galvanic skin response, greater slow-wave activities of the EEG, smaller amplitudes of response to stimulation, and more rapid habituation on average evoked responses to stimuli (Barkley 1990).

Family genetic factors have been implicated as etiological in ADD for some twenty-five years. Heritability is estimated to be between 0.55 to 0.92. Concordance was 51 percent in monozygotic twins and 33 percent in dizygotic twins in one study (Goodman and Stevenson 1989). Family aggregation studies have shown that the ADD syndrome and related problems do run in close family members (Biederman et al. 1989). Adoption studies support that this "running in families" is genetic rather than environmental (Barkely 1990, Cantwell 1975). At this point, no gene has been described or found, but this is an active area of research and is likely to bear fruit in the foreseeable future.

The positive response of ADD individuals to central nervous system (CNS) stimulants and antidepressants logically suggested catecholamine abnormalities in ADD. There is a substantial body of literature reporting both animal and human studies that used blood, urine, and cerebrospinal fluid (CSF), but results are inconsistent (Zametkin and Rapoport 1986). Low dopamine and norepinephrine turnover is suggested by most studies. However, there is interaction between the serotonin and catecholamine systems and any "one drug–one neurotransmitter" hypothesis is too simplistic. Psychosocial factors are not thought to play a primary etiological role. Various types of parent–child relationships and family dysfunction are found in families of children with ADD. Interaction conflicts with their mothers are more common in younger children with ADD than in older children with ADD. In the older adolescent age range, more noncompliant and negative verbalizations are reported in families of children with ADD than in families of normal children. These psychosocial factors are thought to be primarily related to development of oppositional defiant disorder and conduct disorder rather than to the core symptoms of ADD.

Some environmental etiological factors have been proposed. These include various pre- and perinatal abnormalities, toxins such as lead and various food additives, sugar intoxication, and orthomolecular theories of a great need for vitamins and nutrients in children with ADD. None of these has received substantial empirical support (Arnold and Jensen 1995, Barkley 1990).

CORE CLINICAL CRITERIA

Although *DSM-III*, *DSM-III-R*, and *DSM-IV* differ on the exact core symptoms and how they are arranged, they are actually globally quite consistent. There is general agreement that the core symptoms consist of an inattention domain and a hyperactivity/impulsivity domain. *DSM-III* arranged these domains in three separate symptom areas. *DSM-III-R* grouped them in one long symptom list. *DSM-IV* lists them as two core dimensions. There are nine symptoms of each dimension in *DSM-IV*. *DSM-IV* maintains the requirement of an early age of onset (before the age of 7 years), presence for six months or longer (to indicate chronicity), and presence in two or more settings (to indicate pervasiveness of symptoms). *DSM-IV* describes a combined subtype in which the individual has six or more symptoms out of nine from both the inattention dimension and the hyperactive/impulsive dimension. The predominantly inattentive subtype consists of six or more inattention symptoms and five or fewer hyperactive/impulsive symptoms. A predominantly hyperactive/impulsive type consists of six or more symptoms of the hyperactive/impulsive dimension and five or fewer of the inattention dimension. The symptoms must be more frequent and severe than those of children of comparable developmental level and must cause significant functional impairments. Across children, the symptoms may vary in their frequency of occurrence, in their pervasiveness across settings, and in the degree of functional impairment in various areas. Also, with the same child some settings may enhance or decrease symptom manifestation. For example, open classrooms may bring out more symptoms than classrooms that are more structured.

DEVELOPMENTAL PSYCHOPATHOLOGY

The core symptoms of ADD may change over time. Most of our knowledge base comes from studies of elementary school-age boys with ADD. There are fewer studies of younger children and adolescents and a growing body of literature on adults.

In the preschool age range, the most difficult differential diagnostic problem is with normally active, exuberant preschool children. Many parents of normal children describe their children as inattentive and hyperactive. The preschool child with true ADD, which persists over time, generally has such additional symptoms as temper tantrums, argumentative behavior, aggressive behavior (hitting others and taking others' possessions), and fearless behavior that leads to frequent accidental injury and noisy, boisterous behavior. Noncompliance is often a major problem with these youngsters, as is sleep disturbance (Campbell 1990). One follow-up study by Campbell (1990) showed that about one-half of preschool children with a diagnosis of hyperactivity had a clear diagnosis of ADD by age 9. The children with more severe symptoms in preschool were likely to have the most persistent ADD over time.

The various *DSM* criteria have been based on the clinical picture in elementary school–age children. Cognitively effortful work is most difficult for these children. Thus, entering into the academic arena in the elementary school age range puts greater stress on the cognitive domain. In addition, their impulsivity, hyperactivity, and inattention often lead to difficulty in peer relationships, which first becomes manifest in the elementary school age range. Elementary school children also may begin to develop comorbid symptomatology such as noncompliant behavior.

The clinical presentation of ADD in adolescents has not been studied as systematically as in younger children (Barkley 1990). Barkley suggests that not only do the symptom manifestations change with age, but that a lower number of symptoms should be considered as indicative of the diagnosis in the adolescent age range and possibly the adult age range. Adolescents are in junior high school or high school, where they no longer have one teacher in one class, but now have multiple teachers in multiple classes. In addition, adolescent demands for a greater degree of independence and development of both same-sex and opposite-sex peer relationships may present conflicts. The core symptoms may be manifest now as an internal sense of restlessness rather than gross motor activity. Their inattention and cognitive problems may lead to poorly organized approaches to school and work and poor follow-through on tasks. Failing to complete independent academic work is a hallmark in the adolescent age range, and a continuation of risky types of behaviors such as more frequent auto and bike accidents may also be manifestations (Weiss and Hechtman 1994).

The study of the adult syndrome is a much more recent phenomenon. A variety of different symptoms in adults have been described by Wender (1994), Barkley (1995), Conners (1995), and Hallowell and Ratey (1994). The presence of disorganization continues to have an impact in the workplace, often requiring written lists of activities to be used as reminders. Poor concentration may continue to persist into adult life, leading to shifting activities, not finishing projects, and moving from one activity to another. Procrastination is present, as are intermittent explosive outbursts, which may be related to comorbid mood symptomatology or may be a special type of labile mood described by Wender (1994).

COMORBIDITY

Comorbidity is a major problem in children, adolescents, and adults with the ADD syndrome. As many as two-thirds of elementary school–age children with ADD who are referred for clinical evaluation have at least one other diagnosable psychiatric disorder (Arnold and Jensen 1995, Cantwell 1994b, Nottelman and Jensen 1995). The actual comorbid conditions and their prevalence rates may vary across different types of samples, depending on whether the sample is clinical or epidemiological and whether a clinical sample is pediatric or psychiatric. Conduct disorder and oppositional defiant disorder seem to be higher in psychiatric samples, and learning disorders in pediatric samples. The major comorbid conditions include language and communication disorders, learning disorders, conduct and oppositional defiant disorder, anxiety disorders, mood disorders, and Tourette's syndrome or chronic tics (Cantwell 1994b). A type of comorbidity described by Cantwell as "lack of social savoir-faire" is not a diagnosable condition in the *DSM* sense. However, it does describe a common problem that many ADD children, adolescents, and adults have. It is an inability to pick up on social cues, leading to difficulties in interpersonal relationships.

Cormorbidity complicates the diagnostic process and can impact on natural history and prognosis and the management of children, adolescents, and adults with ADD. Assessment and treatment of the comorbid disorder is often equally as important as assessing and treating the ADD symptomatology. It may be that some of the comorbid conditions, such as ADD plus Tourette's syndrome or ADD plus conduct disorder, may identify subgroups of ADD children with different natural histories and possibly different underlying etiological factors and different responses to treatment. At present, the practicing clinician simply must carry a high index of suspicion for other types of disorders when assessing the child who has ADD. In particular, the internalizing problems such as anxiety and mood disorders may be underreported by parents and teachers, who are better able to see the externalizing behaviors.

DIFFERENTIAL DIAGNOSIS AND ASSESSMENT

It should be kept in mind that in the differential diagnosis of ADD in children there are conditions that in some cases may be comorbid and in other cases may mimic "true" ADD. A good example would be absence seizures, which may mimic the clinical presence of ADD in some cases and may be associated with a true ADD syndrome in others. The differential diagnosis must rule out the presence of other psychiatric disorders, developmental disorders, and medical and neurological disorders and determine whether these are comorbid or whether they are mimicking an ADD syndrome.

The diagnosis of ADD is a clinical diagnosis. It is made on the basis of a clinical picture that begins early in life, is persistent over time, is pervasive across different settings, and causes functional impairment at home, at school, or in leisure activity. The is no laboratory test or set of tests that currently can be used to make a definitive diagnosis of ADD (Arnold and Jensen 1995, Barkley 1990). The clinician has a number of diagnostic tools, including parent and child interviews, observations of the parent and child, behavior rating scales, physical and neurological examinations, and cognitive testing. Laboratory studies such as audiology and vision testing may be useful in some cases but not others. Detailed speech and language evaluation may be appropriate in some cases. Developmental questionnaires and behavior rating scales for completion by the teacher and parents can be mailed out prior to the first visit. The initial parent visit should consist of a detailed developmental and symptomatic history and a detailed medical, neurological, family, and psychosocial history. The diagnostic process must occur in a developmental context. Symptoms are considered to be present and meaningful only if they are in excess of what would be expected in a child of the same age and cognitive level.

The nature and content of the interview with the child vary, of course, with age and developmental levels. Nevertheless, the goal is the same: to obtain, both spontaneously and in response to direct questions, the patient's report of various types of psychiatric symptoms and their impact on the patient's life.

In the assessment process a variety of rating scales can be used to gather information from parents, teachers, other significant adults, and in some cases the patient. These can be generally divided into broad- and narrow-range scales. An example of a broad-range scale is the Child Behavior Checklist development by Achenbach (1993). It contains items on a variety of dimensions, not just inattention and hyperactivity. It is useful as a broad-based screener. There is a parent and a teacher version.

More specific scales have been developed for ADD (Hinshaw 1994), such as those by Conners (1995), the SNAP-IV by Swanson, Nolan, and Pelham (Swanson 1995), and the Disruptive Behavior Disorder Scale by Pelham (1992). A diagnosis is not made on the basis of a score on one scale. Rather it is made when the clinician has collected all the available information and on that basis determines that ADD is present, determines whether there is or is not comorbidity, and determines what possibly important biological and psychosocial factors should be considered. Good measures of current intellectual functioning and current level of academic achievement are useful for every child. The need for further testing will then depend on the results of the clinical evaluation.

Specialized tests such as the Continuous Performance Test (in its various permutations), the Wisconsin Card-Sorting Test, the Matching Familiar Figures Test, and subtests of the Wechsler Intelligence Scale for Children–Revised (WISC-R) should not be considered diagnostic of ADD (DuPaul et al. 1992). Tests that measure cognitively effortful work, such as the Paired Associate Learning (PAL) Task, may be useful because they most approximate a laboratory measure of classroom learning. The PAL is likely to pick up "cognitive toxicity" caused by high dosages of medication, which may not be noticed simply by the use of behavior rating scales. However, the PAL is not diagnostic of ADD either. There is no specific diagnostic test of ADD (Cantwell and Swanson 1992).

The core symptoms of ADD may occur in other psychiatric conditions and may be precipitated by medical and neurological conditions. In some cases a child, parent, or teacher may be unreliable as an informant. There may be negative findings in a brief, one-time interview with the child. All of these findings lead to pitfalls in the diagnostic process, but they can be overcome with the proper diagnostic approach. Such a diagnostic approach involves the following (Reiff et al. 1993):

- A comprehensive interview with all parenting figures. This interview should pinpoint the child's symptoms so that the clinician can discern when, where, with whom, and with what intensity these symptoms occur. This should be complemented by a developmental, medical, school, and family social, medical, and mental health history.

- A developmentally appropriate interview with the child to assess the child's view of the presence of signs and symptoms; the child's awareness of and explanation of any difficulties; and, most importantly, at least a screening for symptoms of other disorders, especially anxiety, depression, suicidal ideation, hallucinations, and unusual thinking.

- An appropriate medical evaluation to determine general health status and to screen for sensory deficits, neurological problems, or other physical explanations for the observed difficulties.

- Appropriate cognitive assessment of ability and achievement.
- The use of broad-spectrum and more narrowly ADD focused parent and teacher rating scales. Appropriate adjunct assessments such as speech and language assessment, and evaluation of fine and gross motor function in selected cases (Braswell and Bloomquist 1994).

NATURAL HISTORY

In the past it was believed that all children with ADD "outgrew" their problem. This outgrowing was supposed to occur with puberty. We now know from prospective studies that this is not true. Cantwell (1985) has described three potential types of outcomes. One is described as a "developmental delay" outcome. This may occur in 30 percent of the subjects. With this outcome, sometime early in young adult life the individual no longer manifests any functionally impairing ADD symptoms. The second outcome has been called the "continual display" outcome. This may occur in about 40 percent of child subjects. In this case, functionally impairing symptoms of ADD continue into adult life. In addition, these symptoms may be accompanied by a variety of different types of social and emotional difficulties. The last outcome, which may occur in as many as 30 percent of subjects, Cantwell describes as a "developmental decay" outcome. In these cases not only is there a continual display of core ADD symptoms, but there is the development of more serious psychopathology such as alcoholism, substance abuse, and antisocial personality disorder. One of the strongest predictors of this most negative outcome is the presence of comorbid conduct disorder with ADD in childhood.

Recent studies of adults with retrospectively diagnosed ADD suggest there may be people (particularly females) who had unrecognized ADD in childhood, who were not evaluated in childhood, and yet who seem to make a reasonable adjustment in adult life. They present with a wide range of comorbid adult disorders such as anxiety disorders and mood disorders (Wender 1994), even though they have made a reasonable adjustment without treatment. A combination of psychosocial and medical interventions improves their functioning

(Hallowell and Ratey 1994, Wender 1994). It is interesting that in most samples of those who present as adults with no childhood evaluation or treatment, a substantially greater number of females has been present.

MANAGEMENT

It is now recognized that management of the ADD syndrome requires a multiple-modality approach (American Academy of Child and Adolescent Psychiatry 1991, Braswell et al. 1991, Hechtman 1993, Pelham 1994, Swanson 1992). A multiple-modality approach combines psychosocial interventions and medical interventions. The psychosocial interventions that have proven to be effective for children with ADD can be classified as those psychosocial interventions that focus on the family, the school, and the child. Among the family-focused interventions are education about what ADD is and what it is not. Support groups such as CHADD (Children with Attention Deficit Disorder) and ADDA (Attention Deficit Disorder Association) are quite helpful in the psychoeducation process and are useful for other reasons such as providing group support and knowledge about working with school systems and about resources in the community. A number of books now available for parents, teachers, and the children themselves are useful adjuncts to treatment.

Parent management training is almost a sine qua non of psychosocial interventions with ADD. Training parents to use contingency management techniques and to cooperate with the school in a school–home daily report card and point/token response cost system is highly effective. Parent management training has been shown not only to reduce the child's disruptive behavior in the home setting, but also to increase the parents' own self-confidence in their competence as parents and to decrease family stress. Both individual and group formats have been used for parent management training. Some clinicians such as Brown and Cantwell (1976) have used older siblings in addition to parents to serve as positive reinforcement and to make positive interactions. Assessment and treatment of parental psychopathology and more specific assessment and treatment of family dysfunction such as marital conflict are always indicated.

School-focused intervention should target academic performance. However, classroom behavior and peer relationships are also important. The most appropriate classroom is probably a structured classroom with the child placed in the front of the room, close to the teacher, where he or she may be less easily distracted and more able to focus. Children with ADD respond to predictable, well-organized schedules with rules that are known and clearly reinforced in the classroom setting. Contingency management and daily teacher-completed report cards showing the child's progress in targeted areas of improvement are hallmarks of this type of intervention (Braswell and Bloomquist 1994). Incentives and tangible rewards, reprimands, and time-outs in the classroom setting can also be used in school as well as in the home.

School placement is a crucial issue. While many if not most children with ADD will remain in a regular classroom setting, some may need individual tutoring, some may need a resource program, some may need a self-contained special class (primarily for academic reasons), and some with complex problems may need a special school. The clinician can play a major role in assessing the need for specialized school intervention and in facilitating school placement.

The child-focused interventions include the use of individual psychotherapy to treat any depression, low self-esteem, anxiety, or other types of associated symptomatology. There should be a concerted effort to improve the child's impulse control, anger control, and social skills. Social skills training programs focus on the child's entry into the social group, the development of conversational skills and problem-solving skills, as well as those factors noted above. Impaired social skills are an extremely important part of the negative aspect of children with ADD (Pelham and Bender 1982). Problems caused by the "in your face" type of behavior associated with impulsivity and hyperactivity may be more easily treated than the lack of social savoir-faire described by Cantwell (1994b).

A number of summer treatment programs have been developed in which the child is in an intense school program for eight weeks, eight hours per day. The day involves not only academic work but behavioral management, social skills, and individual work with the child. There is then an attempt to carry over the school program into the regular school by the use of paraprofessionals in the regular class-room setting (Swanson 1992).

The primary psychopharmacological agents used to treat ADD are the CNS stimulants (Cantwell 1994a, Wilens and Biederman 1992). The prototype drugs are dextroamphetamine, methylphenidate, and pemoline. There are a number of amphetamines including metham-phetamine and dextroamphetamine, but dextroamphetamine probably enjoys the greatest use. Methylphenidate is probably used more than any of the other stimulants. At least 70 percent of children will have a positive response to one of the major stimulants on the first trial. If a clinician conducts a trial of dextroamphetamine, methylphenidate, and pemoline, the response rate to at least one of these is in the 85 to 90 percent range, depending on how response is defined (Elia 1993).

While it is clear that the medications target classroom behavior, academic performance (Evans and Pelham 1991), and productivity (Swanson et al. 1991), there is also good evidence to show that ADD children with oppositional and conduct symptomatology and aggres-sive behavior also respond positively in these areas as well. Interac-tions between the child and peers, family, siblings, teachers, and sig-nificant others (such as scout masters and coaches) also improve. In addition, participation in leisure activity, such as playing baseball, improves (Cantwell 1994b). The main message is that stimulants are not "school-time drugs." They should be used throughout the wak-ing day and on the weekends as well. There is no way to pick the first stimulant to be tried because, essentially, they are equally effec-tive (Pelham et al. 1990). Some children respond better to one than to another, but response is idiosyncratic and cannot be predicted.

Side effect profiles may be better for one child with one drug than another, but in general all stimulants share side effects of decreased appetite, insomnia, stomachache, headache, and irritability. Most side effects dissipate with time, and many can be managed with various types of manipulation (Cantwell 1994b). Growth suppression appears to be dose-related, if it occurs at all. There does not seem to be strong evidence that adverse effects on the patient's ultimate height has been present in the long-term follow-up studies that have been done. How-ever, there are individual children who do not seem to be able to adjust and adapt to the growth suppression. There is good evidence that the drugs do not lose their effect after puberty and that tolerance to medication does not develop and lead to substance abuse (Greenhill and Setterberg 1993). While there are some concerns about the use of stimulants in the ADD individuals who themselves have substance abuse in their past history or who have family members who are current substance abusers, this has not been a major problem.

The relationship of stimulant drugs to the development of tics is controversial. It is clear that a substantial number of children with ADD who are referred for clinical evaluation have motor or vocal tics or both. Some of these children experience worsening of their tics when stimulants are used. Recent data by Gadow and colleagues (1995) suggest that a substantial majority of those children return to baseline, even when stimulants are continued. If this does not occur, adjunct treatment of the tics with medications such as haloperidol, pimozide, or clonidine is usually effective.

Rebound is a deterioration in behavior that follows the wearing off of short-acting stimulants (Johnston et al. 1988). This rebound period may be one-half hour or more, and it is actually a worsening of behavior above baseline behavior. This occurs in a minority of children. Rebound can be managed by the use of longer-acting drugs, which seem to have a smoother onset and offset.

Cantwell and Swanson (1992) have reported "cognitive toxicity" in a subgroup of patients at doses at which the behavioral effect of the medication are maximized. Thus, the maximum dosage the child receives for behavioral effects will have less than a maximal effect on cognitive functioning. In these cases the dose should be lowered.

The literature on stimulants consists of more than 100 studies of more than 4,500 elementary school-age children. There are several small studies of preschool children (approximately 130 subjects), a small number of studies of adolescents (approximately 113 subjects), and eight studies of adults (180 subjects). In general, the response rate is 70 percent or more in the elementary school age range and in the adolescent range. A more variable effect has been found in studies with preschool children and with adults (Cantwell 1994b).

The use of nonstimulant medication to treat attention deficit hyperactivity disorder has been reviewed by Cantwell (1994a). The medications that have been evaluated include the antidepressants, antianxiety agents (clonidine and guanfacine), neuroleptics, fenfluramine, lithium, and the anticonvulsants. The best studied of the nonstimulants are the heterocyclic antidepressants (Elia 1991). Some studies suggest that approximately 70 percent of children with ADD will respond to desipramine at dosages up to 5 mg/kg per day with blood levels of 100 to 300 ng/mg per milliliter (Biederman et al. 1989, Pliszka 1987). All of the heterocyclics produce positive effects on hyperactivity, impulsivity, inattention, and most likely on anxiety and depressed mood. There is some question about whether there is a major effect on learning. The major side effects that are of concern are cardiovascular, especially the possible induction of arrhythmias. The report of the sudden death of several young children has led to a reconsideration of the use of the heterocyclics (Riddle et al. 1991).

Bupropion is an antidepressant that is not a serotonin reuptake blocker and is not a tricyclic. The side effect profile is very positive, and efficacy has been suggested in several studies published since 1986 using 5 to 6 mg/kg per day in three divided dosages.

The literature on serotonin reuptake blockers such as fluoxetine, sertraline, paroxetine, and fluvoxamine is limited, but it suggests that some individual children may get a positive response (Barrickman et al. 1991). Gammon and Brown (1993) reported on thirty-two subjects, aged 9 to 17 years, all with a diagnosis of ADD with multiple comorbid conditions. Mood disorders such as dysthymia were present in 78 percent of cases and major depressive disorder in 80 percent of cases. The addition of fluoxetine to the ongoing methylphenidate treatment led to a significant improvement in many measures in thirty of the thirty-two subjects.

Monoamine oxidase inhibitors have been shown in small studies to be effective in a substantial number of children, and in one study (Zametkin et al. 1986) their effect was equal to that of dextroamphetamine; however, multiple possible drug and diet reactions severely limit their use.

Clonidine and guanfacine are alpha-adrenergic agonists. The literature suggesting their efficacy alone in ADD is limited. In conjunction with stimulants, they may offer some adjunctive help in the treatment of associated aggressive hyperactive/hyperarousal behavior and they may benefit those children who have tics. The clonidine-methylphenidate combination has recently been associated with idiosyncratic episodes in a small number of cases; there have been three cases of sudden death. The exact role, if any, of the drugs in these deaths in unclear. Fenfluramine is a synthetic stimulant not shown to be useful in the usual case of ADD. Clinical data suggest a possible positive effect on ADD symptoms (Cantwell 1994a) in those with mental retardation and pervasive developmental disorders.

The mood stabilizers, such as lithium, carbamazepine, and vaproic acid, do not seem to have a positive effect on core ADD symptoms. Symptoms of episodic dyscontrol in some ADD individuals may be positively affected.

Early studies with neuroleptics suggested an effect on certain symptoms. Neuroleptics may be cognitively dulling, although the early studies at smaller doses did not show that. They are very rarely used today because of the negative side effect potential. However, haloperidol or pimozide plus stimulants may be a useful combination for those who have ADD plus Tourette's syndrome or tics.

It is now accepted that a multimodal approach to therapy that uses both psychosocial intervention and medication has the greatest chance of alleviating the multiple symptoms and domains of dysfunction with which ADD children present. Medical treatment and psychosocial treatment have complementary effects. Thus a wider range of symptoms may be treated than with either intervention alone. Psychosocial intervention may improve symptoms during the period of time that medication has worn off. The use of both interventions together may lead to lower medication dosage and a less complex psychosocial intervention program than with either treatment alone.

SUMMARY AND CONCLUSIONS

This chapter has highlighted advances in ADD over the past ten years. Advances have been made on all fronts. Neuroimaging and family genetic studies are providing enticing leads to possible underlying etiological factors. Treatment studies have added to the staple of treatment, which has remained psychostimulant medication. Various psychotherapeutic and psychosocial interventions play a major role in treatment. School-based interventions have become more common and are quite effective. More work needs to be done on long-term results of treatment in childhood. The syndrome of ADD remains a subject of intense research as one of our best-studied child psychiatric problems.

REFERENCES

Achenbach, T. M. (1993). *Empirically Based Taxonomy: How to Use Syndromes and Profile Types Derived from the CBCL from 4 to 18*. TRF and YSR. Burlington, VT: University of Vermont Department of Psychiatry.

American Academy of Child and Adolescent Psychiatry. (1991). Practice parameters for the assessment and treatment of ADHD. *Journal of the American Academy of Child and Adolescent Psychiatry* 30:i–iii.

American Psychiatric Association. (1994). *Diagnostic and Statistical Manual of Mental Disorders*, 4th ed. (*DSM-IV*). Washington, DC: American Psychiatric Association.

Arnold, L. E., and Jensen, P. S. (1995). Attention deficit disorders. In *Comprehensive Textbook of Psychiatry*, ed. H. Kaplan and B. Sadsock, 6th ed., pp. 2295–2310. Baltimore: Williams & Wilkins.

Barkley, R. A. (1990). *Attention Deficit Hyperactivity Disorder: A Handbook in Diagnosis and Treatment*. New York: Guilford.

——— (1995). Attention deficit disorder symptoms in adults. Paper presented to the Bay State Psychiatric Hospital Symposium, Springfield, MA.

Barrickman, L., Noyes, R., and Kuperman, S. (1991). Treatment of ADHD with fluoxetine, a preliminary trial. *Journal of the American Academy of Child and Adolescent Psychiatry* 30:762–767.

Baumgaertel, A. L., Wolraich, M. L., and Dietrich, M. (1995). Comparison of diagnostic criteria for attention deficit disorders in a German elementary school sample. *Journal of the American Academy of Child and Adolescent Psychiatry* 34:629–638.

Biederman, J., Baldessarini, R. J., Wright, V., et al. (1989). A double-blind placebo controlled study of desipramine in the treatment of ADD: I. Efficacy. *Journal of the American Academy of Child and Adolescent Psychiatry* 28:777–784.

Braswell, L., and Bloomquist, M. (1994). *Cognitive Behavior Therapy of ADHD*. New York: Guilford.

Braswell, L., Bloomquist, M., and Pederson, S. (1991). *ADHD: A Guide to Understanding and Helping Children with Attention Deficit Hyperactivity*

Disorder in School Settings. Minneapolis: University of Minnesota Professional Development.

Brown, N. B., and Cantwell, D. P. (1976). Siblings as therapist: a behavioral approach. *American Journal of Psychiatry* 133:447–450.

Campbell, S. B. (1990). *Psychiatric Disorder in Preschool Children.* New York: Guilford.

Cantwell, D. P. (1975). The hyperactive child: epidemiology, classification and diagnosis. In *The Hyperactive Child: Diagnosis, Management, and Current Research,* ed. D. P. Cantwell, pp. 3–50. New York: Spectrum.

—— (1985). Hyperactive children have grown up. What have we learned about what happens to them? *Archives of General Psychiatry* 42:1026–1028.

—— (1994a). *ADHD Treatment with Non-stimulants. Pediatric Psychopharmacology.* Washington, DC: AACAP Press.

—— (1994b). *Therapeutic Management of Attention Deficit Disorder: Participant Workshop,* pp. 4–20. New York: SCP Communication.

Cantwell, D. P., and Swanson, J. (1992). *Cognitive toxicity in ADHD children treated with stimulant medication.* Paper presented at the American Academy of Child and Adolescent Psychiatry Annual Meeting.

Conners, K. (1995). *Attention deficit disorder core criteria in adults.* Paper presented to the Neuroscience Research Seminar, Lake Forest, IL.

DuPaul, G. J., Anastopoulos, A. D., Shelton, T. L., et al. (1992). Multimethod assessment of attention-deficit hyperactivity disorder: the diagnostic utility of clinic-based tests. *Journal of Clinical Child Psychology* 21:194–402.

Elia, J. (1991). Stimulants and antidepressant pharmacokinetics in hyperactive children. *Psychopharmacology Bulletin* 27:411–415.

—— (1993). Drug treatment for hyperactive children. Therapeutic guidelines. *Drugs* 46:863–871.

Evans, S. W., and Pelham, W. E. (1991). Psychostimulant effects on academic and behavioral measures for ADHD junior high school students in a lecture format classroom. *Journal of Abnormal Child Psychology* 19:537–552.

Gadow, K. D., Sverd, J., Spratkin, J., et al. (1995). Efficacy of methylphenidate for attention deficit hyperactivity disorder in children with tic disorder. *Archives of General Psychiatry* 52:444–455.

Gammon, G. D., and Brown, T. E. (1993). Fluoxetine augmentation of methylphenidate for attention deficit and comorbid disorders. *Journal of Child and Adolescent Psychopharmacology* 3:1–10.

Giedd, J. N., Cassenalos, F. X., Korzuch, P., et al. (1994). Quantitative morphology of the corpus callosum in attention deficit hyperactivity disorder. *American Journal of Psychiatry* 15:665–669.

Goodman, R., and Stevenson, J. (1989). A twin study of hyperactivity. II. The etiologic role of genes, family relationships, and perinatal adversity. *Journal of the Child Psychology and Psychiatry* 30:691–709.

Greenhill, L. L., and Setterberg, S. (1993). Pharmacotherapy of disorders of adolescents. *Psychiatric Clinics of North America* 16:793–814.

Hallowell, E., and Ratey, J. (1994). *Driven to Distraction*. New York: Pantheon.

Hechtman, L. (1993). Aims and methological problems in multimodal treatment studies. *American Journal of Psychiatry* 38:458–464.

Hinshaw, S. P. (1994). Behavior rating scales in the assessment of disruptive behavior disorders in childhood. In *Assessment in Child Psychopathology*, ed. D. Shatfer and J. E. Richters, pp. 59–73. New York: Cambridge.

Hynd, G. W., Semrud-Clikeman, M., Lorys, A. R., et al. (1990). Brain morphology in developmental dyslexia and attention deficit disorder with hyperactivity. *Archives of Neurology*, pp. 919–926.

Johnston, C., Pelham, W. E., and Hoza, J. (1988). Psychostimulant rebound in attention deficit disordered boys. *Journal of the American Academy of Child and Adolescent Psychiatry* 27:806–810.

Lou, H. C., Henriksen, L., Bruhn, P., et al. (1989). Striatal dysfunction in attention deficit and hyperkinetic disorder. *Archives of Neurology* 46:48–52.

Nottelmann, E., and Jensen, P. (1995). Comorbidity of disorders in children and adolescents: developmental perspectives. In *Advances in Clinical Child Psychology*, vol 17, pp. 109–155. New York: Plenum.

Pelham, W. E. (1992). Teacher ratings of *DSM-III-R* symptoms from the disruptive behavior disorders. *Journal of the American Academy of Child and Adolescent Psychiatry* 31:210–218.

——— (1994). *Attention Deficit Hyperactivity Disorder: A Clinician's Guide*. New York: Plenum.

Pelham, W. E., and Bender, M. E. (1982). Peer relationships in hyperactive children: description and treatment. In *Advances in Learning and Behavioral Disabilities*, ed. K. Gadow and I. Bailer, pp. 365–436. Greenwich, CT: JAI Press.

Pelham, W. E., Greenslade, K. E., Vodde-Hamilton, M., et al. (1990). Relative efficacy of long-acting stimulants on children with attention deficit-hyperactivity disorder: a comparison of standard methylphenidate, sustained released methylphenidate, sustained released dextroamphetamine, and pemoline. *Pediatrics* 86:226–237.

Pliszka, S. R. (1987). Tricyclic antidepressants in the treatment of children with attention deficit disorder. *Journal of the American Academy of Child and Adolescent Psychiatry* 26:127–132.

Reiff, M. I., Banez, G. A., and Culbert, T. P. (1993). Children who have attentional disorders: diagnosis and evaluation. *Pediatrics in Review* 12:455–465.

Riddle, M. A., Nelson, J. C., Kleinman, C. S., et al. (1991). Sudden death in children receiving Norpramin: a review of three reported cases and commentary. *Journal of the American Academy of Child and Adolescent Psychiatry* 30:104–108.

Steere, G., and Arnsten, A. F. T. (1995). Corpus callosum morphology in ADHD. *American Journal of Psychiatry* 152:1105–1107.

Swanson, J. M. (1992). *School-Based Assessment and Interventions for ADD Students.* Irvine, CA: University of California Child Development Center.
——— (1995). *SNAP-IV Scale.* Irvine, CA. University of California Child Development Center.

Swanson, J. M., Cantwell, D., Lerner, M., and Hanna, G. L. (1991). Effects of stimulant medication on learning in children with ADHD. *Journal of Learning Disabilities* 4:219–230, 255.

Weiss, G., and Hechtman, L. T. (1994). *Hyperactive Children Grown Up*, 2nd ed. New York: Guilford.

Wender, P. (1994). *Attention Deficit Disorder in Adults.* New York: University of Oxford Press.

Wilens, T., and Biederman, J. (1992). The stimulants. *Psychiatric Clinics of North America* 15:191–222.

Wolraich, M. L., Hannah, J. N., and Pinnock, T. Y. (1996). Comparison of diagnostic criteria for attention-deficit hyperactivity disorder in a countywide sample. *Journal of the American Academy of Child and Adolescent Psychiatry* 35:319–324.

Zametkin, A. (1993). Brain metabolism in teenagers with attention deficit hyperactivity disorder. *Archives of General Psychiatry* 50:333–340.

Zametkin, A. J., Nordahl, T. E., Gross, M., et al. (1990). Cerebral glucose metabolism in adults with hyperactivity of childhood onset. *New England Journal of Medicine* 323:1361–1366.

Zametkin, A. J., and Rapoport, J. L. (1986). The pathophysiology of attention deficit disorder with hyperactivity. In *Advances in Clinical Child Psychology*, vol. 9, ed. B. B. Lahey and A. E. Kasdin, pp. 177–216. New York: Plenum.

Zametkin, A. J., Rapoport, J. L., and Murphy, D. L. (1986). Treatment of hyperactive children with monoamine oxidase inhibitors. I. Clinical efficacy. *Archives of General Psychiatry* 42:962–966.

PART II

Assessment of AD/HD in Children and Adolescents

INTRODUCTION TO PART II

The second part of the journey into understanding and treating AD/HD focuses on the assessment of this disorder. Though clinicians know that in order to understand and treat a problem they must first properly diagnose that problem, somehow in the area of AD/HD that step is often bypassed on the way to making treatment recommendations. The AD/HD diagnosis is often based on the patient's describing symptoms that seem to suggest attentional problems. The patient is then told that medication should relieve the symptom. As will be learned in this section of the book, a number of factors need to be considered in making the diagnosis of AD/HD and in determining the appropriate subtype of AD/HD. Without such assessment, the appropriate treatment for this disorder may elude us as clinicians.

This section begins with an article by Terri L. Shelton, Ph.D., and

Russell A. Barkley, Ph.D. Dr. Barkley, another pioneer in the area of AD/HD, together with his associate, Dr. Shelton, have collaborated on a number of articles in this field. They present a thorough review of the field, including traditional methods used to diagnose and treat AD/HD in children and adolescents. They give an excellent review of AD/HD and current practice in this field. They also describe the two-tier approach they believe is essential in the assessment of AD/HD in children. In Chapter 3, James A. Incorvaia, Ph.D., argues for a comprehensive assessment in the diagnosis of AD/HD, which includes various psychological tests to help in not only making the appropriate diagnosis but also differentiating the subtypes of AD/HD and attendant comorbid disorders. In Chapter 4, Donald Tessmer, Ph.D., further explores the area of comorbid dysfunction in AD/HD and presents a test battery that can be used in a clinic setting to differentially diagnose AD/HD from other emotional and learning problems. In Chapter 5, Marcel Kinsbourne, M.D., introduces one subtype of AD/HD—the overfocused child—and offers a questionnaire format for assessing its presence. In Chapter 6, Lawrence Greenberg, M.D., reviews current practices and applications of one of the most popular clinical continuous performance tests used in the assessment of AD/HD. Assessing AD/HD from a different perspective, in Chapter 7, Daniel G. Amen, M.D., discusses his use of single photon emission computed tomography in the differential assessment of AD/HD and introduces five subtypes of this disorder he has detected using this diagnostic procedure. In Chapter 8, Leah Ellenberg, Ph.D., discusses the importance of looking at executive function in assessing AD/HD in young people and describes some of the tests used in assessing these important areas of cognition.

2

The Assessment and Treatment of Attention Deficit/Hyperactivity Disorder in Children

Terri L. Shelton and
Russell A. Barkley

Attention deficit/hyperactivity disorder (AD/HD) is one of the most common psychological or behavioral disorders present in childhood, affecting approximately 3 to 5 percent of the general child population (American Psychiatric Association 1987, 1994, Barkley 1990). Although children with AD/HD may have characteristics in common, there is variability in how these deficits may be manifested in the behavior of different children and in an individual child's behavior across settings. This variability reflects not only the disorder itself, but also the varying definitions of attention and impulsivity in general and the ever-changing diagnostic criteria for the disorder as well. As a result, the diagnosis, assessment, and treatment of AD/HD are

This chapter first appeared in the *Handbook of Pediatric Psychology 2E*, ed. M. C. Roberts, pp. 633–654, copyright © 1995 by The Guilford Press, New York, and is reprinted by permission.

complex tasks. These tasks must take into account not only whether the disorder exists, but the degree to which other behaviors (e.g., oppositional defiant disorder) are present, and the specific ways in which the disorder affects a child's development in all settings (e.g., home, school, and with peers).

OVERVIEW OF THE DISORDER

Behavioral disorders resembling AD/HD have been described for almost 100 years. Still (1902), Tredgold (1908), and others described children who were excessively emotional, showed little behavioral inhibition, and had difficulty sustaining attention. Since then, numerous diagnostic labels have been given to this constellation of behaviors, including hyperkinesis, minimal brain dysfunction, and attention deficit disorder (with or without hyperactivity). Currently, the disorder is termed *attention deficit/hyperactivity disorder*, a name that once again places greater emphasis on the hyperactive and impulsive features of the disorder. The changing labels reflect the evolving understanding of the underlying etiologies and a shifting emphasis on the various behaviors associated with AD/HD. Regardless of the label, however, there have been remarkable consistencies in the characteristics that have come to be identified with AD/HD. Three characteristics—inattention, impulsivity, and hyperactivity—are highlighted to some extent in all definitions of AD/HD.

Basic Characteristics

Children with AD/HD, by definition, display more difficulties with attention than do other children of the same age and sex. In its broadest sense, "attention" refers to the ability of the organism to respond to events in its environment. Attention is also a multidimensional construct (Hale and Lewis 1979, James 1898, Mesulam 1990, Mirsky 1987, Posner 1988). There is general consensus that arousal or alertness, selective or focused attention, and sustained attention or persistence are dimensions of attention. Other components of attention over which there is less agreement include divided attention, in which the individual must pay attention and respond to two different tasks simultaneously; searching, which refers to the strategy employed by the individual to inspect and evaluate the environmental event; and encoding, which refers to the capacity to retain information in working or short-term memory (Barkley 1994, Cooley and Morris 1990). Each of these dimensions appears to have a separate neuroanatomical system responsible for its existence. Furthermore, these dimensions of attention interact and their functions are coordinated, such that a child with one type of inattention can have problems in other areas (including difficulties with alertness, arousal, selectivity, sustained attention, distractibility, or span of apprehension).

Although there is considerable research on attention, less is known about deficiencies in these particular areas of attention. This lack of knowledge has had an impact on our ability to assess these deficits, and, more importantly, on how assessments can lead to treatment recommendations. Research to date suggests that children with AD/HD have their greatest difficulties with sustaining attention to tasks or with vigilance (Douglas 1983). Intertwined with this difficulty in sustained attention is a deficiency in inhibiting behavior in response to situational demands, or impulsivity. Like attention, impulsivity is multidimensional in nature (Milich and Kramer 1985). The problem is often defined as a pattern of rapid, inaccurate responding to tasks (Brown and Quay 1977). It may also be described as poor sustained inhibition of responding, poor delay or gratification, or impaired adherence to commands to regulate or inhibit behavior in social contexts (Rapport et al. 1986).

Hyperactivity has been a hallmark of the diagnosis. Children with AD/HD have been found to be more active, restless, and fidgety than same-aged peers (Porrino et al. 1983). As with poor sustained attention, however, there are significant situational fluctuations in this symptom (Luk 1985). This situational variability suggests that it is the failure to regulate activity level to setting or task demands that may be problematic in the disorder (Routh 1978). More recent studies suggest that it may be the pervasiveness of the hyperactivity across settings that distinguishes AD/HD from other diagnostic categories of children (Taylor 1986).

In addition to inattention, impulsivity, and hyperactivity, there is growing evidence that children with AD/HD have difficulties in following rules and using language to control their own behavior (Barkley 1981, 1990). This may be evidenced as noncompliance with parental and teacher commands or an inability to delay reward or gratification that is not attributable to sensory handicaps (e.g., deafness), impaired language development, or defiance or oppositional behavior. Like the other symptoms, rule-governed behavior is a multidimensional construct (Zettle and Hayes 1982). It is not clear which aspects of this construct present the greatest difficulty for children with AD/HD.

Diagnostic Criteria

The changing names given to attentional disorders and the different behaviors that have been highlighted are reflected in concomitant changes in diagnostic criteria. For example, in the third edition of the *Diagnostic and Statistical Manual of Mental Disorders* (*DSM-III*; American Psychiatric Association 1980), two subtypes of attention deficit disorder were identified: attention deficit disorder with hyperactivity (ADD+H) and attention deficit disorder without hyperactivity (ADD-H). The three primary symptoms of inattention, impulsivity, and hyperactivity still characterized attention deficit disorder with hyperactivity. The disorder without hyperactivity was defined as significant problems with sustained attention alone. The diagnostic criteria were revised again for *DSM-III-R* (American Psychiatric Association 1987). This definition included inclusionary and exclusionary criteria, recognized the situational variability of behaviors associated with AD/HD, and acknowledged the need for documenting that symptoms exceeded developmental expectations. At the time, however, there was little empirical support for two distinct subtypes. As a result, attention deficit disorder without hyperactivity was no longer listed as a subtype. Instead, the label of "undifferentiated attention deficit disorder" was used to characterize those children whose primary difficulty was inattention, and in whom signs of hyperactivity and impulsivity were not present. AD/HD was defined as difficulties with inattention, hyperactivity, and impulsivity that exceeded developmental expectations.

The *DSM-IV* (American Psychiatric Association 1994) represents still another change in diagnostic classification. This change reflects the increasing empirical evidence that attention deficits and hyperactivity-impulsivity are two distinct dimensions, differing in level of impairment, the presence of comorbid features, social and cognitive development, and developmental course. For example, it appears that those children whose primary difficulties lie in impulsivity-hyperactivity may have their principal problem in the response inhibition component of attention (Barkley et al. 1990a, Barkley et al. 1992, Goodyear and Hynd 1992). They are at greater risk for difficulties with peer relations, conduct problems, substance use, abuse, and antisocial personality in adulthood (Barkley et al. 1990b). In contrast, those children whose primary difficulties are with inattention may have their deficit in the selecting/focusing component of attention. These children more closely resemble those with learning disabilities with respect to academic difficulties (Carlson 1986) and associated behavioral difficulties (e.g., anxiety, depression).

The symptoms of inattention, impulsivity, and hyperactivity are still present in the new diagnostic criteria. However, they may occur separately or concurrently, resulting in four subtypes: (1) AD/HD, predominantly inattentive type; (2) AD/HD, predominantly hyperactive-impulsive type; (3) AD/HD, combined type; and (4) AD/HD not otherwise specified (for disorders with prominent symptoms of attention deficit or hyperactivity-impulsivity that do not meet criteria for any of the first three subtypes).

Etiology

To some extent, the changing diagnostic criteria reflect a growing understanding of the factors that do or do not lead to AD/HD. Although brain damage was initially proposed as a chief cause of these symptoms (Strauss and Lehtinen 1947), later reviews of the evidence suggest that fewer than 5 percent of these children have neurological findings consistent with such an etiology. Possible neurotransmitter dysfunctions or imbalances have been proposed, based primarily on the evidence of the responses of children with AD/HD to different drugs. However, little direct evidence is available, and many of the studies are conflicting in their results (Shaywitz et al. 1983, Zametkin and Rapoport 1986). Nevertheless, findings of decreased cerebral blood flow, frontal lobe deficits on neuropsychological tests, and various psychophysiological findings suggest the role of some central nervous system mechanism, probably involving the prefrontal cortex and its connections to the caudate nucleus and limbic system (Anastopoulos and Barkley 1988, Chelune et al. 1986, Hastings and Barkley 1978, Lou et al. 1984). In addition, the lack of inhibitory protection against internal interference frequently seen in humans and animals with damage or dysfunction in the prefrontal cortex (Fuster 1989) contributes further evidence to this theory of a prefrontal lobe origin for AD/HD.

A number of studies support a hypothesis of a genetic predisposition in the phenotypic expression of AD/HD (see Deutsch and Kinsbourne 1990 for a review). Twin studies, some using the Child Behavior Checklist (CBCL; Achenbach and Edelbrock 1983), report heritability estimates of 67 to 80 percent for attention for parent ratings and 72 percent for teacher ratings of attention (Edelbrock et al. 1991). Other studies have reported that from 20 to 32 percent of parents and siblings of AD/HD children also have the disorder (Biederman et al. 1987, Deutsch et al. 1982). However, the manner of transmission has not been determined.

Despite popular opinion, there is little empirical support for the proposition that various environmental toxins, such as food additives, refined sugars, and allergens (Feingold 1975, Taylor 1980), are a major cause of AD/HD (Conners 1980, Gross 1984, Mattes and Gittelman 1981, Wolraich et al. 1985). Furthermore, though chaotic home environments and differences in parenting style can exacerbate AD/HD and comorbid symptomatology, these do not cause AD/HD. Instead, environmental influences play more of a role in the development and maintenance of oppositional defiant behaviors, aggression, and conduct problems in children (August and Stewart 1983, Lahey et al. 1988). Some evidence of a correctional nature shows that elevated blood lead levels in children may be related to excessive activity and inattention (Gittleman and Eskinazi 1983). Nevertheless, the relationship is quite low (correlations ranging from .08 to .15), and a direct causal connection between body lead and AD/HD remains to be established. Maternal alcohol consumption and cigarette smoking during pregnancy (Streissguth et al. 1984) have been correlated with the degree of AD/HD symptoms in the offspring of these mothers.

Prevalence

Although prevalence ratings depend on the manner in which AD/HD is defined, the consensus seems to be that approximately 3 to 5 percent of the childhood population has AD/HD (American Psychiatric Association 1987). However, estimates have varied from 1 to 20 percent (Lambert et al. 1978, Ross and Ross 1982, Szatmari et al. 1989). Rates of occurrence also fluctuate to a small degree across cultures (Ross and Ross 1982) and socioeconomic strata (Taylor 1986). The proportion of males to females varies considerably across studies, from 2:1 to 10:1 (American Psychiatric Association 1980, Ross and Ross 1982), with an average of 6:1 most often cited for clinic-referred samples of children. However, epidemiological studies find the proportion to be approximately 3:1 among nonreferred children displaying these symptoms (Szatmari et al. 1989, Trites et al. 1979a).

Developmental Course and Outcome

Years ago, it was thought that children with AD/HD would outgrow their symptoms as they entered adolescence. A small percentage of children do appear to outgrow their symptoms, in that their later behavior falls within the broadly defined normal range. However, as many as 75 percent (Weiss and Hechtman 1993) continue to have problems with school, home, or community adjustment. As adolescents, these problems may be evidenced in academic underachievement or failure (Brown and Borden 1986, Thorley 1984, Weiss and Hechtman 1993) and increased interpersonal problems (Loney et al. 1981, Weiss and Hechtman 1993). Higher-than-normal levels of substance abuse occur in the adolescent years (Weiss and Hechtman 1993), but these are related more to the presence of aggression and conduct disorder symptoms than to AD/HD.

Less research exists on the young adult outcome of children with AD/HD. What does exist suggests that at least 30 to 60 percent continue to have the disorder, with many more having some residual symptoms into adulthood. These difficulties may be evidenced as interpersonal problems, depression and low self-esteem, criminal convictions, symptoms of adult antisocial personality, and alcohol/drug abuse (Farrington et al. 1987, Loney et al. 1981). The actual outcome may be more positive than these data suggest, as most studies have focused on clinic-referred children. Furthermore, the degree to which early and intensive intervention may minimize the negative outcomes is not clear. Significant predictors of poorer outcomes are lower intelligence and socioeconomic status, past history or high degrees of aggressive and oppositional behavior, poor peer relations, parental psychopathology, and the extent and duration of treatment during adolescence (Loney et al. 1981, Satterfield et al. 1981, Weiss and Hechtman 1993).

Associated Features

Children with AD/HD are more likely than those without AD/HD to have medical, behavioral, emotional, and academic difficulties. Deficits in intelligence, academic achievement, and motor coordination are more prevalent in these children than in matched samples of children without AD/HD or even in siblings (Barkley 1990, Cantwell and Satterfield 1978, Safer and Allen 1976). Depression, low self-esteem, and poor peer acceptance are also more common (Johnston et al. 1985). It has been shown repeatedly that children with AD/HD have a higher incidence of minor physical anomalies, allergies, and accidental injuries than the norm (Hartsough and Lambert 1985, Quinn and Rapoport 1974, Trites et al. 1980). Greater parent stress, family psychopathology, and negative parent–child interactions are often noted in families that have children with AD/HD than in those that do not (Anastopoulos et al. 1992, Barkley et al. 1985, Biederman et al. 1987). Some of the more common associated features are discussed below.

Intellectual Development, Academic Performance, and Learning Disabilities

Studies suggest that children with AD/HD may score an average of seven to fifteen points below same-aged peers and their own siblings on standardized intelligence tests (Fischer et al. 1990, McGee et al. 1989). These differences may be attributable to actual deficits in abilities and/or to impaired test-taking performance. In addition, many of these children are underachieving relative to measured levels of ability (Barkley et al. 1990b). Depending on the definition, approximately 25 percent of children with AD/HD have at least one type of learning disability, in either math, reading, or spelling (Barkley 1990, Safer and Allen 1976).

There is some evidence that children with AD/HD may be at increased risk for language disorders. Some studies have identified early delays (Hartsough and Lambert 1985, Stewart et al. 1966, Szatmari et al. 1989), others have not (Barkley et al. 1990b). Although children with AD/HD are likely to talk more than those without AD/HD, especially during spontaneous conversation (Barkley 1983, Zentall 1989), they may be less verbal and more dysfluent when they must organize and generate their speech in response to a goal or task demand (Hamlett et al. 1987, Zentall 1985).

Conduct and Oppositional Disorders

There is considerable evidence that children with AD/HD display greater difficulties with oppositional defiant behavior, aggressiveness, and conduct problems, and antisocial behavior than children without AD/HD. From 40 to 65 percent of clinic-referred samples meet full diagnostic criteria for oppositional defiant disorder, and from 21 to 45 percent have diagnosable conduct disorder (Barkely 1990). Given this overlap, there has been considerable discussion as to whether AD/HD is a separate disorder. Although there is overlap, the disorders appear to differ in specific characteristics and proposed etiologies (Barkley 1990, Hinshaw 1987).

Assessment

The very nature of AD/HD demands a comprehensive approach to assessment. While it may be possible to choose a set of measures to be used as the core of a standard battery, some researchers have suggested that a decision-making or problem-solving model (e.g., Kanfer and Saslow 1969) may be more useful to accommodate the changing diagnostic criteria for AD/HD, the various characteristics that may be associated with AD/HD, and the child's characteristics (e.g., chronological age, developmental functional levels). The Professional Group for Attention-Related Disorders, the Forum on the Education of Children with Attention Deficit Disorder, and the *Educator's Manual* (Fowler 1992) published by the National Education Committee of the advocacy group Children and Adults with Attention Deficit Disorders (ChADD) have all recommended using such a problem-focused, two-tiered assessment model.

Tier one is designed to rule in or out the presence of AD/HD, including cardinal characteristics, age of onset, and exclusionary criteria. Once a diagnosis of AD/HD is confirmed, tier two focuses on the specific ways in which these symptoms have an adverse impact on a child's functioning in other areas (e.g., cognitive, school, social, home). Using this two-tiered approach as a framework, we now briefly review assessment techniques with proven or promising utility. More extensive reviews of individual instruments are available elsewhere (Barkley 1981, 1987a, 1990, Shelton and Barkley 1993).

Tier One: Determining the Presence of the Disorder

First, the formal diagnostic criteria for AD/HD must drive the choice of measures in this first level of assessment. Therefore, an assessment battery must allow for an evaluation of the three core symptoms: inattention, hyperactivity, and impulsivity. Second, the tools chosen must permit a comparison of skills to a child's developmental level, necessitating that at least some of the measures contain normative data in these three areas. If a child has developmental delays, these must be taken into account in the establishment of expectations for behavior. Third, the assessment battery must sample from a number of settings (e.g., school, home) to determine the pervasiveness and situational variability of symptoms. Fourth, because of the frequency with which other behaviors and difficulties accompany AD/HD, an assessment battery should include measures not only of AD/HD symptomatology but of other behaviors and skills as well (e.g., peer relations, anxiety, depression, oppositional or conduct problems). Finally, the battery must permit other reasons for AD/HD symptomatology to be ruled out. For example, children with auditory comprehension disorders (Wilson and Risucci 1986), including difficulties with auditory discrimination, perception, cognition, and sequential memory, may behave in some ways that are similar to children with AD/HD (e.g., not following directions, inattention, poorer performance in large-group situations). Adverse medication responses and other developmental conditions that may be associated with chronic or transient inattention or impulsivity (e.g., pervasive developmental disorder, or posttraumatic stress disorder) must also be considered. Thus, a multimethod assessment battery usually consists of some combination of interviews, rating scales, laboratory measures, direct observational procedures, and other psychological and/or educational tests.

Interviews

In-depth interviews with parents and primary caregivers, the child, and teachers form the core of the assessment. Although informal or semistructured interviews can be quite useful, the federally funded national resource centers for the study of AD/HD have recommended using one of the well-established structured interviews for assessing AD/HD symptomatology and related behaviors as well. They specifically mention the following: The Diagnostic Interview Schedule for Children (Costello et al. 1982) includes formation for parents as well as children and has recently been revised to include both *DSM-III-R* and *DSM-IV* symptom items (Shaffer et al. 1993). Other interviews have been developed solely for children's responses, such as the Interview Schedule for Children (Kovacs 1982). This instrument was designed mainly to diagnose depression, but it can also assess anxiety disorders and AD/HD in children. The revised Schedule for Affective Disorders and Schizophrenia for School-Age Children (Last 1986) is a brief interview form that taps major affective disorders with reasonable reliability and validity. The Diagnostic Interview for Children and Adolescents (Reich et al. 1992) has recently been revised. The new revision does not yet have reliability and validity data and it requires more skill and training to administer than the others do. Nevertheless, previous versions have been shown to be valuable in genetic studies of children with AD/HD.

In addition to the areas covered by these structured psychiatric interviews, there should be a review of the child's developmental milestones, unusual medical problems, and school history, as well as the family history of any learning or psychiatric problems. Interviewing the child provides information about his or her general appearance, interests in the play and school, language functioning, and social skills; sheds light on the child's view of his or her academic and behavioral strengths and needs, family relations and conflicts, and the reason for this evaluation; and provides a means of establishing rapport.

The interview with the teacher should include questions about the child's current academic achievement, social functioning with classmates and general classroom behavior. Attention should be directed toward the child's attention to tasks, impulse control in various situations, activity level, and ability to follow rules and instructions. Differences in behavior based on academic subject, teacher, class size and the like should be described. Finally, interviews with teachers provide needed information about the child's functioning in other settings and the impact of AD/HD symptomatology on academic areas. Any additional information concerning the child's personality, emotional difficulties, and family problems should be obtained.

Child and Parent Behavior Rating Scales

The clinical utility of child behavior rating scales in the assessment of AD/HD is well established. These scales provide a means of evaluating the developmental deviancy and severity of symptoms, gathering information across setting and informants, and examining not only AD/HD symptomatology but comorbid features as well. They are also helpful in determining competing diagnostic information. An assessment battery should include broad-function scales as well as those specific to AD/HD.

For broad function, the revised CBCL (Achenbach 1991) has proven to be a good adjunct to the structured interviews. There are now comparable forms for parents and teachers of children aged 4 to 18, a parent form for children aged 2 to 3, and a child self-report form as well. The courses provide a profile of the child's behavior relative to other children the same age and sex for a wide range of behaviors, including both internalizing (e.g., depression, anxiety) and external-izing (e.g., conduct problems) behaviors, as well as social competence. The federally funded AD/HD national centers also suggest that the Behavior Assessment System for Children (BASC; Reynolds and Kamphaus 1992) holds promise. Similar to the CBCL, the BASC is a multimethod assessment system that contains a self-report form and separate parent and teacher forms. In addition, there is a structured developmental history and a form for recording and classifying directly observed classroom behavior.

For evaluating AD/HD symptomatology exclusively, the revised Conners Parent and Teacher Rating Scales (Goyette et al. 1978) provide a profile of child behavior in five categories (conduct problems, learning problems, psychosomatic problems, impulsivity-hyperactivity, and anxiety) from ages 3 through 17, as well as a hyperactivity index. The Attention Deficit Disorders Evaluation Scale (McCarney 1989) has home and school versions, and the AD/HD Rating Scale (DuPaul 1991) provides a quick screening of the number and severity of AD/HD symptoms.

Edelbrock (1985) has developed a rating scale, known as the Child Attention Profile, composed of items from the CBCL that assess attention and overactivity. It includes normative data for 1,100 children aged 6 through 16, and could be quite helpful in using the *DSM-IV* criteria (see Barkley 1990). Other measures of AD/HD symptomatology with normative data include the Werry-Weiss-Peters Activity Rating Scale (Werry and Sprague 1970) and the ADD-H Comprehensive Teacher Rating Scale (Ullmann et al. 1984).

Laboratory Measures

Although interviews and ratings scales are essential, there are potential limitations to these measures. Interviews and rating scales typically do not provide a fine-grained analysis of attention that permits its separation into the components described earlier (Barkley 1994). Parent and teacher rating scales of behavior often identify only one dimension that can be considered as assessing attention. This dimension often contains items that pertain to hyperactive and impulsive behavior as well as attention, suggesting that parents and teachers may judge attentional problems in a very general or global manner.

Laboratory measures can be more helpful, in that they can differentiate the components of attention. These measures are not without their problems either and are not purely objective measures of AD/HD. Performance on them is likely to be confounded by other factors (e.g., memory, intelligence, language abilities, and executive functions). In addition, laboratory measures have low to moderate ecological validity; may be less accurate in their ability to predict attentional problems in natural settings such as school (Barkley 1992); and lack appropriate normative data, which are essential for clinical diagnostic and assessment purposes. Nevertheless, it would appear that with additional normative data, laboratory tests of AD/HD symptoms may become a useful part of a comprehensive battery as detailed below.

Vigilance and Sustained Attention

One of the most widely used instruments for assessing vigilance has been the continuous performance test (CPT). Numerous versions exist (e.g., the Conners Continuous Performance Task [Conners 1994], the Gordon Diagnostic System [Gordon 1983, Klee and Garfinkel 1983]), but most involve having the child observe a screen while individual letters or numbers are projected onto the screen at a rapid pace. The child is required to press a button when a certain stimulus appears.

Although CPTs are intuitively appealing, the research on the clinical utility of these measures remains to be established. Further, they give high numbers of false-positive and false-negative results (DuPaul et al. 1992, Trommer et al. 1988). These instruments may be most helpful in evaluating responses to stimulant medication.

Impulsivity

Several laboratory methods have been used in assessing impulsivity in AD/HD children. The best known of these is the Matching Familiar Figures Test (Kagan 1966). Although the measure has discriminated children with AD/HD from those without in some studies (Campbell et al. 1971), it has not done so reliably across studies and has been criticized as being heavily confounded by general mental ability or IQ (Milich and Kramer 1985). Its sensitivity to stimulant drug effects is also unreliable (Barkley 1977). Also used quite frequently are the CPTs described above, in which the score of commission errors is taken as an indicator of poor response inhibition. Many studies have used the Porteus Mazes to evaluate planning and impulse control in AD/HD children (Douglas 1983). A major problem with all of these instruments is their low intercorrelation, which implies that each measures a different facet of impulsivity (Milich and Kramer 1985). Behavioral ratings of impulsivity appear to have more diagnostic utility at this time.

Activity Level

Numerous measures of activity level have been employed in research spanning a variety of types of activity, such as the motion of arms, legs, or trunk; locomotion; total body movement; and so forth (Tryon 1984). The lack of normative data, low reliability in some cases, low intercorrelation, and poor relationship to parent and teacher ratings of activity level have argued against the use of activity measures in clinical practice. The inability of these instruments to take into account important situational influences on activity level makes them unlikely to contribute to decisions surrounding treatment planning.

Direct Observational Procedure

Although costly, and therefore not often included in a standard assessment, a direct assessment of the child performing independent academic work in the school yields information that cannot be gathered through other assessment modalities. Not only can the observation be helpful in documenting problems with inattention, impulsivity, and restlessness that have been mentioned by parents and teachers, it can also yield invaluable information for treatment, including the physical structure of the classroom setting and the instructional style of the teacher. When direct classroom observation is not possible, analogue situations in the clinic can yield some of this information.

Various behavioral observation codes are available for observing children with AD/HD. Notable among these are the systems developed by Jacob and colleagues (1978), and Abikoff and colleagues (1977) for classroom observations, and Roberts (1979) and Barkley (1990) for clinic analogue situations. These coding systems record behaviors such as being off task, being out of one's seat, fidgeting, locomotion, vocalizations, and attention shifts-behaviors, which are noted to occur far more often in children with AD/HD than in those without AD/HD.

Overall Considerations

In choosing a battery, the length of time required to complete the assessment and the degree of overlap between measures must be taken into consideration. In addition, when interpreting the inevitable differences that can arise when using multiple information, one must be careful not to reject one set of ratings out of hand. The low agreement between parent and teacher ratings of child behavior problems is well established (Achenbach et al. 1987). Parents and teachers have different perspectives, and behavior varies by context. In addition, disagreements may be attributable to the particular symptom or age of the child (Achenbach et al. 1987, Shelton et al. 1994, Touliatos and Lindholm 1981). The differences can offer useful information about the ways in which AD/HD is manifested in a particular child, as well as the environments that support the child's strengths; such information also can be used for treatment planning.

Tier Two: Determining the Impact of the Disorder on Adaptive Functioning

The second level of assessment is particularly important for generating treatment recommendations and determining legal eligibility for special educational services (see Zirkel 1992 for legal eligibility guidelines). Some of the assessment tools mentioned for use in making the diagnosis are applicable here. In conducting the second level, consideration should be given to examining the impact of AD/HD on the child's academic/school performance, his or her relations with peers, the development of self-help and home-related responsibilities, and the child's participation within the larger social community (e.g., clubs, sports, organizations).

Impact on Academic/School Performance

Because of the relatively high incidence of learning disabilities among children with AD/HD, intelligence and academic achievement should be assessed. This can be accomplished through the administration of well-standardized tests, the use of screening measures with referrals for more intensive evaluations, and/or (at the very least) a review of recently administered tests. In the case of complex, mixed, or unusual learning disorders, neuropsychological testing may be necessary to gain a clearer picture of the child's cognitive strengths and deficits. Such tests as the Stanford-Binet Intelligence Scale, fourth edition (Thorndike et al. 1986), the various Wechsler intelligence scales (Wechsler 1989a,b, 1992), and the Woodcock-Johnson Psycho-Educational Battery–Revised (Woodcock and Johnson 1990) provide adequate coverage of the major domains of general mental development (verbal, performance, and perceptual-motor domains).

For academic achievement, and more specifically for predicting achievement from intellectual abilities, the Woodcock-Johnson Psycho-Educational Battery-Revised (Woodcock and Johnson 1990) or the Wechsler Individual Achievement Test (Wechsler 1992) can be quite helpful. Although these measures should not be used for diagnosing AD/HD (Anastopoulos et al. 1994, Greenblatt et al. 1991), they can be used in conjunction with the cognitive ability index generated from the Woodcock-Johnson or the Wechsler Intelligence Scale for Children, third edition, respectively, to examine the degree to which the child's academic ability may be affected by the AD/HD and the degree to which additional learning disabilities may be present.

Classroom observations may also be included, especially during individually performed assignments completed by the child independently of the teacher, as well as during lectures. Being off task, fidgeting, being out of one's seat, vocalizing, and playing are some of the behaviors that should be recorded. Whenever possible, observation of peers should be completed to ensure that the child is compared to typical children within his or her age group. Such a comparison controls for confounding factors such as class structure, size, and teacher style.

Impact on Peer Relationships

For some children with AD/HD, their impulsivity, inattention, and/or overactivity, as well as characteristics that frequently accompany AD/HD (e.g., oppositionality), may interfere with the development of positive friendships. There are many methods for obtaining information about this area, including interviews, behavior rating scales, sociometric ratings, structured role playing, and direct observation, which can be easily combined with the initial diagnostic evaluation (see Guevremont 1990 for a review).

Impact on Home

There is increasing evidence of the impact of AD/HD on the home, as well as of the important role that parents/caregivers play in exacerbating or lessening the negative impact of AD/HD on the child's development. Children with AD/HD can place a tremendous strain upon family functioning. As a result, not only is the normal parenting process disrupted, but parent–child relations, sibling relations, material relations, and/or parental personal functioning may suffer as well. Thus, it is valuable to include parent self-report measures as part of the assessment. For marital relations and parent functioning, the Symptom Checklist 90–Revised (Derogatis 1986), the Beck Depression Inventory (Beck et al. 1979), and the Locke-Wallace Marital Adjustment Scale (Locke and Wallace 1959) have proven to be useful for both research and clinical purposes. To evaluate behavior management practices and parenting stress, the Parenting Practices Scale (Strayhorn and Weidman 1988) and the Parenting Stress Index (Abidin 1986), among others, are useful.

TREATMENT

Because of the multidimensional nature of AD/HD, treatment, as well as assessment, should be multimethod in nature if significant and long-standing improvement is to be maintained. In developing a comprehensive treatment plan, it is important to keep in mind that there is no cure for AD/HD; in this sense, AD/HD is very much a developmental disability. Nevertheless, there are a number of effective treatments. Some reduce AD/HD symptomatology specifically. Others prevent, reduce, or ameliorate the other problems that so often accompany AD/HD (e.g., academic underachievement, low self-esteem, oppositional behavior, parenting stress). Treatment effectiveness, however, depends on these treatments being monitored and, in some cases, maintained over time (Satterfield et al. 1981).

Interventions should be directed at (1) adapting the child's environment to support the child's strengths and to minimize the expression of AD/HD symptoms, and (2) giving the child and those around him or her new skills to mediate or ameliorate the difficulties that sometimes accompany AD/HD. The information obtained through the second level of assessment can be helpful in developing a comprehensive treatment plan.

Many different treatments have been attempted with these children over the past century (see Ross and Ross 1976, 1982 for reviews). Among those lacking strong empirical support for reducing AD/HD symptoms are vestibular stimulation (Arnold et al. 1985), running (Hales and Hales 1985), biofeedback and relaxation training (Richter 1984), and play therapy (Ross and Ross 1976). Although the various dietary treatments—such as removal of additives, colorings, or sugar from the diet, or addition of high doses of vitamins—are popular, they also have minimal scientific support (Conners 1980, Haslam et al. 1984, Milich et al. 1986). Those treatments with some proven efficacy are psychopharmacological therapy (Barkley 1990); parent training in contingency management methods (Barkley 1981, 1987b); classroom applications of contingency management techniques (Ayllon and Rosenbaum 1977), as well as special educational resources; individual or group psychotherapeutic interventions with children; and combinations of these approaches.

Medication

Stimulant medication is the most frequently recommended intervention for AD/HD. It is estimated that from 60 to 90 percent of children with AD/HD receive stimulant therapy at some point (Whalen and Henker 1991), and that from 2 to 6 percent of public school students (10 percent of boys) receive such therapy (Jacobvitz et al. 1990, Safer and Krager 1988). As a result of this widespread use, medication therapy is the most widely researched treatment for AD/HD. There are a number of comprehensive reviews of the benefits and limitations of this treatment (Carlson and Brunner 1993, DuPaul and Barkley 1990, Hinshaw 1991, Jacobvitz et al. 1990, Swanson 1993, Swanson et al. 1992).

The three most commonly used stimulants are methylphenidate (Ritalin), dextrodamphetamine (Dexedrine), and pemoline (Cylert). Methylphenidate is the most commonly used (Safer and Krager 1988). Although the precise mechanism of their operation is not completely understood, psychostimulant medications are thought to increase the arousal or alertness of the central nervous system, possibly by increasing the availability of norepinephrine and/or dopamine at the synaptic cleft (Donnelly and Rapoport 1985). In the past, it was thought that the primary locus of action was the brain stem. However, recent cerebral blood flow studies suggest that the midbrain or frontal cortex, including the striatum and connections between the orbital-frontal and limbic regions (Barkley et al. 1992, Lou et al. 1984, Lou et al. 1989), may be the primary location.

Stimulant medications are quickly absorbed, with methylphenidate reaching peak plasma levels within 1.5 to 2.5 hours. The plasma half-life is between 2 and 3 hours, and the drug is entirely metabolized within 12 to 24 hours (Diener 1991). The behavioral effects occur within 30 to 60 minutes, peak within 1 to 3 hours, and dissipate within 3 to 5 hours (Barkley 1990). In the past, medication was typically prescribed on the basis of body weight. However, recent research suggests that it may be more effective to identify an individual child's optimal dose using a double-bind drug-placebo trial (Rapport et al. 1989).

Occasionally, antidepressants such as desipramine (Norpramin) and imipramine (Tofranil), and, less frequently, monoamine oxidase inhibitors have been shown to reduce AD/HD symptomatology (see Pliszka 1987, 1991, for reviews; Zametkin et al. 1985). These medications may be particularly helpful for children who do not respond to stimulants. However, the potential side effects (e.g., increased blood pressure, and heart rate, slowing of intracardiac conduction) must be carefully considered.

For those children who do respond to medication, it can result in temporary improvement in the ability to modulate motor behavior, increased concentration or effort on tasks, improved self-regulation, increased effort and compliance, decreased physical and verbal hostility, decreased negative social interactions, and increased amount and accuracy of work when performing previously learned skills. There are limitations, however, to the direct benefits of medication alone. For example, long-term beneficial effects have not been supported by research. Medication alone is not likely to effect a long-term improvement in academic achievement, antisocial behavior, or higher-order cognitive processes. Some children also experience side effects; eating and sleeping difficulties are the most frequently mentioned. If the sleeping and eating difficulties are not monitored, there can be growth inhibition as well. However, these concerns can be addressed by modifying dosage and mealtimes. Although such cases are infrequent, a few children may develop tics or have an increase in tics, particularly when there is a positive family history. At overly high doses, negative psychological effects on cognitive and attribution are possible. Many of the negatives, however, can be eliminated or minimized through a responsible approach to prescribing and monitoring the medication dosage (see DuPaul and Stoner 1994, for review of medication evaluation procedures). Medication should not be considered a permanent solution to AD/HD. Rather, it should be combined with one or more of the interventions reviewed below.

Parent Training and Support Groups

Although parents and caregivers of children with AD/HD may have more negative interactions with these children, AD/HD is not caused by poor parenting per se. Rather, negative parent–child interactions are more likely to be reactions to the behavioral difficulties associated with AD/HD (Barkley and Cunningham 1980, Barkley et al. 1984, 1985). Nevertheless, parents play an essential role in the establishment and maintenance of a "prosthetic social environment" (Barkley 1990). The exacerbation and continuation of AD/HD symptoms and especially the maintenance of oppositional behavior in these children seem to be related to parents' use of commands and criticism (Campbell 1987, 1990). Because these patterns are learned, it is thought that more adaptive parent influences can be developed through treatment.

Parent Training

Parent training has been found to reduce the increased stress experienced by the parent of children with AD/HD; to support behavioral improvements initially induced through medication; to address behavioral difficulties in the 20 to 30 percent of the school-aged population (and the even high percentage of the preschool population) who do not respond to medication or who may evidence undesirable side effects; to manage the behavior of children when medication is not being taken; and to address the other psychosocial difficulties, such as aggression, oppositional defiant behavior, conduct disturbance, academic underachievement, diminished self-esteem, depression, peer relationship problems, enuresis, and encopresis, that accompany AD/HD (Anastopoulos et al. 1993, Barkley 1990). In addition, parent training can be particularly effective in enhancing classroom management techniques, such as providing additional incentives for successful compliance in school (e.g., daily report card). The information parents gain about AD/HD within parent training can also be instrumental in education the child's teachers, who may be less informed about the disorder. Finally, informed parents can be more effective advocates on behalf of a child with AD/HD.

Various parent-training programs have been developed specifically for the remediation of oppositional and/or aggressive behaviors, and these programs have been applied to the treatment of children with AD/HD. Three such approaches—Barkley's (1987b) method, described in his book *Defiant Children*; Patterson's and the Oregon Social Learning Center's approach to parent training (Patterson 1976, 1982a,b); and Forehand and McMahon's (1981) approach, described in their book *Helping the Noncompliant Child*—share many elements, being based on Hanf's (1969) two-stage behavioral program for child noncompliance. The programs differ in their use of social reinforcement and contingency management, treatment formats (e.g., individual vs. group), and punishment procedures. However, all in-

clude training in ways to increase positive interactions, to set up token economy programs, and to use time out and punishment procedures. (See Newby et al. 1991, for a review and comparison of these
approaches.)

Parent Support Groups

In addition to the benefits of parent training in the treatment of
children with AD/HD, many parents find the support and resources
available from parent support groups (such as group parent training)
provide support as well as training. The support that another parent
offers is unique. Parent support groups can serve many functions,
from mutual support for parents managing their children's conditions,
to advocating for service, to relief from isolation.

There are a number of national networks such as ChADD and
the Attention Deficit Disorders Association in the United States and
Canada, as well as regional and local chapters/associations that provide support and information. In addition, these groups have been
particularly active in educating the public about AD/HD and in advocating at the local and federal levels for supportive services.

Classroom-Focused Interventions

Because of the amount of time the child spends in the classroom
setting and the likelihood that classroom performance will be disrupted because of the AD/HD symptoms, classroom interventions
are a common part of a comprehensive treatment plan. These interventions can be broadly divided into two categories: (1) interventions
aimed at changing the classroom structure and task demands, and (2)
interventions aimed at increasing the frequency and contingent nature of feedback in the classroom.

Changing Task Demands

There is a large body of literature identifying factors that either
enhance or diminish the attention span and academic performance of
students with AD/HD (Pfiffner and Barkley 1990, Whalen et al. 1979,

Zentall 1985, Zentall and Meyer 1987). This research points to a number of environmental changes that can be made in classroom instruction that do not require a more elaborate behavioral program:

- Match the tasks to the child's ability.

- Increase task novelty and interest level through color, shape, and texture.

- Present material using multiple modalities; alternate low-interest or passive tasks with high-interest or active tasks.

- Divide long assignment into shorter segments.

- Permit the child to complete less than the entire assignment when it is clear that he or she has mastered the material and achieved the automaticity required.

- Use enthusiastic and brief instruction during group lessons; allow frequent and active child participation.

- Schedule more difficult academic instruction in the morning hours.

- Augment regular classroom instruction with computer-assisted instruction.

- Permit the child to tape-record lectures and use word processing to minimize frustration resulting from handwriting difficulties.

- Provide preferential seating whenever possible to enhance eye contact.

- Provide a moderate amount of visual and auditory stimulation in the classroom. Too little stimulation (restricted cubicles) or too much (noisy, open classroom) can result in decreased attention and performance.

- Provide organized classroom structure, posting a daily schedule and classroom rules.

- Give assignments and directions as brief commands rather than longer requests.

- Minimize transitions whenever possible. Attempt to schedule "pull-out" therapies (e.g., speech/language, occupational) during the least disrupted academic periods. Plan for the child's reintegration into the flow of classroom instruction.

- Use a "priming" procedure prior to giving academic assignments.

Formal Behavior Modification Programs

A number of school-based behavioral programs have been developed specifically for children with AD/HD (Burcham and Carlson 1993, DuPaul and Stoner 1994, Parker 1992, Pfiffner and Barkley 1990, Rief 1993, Shelton and Crosswait 1992, in press). All involve the alteration of the schedule, timing, and salience of behavioral consequences used to increase and suppress target behavioral patterns. Both a review of the available research literature and the recommendations from the Federal Resource Center at the University of Kentucky, charged with identifying promising practices in classroom intervention (Burcham and Carlson 1993), indicate that successful classroom-based programs should incorporate as many of the following characteristics as possible:

- Interventions should be empirically based.

- Interventions should take into account the child's developmental age, along with the typical developmental challenges of that age.

- Academic and behavioral strengths as well as needs should be considered.

- Interventions should be practical and, whenever possible, should be "transplanted" into regular educational settings.

- Positive and proactive interventions to increase and support positive behaviors should be used, in addition to response cost or punishment procedures to decrease negative behaviors.

- Intervention strategies should be targeted to specific AD/HD symptomatology evident in the child.

- Interventions should be implemented across settings, not for only one part of the day.
- The effectiveness of and need for interventions should be monitored regularly. Treatments should not be discontinued as soon as the child shows improvement.
- Access to preferred activities should be used instead of concrete reinforcers (e.g., candy) whenever possible to increase generalization.

Educational Placement and Teacher Support

Many of the successful behavioral interventions that have been cited in the research literature involved placing the child in a substantially separate classroom, such as a behavior disorders/special educational placement or a research-funded site. However, the present educational philosophy of full inclusion and dwindling special education budgets are resulting in the placement of more and more students with AD/HD in regular classroom settings. Although the philosophy of "least restrictive environment" has documented advantages, there are potential disadvantages to this approach, especially if regular education teachers are not trained in successful interventions and if the successful interventions cannot be transplanted into regular educational settings. As a result, many state education agencies are using a "prereferral intervention" model (Parker 1992). In a prereferral model, there is a systematic and collaborative effort to assist regular education teachers in using relatively easy modifications of the classroom environment or instructional program (see list above).

Because of the demand on regular and special education classroom teachers to implement behavioral programs, many school systems are also developing programmatic student and teacher support systems (DuPaul and Stoner 1994). These include ongoing support and preparation to enable students with AD/HD to participate successfully in the future; supervision and monitoring across classrooms and other school settings; support for teachers to implement these programs (stress management); instructional accommodations when necessary; and comprehensive transition and coordination services (case management).

A consideration of interventions within regular classroom settings should not preclude a consideration of the legal right of students with AD/HD to special education services. On September 16, 1991, the U. S. Department of Education issued a policy clarification memorandum expressly recognizing children with AD/HD as eligible for special education and related services under Public Law 94-142 (Part B of the Individuals with Disabilities Education Act/IDEA) and Section 504 of the Federal Rehabilitation Act of 1973. This memorandum states that children with AD/HD meet the law's "other health impairment" disability definition, with AD/HD being a "chronic or acute health problem resulting in limited alertness (i.e., attention which adversely affects educational performance)" (p. 3). Having AD/HD does not automatically qualify a child for the assistance; it must be documented that the AD/HD results in an adverse effect on educational performance. This fact further supports the advantages of the two-tiered assessment approach described earlier. Obviously, the availability of special education services will be reviewed on a case-by-case basis. ChADD's *Educator's Manual* (Fowler 1992) and *Attention Deficit Disorder and the Law* (Latham and Latham 1992) contain helpful overviews of pertinent federal laws and legal opinions.

Individual or Group Interventions with Children

Social Skills Training

As mentioned, children with AD/HD tend to have more difficulties than their peers in getting along with others and maintaining close friendships (Barkley 1990, Guevremont 1990). The impulsivity or inattention that can interfere with classroom performance can also result in disruptive behavior on the playground, low frustration tolerance and temper tantrums, and difficulty following the rules of games. Most children with AD/HD are able to articulate the skills necessary for successful social interaction; they seem to have their greatest difficulty in using these skills in a successful way. Because of these performance deficits, interventions that target the acquisition of skills rather than the performance of these skills have failed to show generalization from the therapy session to in vivo situations (DuPaul and Eckert 1994, Guevremont 1990).

Several promising social skills interventions attempt to overcome these shortcomings (Guevremont 1990, Hinshaw et al. 1984, Pelham and Bender 1982, Shelton and Crosswait, in press). Although the approaches vary in the target age of the child, the setting for intervention (e.g., clinic, camp, and classroom), and specific techniques, all attempt to address generalization and maintenance. Important components include anger control, conversational skills and entry into peer group activities, teacher-led social skills training generalized across the academic curriculum, and strategic use of peers.

Cognitive-Behavioral Interventions

Cognitive-behavioral approaches, based on the work of Russian neuropsychologists (Luria 1961, Vygotsky 1962), address the supposed deficits of children with AD/HD in developing self-directed speech. The absence of self-directed speech is thought to be evidenced in the children's lack of behavioral control, their difficulty in generating solutions to problems, and their impulsivity. Numerous cognitive-behavioral treatment approaches have been developed (Braswell and Bloomquist 1991, Camp 1980, Kendall and Braswell 1984, Meichenbaum 1988) on the basis of this theory. Although intuitively appealing, recent research has failed to yield strong empirical support for this approach, particularly in the maintenance and generalization of treatment gains seen in the therapy session to other settings (e.g., home, school). While not as successful as once thought, these techniques can be a helpful adjunct to an overall treatment package if certain considerations are kept in mind. First, the child's cognitive abilities must be considered. Cognitive-behavioral interventions are more likely to be successful with older children whose cognitive abilities are solidly within Piaget's concrete operational stage. Second, the use of cognitive-behavioral/self-monitoring strategies must be reinforced at home and school. This can be accomplished by rewarding the use of such strategies, as well as having the adults in a child's life model a similar "task analysis" approach. Third, these strategies can be helpful in remediating some of the difficulties that can accompany AD/HD, such as social skills deficits, depression, low self-esteem, misattributions for success and failure (e.g., medication effects), and anxiety.

CONCLUSION

AD/HD is a developmental disability manifested in difficulties with sustained attention, impulse control, and the regulation of activity level to situational demands. It develops early in childhood, is relatively pervasive and cross-situational, and is typically chronic in nature. Current research supports a biological predisposition to the disorder; however, there may be multiple pathways toward the development of the disorder. Although environmental influences are not a major cause, they appear to play a role in determining the severity of AD/HD symptoms, the development of oppositional and defiant behavior as well as conduct problems, and the long-term prognosis for the disorder.

As a result of the clinical picture of AD/HD, the assessment, diagnosis, and treatment of the disorder must necessarily be multidimensional. Interviews, standardized child behavior rating scales, psychometric measures of intelligence and achievement, and direct behavioral observations of the AD/HD symptoms in natural or analogue settings should be considered as part of an assessment battery, incorporating the opinions of several informants (parent and teachers). The treatment of AD/HD requires expertise in many different treatment modalities, no single one of which can address all of the difficulties likely to be experienced by such children. Among available treatments, stimulant medication, parent training in effective child management, classroom behavior modification, special educational placement, and in some cases individualized self-control and social skills training appear to have the greatest efficacy. Nevertheless, to be effective in altering prognosis, treatment must be evaluated periodically and, when necessary, maintained over an extended time.

REFERENCES

Abidin, R. R. (1986). *The Parenting Stress Index*, 2nd ed. Charlottesville, VA: Pediatric Psychology Press.

Abikoff, H., Gittelman-Klein R., and Klein, D. (1977). Validation of classroom observation for hyperactive children. *Journal of Consulting and Clinical Psychology* 45:772–783.

Achenbach, T. M. (1991). *Manual for the Revised Child Behavior Checklist.* Burlington: University of Vermont, Department of Psychiatry.

Achenbach, T. M., and Edelbrock, C. (1983). *Manual for the Child Behavior Checklist and Revised Child Behavior Profile.* Burlington: University of Vermont, Department of Psychiatry.

Achenbach, T. M., McConaughy, S. H., and Howell, C. T. (1987). Child/adolescent behavior and emotional problems: implications of cross-informant correlations for situational specificity. *Psychological Bulletin* 102:213–232.

American Psychiatric Association. (1980). *Diagnostic and Statistical Manual of Mental Disorders*, 3rd ed. *(DSM-III).* Washington, DC: American Psychiatric Association.

—— (1987). *Diagnostic and Statistical Manual of Mental Disorders*, 3rd ed. revised. *(DSM-III-R).* Washington, DC: American Psychiatric Association.

—— (1994). *Diagnostic and Statistical Manual of Mental Disorders*, 4th ed. *(DSM-IV).* Washington, DC: American Psychiatric Association.

Anastopoulos, A. D., and Barkley, R. A. (1988). Biological factors in attention deficit hyperactivity disorder. *Behavior Therapist* 11:47–53.

Anastopoulos, A. D., Guevremont, D. C., Shelton, T. L., and DuPaul, G. J. (1992). Parenting stress among families of children with attention deficit hyperactivity disorder. *Journal of Abnormal Child Psychology* 20:503–520.

Anastopoulos, A. D., Shelton, T. L., DuPaul, G. J., and Guevremont, D. C. (1993). Parent training for attention deficit hyperactivity disorder: its impact on parent functioning. *Journal of Abnormal Child Psychology* 21:581–596.

Anastopoulos, A. D., Spisto, M. A., and Maher, M. (1994). The WISC-III third factor: its utility in identifying children with attention deficit hyperactivity disorder. *Psychological Assessment* 6:368–371.

Arnold, L. E., Clark, D. L., Sachs, L. A., et al. (1985). Vestibular and visual rotational stimulation as treatment for attention deficit and hyperactivity. *American Journal of Occupational Therapy* 39:84–91.

August, G. J., and Stewart, M. A. (1983). Family subtypes of childhood hyperactivity. *Journal of Nervous and Mental Disease* 171:362–368.

Ayllon, T., and Rosenbaum, M. (1977). The behavioral treatment of disruption and hyperactivity in school settings. In *Advances in Clinical Child Psychology*, vol. 1, ed. B. Lahey and A. Kazdin, pp. 83–118. New York: Plenum.

Barkley, R. A. (1977). A review of stimulant drug research with hyperactive children. *Journal of Child Psychology and Psychiatry* 18:137–165.

—— (1981). *Hyperactive Children: A Handbook for Diagnosis and Treatment.* New York: Guilford.

—— (1987a). Child behavior rating scales and checklists. In *Assessment and Diagnosis in Child Psychopathology*, ed. M. Rutter, A. H. Tuma, and I. S. Lann, pp. 113–155. New York: Guilford.

—— (1987b). *Defiant Children: A Clinician's Manual for Parent Training.* New York: Guilford.

—— (1990). *Attention-Deficit Hyperactivity Disorder: A Handbook for Diagnosis and Treatment.* New York: Guilford.

—— (1992). The ecological validity of laboratory and analogue assessments of AD/HD symptoms. *Journal of Abnormal Child Psychology* 19:149–178.

—— (1994). The assessment of attention in children. In *Frames of Reference for the Assessment of Learning Disabilities: New Views on Measurement Issues*, ed. G. R. Lyon, pp. 110–141. Baltimore: Paul H. Brookes.

Barkley, R. A., and Cunningham, C. (1980). The parent-child interactions of hyperactive children and their modification by stimulant drugs. In *Treatment of Hyperactive and Learning Disabled Children*, ed. R. Knights and D. Bakker, pp. 210–236. Baltimore: University Park Press.

Barkley, R. A., Cunningham, C., and Karlsson, J. (1983). The speech of hyperactive children with their mothers: comparisons with normal children and stimulant drug effects. *Journal of Learning Disabilities* 16:105–110.

Barkley, R. A., DuPaul, G., and McMurray, M. (1990a). A comprehensive evaluation of attention deficit disorder with and without hyperactivity as defined by research criteria. *Journal of Consulting and Clinical Psychology* 58:775–789.

Barkley, R. A., Fischer, M., Edelbrock, D. S., and Smallish, L. (1990b). The adolescent outcome of hyperactive children diagnosed by research criteria: I. An 8-year prospective follow-up study. *Journal of the American Academy of Child and Adolescent Psychiatry* 29:546–557.

Barkley, R. A., Grodzinsky, G., and DuPaul, G. J. (1992). Frontal lobe functions in attention deficit disorder with and without hyperactivity: a review and research report. *Journal of Abnormal Child Psychology* 20:163–188.

Barkley, R. A., Karlsson, J., and Pollard, S. (1985). Effects of age on the mother–child interactions of hyperactive children. *Journal of Abnormal Child Psychology* 13:631–638.

Barkley, R. A., Karlsson, J., Strzelecki, E., and Murphy, J. (1984). Effects of age and Ritalin dosage on the mother–child interactions of hyperactive children. *Journal of Consulting and Clinical Psychology* 52:750–758.

Beck, A. T., Rush, A. J., Shaw, B. F., and Emery, G. (1979). *Cognitive Therapy for Depression.* New York: Guilford.

Biederman, J., Munir, K., Knee, D., et al. (1987). High rate of affective disorders in probands with attention deficit disorders and in their relatives: a controlled family study. *American Journal of Psychiatry* 144:330–333.

Braswell, L., and Bloomquist, M. L. (1991). *Cognitive-Behavioral Therapy with AD/HD Children: Child, Family, and School Interventions.* New York: Guilford.

Brown, R. T., and Borden, K. A. (1986). Hyperactivity at adolescence: some misconceptions and new directions. *Journal of Clinical Child Psychology* 5:194–209.

Brown, R. T., and Quay, L. A. (1977). Reflection-impulsivity of normal and behavior disorder children. *Journal of Abnormal Child Psychology* 5:457–462.

Burcham, B., and Carlson, L. (1993). *Promising Practices in the Identification and Education of Children with Attention Deficit Disorder.* Lexington: University of Kentucky.

Camp, B. W. (1980). Two psychoeducational treatment programs for young aggressive boys. In *Hyperactive Children: The Social Ecology of Identification and Treatment,* ed. C. Whalen and B. Henker, pp. 191–220. New York: Academic Press.

Campbell, S. B. (1987). Parent-referred problem three-year-olds: developmental changes in symptoms. *Journal of Child Psychology and Psychiatry* 28:835–846.

——— (1990). *Behavior Problems in Preschool Children: Clinical and Developmental Issues.* New York: Guilford.

Campbell, S. B., Douglas, V. I., and Morgenstern, G. (1971). Cognitive styles in hyperactive children and the effect of methylphenidate. *Journal of Child Psychology and Psychiatry* 12:55–67.

Cantwell, D. E., and Satterfield, J. H. (1978). The prevalence of academic underachievement in hyperactive children. *Journal of Pediatric Psychology* 3:168–171.

Carlson, C. (1986). Attention deficit disorder without hyperactivity: a review of preliminary experimental evidence. In *Advances in Clinical Child Psychology,* vol. 9, ed. B. Lahey and A. Kazdin, pp. 153–176. New York: Plenum.

Carlson, C., and Brunner, M. R. (1993). Effects of methylphenidate on the academic performance of children with attention-deficit hyperactivity disorder. *School Psychology Review* 22:184–198.

Chelune, G. J., Ferguson, W., Koon, R., and Dickey, T. O. (1986). Frontal lobe disinhibition in attention deficit disorder. *Child Psychiatry and Human Development* 16:221–234.

Conners, C. K. (1980). *Food Additive and Hyperactive Children*. New York: Plenum.

——— (1994). *The Continuous Performance Test (CPT): use as a diagnostic tool and measure of treatment outcome*. Paper presented at the annual meeting of the American Psychological Association, Los Angeles, CA, August.

Cooley, E. I., and Morris, R. D. (1990). Attention in children: a neuropsychologically based model for assessment. *Developmental Neuropsychology* 6:239–274.

Costello, A. J., Edelbrock, C. S., Kalas, R., et al. (1982). *The NIMH Diagnostic Interview Schedule for Children (DISC)*. Pittsburgh: University of Pittsburgh, Department of Psychiatry.

Derogatis, L. (1986). *Manual for the Symptom Checklist 90-Revised (SCL-90-R)*. Baltimore: Author.

Deutsch, C. K., and Kinsbourne, M. (1990). Genetics and biochemistry in attention deficit disorder. In *Handbook of Developmental Psychopathology*, ed. M. Lewis and S. M. Miller, pp. 93–107. New York: Plenum.

Deutsch, C. K., Swanson, J. M., and Bruell, J. M. (1982). Overrepresentation of adoptees in children with the attention deficit disorder. *Behavioral Genetics* 12:231–238.

Diener, R. M. (1991). Toxicology of ritalin. In *Ritalin: Theory and Patient Management*, ed. L. L. Greenhill and B. B. Osman, pp. 34–43. New York: Mary Ann Liebert.

Donnelly, M., and Rapoport, J. L. (1985). Attention deficit disorders. In *Diagnosis and Psychopharmology of Childhood and Adolescent Disorders*, ed. J. M. Wiener, pp. 179–197. New York: Wiley.

Douglas, V. I. (1983). Attention and cognitive problems. In *Developmental Neuropsychiatry*, ed. M. Rutter, pp. 280–329. New York: Guilford.

DuPaul, G. (1991). Parent and teacher ratings of AD/HD symptoms: psychometric properties in a community-based sample. *Journal of Clinical Child Psychology* 20:245–253.

DuPaul, G. J., Anastopoulos, A. D., Shelton, T. L., et al. (1992). Multimethod assessment of attention deficit hyperactivity disorder: the diagnostic utility of clinic-based tests. *Journal of Clinical Child Psychology* 21:394–402.

DuPaul, G. J., and Barkley, R. A. (1990). Medication therapy. In *Attention-Deficit Hyperactivity Disorder: A Handbook for Diagnosis and Treatment*, ed. R. A. Barkley, pp. 573–612. New York: Guilford.

DuPaul, G. J., and Eckert, T. L. (1994). The effects of social skills curricula: now you see them, now you don't. *School Psychology Quarterly* 9(2):113–132.

DuPaul, G. J., and Stoner, G. (1994). *AD/HD in the Schools.* New York: Guilford.

Edelbrock, C. S. (1985). The Child Attention Problems (CAP) Rating Scale. In *Attention-Deficit Hyperactivity Disorder: A Handbook for Diagnosis and Treatment,* ed. R. A. Barkley. New York: Guilford, 1990.

Edelbrock, C. S., Render, R., Plomin, R., and Thompson, L. A. (1991). Genetic and environmental effects on competence and problem behavior in childhood and early adolescence. Unpublished manuscript, Pennsylvania State University.

Farrington, D. P., Loeber, R., and van Kammen, W. B. (1987). *Long-term criminal outcomes of hyperactivity-impulsivity-attention deficit and conduct problems in childhood.* Paper presented at the meeting of the Society of Life History Research, St. Louis, MO, October.

Feingold, B. (1975). *Why Your Child is Hyperactive.* New York: Random House.

Fischer, M. E., Barkley, R. A., Edelbrock, C. S., and Smallish, L. (1990). The adolescent outcome of hyperactive children diagnosed by research criteria; III. Academic attention, and neuropsychological status. *Journal of Consulting and Clinical Psychology* 58:580–588.

Forehand, R., and McMahon, R. (1981). *Helping the Noncompliant Child: A Clinician's Guide to Parent Training.* New York: Guilford.

Fowler, M. (1992). *Educator's Manual.* Plantation, FL: Children and Adults with Attention Deficit Disorders.

Fuster, J. M. (1989). A theory of prefrontal functions: the prefrontal cortex and the temporal organization of behavior. In *The Prefrontal Cortex: Anatomy, Physiology, and Neuropsychology of the Frontal Lobe,* ed. J. M. Fuster, pp. 157–196. New York: Raven.

Gittelman, R., and Eskinazi, B. (1983). Lead and hyperactivity revisited. *Archives of General Psychiatry* 40:827–833.

Goodyear, P., and Hynd, G. (1992). Attention deficit disorder with (ADD/H) and without (ADD/WO) hyperactivity: behavioral and neuropsychological differentiation. *Journal of Clinical Child Psychology* 21:273–304.

Gordon, M. (1983). *The Gordon Diagnostic System.* Boulder, CO: Clinical Diagnostic Systems.

Goyette, C. H., Conners, C. K., and Ulrich, R. F. (1978). Normative data for Revised Conners Parent and Teacher Rating Scales. *Journal of Abnormal Child Psychology* 6:221–236.

Greenblatt, E., Mattis, S., and Trad, P. V. (1991). The ACID pattern and the freedom from distractibility factor in a child psychiatric population. *Developmental Neuropsychology* 7:121–130.

Gross, M. D. (1984). Effects of sucrose in hyperkinetic children. *Pediatrics* 74:876–878.

Guevremont, D. C. (1990). Social skills and peer relationship training. In *Attention-Deficit Hyperactivity Disorder: A Handbook for Diagnosis and Treatment*, ed. R. A. Barkley, pp. 540–572. New York: Guilford.

Hale, G. A., and Lewis, M. (1979). *Attention and Cognitive Development*. New York: Plenum.

Hales, D., and Hales, R. (1985). Using body to mend the mind. *American Health* 6:27–31.

Hamlett, K. W., Pellegrini, D. S., and Conners, C. K. (1987). An investigation of executive processes in the problem-solving of attention deficit disorder-hyperactive children. *Journal of Pediatric Psychology* 12:227–240.

Hanf, C. (1969). *A two-stage program for modifying maternal controlling during mother–child (M-C) interaction.* Paper presented at the meeting of the Western Psychological Association, Vancouver, British Columbia, April.

Hartsough, C. S., and Lambert, N. M. (1985). Medical factors in hyperactive and normal children: prenatal, developmental, and health history findings. *American Journal of Orthopsychiatry* 55:190–201.

Haslam, R. H. A., Dalby, J. T., and Rademaker, A. W. (1984). Effects of megavitamin therapy on children with attention deficit disorders. *Pediatrics* 74:103–111.

Hastings, J. E., and Barkley, R. A. (1978). A review of psychophysiological research with hyperactive children. *Journal of Abnormal Child Psychology* 7:413–447.

Hinshaw, S. (1987). On the distinction between attentional deficits/hyperactivity and conduct problems/aggression in child psychology. *Psychological Bulletin* 101:443–463.

—— (1991). Stimulant medication and the treatment of aggression in children with attention deficits. *Journal of Clinical Child Psychology* 20:301–312.

Hinshaw, S., Henker, B., and Whalen, C. K. (1984). Self-control in hyperactive boys in anger-inducing situations. Effects of cognitive-behavioral training and of methylphenidate. *Journal of Consulting and Clinical Psychology* 52:739–749.

Jacob, R. G., O'Leary, K. D., and Rosenblad, C. (1978). Formal and informal classroom settings: effects on hyperactivity. *Journal of Abnormal Child Psychology* 6:47–59.

Jacobvitz, D., Sroufe, L., Steward, M., and Leffert, N. (1990). Treatment of attentional and hyperactivity problems in children with sympathomimetic drugs: a comprehensive review. *Journal of the American Academy of Child and Adolescent Psychiatry* 29:677–688.

James, W. (1898). *Principles of Psychology*, 2 vols. New York: Henry Holt.

Johnston, C., Pelham, W. E., and Murphy, H. A. (1985). Peer relationships in ADDH and normal children: a developmental analysis of peer and teacher ratings. *Journal of Abnormal Child Psychology* 13:89–100.

Kagan, J. (1966). Reflection-impulsivity: the generality and dynamics of conceptual tempo. *Journal of Abnormal Psychology* 71:17–24.

Kanfer, F. H., and Saslow, G. (1969). Behavioral diagnosis. In *Behavior Therapy: Appraisal and Status*, ed. C. M. Franks, pp. 417–444. New York: McGraw-Hill.

Kendall, P. E., and Braswell, L. (1984). *Cognitive-Behavioral Therapy for Impulsive Children*. New York: Guilford.

Klee, S. H., and Garfinkel, B. D. (1983). The computerized continuous performance task: a new measure of attention. *Journal of the American Academy of Child Psychiatry* 11:487–496.

Kovacs, M. (1982). *The Longitudinal Study of Child and Adolescent Psychopathology: I. The Semistructured Psychiatric Interview Schedule for Children (ISC)*. Pittsburgh: Western Psychiatric Institute.

Lahey, B. B., Piacentini, J. C., McBurnett, K., et al. (1988). Psychopathology in the parent of children with conduct disorder and hyperactivity. *Journal of the American Academy of Child and Adolescent Psychiatry* 27:163–170.

Lambert, N. M., Sandoval, J., and Sassone, D. (1978). Prevalence of hyperactivity in elementary school children as a function of social system definers. *American Journal of Orthopsychiatry* 48:446–463.

Last, D. G. (1986). Modification of schedules for affective disorder and schizophrenia for school-age children (K-SADS). Unpublished manuscript.

Latham, P. S., and Latham, P. H. (1992). *Attention Deficit Disorder and the Law*. Washington, DC: JKL Communications.

Locke, H. J., and Wallace, K. M. (1959). Short-term marital adjustment and prediction tests: their reliability and validity. *Journal of Marriage and the Family Living* 21:251–255.

Loney, J., Whaley-Klahn, M. A., Kosier, T., and Conboy, J. (1981). *Hyperactive boys and their brothers at 21: predictors of aggressive and antisocial outcomes*. Paper presented at the meeting of the Society for Life History Research, Monterey, CA, November.

Lou, H. C., Henriksen, L., and Bruhn, P. (1984). Focal cerebral hypoperfusion in children with dysphasia and/or attention deficit disorder. *Archives of Neurology* 41:825–829.

Lou, H. C., Henriksen, L., Bruhn, P., et al. (1989). Striatal dysfunction in attention deficit and hyperkinetic disorder. *Archives of Neurology* 46:48–52.

Luk, S. (1985). Direct observations studies of hyperactive behaviors. *Journal of the American Academy of Child Psychiatry* 24:338–344.

Luria, A. R. (1961). *The Role of Speech in the Regulation of Normal and Abnormal Behavior.* Elmsford, NY: Pergamon Press.

Mattes, J. A., and Gittelman, R. (1981). Effects of artificial food colorings in children with hyperactive symptoms. *Archives of General Psychiatry* 38:714–718.

McCarney, S. B. (1989). *Attention Deficit Disorders Evaluation Scale Technical Manual.* Columbia, MO: Hawthorne Educational Services.

McGee, R., Williams S., Moffitt, T., and Anderson, J. (1989). A comparison of 13-year-old boys with attention deficit and or reading disorder on neuropsychological measure. *Journal of Abnormal Child Psychology* 17:37–53.

Meichenbaum, D. (1988). Cognitive behavioral modification with attention deficit hyperactive children. In *Attention Deficit Disorder: Criteria, Cognition, and Intervention,* ed. L. Bloomingdale and J. Sergeant, pp. 127–140. Elmsford, NY: Pergamon Press.

Mesulam, M. A. (1990). Large-scale neurocognitive networks and distributed processing for attention, language, and memory, *Annals of Neurology* 28:597–613.

Milich, R., and Kramer, J. (1985). Reflections on impulsivity: an empirical investigation of impulsivity as a construct. In *Advances in Learning and Behavioral Disabilities,* vol. 3, ed. K. Gadow and I. Bialer, pp. 117–150.

Milich, R., Wolraich, M., and Lindgren, S. (1986). Sugar and hyperactivity: a critical review of empirical findings. *Clinical Psychology Review* 6:493–513.

Mirsky, A. F. (1987). Behavioral and psychophysiological markers of disordered attention. *Environmental Health Perspectives* 74:191–199.

Newby, R. F., Fischer, M., and Roman, M. A. (1991). Parent training for families of children with attention deficit-hyperactivity disorder. *School Psychology Review* 20:252–265.

Parker, H. C. (1992). *The ADD Hyperactivity Handbook for Schools.* Plantation, FL: Impact.

Patterson, G. R. (1976). *Living with Children: New Methods for Parents and Teachers.* Champaign, IL: Research Press.

——— (1982a). *Coercive Family Process.* Eugene, OR: Castalia.

——— (1982b). *A Social Learning Approach to Family Intervention,* vol. 3. Eugene, OR: Castalia.

Pelham, W. E., and Bender, M. E. (1982). Peer relationships in hyperactive children: description and treatment. In *Advances in Learning and Behavioral Disabilities,* vol. 1, ed. K. D. Gadow and I. Bialer, pp. 365–436. Greenwich, CT: JAI Press.

Pfiffner, L. J., and Barkley, R. A. (1990). Educational placement and classroom management. In *Attention-Deficit Hyperactivity Disorder: A Handbook for Diagnosis and Treatment*, ed. R. A. Barkley, pp. 498–539. New York: Guilford.

Pliszka, S. R. (1987). Tricyclic antipressants in the treatment of children with attention deficit disorder. *Journal of the American Academy of Child and Adolescent Psychiatry* 26:127–132.

———— (1991). Antidepressants in the treatment of child and adolescent psychopathology. *Journal of Clinical Child Psychology* 20:313–320.

Porrino, L. J., Rapoport, J. L., Behar, D., et al. (1983). A naturalistic assessment of the motor activity of hyperactive boys. *Archives of General Psychiatry* 40:681–687.

Posner, M. (1988). Structures and function of selective attention. In *Clinical Neuropsychology and Brain Function: Research, Measurement, and Practice*, ed. M. Dennis, E. Kaplan, M. Posner, et al., pp. 169–201. Washington, DC: American Psychological Association.

Quinn, P. O., and Rapoport, J. L. (1974). Minor physical anomalies and neurologic status in hyperactive boys. *Pediatrics* 53:742–747.

Rapport, M. D., DuPaul, G. J., and Kelly, K. L. (1989). Attention-deficit hyperactivity disorder and methylphenidate: the relationship between gross body weight and drug response in children. *Psychopharmacology Bulletin* 25:285–290.

Rapport, M. D., Tucker, S. B., DuPaul, G. J., et al. (1986). Hyperactivity and frustration: the influence of control over and size of rewards in delaying gratification. *Journal of Abnormal Child Psychology* 14:191–204.

Reich, W., Shayka, J. J., and Taibleson, C. (1992). *Diagnostic Interview for Children and Adolescents (DICA-R-A)*. St. Louis, MO: Washington University.

Reynolds, C. R., and Kamphaus, R. W. (1992). *Behavior Assessment System for Children*. Circle Pines, MN: American Guidance Service.

Richter, N. C. (1984). The efficacy of relaxation training with children. *Journal of Abnormal Child Psychology* 2:319–344.

Rief, S. F. (1993). *How to Reach and Teach ADD/AD/HD Children*. New York: Simon & Schuster.

Roberts, M. A. (1979). *A Manual for the Restricted Academic Playroom Situation*. Iowa City, IA: Author.

Ross, D. M., and Ross, S. A. (1976). *Hyperactivity: Research, Theory, and Action*. New York: Wiley.

———— (1982). *Hyperactivity: Current Issues, Research, and Theory*, 2nd ed. New York: Wiley.

Routh, D. K. (1978). Hyperactivity. In *Psychological Management of Pediatric Problems,* ed. I. P. Magrab, pp. 3–48. Baltimore: University Park Press.

Safer, D. J., and Allen, R. (1976). *Hyperactive Children.* Baltimore: University Park Press.

Safer, D. J., and Krager, J. M. (1988). A survey of medication treatment for hyperactive/inattentive students. *Journal of the American Medical Association* 260:2256–2258.

Satterfield, J. H., Satterfield, B. T., and Cantwell, D. P. (1981). Three-year multimodality treatment study of 100 hyperactive boys. *Journal of Pediatrics* 98:650–655.

Shaffer, D., Schwab-Stone, M., Fisher, P., et al. (1993). The Diagnostic Interview for Schedule for Children–Revised Version (DISC-R): I. Preparation, field testing, interrater reliability, and acceptability. *Journal of the American Academy of Child and Adolescent Psychiatry* 32:643–650.

Shaywitz, S. E., Shaywityz, B. A., Cohen, D. J., and Young, J. G. (1983). Monoaminergic mechanisms in hyperactivity. In *Developmental Neuropsychiatry*, ed. R. Rutter, pp. 330–347. New York: Guilford.

Shelton, T. L., Anastopoulos, A. D., and DuPaul, G. J. (1994). *Correspondence between parent and teacher ratings of AD/HD symptomatology: developmental considerations.* Paper presented at the annual meeting of the Society for Research in Child and Adolescent Psychiatry, London, June.

Shelton, T. L., and Barkley, R. A. (1993). Assessment of attention-deficit hyperactivity disorder in young children. In *Testing Young Children*, ed. J. L. Culbertson and D. J. Willis, pp. 290–318. Austin, TX: Pro-Ed.

Shelton, T. L., and Crosswait, C. R. (1992). Prevention/treatment program for kindergarten students with or at risk for AD/HD. *Chadder*, pp. 16–18, 33.

——— (in press). *Managing Disruptive Behaviors in the Classroom.* New York: Guilford.

Stewart, M. A., Pitts, F. N., Carig, A. G., and Dieruf, W. (1966). The hyperactive child syndrome. *American Journal of Orthopsychiatry* 36:861–867.

Still, G. F. (1902). Some abnormal psychical conditions in children. *Lancet* 1:1008–1012, 1077–1082, 1163–1168.

Strauss, A. A., and Lehtinen, L. W. (1947). *Psychopathology and Education of the Brain-Injured Child.* New York: Grune & Stratton.

Strayhorn, J. M., and Weidman, C. S. (1988). A parent practices scale and its relations to parent and child mental health. *Journal of the American Academy of Child and Adolescent Psychiatry* 27:613–618.

Streissguth, A. P., Martin, D. C., Barr, H. M., et al. (1984). Intrauterine alcohol and nicotine exposure: attention and reaction time in 4-year-old children. *Developmental Psychology* 20:533–541.

Swanson, J. (1993). *The Effects of Medication on Children with Attention Deficit Disorder: The University of California at Irvine ADD Center's Review of Reviews.* Irvine: University of California at Irvine.

Swanson, J., Cantwell, D., Lerner, M., et al. (1992). Treatment of AD/HD: beyond medication. *Beyond Behavior* 4:13–22.

Szatmari, P., Offord, D. R., and Boyle, M. H. (1989). Ontario Child Health Study: prevalence of attention deficit disorder with hyperactivity. *Journal of Child Psychology and Psychiatry* 30:219–230.

Taylor, E. A. (1986). Childhood hyperactivity. *British Journal of Psychiatry* 149:562–573.

Taylor, J. F. (1980). *The Hyperactive Child and the Family.* New York: Random House.

Thorley, G. (1984). Review of follow-up and follow-back studies of childhood hyperactivity. *Psychological Bulletin* 96:116–132.

Thorndike, R. L., Hagen, E. P., and Sattler, J. M. (1986). *Guide for Administering and Scoring the Stanford-Binet Intelligence Scale*, 4th ed. Chicago: Riverside.

Touliatos, J., and Lindholm, B. W. (1981). Congruence of parents' and teachers' ratings of children's behavior problems. *Journal of Abnormal Child Psychology* 9:347–354.

Tredgold, A. F. (1908). *Mental Deficiency (Amentia).* New York: W. Wood.

Trites, R. L., Dugas, F., Lynch, G., and Ferguson, B. (1979a). Incidence of hyperactivity. *Journal of Pediatric Psychology* 4:179–188.

Trites, R. L., Tryphonas, H., and Ferguson, B. (1979b). Incidence of hyperactivity. *Journal of Pediatric Psychology* 4:179–188.

——— (1980). Diet treatment for hyperactive children with food allergies. In *Treatment of Hyperactive and Learning Disordered Children*, ed. R. Knight and D. Bakker, pp. 151–166. Baltimore: University Park Press.

Trommer, B. L., Hoeppner, J. B., Lorber, R., and Armstrong, K. (1988). Pitfalls in the use of a continuous performance test as a diagnostic tool in attention deficit disorder. *Journal of Developmental and Behavior Pediatrics* 9:339–345.

Tryon, W. W. (1984). Principles and methods of mechanically measuring motor activity. *Behavioral Assessment* 6:129–140.

Ullmann, R., Sleator, E., and Sprague, R. (1984). A new rating scale for diagnosis and monitoring of ADD children. *Psychopharmacology Bulletin*, 20:160–164.

U. S. Department of Education. (1991, September 16). *Policy Clarification Memorandum.* Washington, DC: Office of Special Projects and Rehabilitation Services.

Vygotsky, L. S. (1962). *Thought and Language.* Boston: MIT Press.

Wechsler, D. (1989a). *Manual for the Wechsler Preschool and Primary Scales of Intelligence.* San Antonio, TX: Psychological Corporation.

———— (1989b). *Manual for the Wechsler Intelligence Scale for Children,* 3rd ed. San Antonio, TX: Psychological Corporation.

———— (1992). *The Wechsler Individual Achievement Test.* San Antonio, TX: Psychological Corporation.

Weiss, G., and Hechtman, L. T. (1993). *Hyperactive Children Grown Up,* 2nd ed. New York: Guilford.

Werry, J. S., and Sprague, R. L. (1970). Hyperactivity. In *Symptoms of Psychopathology,* ed. C. G. Costello, pp. 397–417. New York: Wiley.

Whalen, C. K., and Henker, B. (1991). Social impact of stimulant treatment for hyperactive children. *Journal of Learning Disabilities* 24:231–241.

Whalen, C. K., Henker, B., Collins, B. E., et al. (1979). A social ecology of hyperactive boys: medication effects in structured classroom environments. *Journal of Applied Behavior Analysis* 12:65–81.

Wilson, B. C., and Risucci, D. A. (1986). A model for clinical-quantitative classification: generation I. Application to language-disordered preschool children. *Brain and Language* 27:281–309.

Wolraich, M., Milich, R., Stumbo, P., and Schultz, F. (1985). The effects of sucrose ingestion on the behavior of hyperactive boys. *Pediatrics* 106:675–682.

Woodcock, R. W., and Johnson, M. B. (1990). *Woodcock-Johnson Psycho-Educational Battery-Revised.* Allen, TX: DLM Teaching Resources.

Zametkin, A. J., and Rapoport, J. L. (1986). The pathophysiology of attention deficit disorder with hyperactivity: a review. In *Advances in Clinical Child Psychology* vol. 9, ed. B. Lahey and A. Kazkin, pp. 177–216. New York: Plenum.

Zametkin, A., Rapoport, J. L., Murphy, D. L., et al. (1985). Treatment of hyperactive children with monoamine oxidase inhibitors: I. Clinical efficacy. *Archives of General Psychiatry* 42(9):73–118.

Zentall, S. S. (1985). A context for hyperactivity. In *Advances in Learning and Behavioral Disabilities,* vol. 4, ed. K. D. Gadow and I. Bialer, pp. 273–343. Greenwich, CT: JAI Press.

———— (1989). Production deficiencies in elicited language but not in the spontaneous verbalization of hyperactive children. *Journal of Abnormal Child Psychology* 16:657–673.

Zentall, S. S., and Meyer, M. J. (1987). Self-regulation of stimulation for ADD-H children during reading and vigilance task performance. *Journal of Abnormal Child Psychology* 15:519–536.

Zettle, R. D., and Hayes, S. C. (1982). *Rule-Governed Behavior: A Potential Theoretical Framework for Cognitive-Behavioral Therapy. Advances in Cognitive-Behavioral Research*, vol. 1, pp. 73–118. New York: Academic Press.

Zirkel, P. A. (1992). A checklist for determining eligibility of ADD/AD/HD students. *Special Educator* 8:93–97.

3

The Need for Psychological Diagnostic Testing in the Assessment of AD/HD in Children and Adolescents

James A. Incorvaia

Attention deficit disorder (ADD) has more recently been labeled AD/HD by the American Psychiatric Association's *Diagnostic and Statistical Manual of Mental Disorders* (*DSM-IV*) (American Psychiatric Association 1994). Barkley (1990), considered to be one of the leading experts in this area, has given this disorder the following consensus definition:

> Attention deficit/hyperactivity disorder is a developmental disorder characterized by developmentally inappropriate degrees of inattention, overactivity, and impulsivity. These often arise in early childhood; are relatively chronic in nature; and are not readily accounted for on the basis of gross neurological, sensory, language, or motor impairments, mental retardation, or severe emotional disturbance. These difficulties are typically associated with deficits in rule-governed behavior and in maintaining a consistent pattern of work performance over time. [p. 47]

AD/HD is the most popular and most diagnosed disorder in children and adolescents in the United States today. Fitzsimmons (1996), in a recent *San Diego Union Tribune* article, estimated that nationwide about two million youth, 5 percent of all school-age children, suffer from AD/HD. Amen (1995) estimates the incidence as even greater, 17 million people in the United States alone, including 5 to 10 percent of the childhood population. He also states that it affects 50 percent of those children and adolescents who come to mental health clinics for evaluation. Blau (1995) concurs, adding that AD/HD is "the leading psychiatric diagnosis among children, but the condition is also commonly misdiagnosed" (p. 45).

In fact, AD/HD is fast becoming one of the most used, and, some feel, most abused, diagnoses currently given to young people around the world. It is not surprising, then, that there are many detractors, including some who even question the existence of AD/HD.

Blau (1995) suggests that detractors have three concerns:

1. The diagnosis of AD/HD is being "strongly encouraged by the drug companies, who have the most to gain because of the widespread use of psychoactive medications particularly stimulants like Ritalin" (p. 44).

2. The diagnosis of AD/HD is "the latest disease of the week and a convenient catchall diagnosis for children whose busy parents weaned them on the sound bytes of Sesame Street" (p. 44).

3. The diagnosis of AD/HD is the "latest cash cow of the mental health industry" (p. 44).

Those who question the existence of this diagnosis make others in the mental health field wonder why AD/HD, a relatively new category of dysfunction, has not been heard of in past decades in the assessment of children and adolescents. To answer that, one must look at its history. Wallis (1994) reports that the history of this disorder began in 1902, when British pediatrician George Still published an account of twenty children in his practice who were passionate, defiant, spiteful, and lacking in inhibitory volition. He suspected a subtle brain injury. This theory gained credence in the years following the 1917 epidemic of viral encephalitis, in which doctors observed that the infection left some children with impaired attention, memory, and control over their impulses. In the 1940s and 1950s this same constellation of symptoms was called minimal brain damage and later minimal brain dysfunction. In 1937 a Rhode Island pediatrician reported that giving stimulants called amphetamines to children with these symptoms had the unexpected effect of calming them down. By the mid-1970s, Ritalin had become the most prescribed drug for what was eventually termed AD/HD.

The diagnostic category of minimal brain dysfunction (MBD), though used with children and adolescents for some time, was not a popular diagnosis. First, the term *brain damage/brain dysfunction* was one against which parents recoiled. Additionally for professionals, Pennington (1991) points out that the use of MBD as a syndrome was too vague and too overinclusive, and that the developing brain was much too complex to continually result in the same set of symptoms when it was perturbed. The term *AD/HD*, adopted in 1987, seemed to be more specific and less negative a term for parents and professionals alike. It acquired a slash in *DSM-IV* (1994) and has been the official diagnostic label since then.

However, since the diagnosis is given so frequently and, at the same time, considered by some not even to exist as a separate diagnosis, it seems especially important to more fully understand just what AD/HD is, particularly in children and adolescents. In defining AD/HD in children, Pennington (1991) states that the primary problems are "inattention, impulsivity, and hyperactivity" (p. 98). He goes on to note that all the following behaviors are also consistent with the diagnosis: "Fidgetiness, poor attention, difficulty with limits, impulsive response style on tasks requiring self-monitoring and persistence (such as on drawing tasks), perseveration, other indicators of difficulty shifting cognitive set, difficulty with new/abstract concepts, concrete responses, and emotional lability" (p. 99).

Barkley (1995) has more recently suggested a new theory of AD/HD that would assume that humans develop a capacity to inhibit their responses and protect their delay in responding from interferences by competing activities while they engage in a series of self-directed actions that modify their own behavior. He goes on to say, "The disinhibition of AD/HD disrupts the self-directed actions. The action that leads to immediate reward or escape from immediate aversive events (prepotent response) must be inhibited. And that inhibition must be sustained through interference control" (p. 4). He calls this form of sustained attention "goal-directed persistence," and he now feels that this is what is impaired in those with AD/HD. Yet his idea does not appear to be a totally new concept, as there has been a large body of data that demonstrates it is the AD/HD child's lack of persistence, not just distractions in the environment, that throws him/her off task (Douglas 1972). Pennington (1991) credits Douglas with developing her theory of AD/HD in the early 1970s as he notes in summarizing her work on this disorder that it supports the hypothesis that

> AD/HD children have a generalized self-regulatory deficit that affects the organization of information processing, the mobilization of attention throughout information processing, and the inhibition of inappropriate responding, and that this self-regulatory deficit is present across visual, auditory, motor, and perceptual-motor modalities. In her formulation, organization of information processing encompasses planning, executive function, metacognition, optimum set maintenance, regulation of arousal and alertness, and self-monitoring. [p. 93]

To make things even more complex, others, such as Kinsbourne (1991) and Amen (1995), have expanded the conceptualization of AD/HD as they suggest that there is also a form of this dysfunction that appears to be the opposite of the under–self-regulated, hyperactive child with little persistence—the overfocused AD/HD.

Since the diagnosis of AD/HD is most often made on the basis of observable symptoms, Blau (1995) suggests the following symptoms, some noted by parents and some by siblings and peers, be used to detect AD/HD in children:

1. Parents should notice:
   a. willfulness and self-centeredness
   b. uncooperativeness
   c. inability to concentrate
   d. unwillingness/inability to listen
   e. refusal to pay attention

    f. inability to follow the rules
2. Siblings and peers should notice:
    a. playing/being too rough
    b. being bossy
    c. being hyperactive (unable to sit still and talking excessively or out of turn)
    d. being weird and unpredictable, throwing out non sequiturs and acting like they are from another planet.

Quinn and Stern (1991) expand on the symptoms that make up AD/HD in children as they note the following problems, which seem to include the overfocused child mentioned above by both Kinsbourne and Amen:

1. Trouble focusing on just one thing, as other thoughts, sounds, and sights keep interrupting, which leads to difficulty concentrating, problems paying attention to the teacher, and many thoughts popping into their heads (a symptom they coined as "channel flicking").

2. Trouble paying attention, with a short attention span, especially if what they are attending to is not something they are interested in, such as a difficult or uninteresting subject.

3. Trouble thinking before they act, and often doing or saying things in an impulsive manner without thinking.

4. Trouble keeping still, as they always need to be moving or to stand up or to wiggle and move around. If they are not permitted to do so, they become very upset, as they also can be when tired or sleepy.

5. Trouble keeping track of things such as school assignments, chores, and time and/or its management. They can be very disorganized, often making it difficult for them to be ready when the bus comes to pick them up or to be ready with assignments, as they often wait until the last minute and then try to rush through them. Thus, the work they turn in does not reflect all they know about the subject.

6. Trouble learning in school, which makes it necessary for them to either have a tutor or take special classes.

What seems to be the most complete list of signs and symptoms found in children and adolescents with AD/HD is given by Wender (1995), whose nine categories of functioning I have summarized:

A. Attentional difficulties

    1. short attention span

    2. not sticking to things

    3. rushing from one game/activity to another—never playing one game for long

    4. as toddlers, pulling every toy from shelf, then being at loss for what to do

    5. in school, inattentiveness is evidenced by:

        a. not sticking with things for long

        b. always wool gathering/daydreaming

        c. unmotivated

        d. lacking in "stick-to-it-iveness"

        e. can't follow instructions

    6. at home, inattentiveness is evidenced by:

        a. not listening for long

        b. not paying attention

        c. not remembering

        d. parents must hover over child to get him/her to do what they want

        e. in the middle of one assignment/chore will begin another

        f. fails to complete assignments/homework unless nagged at

        g. easily distracted from tasks

(AD/HD children can attend one-to-one in class or evaluations for a while and can attend to materials they find interesting. As they grow older, there is less ability to focus attention where it is required, even though the pressure is internalized, in that they themselves insist that they do certain uninteresting things.)

   B. Motor abnormalities: hyperactivity and impaired coordination

      1. gross and fine motor hyperactivity as if driven by a motor

        a. kicks feet, drums fingers, twists in seat, rushes (though not noticed on the playground, is definitely seen in the classroom)

      2. may kick vigorously in utero

      3. active and restless in infancy and toddlerhood—into everything

        a. inadvertently breaks toys and objects

        b. requires supervision at all times for own protection and that of others

      4. as an older child constantly fidgets—unable to sit at dinner table or TV set

      5. overtalkativeness—"motor mouth"

      6. in many children, impaired coordination—slow to learn to button, zip, tie shoes, cut and color along the lines

      7. printing legible at times, but script is hard to read

      8. on the playing field—poor hand-eye coordination, which affects sports (though not seen in that many AD/HD children)

(All of these are developmental and may change with age and growth.)

   C. Impulsivity—decrease in ability to delay gratification/low frustration tolerance

1. impatient

2. quickly upset when people do not behave as expected

3. blurts out things in class

4. interrupts others

5. commits other disruptive "peccadilloes"

6. outside of class is:

    a. reckless

    b. shows no concern for bodily safety

    c. often has head and other injuries

    d. impulsively going along with antisocial behavior

D. Disorganization—often massively so

1. school papers are often a sensitive measure of this

2. assignments are not written down or are copied inaccurately

3. assignments are not finished on time or are not done at all

4. writing is arranged unsystematically; for example, a complete composition can be placed in one-fourth of page

5. columnar arrangements of math calculations is chaotic

6. disorganization is also noted in desks, lockers, and bedroom

7. as preadolescents are much more than just ordinarily sloppy

E. Altered response to social reinforcements, with repeated failure to comply with requests

1. failure to do what is asked due to forgetfulness or distraction (if reminded can be apologetic/tearful)

2. temperamentally act like they are locked in "the terrible twos" stage of life

    a. disciplinary measures are seen as unsuccessful whether they be rewards, deprivation of privileges, physical punishment

    b. want their own way

    c. never learn from their own mistakes

    d. can't reach them

    e. almost immune to punishment

    f. obstinate, stubborn, negativistic, and do not pay attention

    g. negative

    h. forgetful

(They do respond to immediate positive reinforcement but the effects do not last, as reinforced behaviors extinguish rapidly. Thus, parents are often inconsistent, because things don't work. Parents' criticism often amplifies the maladaptive behavior, with deviation amplifying the feedback in what becomes a vicious circle.)

F. Altered interpersonal relations:

    1. bossy—wanting to play games their own way or with their own rules

    2. domineering

    3. stubborn

    4. bullying

    5. have few friends, as they show social immaturity, are unable to give, exhibit athletic clumsiness; thus, others reject them

    6. have an insatiable demand for attention and a strong reaction to rejection (in some cases, from birth), which can lead to their becoming the class clown or to "buying" friendships

    7. often teased by others about their incompetence or deficits

8. grossly overreactive and thus a ripe target, as others know they can get a rise out of them

9. show inappropriate interpersonal sensitivity for their age, as they are awkward dealing with others' feelings, behaviors, and motivation

G. Altered emotionality in both temper and mood as they are:

1. very labile with mercurial mood going from dysphoric to overexcited (excitement is not euphoric but more a feeling of being out of control or just unwinding)

   a. stimulus-rich situations can cause excessive excitement (where normals would get pleasure) and unpleasant ones can cause temper outbursts

   b. excessive anger and hot temper, with a short fuse/low flash point

2. have a decreased ability to experience pleasure—hypohedonic

3. can feel demoralized and helpless as adolescents, as they are often ineffectual, unable to solve problems, work too hard, and are seen as boring by their peers

4. have low self-esteem due to constant negative input, but can also be physiological, based on mood

H. Stress intolerance—showing low frustration tolerance, a lack of sticking to things, and a tendency to give up under pressure

I. Response to medication (stimulants): 60 to 80 percent of them respond positively with:

1. diminished inappropriate hyperactivity and restlessness

2. improved attention, concentration, and memory

3. decreased impulsivity everywhere

4. decreased lability and reduced temper outbursts both in degree and frequency

Swanson (1992) suggests that to avoid making a diagnosis based on misleading symptoms, one should consider a number of characteristics of what he calls a "bona fide" AD/HD child:

1. early onset (before age 7)

2. persistent presence of developmentally inappropriate behaviors over time and across stages of development

3. functional impairments that are severe enough to disrupt daily activities at school and home

4. the AD/HD must be primary in status and precede rather than follow from or be secondary to the appearance of other, comorbid disorders, such as learning disabilities, depression, and anxiety

Zablow (1996) urges professionals to realize that AD/HD can occur in quiet and cooperative children, and even in those who are A students who have overcompensated by studying twice as long as their peers or have had major tutoring to get them through their classes.

Finally, Amen (1995) lists five subtypes of AD/HD in children, adolescents, and adults that correlate with problems in different areas of the brain:

1 and 2. Attention-deficit/hyperactivity disorder and attention-deficit predominantly inattentive type, both caused by problems in the prefrontal cortex system. The latter type often does not appear until later childhood or adolescence. The brighter the child, the later it seems to become a problem. These children are often labeled willful, uninterested, or defiant and are not offered help. They complain about being bored, appear unmotivated or apathetic, are frequently sluggish or slow moving, can be "couch potatoes," and appear spacey or internally preoccupied.

3. Overfocused: These children tend to get locked into things and have trouble shifting their attention from thought to thought, which can lead to obsessive or repetitive negative thoughts, compulsive behaviors, oppositionalism, or difficulty making

changes. This subtype is attributed to problems in the cingulate system, with very specific brain patterns showing increased blood flow in the top center portion of the frontal lobes.

4. Depressive, which emanates from problems in the limbic system. It is important to differentiate this subtype from clinical depression. The latter is cyclical and may have a later onset, while this subtype is consistent over time and is in evidence in childhood and adolescence.

5. Explosive, caused by problems in the temporal lobe. Ten to 15 percent of patients with AD/HD have temporal lobe symptoms, and these are among the most painful to deal with because of periods of panic and fear for no reason, periods of spaciness and confusion, with dark and suicidal or homicidal thoughts, significant social withdrawal, frequent periods of déjà vu, irritability, rages, and the experience of visual changes.

The literature suggests that within the AD/HD diagnostic category there are specific age-related or developmentally different symptoms (Barkley 1990, Goldstein and Goldstein 1990, Pennington 1991, Wender 1995). Though *DSM-IV* requires that symptoms of AD/HD must be present by age 7 (APA 1994), they are usually present early in life. In fact, some feel that there should be an onset earlier than age 7, and if not present by first grade, the symptoms should be considered secondary to other difficulties, such as reading problems (Pennington 1991).

Cantwell (1975) and Pennington (1991) suggest many differences in symptoms in the preschool versus the latency-age AD/HD child. Infants show high activity levels, less need for sleep, frequent crying, and difficulty being soothed. Toddlers show difficulty sensing dangerous situations, more than the usual energy, and moving from one activity to another quickly. Parents also note that these children wear out their shoes, clothing, and toys much faster than others their age. In the preschool and early elementary years, AD/HD children frequently leave their seats, talk more than most young people their age, have problems with keeping their hands to themselves, and have difficulty finishing their school and homework assignments. Without these symptoms being present in the early years of school, one must question if AD/HD is present or may have been acquired later due to head injury or illness (Pennington 1991).

Campbell and colleagues (1982) list the following observational behaviors in preschool settings that can suggest AD/HD:

1. inattention, shifting activity more readily in free-play

2. exhibiting more restlessness

3. in and out of seat, exhibiting off-task behaviors in structured situations where reflection and sustained attention are required

Fitzsimmons (1996) lists the following symptoms in school-age children as being indicative of AD/HD:

1. constantly saying they are bored

2. having to repeat kindergarten because they are "too immature," even though they are the right age

3. repeatedly "jumping the gun" by acting first and then thinking

4. having a very limited ability to focus attention on something, as they are often in a fog or are daydreaming

5. are disorganized, with cluttered desk, jumbled backpack, and tornado-like strewn bedroom, and if asked to clean it up, they seem to get lost playing with each item, never finishing the task

6. regularly losing things, and having little patience with waiting

7. having trouble condensing their thoughts in writing, but very able to talk at length about things

8. making careless mistakes in math, such as ignoring the signs

9. having very messy handwriting

As to symptoms in adolescents, Noshpitz (1991) notes,

The adolescent with this syndrome is usually diagnosed during latency in connection with school difficulties. The youngsters display characteristic patterns of hyperactivity, distractibility, poor attention span, difficulty in certain patterns of movement, and in many cases specific learning deficits. They seem to have egos which are constitutionally incapable of mastering their drives. Even when well socialized, these youngsters show a good deal of difficulty in "putting on the brakes" especially when excited. . . . As these youngsters move into adolescence, the hyperactivity seems to diminish, but the awkwardness may persist. More than that the "ADD" remains and continues to plague these youths' attempts to cope with school. . . . They become depressed, morose, and often irritable and resentful. Their constitutionally weak impulse control apparatus sometimes results in serious eruptions. [pp. 154, 156]

Noshpitz's description of AD/HD in adolescents sounds very different from some of the above descriptions of AD/HD in children. These developmental differences and the manner in which AD/HD is often assessed have added to the criticism of the diagnosis of AD/HD. Therefore, given that there are numerous symptoms and that developmentally the symptoms differ, it is important to consider all these factors in the assessment of AD/HD in children and adolescents.

Related to this, Craighead and colleagues (1994) set out specific goals for an AD/HD assessment in children:

1. Gather information about the developmental deviances of AD/HD symptoms or other problem behaviors;

2. Rule out other psychiatric, learning, or emotional problems that may be causing inattention, impulsivity, and/or overactivity;

3. Determine the degree of consistency between sources and across situations with respect to reports of behaviors associated with AD/HD;

4. Identify and prioritize targets for intervention. [p. 238]

To accomplish this, professionals must do more than just ask parents about the behavior of their child or have them fill out questionnaires. What seems to be needed is a comprehensive evaluation to determine the presence of AD/HD and, based on that, to prescribe appropriate interventions.

Baren (1994) warns, "Diagnosis of AD/HD is not a simple matter. It's a mistake for a 'snap' diagnosis to be made or to try to intervene before all the facts are known" (p. 11). He goes on to note that it is important to investigate all the possibilities that could explain a child's behavior; to explore whether there are any other problems, in addition, such as learning disabilities, conduct disorder, depression, anxiety, or any physical illness; to know the family structure, classroom situation, and any other condition or problems; and to have a good idea about the child's thinking ability and academic skills.

Pennington (1991) further notes that because AD/HD children may not manifest their problematic behaviors in a novel or structured situation, the absence of AD/HD symptoms in the clinician's office does not necessarily rule out the diagnosis.

Goldstein and Goldstein (1990) concur:

> Attention deficit does not fit into this mode of medical evaluation and treatment. The information required to make a proper diagnosis cannot be obtained simply as a result of a brief conversation between the physician and a parent or the physician and the child. . . . In children with suspected AD/HD, the physician's direct observations may be misleading. . . . A comprehensive multidisciplinary evaluation of attention and arousal-level problems in children [is needed]. This type of assessment is essential because the symptoms characteristic of AD/HD may also be caused by a variety of other medical, developmental, and psychological problems. [pp. 49, 51]

Blau (1995) agrees:

> A host of other conditions can mimic AD/HD, be a by-product of the disorder, or can co-exist with it. Therefore the only way to determine if a child has pure AD/HD is to first rule out everything else, determining what the child doesn't have. A comprehensive evaluation, explains Wade Hoen, a clinical psychologist and the executive director of CHADD (Children and Adults with Attention Deficit Disorder) begins with a thorough developmental history, establishing that the symptoms were present before age six or seven. Then you need an assessment of the child's current behavior. . . . Because AD/HD often mimics a learning disability, a competent evaluation must try to tease apart the two conditions. [pp. 47–48]

Craighead and colleagues (1994) concur: "A comprehensive evaluation of AD/HD in children will include multiple assessment techniques conducted across sources (i.e., parents, teachers) and settings" (p. 238).

In diagnosing AD/HD, Gordon (1995) suggests:

> From my point of view a well-conceived and executed evaluation can be cost effective and clinically justified for most cases. It can increase the chances that only children who need help will get it and that the interventions prescribed are sensible and targeted. An evaluation can also serve as a baseline against which one can judge treatment response. . . . But, at least for the cases referred to our setting where co-morbidity reigns and complications abound, I am convinced that diagnosis does, indeed, make the difference. [p. 4]

Though there is a strong consensus among these professionals as to the need for a comprehensive evaluation of the child or adolescent suspected of having AD/HD, there needs also to be some consensus as to what such an evaluation entails. Kirkman and Peltoman (1991) state, "Attention disorder is likely to be a heterogeneous entity which may take various forms, depending on which components of attention are deficient. In the assessment of attentional problems the various components of attention should be differentially evaluated in order to specify their relevant strengths and weaknesses" (p. 461). Downing (1995) also feels that specialized tests are needed for assessing attentional problems, and suggests including tasks of thinking and reasoning, shifting of attention, inhibitory control, mental control, concentration, and a continuous performance test.

One area in the assessment of AD/HD that has been frequently discussed in the literature is, not surprisingly, that of attention, for, after all, the diagnosis itself is called attention deficit disorder. Goldstein and Goldstein (1990) suggest that an AD/HD evaluation should include "tests sensitive to sustained attention and organizational skills that require the child to locate stimulus items that are hidden in a larger visual field. They also require adequate visual-perceptive skills" (p. 127). They recommend the Children's Embedded Figures Test and the Visual Closure Test of the Illinois Test of Psycholinguistic Abilities (ITPA) to sensitively discriminate between inattentive and normal children. They also recommend including complex visual tasks that require a degree of reflective strategizing for successful performance and that are at the same time designed to produce frustration. A maze test is an example of this type of test, which, along with the Matching Familiar Figures Test, can significantly discriminate between AD/HD and normal children.

Pennington (1991) indicates there are selective deficits in sustained attention—a right frontal function. "AD/HD children are no more vulnerable to extraneous stimuli that engage orienting attention than are normals. In contrast, on measures of vigilance or sustained attention, AD/HD children have a clear deficit especially when prolonged attention is required and the time of presentation is experimenter paced" (p. 93).

Barkley (1995) disagrees:

> Deficit in attention is not in the manner in which we attend to information in the environment (input) and/or in the way it is processed as implied in the terms of focused attention, selective attention, or span of attention (how much information you can attend to at one time). Consequently, thinking of AD/HD as some kind of "input" or "filtering" disorder, where the individual is bombarded with excessive stimulation and has difficulty sorting it out, is certainly erroneous. . . . The problem with sustained attention in AD/HD, then, seems to pertain to the relative schedule of reward and interest level (appeal) between the assigned task and other activities freely available in the same context. [pp. 1–2]

He goes on to warn that professionals must differentiate between contingency-shaped sustained attention (sustained attention directly to the task and directly dependent on the novelty, intrinsic interest, value, and extrinsically provided consequences), and sustaining attention (responding) to that task or activity. He feels that AD/HD children have no difficulty with this type of sustained attention. They do, however, have problems with persistence that is goal directed (behavior that is self-regulated):

> The challenge for those with AD/HD arises when there is a clear conflict between the immediate and temporally distant consequences for a behavior. . . . Many tasks involve little or no immediately available reinforcement for persisting in the activity or may involve even the need to face aversive events in doing the task, yet there is an important but delayed consequence for doing so. These circumstances often require that the individual actively deprive himself of other immediately available rewards that are associated with different ac-

tivities, in order to accomplish this unrewarding task and achieve a larger but greater reward . . . deferred gratification. Equally troublesome are tasks where an immediate reward is available but the individual must inhibit the response that would obtain it, denying [himself] the reward, in order to avoid a later and more serious harm. This is often thought of as self-discipline or willpower. These are the types of tasks or settings that are so difficult for those with AD/HD to succeed [at]. [pp. 2–3]

On the other hand, Kirkman and Peltoman (1991) assert that in AD/HD mechanisms of attention must be assessed including the following: alertness/arousal, selective attention, inhibitory control of behavior, sustained attention, search and application of strategies of performance, and apprehension span (the ability to attend to many relevant stimuli simultaneously). To do this, Goldstein and Goldstein (1990) suggest the following tests be used for attentional skills:

Vigilance measures

1. Detroit Test of Word Sequences—measuring auditory attention span for unrelated words

2. Detroit Test of Visual Attention Span for Objects—measuring visual vigilance

3. Digit Span on the Wechsler Intelligence Scale for Children (WISC-III)—measuring vigilance and auditory sequential memory

4. Seashore Rhythm Test—measuring auditory vigilance and memory

5. Speech-Sounds Perception Test—measuring words

6. Continuous Performance Test (CPT)

Sustained attention measures

1. Cancellation of Rapidly Recurring Target Figures Test

2. Coding on the WISC-III

3. Symbol Digit Modalities Test

4. ITPA Visual Closure Test

5. Gardner Steadiness Test

Focused attention measures

1. Trail Making Test parts A and B
2. Stroop Color Discrimination Test

Divided attention measures

1. Trail Making Test part B
2. Arithmetic subtest of the WISC-III

Impulsivity measures (the inability to use reflection)

1. Matching Familiar Figures Test
2. Mazes subtest of the WISC-III
3. Gordon's Diagnostic System—delay task

Another area that should be assessed in the diagnosis of AD/HD is memory. Goldberg (1995) notes:

Adolescents with attentional deficits are especially susceptible to undue strain upon their memory in school. Because of inconsistencies in their attentional patterns, these students are likely to register and consolidate nonsalient data in memory. They are apt to have difficulty determining and remembering what is relevant when reading a text or studying for an examination. . . . Additionally, many students with attentional deficits exhibit a divergent approach to memory. That is they prefer to roam about their storehouse of knowledge and talk about what they find rather than being confronted with direct questions for which there is only one correct answer (convergent memory). . . . Not surprisingly, students with attentional deficits are likely to have their greatest difficulty in classes that stress cumulative and precise memory (math, science, foreign language being harder than English and social studies [discontinuous subjects]). [pp. 61–62]

Noshpitz (1991) suggests that a third area to assess in AD/HD evaluations is ego functioning:

Ego pathology is central to this disorder. Many ego functions are affected: perception is distorted; short-term memory is often weakened; integration of perceptual and expressive patterns is deficient; regulation of attention and concentration is seriously awry; the ability to screen out extraneous stimuli and keep figure from ground is abnormal; management of emotions is poorly accomplished; and the inhibition of impulse is faulty. Motor patterns may be affected with dysregulation of motor integration, often present, in that the child's motor behavior is often jerky, awkward, and/or twitching. [p. 156]

Additionally, one needs to use evaluative measures to assess both the types of AD/HD and differential diagnoses, given that there appears to be more than one form of AD/HD and that many of the symptoms that occur in AD/HD children and adolescents also can occur in other disorders. Goldberg (1995) summarizes the differences between the hyperactive (AD/HD) and the nonhyperactive (AD/HD-H) child with AD/HD:

We describe a typical AD/HD child as having problems sustaining their attention while the consensus in publications is that the nonhyperactives have difficulty focusing their attention. The AD/HD-H had fewer problems with off-task behaviors than the AD/HD group. The AD/HD-H group's performed worse on the Coding of the WISC-R and had greater problems on measures of retrieval of verbal information from memory. Though both groups show impairment of vigilance, the AD/HD group committed 2x the number of impulsive errors. The AD/HD-H group had more trouble with focused components of attention and in the area involving cognitive processing speed. . . . The two types of ADD/AD/HD may be separate and distinct childhood disorders rather than the two subtypes of a common attention deficit. [p. 62]

Using a battery of neuropsychological tests, Conners and Wells (1986) found a number of different subtypes of hyperkinetic children. In one group, which had no cognitive or academic problems, the hyperactivity appeared to be due to anxiety. Another group showed learning disabilities; in this group AD/HD was secondary to this dysfunction. A third group had an isolated motor impulsivity deficit. A fourth group had a visual-spatial pattern of deficits like those addressed in children with nonverbal learning disabilities. A fifth group had frontal lobe dysfunction; these children appeared to have problems with their executive functioning more reminiscent of those typically thought of as AD/HD.

Finally, there is the area of comorbidity in the assessment of AD/HD that must be considered in any comprehensive evaluation of this disorder. Pennington (1991) refers to the following symptoms as secondary or comorbid with AD/HD in children: aggressive behavior, conduct disorder, learning disabilities, depression, poor self-esteem, poor social skills, and substance abuse. He also feels that because of the continual school failures of dyslexic children, they can have secondary AD/HD symptoms of inattention, distractibility, and impulsivity. He also feels that genetic and environmental-social factors can lead to secondary AD/HD.

In discussing comorbidity in his AD/HD patients, Gordon (1995) notes, "30% of children have both AD/HD and internalizing problems such as anxiety and depression. It also turns out that AD/HD children with co-morbid internalizing problems are less likely to respond to stimulant medication" (p. 9).

Baren (1994) lists many conditions that can occur together with AD/HD:

Additional behavioral disorders

Anxiety

Depression

Tourette's syndrome

Bed-wetting or soiling

Developmental delays in areas such as motor coordination

Speech and language disorders

Allergies

Sleep disturbance or night terrors

Hearing loss from earlier ear infections

Learning disabilities

Baren points out that 15 to 20 percent of those with AD/HD also have a learning disability, and that 50 percent of those with learning disabilities have AD/HD.

Keller (1992) warns that one must at times also differentiate forms of AD/HD from auditory processing problems, and suggests the following tests for screening in this area: Goldman Fristoe Woodcock Test of Auditory Discrimination, Selective Attention Test, Psychological Corporation's Screening Test for Auditory Processing Disorders (SCAN), Speech Sounds Perception Test, Rhythm Test (from Halsted-Reitan Neuropsychological Test Battery), and the Noise Subtest of the Test of Auditory Discrimination.

Glasser (1995) recommends that one assess comorbid disorders as well as the differential diagnosis of these disorders with AD/HD to determine proper treatment. He suggests that manic and depressive disorders can be either a differential diagnostic category or a subtype of AD/HD. He mentions that in children depression is often expressed with different symptoms than in adults. Children rarely look or complain about being depressed. Instead they often cry and are irritable. Manic behavior in children is also different from that in adults in that children are more irritable and aggressive and have emotional lability, and if there is grandiosity, it is seen more as being extremely hostile to adults or anyone who has to make rules in the home or at school—preferring to act as if they were in charge. Bipolar disorders in children with AD/HD may find them experiencing temper tantrums and aggressive behavior. What can trigger AD/HD behavior in these children is sensory or emotional overstimulation, or it can be a reaction to limit setting (responding to "no" with extremely angry reactions may be showing evidence of grandiosity). He also notes that irritability in prepubescent children with mania-like symptoms can be very severe and can lead them to be assaultive. Finally he notes that a combination of AD/HD and bipolar disorders is particularly lethal, with a higher suicide rate. He concludes, "Subgroups of patients with AD/HD and comorbid disorders may respond differently to different therapeutic interventions. Therefore, determining the subgroups is important in terms of early intervention. Clearly there are important consequences to identifying which children with AD/HD may be part of a subgroup with bipolar disorder " (pp. 8–9).

Finally, in terms of comorbidity, Zablow (1996) notes that over 70 percent of AD/HD children and adults also have symptoms of anxiety, depression, or adjustment problems.

To assess the many areas that have been suggested in the literature and to check for comorbidity and differential diagnosis, a comprehensive psychological testing assessment is needed. More typically, however, only two test measures are being used in assessing AD/HD: rating scales and continuous performance tests.

Craighead and colleagues (1994) list the typical assessment techniques that should be used in diagnosing AD/HD:

> Interviews with the parents, teacher, and child; parent and teacher rating scales of child behaviors; self-report ratings of older children and adolescents; clinic-based measures of AD/HD symptoms; direct observational techniques; parent self-report measures of relevant psychiatric conditions. In addition psychological testing, especially intelligence and achievement may be required for 30–40 percent of all AD/HD children because of co-existing learning disabilities. [p. 238]

Of rating scales used to assess AD/HD, Anastophoulos (1993) suggests, "The Child Behavior Checklist (CBCL) is one of the most frequently employed measures of this sort" (p. 3). He goes on to mention, "In using the CBCL's Attention Problems subscale, consider using a T score of 65 as a cutoff a recommended by Dr. Achenbach" (p. 4). Interestingly, Achenbach, who developed the CBCL, and Edelbrock (1981) reported that rates of attentional problems, restlessness, and social immaturity (all symptoms of AD/HD) were found in over 30 percent of normal children ages 4 to 16 based on parental reporting.

For this and other reasons, rating scales, long used as a primary measure for diagnosing AD/HD, have been criticized in the literature. Gordon (1993) warns,

> Although criteria based on rating scales and historical information are unquestionably useful, they fall short of absolute reliability. For any particular child referred to a practitioner for an evaluation, there is no certainty, whatsoever, that his parent or teacher will be able to provide wholly accurate information, unbiased by expectations, internal norms, or political agenda. Indeed there is ample evidence of the extent to which the accuracy of behavioral ratings and retrospective reports can be affected by a host of influences, ranging from maternal depression to geographical locale. [p. 5]

Pennington (1991) concurs: "Diagnoses of AD/HD based on behavioral checklists alone run the risk of misdiagnosing children who really have dyslexia, anxiety, and so on" (p. 100).

Though CPTs are only now becoming popular in the assessment of AD/HD children, they have been known to be a very sensitive measure of vigilance and reflective capability since their inception in the mid-1950s (Douglas 1972). Barkley (1990) expresses his belief in the value of continuous performance tasks in the assessment of AD/HD: "Sufficient to say here that the most useful among them at this point in time seems to be vigilance or continuous performance tests (CPTs) and direct, systematic behavioral observations of AD/HD symptoms in the home and classroom" (p. 327). Hallowell and Ratey (1994) comment, "Others use a test called the continuous performance tasks. . . . Examiners use the T.O.V.A.—Test of Variables of Attention . . . to quantify attention, distractibility, and impulsivity" (p. 207). Craighead and colleagues (1994) concur, noting, "Clinic based tests of attention span and impulse control are becoming more relevant in the assessment of AD/HD. These include tasks such as the CPT" (p. 239).

Blau (1995) points out, however, that according to Arnold Cohen, a child psychiatrist at Mt. Sinai Hospital in New York, "Sometimes a CPT is also used [in the evaluation of AD/HD]. CPTs have proved to be about seventy percent accurate" (p. 48).

Gordon (1995), who has developed his own CPT, explains why he feels CPTs are useful: "But like all psychological testing, the goal of administering computerized measures is to gather information in a standardized fashion about an important area of functioning so that we can construct a sense of the child's strengths and weaknesses" (p. 32). In another article, Gordon (1993) first explains,

Our goal in developing the Gordon Diagnostic System [Gordon's own CPT test] was to provide . . . a reliable and well-standardized measure of attention and impulse control . . . within a comprehensive assessment protocol. . . . never be used in isolation, but only as one component of a credible AD/HD evaluation. [p. 5]

He then goes on to summarize his experiences with CPTs:

Overall, . . . the GDS serves, if nothing else, (as) a valid role in confirming the diagnosis. . . . Clinicians gain confidence in their diagnosis when it is supported by data gathered from the child's actual behavior on a psychological test. [pp. 5–6]

But he then suggests a more specific use of CPTs in AD/HD evaluations:

A recent study of children diagnosed as AD/HD but who had normal GDS scores were brighter, older, generally less impaired according to teacher rating than those classified by both diagnosis and this test score as having AD/HD. Children rated as non-AD/HD yet had at least one abnormal score on the GDS looked very different from children who were normal across the board. Teachers rated them as having higher levels of internalizing problems (anxiety and depression) and higher levels of non-compliance (measured by the School Situations Questionnaire and the Actors). [p. 6]

Finally, Anastophoulos and Costabile (1995), after reviewing a particular CPT, strongly state, "We still continue to include the CPT in our multi-method assessment battery" (p. 8).

Though rating scales and CPT tests are useful, and should be a part of a comprehensive assessment for AD/HD, what is needed is a multimethod assessment battery—a comprehensive battery of tests that can assess the appropriate areas to determine the presence or absence of AD/HD and to further assess concomitant dysfunctions and differential diagnoses in order to determine the best treatment course for the child or adolescent.

Though some think that a battery of psychological tests to assess AD/HD is unnecessary (Barkley 1990, 1996), and others that it is not possible to develop (Gardner 1982), Goldstein and Goldstein (1990) report,

The development of a norm-referenced psychometric assessment battery for attention problems has been an elusive goal for researchers and practitioners. . . . This text's [their book on AD/HD] definition of attention disorders incorporates the proposition that the child's attention and reflection disabilities must be observed on standardized, norm-referenced assessment instruments. Structured psychometric testing also affords the practitioner the opportunity to interact with the child in a well-defined situation which adds additional quantifiable data. [p. 124]

These authors later expand on their ideas about what should be included in an AD/HD test battery:

In response to their increased problems dealing successfully with the environment, AD/HD children present an increased risk for the development of helplessness, depression, poor self-esteem and oppositional problems. As part of the evaluation for attention disorders, it is recommended that the practitioner obtain at least a general overview of the AD/HD child's self-awareness, emotional adjustment, coping and problem solving skills. [p. 145]

They go on to suggest the use of a clinical interview and tests such as the Incomplete Sentence Blank, Sentence Completion Test, the Thematic Apperception Test (TAT) or Children's Apperception Test (CAT), and/or the Roberts.

Kelley and Ramundo (1993) also recommend testing in the assessment of AD/HD: "Since there are no lab tests available to confirm the ADD diagnosis, mental health professionals often rely on educational and psychological testing. They provide a more unbiased, objective method of diagnosis than observation and history alone" (p. 110).

Small (1982) concurs with the need for psychological testing to assess AD/HD, in discussing its precursor—minimal brain dysfunction (MBD):

Psychological testing makes major contributions to the diagnosis of MBD. . . . [The tests] identify capabilities and dysfunctions. They can highlight specific types of disabilities in dysfunctional areas and they can direct remedial efforts more specifically than would be possible without them. . . . They are capable of elucidating a wider array of brain-behavior aspects than are achievement tests; more specifically assessing sensory, motor, intrasensory, language and other higher-level cognitive processes. . . . including illuminating the emotional impact of MBD and LD [learning disability], particularly identifying defensive reactions and ego resources for coping. [p. 103]

Wohl (1980) also suggests that a battery of tests be given to best understand the MBD child:

Psychoeducational assessment has been examined and discussed as a dynamic process concerned with the whole child and addressing itself not only to the identification and description of perceptual, integrative, and expressive functions but also to the etiology and ongoing flexible prognosis and treatment. . . . Etiologic preoccupation must give way to an approach which will permit the orderly description of a child from a large number of different dimensions . . . in order to make inferences regarding cognitive and emotional experiences. . . . Projective tests and questioning are useful in helping to analyze the process of perception and often give valuable insights as to how a child's affect influences his intellectual functioning . . . and bring empathy, flexibility and sensitivity to the study of the MBD child. . . . This writer is convinced that the MBD child requires and deserves such a detailed and intensive assessment. [pp. 382–383]

Levinger and Ochrach (1981) support both Small's and Wohl's contention about the value of and need for comprehensive psychological testing in MBD:

A special contribution of the psychologist, as a member of the diagnostic team, is the comprehensive evaluation and integration of various aspects of the child so that he/she becomes a whole child rather than an appendage of his/her pathology. In order to get a rounded picture of the child's functioning, the psychologist must evaluate the child's coordination, control of mobility, perceptual-motor functioning, graphomotor skills, auditory functioning, speech and language, cognitive functioning, and personality. The psychological test battery for children usually includes: figure drawings, the Bender-Gestalt Test, individually administered intelligence tests (WISC), Rorschach, and Children's Apperception Test (CAT) or the Thematic Apperception Test (TAT). There are also a host of special tests that check specific areas in which deficits may appear. [p. 104]

Goldstein and Goldstein (1990) suggest, for an AD/HD evaluation, "a comprehensive psychometric or psychological battery for such a child might additionally include the full administration of the WISC; measures of motor, perceptual, and academic skills and an in-depth assessment of the child's personality" (p. 125). They also suggest that to find possible AD/HD in children not necessarily suspected of having AD/HD, "During an in-depth assessment of a child experiencing attention, learning and/or behavior problems, measurements of and observations of attention and reflection skills must be integrated into the overall evaluation" (p. 125).

Pennington (1991) adds further support for testing: "By requiring both a positive history and positive test results, false positives can be greatly reduced. It is likewise important to rule out dyslexia in a child suspected of AD/HD" (p. 100). He states that among the test findings that suggest AD/HD are depression of IQ, impulsive performance on visual-motor tasks, and lower functioning on measures of executive functions such as the continuous performance tasks and one other test he includes in his studies, the Contingency Naming Test (Taylor 1988).

Though warning about possible false negatives in psychological testing, Hallowell and Ratey (1994) state:

> Psychological testing can be very helpful in elucidating any associated learning disabilities or uncovering other problems that may not have surfaced in the history, such as hidden depression or problems with self-image or a hidden thought disorder or psychosis. For example, projective testing examines what the subject projects. Psychological testing can also offer evidence that helps to confirm the diagnosis of ADD. Certain subclasses of the Wechsler tests of intelligence called the WISC in children and the WAIS in adults are typically low in people with ADD.... there is no standard battery but rather a range of tests from which the tester may select. [pp. 205–206]

In using the Wechsler tests in the assessment of AD/HD, many clinicians focus on the "third factor"—the distractibility factor—developed by Kaufman (1994). There is considerable debate as to its utility as Barkley (1996) warns, "I would urge considerable caution in the interpretation of the third factor scores ... as being of diagnostic value in the assessment of children with AD/HD" (p. 8). At the same time Wielkiewicz and Palmer (1996) reviewed the third factor and found that it was "consistently lower in AD/HD children than other factors. We believe the WISC-III third factor should not be ignored when assessing children with AD/HD. The depressed third factor should be given the same weight as other individual criteria or test scores obtained during an assessment" (p. 5). The use of the third factor was supported but qualified developmentally by Massman and colleagues (1988), who found that in children of ages 6 to 8 there was no significant relationship between poor performance on the three subtests of the WISC called the "freedom from distraction factor" by Kaufman (1994) and hyperactivity or attentional problems. However, in children of ages 9 to 12 this was not the case, as there was a strong correlation for such attentional problems and poor performance on these subtests of the Wechsler. These results suggest that AD/HD problems may have an increasingly negative effect on this triad with age. These authors found similar results with the arithmetic subtest of the Wide Range Achievement Test (WRAT-R).

In further refining the use of psychological testing in an AD/HD evaluation, Gordon (1995) shows how psychological testing can help with the diagnosis of AD/HD:

> When I think of how psychological testing might help me make decisions for children coming to my ADD clinic, these questions come to mind:
>
> 1. Does the child demonstrate deficits in the ability to inhibit responding and sustain attention?
>
> 2. What is the child's overall level of intellectual functioning?
>
> 3. What is the child's overall level of academic attainment?
>
> 4. Is there any evidence of a specific learning disability?
>
> 5. Is there any evidence of serious emotional problems? [pp. 13–14]

Gordon goes on to suggest doing IQ testing and a psychoeducational evaluation, and looking at possible psychiatric problems. He then adds, "If I see the case privately . . . I might well take that further look myself and administer testing oriented toward characterizing levels of pathology" (p. 16). In another article, Gordon (1993) concludes, "In my opinion, then, practitioners and researchers alike would do well to look beyond just the extent to which a psychological test agrees with other information. Accurate identification of my particular child lurks not within any single scale, test or interview format. Rather, it arises from a sensible integration of information from all of these sources" (p. 6).

Pennington (1991) lists specific cognitive tasks on which AD/HD children and adolescents may have trouble during testing. They include monitoring tasks, such as the CPT tests; perceptual search tasks, such as the Matching Familiar Figures Test; logical search tasks, such as Raven's Progressive Matrices; motor control and visual-motor tasks, such as the Porteus Mazes, Bender Gestalt Test, and the Rey Osterreith Complex Figure; prefrontal functions, such as measured by the Wisconsin Card Sort Test; planning tasks, such as the Tower of Hanoi; and conflictual motor responding tasks, such as the "Go-No-Go" Paradigm.

Though it has been my experience that more time is needed to do an adequate and comprehensive psychological assessment for AD/HD, Barkley (1990), at times critical of psychological testing, has suggested, in terms of the time it takes to do an AD/HD assessment, "It is my experience that approximately 2–4 hours are more than adequate to evaluate the typical AD/HD child. This figure does not include time that may be required to do more extensive assessment of learning disabilities or neurological functioning" (p. 353).

In terms of the cost for such a comprehensive psychological evaluation, while Blau (1995) notes that in New York a thorough academic and psychological evaluation for AD/HD costs anywhere from $600 to $1,800, Wallis (1994) suggests that the cost of a psychological testing for AD/HD can cost even more, "anywhere from $500–3,000 depending on the thoroughness of the testing" (p. 47).

The importance of a comprehensive evaluation for AD/HD has one very significant purpose—to make the appropriate diagnosis/diagnoses in order to determine the treatment needed. Some feel that the only treatment for AD/HD is Ritalin. Others go even further and ask why go to the trouble and expense of doing a thorough diagnostic evaluation, why not just give the child the medication and see what happens. Mental health professionals must appreciate that this area is far more complex, and an accurate diagnosis is needed so that one knows what one is treating and does not miss other significant comorbid conditions, a number of which may contraindicate Ritalin or other psychostimulants as the treatment of choice.

Additionally, there are other interventions beside medications such as Ritalin. There is biofeedback, which has had some success with

AD/HD. But, as Blau (1995) notes, however, "Even biofeedback researcher Joel F. Lubar, psychologist at the University of Tennessee, says, biofeedback 'has proved to be most effective when integrated with other forms of treatment including medication' " (p. 49). Therefore, since medication is most frequently a part of the therapeutic program for the treatment of AD/HD in children and adolescents, it is important to also explore the literature regarding the differential effect of medications in treating AD/HD in children and adolescents.

In terms of medication, Fitzsimmons (1996) notes that more than one million school-age children take the controversial drug Ritalin to help keep their symptoms under control. Judith Rapaport, chief of psychiatry at the National Institute of Mental Health (NIMH)–Bethesda reports that in at least one-third of those children taking Ritalin, the side effects of the drug can be dramatic and include nervousness, insomnia, stomachaches, headaches, nausea, rashes, loss of appetite, and feelings of agitation. She also suggests that if a child looks glazed over or glassy eyed, the dosage of medication needs to be lowered or the type of medication changed (Blau 1995).

While stimulant medication has been shown to have beneficial behavioral effects, with 70 to 90 percent of hyperkinetic children showing improvement (Blau 1995, Barkley 1990, Conners and Werry 1979) with what these authors consider minimal side effects, those nonhyperkinetic AD/HD young people seem to not fare as well, especially in the area of cognitive development (Pelham 1988).

Gordon (1993) further notes that he has found that those children and adolescents who were diagnosed as AD/HD but who had normal CPT scores were two times as likely as those who were positive on both diagnosis and the CPT as having AD/HD to be nonresponders to medication and half as likely to receive a recommendation for a high dose of stimulant medication.

Conners and Wells (1986) found that their subtypes of hyperkinetic children had different reactions to typical AD/HD medication. The group whose AD/HD symptoms appeared to be due mainly to learning disabilities did not benefit at all from stimulant medication, nor did the group with isolated motor impulsivity. It was the frontal lobe dysfunction group that seemed to fully benefit from stimulant medications, with improvements in the inhibition of socially inappropriate responses.

Recently, Amen (1995) has also proposed five subtypes, as noted above, and he feels that a differential diagnosis of these subtypes is very important so that the appropriate medication can be recommended for proper treatment. He has found each subtype works better with specific medications:

1. The AD/HD child with hyperactivity is very responsive to stimulant medication such as Ritalin, Dexedrine, Cylert, Desoxyn, and Adderal, which seem to "turn on" the frontal lobes.

2. The AD/HD primarily inattentive type also responds well to the stimulant medication recommended for the first subtype, but to a lesser degree of success.

3. The overfocused type shows a specific increase of blood flow in the top center portion of the frontal lobes and seems to be very responsive to the newer antiobsessive antidepressants such as Prozac, Paxil, Zoloft, Anafranil, and Effexor.

4. The depressive subtype seems to respond to the standard antidepressants such as Tofranil (imipramine), Norpramin (desipramine), and Pamelor (nortriptyline). They also respond well to Prozac and Wellbutrin (buprion) as well as to stimulants. Amen makes a point of noting that it is important to differentiate this subtype from clinical depression because stimulant medications work so very well with this subgroup but not so with clinical depression.

5. The explosive subtype is responsive to antiseizure medications such as Tegretol and Depakote as well as the stimulant Cylert.

Glasser (1995) found that some children who have an hypnotic effect to stimulant medication may have depression, and that this particular type can progress into a bipolar disorder.

Warning that the sole use of medication to treat AD/HD must be tempered, Blau (1995) suggests that because psychoactive drugs like Ritalin are so widespread, "the most vocal antagonists accuse parents and professionals of drugging kids into submission" (p. 51).

Thus the differential effects of medication on various subtypes of

AD/HD and the differential diagnoses of symptoms that appear AD/HD-like further support the need for a more comprehensive assessment of AD/HD using standardized tests to help with this assessment.

Because we at the Reiss-Davis Child Study Center concur with those who advocate the need for comprehensive psychological testing as an integral part of the diagnosis of AD/HD, the following is an example of the test battery used in our AD/HD clinic to assess attentional problems in children and adolescents:

Rorschach

Thematic Apperception Test (TAT) or Children's Apperception Test (CAT)

Trail Making Test (A and B)

Rhythm Test (from Halstead Reitan Battery)

Stroop Test or Fruit Discrimination Test

Test of Variables of Attention (TOVA)

Intermediate Visual and Auditory Continuous Performance Test (IVA)

Cognitive Control Battery (CCB)

Achenbach's Children's Behavioral Checklist (CBCL)

Achenbach's Teacher's Report Form

Wide Range Achievement Test-R (WRAT-R)—selected subtests

Woodcock-Johnson Psychoeducational Battery (WJ-R)

Matching Familiar Figures Test

Incomplete Sentence Blank

Wide Range Assessment of Memory and Learning (WRMAL-R)/ Test of Memory and Learning (TOMAL)—selected subtests

SUPPLEMENTAL TESTS AS NEEDED:

Contingency Naming Test

Wisconsin Card Sort Test

Family Relations Test

Goldman Friscoe-Woodcock Test of Auditory Discrimination

Selective Attention Test

SCAN

Children's Embedded Figures Test

Verbal Closure Test (from the ITPA)

Ray-Osterreith Visual-Motor Test

Porteus Mazes

Raven's Progressive Matrices Test

Tower of Hanoi Test

Go–No–Go Paradigm

Detroit Test of Word Sequencing

Detroit Test of Visual Attention of Specific Objects

Seashore Rhythm Test

Speech-Sound Perception Test

Cancellation of Rapidly Recurring Target Figures Test

Symbol Digit Modalities Test

Gardner Steadiness Test

With the use of the standard battery and, as needed, supplemental tests we feel more confident in not only assessing the presence or absence of AD/HD, but, in those cases where it is present, in further assessing the appropriate subtype and any comorbid features. Then the most accurate treatment plan can be developed including, where indicated, the appropriate medication for the identified subtype of AD/HD.

As more is being discovered daily about the etiology or etiologies of AD/HD and its various subtypes, additional assessment tools may be needed. For example, Eck (1993) found evidence of biochemical imbalances in the AD/HD child and adolescent. Thus, in the future hair analysis may be useful for assessing such deficiencies.

Another area that is exploring the etiology and treatment of attentional dysfunction, and one that is slowly gaining ground in AD/

HD, is mind-body integration and alternative medicine. One book on the use and avoidance of specific foods related to AD/HD written by William Crook (1991) suggests that diet must be considered carefully and that avoidance of certain foods will lessen and in some cases eliminate AD/HD in a child/adolescent. This and other interventions (Goldberg 1995) suggest that it is the immune system that is problematic in the AD/HD child/adolescent, and that the avoidance of stressful foods, which act as toxins to the system, along with immune-strengthening alternative medicine interventions, can help eliminate the dysfunction.

Additionally, Pennington (1991) notes that there are many other factors that can cause AD/HD symptomatology, including neurological factors (head injury; infectious insults to the brain, such as encephalitis; and anoxia at birth or due to head injuries); genetic factors (part of Turner syndrome in females and the fragile X syndrome in males, neurofibromatosis, and early treated phenylketonuria); environmental factors (exposure to lead); and deleterious social factors (inadequate environmental stimulation, large family size, social disability). Though he feels that AD/HD is etiologically heterogeneous, he offers "one plausible theory of brain mechanisms in AD/HD [that] proceeds as follows. The executive function deficit of AD/HD children is caused by functional hypofrontality, which in turn is caused by either structural and/or biochemical changes in the prefrontal lobes, and is detectable as reduced frontal blood flow" (p. 91). He further suggests that more research is necessary because "one subtype of AD/HD children may have hypoarousal of the right posterior hemisphere secondary to norepinephrine depletion, whereas others may have the hypofrontal subtype of AD/HD described here. Although posterior and anterior attentional systems interact, separate deficits in each system are possible" (p. 92). Lou and colleagues (1984) also found decreased blood flow in the frontal lobes of children with AD/HD, but with Ritalin the blood flow increased. At the same time, they note, "Ritalin treatment also decreased blood flow to the motor cortex and primary sensory cortex, suggesting an inhibition of function of these structures, seen clinically as less distractibility and decreased motor activity during treatment" (p. 829). In a later study, Lou and colleagues (1989) found the locus of reduced blood flow in the basal ganglia of these children. Goldberg's (1995) discussion of Mena's new and exciting work at UCLA and Harbor General with the NeuroSPECT in differentiating types of AD/HD and the resulting differentiating of appropriate medication for each type concurs with some of the findings above and is one of the most promising methods of studying the actual causality and differentiation of the often used and frequently misunderstood diagnostic category of AD/HD.

At the present time, however, a comprehensive AD/HD evaluation that includes a multimethod psychological testing assessment battery appears to be the most accurate and ultimately economical method for diagnosing AD/HD in children and adolescents, and should be considered before initiating any attempt at treatment.

REFERENCES

Achenbach, T. M., and Edelbrock, C. S. (1981). Behavioral problems and competencies reported by parents of normal and disturbed children aged 4–16. *Monographs of the Society for Research in Child Development* 46 (188).

Achenbach, T. M., and Wells, K. C. (1986). *Hyperactive Children: A Neuropsychosocial Approach.* Beverly Hills, CA: Sage.

Amen, D. (1995). *Windows into the ADD Mind: Understanding and Treating Attention Deficit Disorder in the Everyday Lives of Children, Adolescents, and Adults.* Fairfield, CT: Mindworks.

American Psychiatric Association. (1994). *Diagnostic and Statistical Manual of Mental Disorders*, 4th ed. *(DSM-IV)*. Washington, DC: American Psychiatric Association.

Anastophoulos, A. D. (1993). Assessing AD/HD with the child behavior checklist. *AD/HD Report* 1(3):3–4.

Anastophoulos, A. D., and Costabile, A. A. (1995). The Conners' Continuous Performance Test: a preliminary examination of its diagnostic utility. *AD/HD Report* 3(1):7–8.

Baren, M. (1994). *Hyperactivity and Attention Disorders in Children.* Irvine, CA: Health Information Network.

Barkley, R. A. (1990). *Attention-Deficit Hyperactivity Disorder: A Handbook for Diagnosis and Treatment.* New York: Guilford.

——— (1995). Is there attention deficit in AD/HD? *AD/HD Report* 3(4):1–4.

——— (1996). Clinical use of the third factor—proceed with caution. *AD/HD Report* 4(3):6–8.

Blau, M. (1995). AD/HD—the scariest letters in the alphabet. *New Yorker,* December 13, pp. 44–51.

Campbell, S. B., Szumowski, E. K., Ewing, L. J., et al. (1982). A multidimensional assessment of parent-identified behavior problems in toddlers. *Journal of Abnormal Child Psychology* 10:569–591.

Cantwell, D. P. (1975). Genetics of hyperactivity. *Journal of Child Psychology and Psychiatry* 16:261–264.

Conners, C. K., and Wells, K. C. (1986). *Hyperkinetic Children: A Neuropsychosocial Approach.* Beverly Hills, CA: Sage.

Conners, C. K., and Werry, J. S. (1979). Pharmacotherapy. In *Psychopathological Disorders in Childhood*, ed. H. C. Quay and J. S. Werry, pp. 336–386. New York: Wiley.

Craighead, L. W., Craighead, W. E., Kazden, A. E., and Mahoney, M. J. (1994). *Cognitive and Behavioral Interventions.* Boston: Allyn and Bacon.

Crook, W. (1991). *Help for the Hyperactive Child.* Jacksonville, FL: Professional Books.

Douglas, V. I. (1972). Stop, look and listen: the problem of sustained attention and impulse control in hyperactive and normal children. *Canadian Journal of Behavioral Science* 4:259–282.

Downing, S. (1995). Neuropsychological contributions of AD/HD assessment. *AD/HD Report* 3(5):5–6.

Eck, P. (1993). Attention deficit disorder and hyperactivity. *Eck Institute Newsletter* 9(12):1–3.

Fitzsimmons, B. (1996). ADD, a daunting dilemma. *San Diego Union Tribune*, September 4, p. E3.

Gardner, R. A. (1982). *Stimulant medication assessment battery.* Unpublished.

Glasser, J. M. (1995). Differential diagnosis of AD/HD and bipolar disorder. *AD/HD Report* 3(3):8–10.

Goldberg, M. J. (1995). *Chronic Fatigue Syndrome in Children and Adults and Its Connection to AD/HD.* Tarzana, CA: Goldberg Publications.

Goldstein, S., and Goldstein, M. (1990). *Managing Attention Disorders in Children: A Guide for Practitioners.* New York: Wiley.

Gordon, M. (1993). Do computerized measures of attention have a legitimate role in AD/HD evaluations? *AD/HD Report* 1(6):5–6.

——— (1995). *How to Operate an AD/HD Clinic.* De Witt: GSI.

Hallowell, E. M., and Ratey, J. J. (1994). *Driven to Distraction.* New York: Touchstone.

Kaufman, A. S. (1994). *Intelligent Testing with the WISC-III.* New York: Wiley.

Keller, W. D. (1992). Auditory processing disorder or attention-deficit disorder. In *Central Auditory Processing: A Transdicipliary View*, ed. J. Katz, N. Stecker, and D. Henderson, pp. 107–114. Chicago: Mosby.

Kelley, K., and Ramundo, P. (1993). *You Mean I'm Not Lazy, Stupid or Crazy?* New York: Scribner.

Kinsbourne, M. (1991). Overfocusing: an apparent subtype of attention deficit-hyperactivity disorder. In *Pediatric Neurology: Behavior and Cognition of the Child with Brain Dysfunction*, ed. N. Amir, I. Rapin, and D. Branski, pp. 18–35. Basel: Karger.

Kirkman, M., and Peltoman, K. (1991). Patterns of test findings predicting attention problems at school. *Journal of Abnormal Child Psychology* 19(4):451–467.

Levinger, L., and Ochrach, R. (1981). Psychological diagnosis of children with MBD. In *Diagnosis and Treatment of MBD in Children*, ed. R. Ochrach, pp. 101–126. New York: Human Sciences Press.

Lou, H. C., Henricksen, L., and Bruhn, P. (1984). Focal cerebral hyopoperfusion and/or attention deficit disorder. *Archives of Neurology* 41:825–829.

Lou, H. C., Henricksen, L., Bruhn, P., et al. (1989). Striatal dysfunction in attention deficit and hyperkinetic disorder. *Archives of Neurology* 46:48–52.

Massman, P. J., Nussbaum, N. L., and Bigler, E. D. (1988). The mediating effect of age on the relationship between child behavior checklist hyperactivity scores and neuropsychological test performance. *Journal of Abnormal Child Psychology* 16:89–95.

Noshpitz, J. D. (1991). Disturbances in early adolescence. In *The Course of Life*, vol. 4, ed. S. I. Greenspan and G. H. Pollock, pp. 119–180. Madison, CT: International Universities Press.

Pelham, W. J. (1988). The effects of psychostimulant drugs on the learning and academic achievement in children with attention deficit disorder and learning disabilities. In *Psychological and Educational Perspectives on Learning Disabilities*, ed. J. K. Torgensen and B. Wong, pp. 259–295. New York: Academic Press.

Pennington, B. F. (1991). *Diagnosing Learning Disorders: A Neuropsychological Framework.* New York: Guilford.

Quinn, P. O., and Stern, J. M. (1991). *Putting on the Brakes—Young People's Guide to Understanding AD/HD.* New York: Magination.

Santostefano, S. (1988). *Cognitive Control Battery—Manual.* Los Angeles: Western Psychological Services.

Small, L. (1982). *Minimal Brain Dysfunction—Diagnosis and Treatment.* New York: The Free Press.

Swanson, J. M. (1992). *School Based Assessment and Interventions for ADD Students.* Irvine, CA: KC Publishing.

Taylor, H. G. (1988). Learning disabilities. In *Behavioral Assessment of Childhood Disorders*, ed. S. J. Mash and L. G. Terdal, pp. 402–450. New York: Guilford.

Wallis, C. (1994). Disorganized? Distracted? Discombobulated? Doctors say you might have attention deficit disorder. *Time*, July 18, pp. 43–49.

Wender, P. H. (1995). *Attention Deficit Hyperactivity Disorder in Adults*. New York: Oxford University Press.

Wielkiewicz, R. M., and Palmer, C. M. (1996). Can the WISC-R/WISC-III third factor help in understanding AD/HD? *AD/HD Report* 4(3):4–6.

Wohl, T. H. (1980). Psychological and psychoeducational assessment techniques. In *Handbook of MBD—A Critical View*, ed. H. E. Rie and E. D. Rie, pp. 362–387. New York: Wiley.

Zablow, S. (1996). Community connection gains doctor's attention. *San Diego Union Tribune*, June 24, p. A6.

4

A Diagnostic Assessment Approach to Attention Deficit Disorder: Problems in Differential and Comorbid Diagnosis

Donald Tessmer

Symptoms of attention deficit/hyperactivity disorder (AD/HD) as a descriptor of children with problems in attention and impulsiveness and with high activity levels has been with us for most of the twentieth century. The disorder has previously been identified as minimal brain damage or the hyperactive child syndrome. These labels traditionally focused mostly on the hyperactive qualities of these individuals. However, beginning in the 1970s, more research was devoted to the attentional and impulsive aspects of these patients.

This chapter reviews some of the literature on diagnosing attention deficit disorder, compares it to other psychiatric disorders that share similar profiles and thus make diagnostic statements difficult. The chapter also illustrates the current assessment process developed and used at Reiss-Davis in addressing the problems of differential and comorbid diagnosis in this often confusing population of children, adolescents, and adults, and summarizes the many intervention areas that should be considered while formulating a treatment plan when a diagnosis of attention deficit disorder is made. ·

DIAGNOSIS

Much of the current evidence suggests that attention deficit disorder is a syndrome of several types of problems, and failure to address the entire picture can lead to frustration on the part of patient, family, and professionals. The *Diagnostic and Statistical Manual of Mental Disorders* from *DSM-III* (1980), *DSM-III-R* (1987), to *DSM-IV* (1994) have delineated changes in thinking and research regarding this frequently diagnosed problem usually first seen in childhood, although lately more and more diagnosed in adolescence and adulthood. *DSM-IV* has returned to a *DSM-III* conceptualization of this disorder and recognizes these subtypes:

314.01 Attention deficit/hyperactivity disorder, combined type
314.00 Attention deficit/hyperactivity disorder, predominantly inattentive type
314.01 Attention deficit/hyperactivity disorder, predominantly hyperactive-impulsive type [p. 83]

This is opposed to the more global or singular view of AD/HD in *DSM-III-R* and connects *DSM-III* with *DSM-IV* in the conceptualization of this disorder.

The following is the *DSM-IV* diagnostic criteria for attention deficit/hyperactivity disorder.*

A. Either (1) or (2):

(1) six (or more) of the following symptoms of *inattention* have persisted for at least six months to a degree that is maladaptive and inconsistent with developmental level:

Inattention

(a) often fails to give close attention to details or makes careless mistakes in schoolwork, work, or other activities

---

*Reprinted with permission from the *Diagnostic and Statistical Manual of Mental Disorders, Fourth Edition*. Copyright © 1994 by the American Psychiatric Association.

(b) often has difficulty sustaining attention in tasks or play activities

(c) often does not seem to listen when spoken to directly

(d) often does not follow through on instructions and fails to finish schoolwork, chores, or duties in the workplace (not due to oppositional behavior or failure to understand instructions)

(e) often has difficulty organizing tasks and activities

(f) often avoids, dislikes, or is reluctant to engage in tasks that require sustained mental effort (such as schoolwork or homework)

(g) often loses things necessary for tasks or activities (e.g., toys, school assignments, pencils, books, or tools)

(h) is often easily distracted by extraneous stimuli

(i) is often forgetful in daily activities

(2) six (or more) of the following symptoms of *hyperactivity-impulsivity* have persisted for at least six months to a degree maladaptive and inconsistent with developmental level:

Hyperactivity

(a) often fidgets with hands or feet or squirms in seat

(b) often leaves seat in classroom or in other situations in which remaining seated is expected

(c) often runs about or climbs excessively in situations in which it is inappropriate (in adolescents or adults, may be limited to subjective feelings of restlessness)

(d) often has difficulty playing or engaging in leisure activities quietly

(e) is often "on the go" or often acts as if "driven by a motor"

(f) often talks excessively

Impulsivity

> (g) often blurts out answers before questions have been completed

> (h) often has difficulty awaiting turn

> (i) often interrupts or intrudes on others (e.g., butts into conversations or games)

B. Some hyperactive-impulsive or inattentive symptoms that caused impairment were present before age 7 years.

C. Some impairment from the symptoms is present in two or more settings (e.g., at school [or work] and at home).

D. There must be clear evidence of clinically significant impairment in social, academic, or occupational functioning.

E. The symptoms do not occur exclusively during the course of a pervasive developmental disorder, schizophrenia, or other psychotic disorder and are not better accounted for by another mental disorder (e.g., mood disorder, anxiety disorder, dissociative disorder, or a personality disorder). [pp. 83–84]

ADD+H (with hyperactivity) is usually much easier to diagnose than ADD-H (without hyperactivity) and many of the current diagnostic dilemmas with children presenting with symptoms are around issues of differential diagnosis between disorders and comorbidity, that is, the one disorder of AD/HD with a high likelihood of having a second diagnosable disorder.

The prevalence of attention deficit/hyperactivity disorder is estimated at 3 to 5 percent in school-age children (*DSM-IV*). However, information on the prevalence for adolescence and adulthood is less specific.

DSM-IV states that the disorder is much more frequent in males than in females, with male-to-female ratios ranging from 4 to 1 to 9 to 1, depending on the setting (i.e., general population or clinics). Our experience at Reiss-Davis is that girls are more likely to be seen with ADD-H than ADD+H.

Barkley (1990) describes ADD-H:

Cognitively, these children appear somewhat sluggish in responding to tasks; often have their awareness focused on internal events rather than external demands; and are typically much slower in completing pencil and paper tasks, such as the coding subtest on the Wechsler Intelligence Scale for Children-III. They also have considerably greater inconsistency in memory recall, particularly on verbal tasks. In their behavioral presentation, they are viewed by many as day-dreaming, confused or lost in thought, apathetic or unmotivated, and at times slow moving. They frequently stare. They are less active, by definition, than AD/HD children and apparently less disruptive of others' activities. They do not show a pattern of behavioral disin-hibition, and hence are not impulsive, intrusive, or unable to delay gratification to a degree that is abnormal for their mental age. Con-sequently, these children are rarely socially aggressive or oppositional and defiant and so they probably have somewhat better social accep-tance than AD/HD children. Their social acceptance, however, is not necessarily normal as they do appear to be more socially neglected or overlooked whereas AD/HD children appear to be more rejected. [pp. 181–182]

Barkley also states that ADD–H children are as likely as ADD + H children to have academic difficulties. He notes that they are often described as underachieving or working below expected academic levels and cites that as many as 25 to 35 percent may have learning disabilities in reading, math, writing, or language.

A learning disability (LD) is typically defined as a significant dis-crepancy between one's intelligence or general ability levels and one's academic achievement levels, such as in the areas of reading, math, spelling, written language, and expressive/receptive language. The issue of what is a significant discrepancy is usually defined by state depart-ments of special education as opposed to psychiatric or psychologi-cal organizations. The manual for the Wechsler Intelligence Scale for Children–III (1991) reports a study that examined differences between groups of learning-disabled, reading-disordered, and attention deficit/ hyperactivity disordered children, and all three groups showed the lowest scores in the areas of freedom from distractibility index and processing speed index. The AD/HD group had the lowest mean subtest scores for coding (7.7) and digit span (8.2) subtests. This study points out some of the diagnostic cognitive similarities between these different groups. When there are diagnosis of AD/HD and LD in the same individual, multiple interventions are needed and one must not ignore one diagnosis over the other.

Barkley (1990) also notes that, in his experience, anxious children may display similar attentional problems to the ADD–H child, thus, again raising another issue in differential or comorbid diagnosis. He states that excessive anxiety is not typically a symptom of the majority of AD/HD children. He does state that anxious children may be "restless, fidgety, and less able to concentrate, but they do not show the persistent and pervasive pattern of behavioral disinhibition, hyperactivity, and poor sustained attention from early childhood so typical of AD/HD" (p. 191). He states that they are rarely impulsive or acting out as compared to the AD/HD child who typically is so. Another feature noted by Barkley is that the anxious child does not usually show neuromaturational delays. Our experience at Reiss-Davis has been that while this general pattern is likely true of the ADD+H child, this may not be as true of the ADD–H child.

Biederman and colleagues (1992) note a comorbid association of approximately 25 percent between AD/HD and anxiety disorders in children. He cites Lahey and colleagues (1987, 1988): "Children with DSM-III diagnosis of ADD–H had higher rates of anxiety disorders than those with ADD+H" (p. 720).

Barkley (1990) states that AD/HD children or adolescents may be more at risk for a comorbid diagnosis of dysthymia and that studies have shown there are greater incidences of this diagnosis in immediate family members. He also cautions about the use of stimulant medication for children who are depressed, because this may accelerate feelings of sadness or depression. Certainly, the AD/HD child or adolescent is more prone to experience low self-esteem because of the potential academic difficulties or peer problems he/she may encounter.

The DSM-IV diagnostic criteria for 300.40, dysthymic disorder, lists the following as a partial criteria. There is the presence, while depressed, of two (or more) of the following:

1. Poor appetite or overeating;

2. Insomnia or hypersomnia;

3. Low energy or fatigue;

4. Low self-esteem;

5. Poor concentration or difficulty making decisions;

6. Feelings of hopelessness. [p. 349]

Here are the *DSM-IV* diagnostic criteria for 300.02, generalized anxiety disorder: the anxiety and worry are associated with two (or more) of the following six symptoms (with at least some symptoms present for more days than not for the past six months). Note: Only one item is required in children.

1. Restlessness or feeling keyed up or on edge;

2. Being easily fatigued;

3. Difficulty concentrating or mind going blank;

4. Irritability;

5. Muscle tension;

6. Sleep disturbance (difficulty falling or staying asleep, or restless, unsatisfying sleep).

The *DSM-IV* also notes that such individuals find it difficult to keep worrisome thoughts from interfering with attention to tasks at hand and they have difficulty stopping the worry. [pp. 435–436]

DSM-IV states that studies also suggest there is a higher prevalence of mood and anxiety disorders, learning disorders, substance-related disorders, and antisocial personality disorder in family members of individuals with AD/HD.

DSM-IV does state that AD/HD is not diagnosed if the symptoms are better accounted for by another mental disorder (e.g., mood disorder, anxiety disorder, dissociative disorder, personality disorder, personality change due to a general medical condition, or a substance-related disorder): "In all these disorders, the symptoms of inattention typically have an onset after age 7 years, and the childhood history of school adjustment, generally, is not characterized by disruptive behavior or teacher complaints concerning inattentive, hyperactive, or impulsive behavior. When a mood disorder or anxiety disorder co-occurs with AD/HD, each should be diagnosed" (p. 83). This statement, though, is rather biased toward the hyperactive type of AD/HD.

Lahey and Carlson (1992) state that clinic-referred children who meet *DSM-III-R* criteria for ADD–H have been shown to exhibit less serious conduct problems, are less impulsive, are more likely to be characterized as sluggish and drowsy, are less rejected by their peers but more socially withdrawn, and are more likely to exhibit depressed mood and symptoms of anxiety disorder than are children with ADD+H. Erk (1995) states that clients with ADD–H tend to experience more depression, moodiness, and restricted affect than many of their counterparts with AD/HD. He states that therapists should be aware that this population is often concrete, operates mostly in the here and now, are not especially verbal (they often have difficulty with internal speech and verbalizing), and after the initial session or two typically find that counseling lacks novelty or uniqueness.

Kinsbourne (1992) describes another type of child, the overfocused, as "one who attends lengthily, ponders decisions long and hard, hesitates to follow an impulse, shuns turmoil, excitement and change, and whose movements are thoroughly predictable" (p. 23). Kinsbourne feels that these patterns of behavior are not generally recognized, although they are not uncommon and can be mistaken for AD/HD. He feels that it is a disorder "of the same system that is affected in AD/HD, but in the opposite direction" (p. 23). Kinsborne quoted the following descriptions by parents of such children:

- He will eat only five different foods and wear two different pairs of trousers.
- He likes sameness and no surprises.
- He is oblivious, has no idea whether anyone is listening to him, does not attend to physical objects.
- He was unable to finish school assignments on time because he did not like to leave a task unfinished once begun.
- He has difficulty following verbal instructions and would lose the gist if he was told more than one thing at a time.
- When excited, he wriggles and talks nonstop. He mostly gets excited "in his head."

- His style is to be totally focused on one activity at a time, his perseverance being to the exclusion of anyone else's needs.

- He has the worst difficulty in making decisions such as what to eat. This is for fear of making an incorrect decision. [p. 23]

Kinsbourne describes these individuals in terms of the internal regulation for maintaining one's arousal system at a normal setting. He describes how some individuals' arousal systems are set lower than they would prefer, and by their actions they enhance arousal. He describes such individuals as sensation-seeking or novelty-seeking and that they are often attention deficit disordered. He maintains that overfocused AD/HD could be part of this set. Kinsbourne also describes other individuals whose arousal systems seem to overflow even when the environment seems normal to most people. He states that these individuals strive to dampen their arousal so as to keep it under control. Kinsbourne feels that this type of overfocused ADD individual avoids situations and interactions that they may find too arousing. He states that they "continually attempt to safeguard their arousal level, and keeping it within tolerable bounds takes priority over meeting goals set by the external environment, both academic and social" (p. 24). Kinsbourne also describes how the overfocused individual will narrow his focus of attention. There is a constricted interaction with the environment that may result in avoidant types of behavior. Such an individual is described as resenting novelty because there is not a broad enough base of attention to "anticipate and adapt to the arrival of unexpected stimuli" (p. 25). With this type of description, it is not uncommon that such overfocused children will likely present with personality or behavioral difficulties since they may be seen as odd or as more generally pathological.

Kinsbourne states that children who are overfocused almost always present with attentional problems, but these are quite different problems than that of the typical AD/HD child. For example, the overfocused individual will not have difficulty in finishing things that are begun. However, they may appear more perseverative in what they are attempting to do. They will not look impulsive in their actions and may look more compulsive. Kinsbourne states that "overfocusers act impulsively only when trapped in situations in which they cannot avoid being overstimulated" (p. 25). He also describes these individuals as often staying on the fringes of peer activities and thus not having such difficulties as waiting turns or interrupting other kids' play or activities. In general, Kinsbourne states, "These individuals have no particular difficulty sustaining attention. Indeed, they sustain it to excess" (p. 25).

Kinsbourne states that overfocused children can often attend very well, but it may not be to what the adult would prefer. He writes that they may appear inattentive in the classroom, or restless, and therefore may be labeled as hyperactive, although he notes that they move differently from the typical AD/HD child, more so by rapidly rotating both hands at the wrist. He notes that they may also have learning problems but that this is often due to organizational difficulties and more inefficient cognitive styles. Also, "because they are so meticulous, they may be considered compulsive, but they are not orderly in general, often quite the reverse, only meticulous in certain self-selected areas" (p. 26).

From my own work these children described by Kinsbourne may also be partially explained by the high lambda score on the Exner scoring system of the Rorschach. Such a child would appear guarded, constricted, avoidant because of a narrowing of the stimulus field in an attempt to oversimplify and make things more manageable. Also, there is the child with this overincorporative cognitive style who is very methodical and does not like to make decisions without a great deal of information. Such a child can also appear cautious or ruminative and wishes to evaluate carefully before responding. That child does not like time pressures and, in the extreme, may seem obsessive-compulsive.

Bipolar disorder is another example of similar-appearing symptoms to AD/HD, which can confuse a proper diagnosis. Popper (1989) offers the following "clinical pointers" in helping to differentiate between ADD+H and bipolar disorder. He states that both of these disorders have many characteristics in common: impulsivity, inattention, hyperactivity, physical energy, behavioral and emotional lability, frequent comorbid conduct disorder and oppositional defiant disorder, and learning disorders. Popper notes that, generally speaking, children with AD/HD do not have psychotic symptoms, and that the presence of primary process thinking, except where it is age or developmentally appropriate, would rule out AD/HD as a diagnosis. Such gross distortions in perceiving reality are not normal for the AD/HD child, even when angry.

Popper (1989) notes that destructiveness may be seen with both of these populations, but arising from different causes. AD/HD children may break things because of carelessness, whereas bipolar children may do so because of extreme temper outbursts, "approaching psychotic degrees of disorganization and releasing manic quantities of physical and emotional energy, sometimes with violence and property destruction" (p. 6). As such, he observes the distinction between the carelessness of the AD/HD child and the anger of the bipolar child. In this regard, he states that the temper tantrums or angry outbursts of AD/HD children usually last no more than twenty to thirty minutes, whereas bipolar children will likely go beyond this, perhaps for periods of hours. Bipolar children are also seen to regress much more during angry episodes. Temper tantrums for AD/HD children may be the result of overstimulation, whereas bipolar children typically react in an angry manner to limit-setting. Bipolar children are seen to be much more irritable, especially upon awakening in the morning, whereas AD/HD children tend to wake up rather quickly and attain normal alertness within minutes, while children with mood disorders may show very slow morning arousal.

Aggressiveness is another area of distinction. The AD/HD child may "stumble" into a fight, whereas Popper describes the bipolar child as looking for a fight and "relishing the power struggle" (p. 5).

AD/HD children may find themselves in dangerous situations without noticing the danger or how they arrived there, while bipolar children are described as more counterphobic and intentionally daredevilish. Also, the danger-seeking may be characterized as grandiosity in bipolar children.

As a final caution regarding comorbidity, Popper notes that AD/HD and bipolar disorder may coexist in the same individual. Popper states, "There is no contradiction in treating both AD/HD and bipolar disorder in the same child" (p. 5). He suggests that stimulants may be used in combination with lithium to treat such children, but cautions that stimulants can destabilize a bipolar patient.

Glasser (1995) also notes that the differential diagnosis between AD/HD and bipolar disorder can be difficult because they may occur together. Her review of the research finds that 24 percent of adolescent patients with bipolar I disorder had a history of AD/HD. "One or more major depressive episodes are often seen in the clinical course" (p. 350).

Neiman and DeLong (1987) distinguish between these disorders by referring to comorbid psychotic and aggressive symptoms. They note that manic children are likely to have a long-standing history of depression with greater emotional difficulties and evidence of psychotic symptoms or significant disturbances in thinking and mood. These children are described as very asocial, perhaps even approaching schizoid in their social relationships, which is not a typical pattern for AD/HD children. They also note that levels of aggression with the bipolar group are much higher than those characteristic of AD/HD children of the same age.

Barkley (1990) states, "It is not enough simply to know the criteria for the diagnosis of AD/HD; the clinician must be able also to distinguish its symptoms from other psychiatric conditions that may bear a superficial resemblance to them" (p. 169). Research and clinical evidence is abundant with examples of children who have multiple types of disorders that coexist with their AD/HD upon initial presentation. Barkley feels it is no longer necessary to try and answer the question of which may be a primary disorder and which may be secondary. Such comorbid disorders, when they occur with AD/HD, can certainly interact and accelerate one another, which Barkley describes as perhaps changing the developmental course. His belief, though, is that if more than one condition is present, they all should be acknowledged and diagnosed.

The etiologies for AD/HD are a much researched area and there is strong evidence for a genetic transfer. Neurological studies are pointing to findings that show that a "dysfunction in the orbital-limbic pathways of the frontal area (and particularly the striatum) is the probable impairment that gives rise to the primary features of AD/HD, particularly its behavioral disinhibition and diminished sensitivity to behavioral consequences or incentive learning" (Barkley 1990, p. 98).

Regarding the course of AD/HD, Barkley (1990) states that there is a developmental decline in hyperactivity levels and some improvement in attention span and impulse control. However, 70 to 80 percent of AD/HD children are likely to continue to display such symptoms into adolescence to an extent inappropriate for their age group.

Barkley (1990) reports a study by Ross and Ross (1976) that indicated, "The adolescent years of AD/HD individuals may be some of the most difficult because of the increasing demands for independent, responsible conduct, as well as the emerging social and physical changes inherent in puberty. Issues of identity, peer-group acceptance, heterosocial dating and courtship, and physical development and appearance erupt as a new source of demands and distress with which the AD/HD adolescent must now cope" (pp. 72–73).

Werry (1992) discusses the longitudinal research on children diagnosed with ADD into adolescence. He states, "Symptoms shift away from hyperactivity toward more attentional-impulsive problems and derived or associated problems such as poor motivation, demoralization, and delinquent activities that make the syndrome itself less easy to detect" (p. 299).

Regarding hyperactivity, Werry discusses the shift from the more typical gross broader overactivity that is characteristic of preschool children through the first few grades. He states, "After that, locomotion is less of a problem than fidgeting, turning in the seat, talking, poking other children, mouthing pencils, and so on. By adolescence, except in a minority of cases, frank hyperactivity is no longer a problem" (p. 307). He notes that incessant talking or interrupting may be more typical of a motor behavior. Werry also states that by adolescence inattention is most often the major core symptom of AD/HD, although it may be somewhat difficult for a classroom teacher to detect because of the departmentalized nature of junior and senior high school, whereby a child sees a new teacher every hour.

Silver (1992) cites evidence that shows, about two-thirds of children with the disorder of attention deficit who were followed into adulthood still had disabling symptoms of the disorder, including many who had all three behaviors associated with AD/HD (inattention, impulsivity, and hyperactivity). Silver cites a study done at the University of Massachusetts AD/HD clinic (Kane et al. 1990) that identified the most frequent presenting complaints of adults evaluated for AD/HD:

Difficulty in finding and keeping jobs.

Performance on job below level of competence.

Inability to perform up to intellectual level in school.

Inability to concentrate.

Lack of organization.

Inability to establish and maintain a routine.

Poor discipline.

Depression, low self-esteem.

Forgetfulness or poor memory.

Confusion, trouble thinking clearly. [p. 622]

Two other disorders that coexist with quite a high degree of probability with AD/HD are oppositional defiant disorder (ODD) and conduct disorder (CD). Barkley (1990) cites his own research in which over 65 percent of children diagnosed with AD/HD are likely to develop sufficient levels of oppositional behavior that they also qualify for the comorbid diagnosis of ODD. Barkley's research on conduct disorder found that approximately 20 to 30 percent of AD/HD children manifest enough signs of antisocial behavior to qualify for a diagnosis of CD. He notes, though, that by adolescence between 40 and 60 percent of the AD/HD children could be diagnosed as CD, with the majority of these also having a diagnosis of ODD.

Biederman and colleagues (1992) cite studies that found that AD/HD and CD co-occur in 30 to 50 percent of cases in both epidemiological and clinical samples. Biederman and colleagues also cite Loney and colleagues (1981), who found that symptoms of hyperactivity and aggression "were not highly correlated and showed different patterns of concurrent and predictive validity, suggesting that they were separate dimensions. In those studies, the presence of CD in childhood, whether associated with AD/HD or not, was significantly correlated with aggressive behavior and delinquency in adolescence, whereas childhood AD/HD without CD was correlated with cognitive and academic deficits" (p. 381).

Many children with AD/HD present with a fairly straightforward, identifiable diagnosis; however, the differential diagnosis, especially of ADD–H youngsters, can be difficult. Both groups can be confounded by the variability in performance that these children typically display. They do much better with novel tasks or situations and perform rather poorly with rote activities. They often begin the school year with few reported problems, but then deteriorate as the year progresses.

ASSESSMENT PROCESS

The assessment process we have developed at Reiss-Davis addresses the problems in differential and comorbid diagnosis of attention deficit disorder.

Our philosophy for assessment at the Reiss-Davis ADD clinic is that a careful evaluation of our population is necessary because of the frequency of the comorbid issues. In addition to a psychological and psychiatric evaluation, parents' and teachers' input is critical. We have noticed, though, that many times parents see their own child differently (usually, the mother has more problems with the child) and that teachers may report differently from one to another, as well as from the parents. Parents and teachers may both have a positive halo effect for a child that they like, and conversely can report quite negatively on a child they do not like. Our experience has also shown that some teachers are reluctant to state in writing their true feelings about a child. Some may feel that direct feedback could reflect poorly on their teaching if the child is perceived as failing in some way.

The first step in our evaluation at Reiss-Davis is taking a careful and thorough history. This should focus on the AD/HD symptoms, but also needs to include developmental information, medical history, family interaction, social/emotional adjustment, and school performance.

Erk (1995) suggests that in reviewing a client's history the following behaviors typically found in ADD–H should be addressed:

1. Often daydreams or is "lost in a fog."

2. Frequently seems to be internally preoccupied.

3. Often seems to be apathetic or unmotivated.

4. Often confused or lost in thought.

5. Frequently low in energy, sluggish, or slow-moving.

6. Often stares in such a way that this behavior is noticeable. [p. 138]

The Child Behavior Checklist developed by Thomas Achenbach (1991), as well as our own informal checklist based on *DSM-IV* criteria, are given to parents and teachers in order to evaluate the child's performance in other settings. Achenbach also has a Youth Self-Report Checklist (1991) for ages 11 through 18, which is helpful. Erk (1995), however, states that ADD checklists or scales available to practitioners do not have sufficient technical data to support a separate factor or subscale specific to inattentiveness or ADD–H, thus impairing their diagnostic utility.

It has been our experience at Reiss-Davis that teachers and parents often interpret inadequate self-application to tasks as signs of character problems in a child rather than as a medical or psychiatric issue. *DSM-IV* corroborates that inadequate self-application to tasks that require sustained effort is often interpreted by others as indicating laziness, a poor sense of responsibility, and oppositional behavior. One of the hallmarks of ADD and/or AD/HD is the variability in sustained attention that the individual has in relation to their symptoms, and this may then lead adults to interpret their behavior as more willful and controlled.

The psychological evaluation that we developed at Reiss-Davis consists of observations of the child during testing, using the following instruments:

1. *Bender-Gestalt Test of Visual/Motor Integration*—Fine motor and visual motor delays are more frequent in the AD/HD population.

2. *Wechsler Intelligence Scale for Children–III (WISC-III)*—We evaluate intertest and intratest scatter (variability between subtests

and within a subtest), learning style, memory, and verbal and perceptual patterns, as well as examining the processing speed and freedom from distractibility indices. We also still apply the old distractibility index of arithmetic, digit span, and coding. As Barkley (1990) has noted, the essential feature of ADD-H is not behavioral disinhibition, but a primary deficit in focused attention and perceptual processing speed. There are approximately fifty factors from the WISC-III that we at Reiss-Davis find helpful in understanding the cognitive patterns of strength and weaknesses so that this information can be applied in school. Our experience has been that ADD and/or comorbid emotional issues can lower Wechsler scores and yield a lower and inaccurate estimate of intelligence.

Erk (1995) writes that ADD can cause a child not to reach his or her full potential, and it is not unusual that by the third grade an intelligence score has dropped significantly when compared with an earlier score (Copeland and Love 1991).

3. *Achievement Testing*—If the history suggests academic problems, then testing is done in this area to determine achievement levels in relation to cognitive ability, so that learning disabilities can be assessed.

4. *Continuous Performance Tests (CPT's)*—The Intermediate Visual and Auditory (IVA) and Test of Variables of Attention (TOVA) are administered as part of the testing battery. The authors have strongly noted that these tests should only be used as part of a battery, and that a diagnosis should not be made solely on these test results. The TOVA has been shown to be helpful in titrating medication levels so that optimum performance on this CPT corresponds to the proper dosage of medicine.

5. *Emotional*—A screening is done in this area using the Rorschach. This helps with the problem of differential diagnosis and/or comorbid emotional issues and also provides baseline data if the child needs psychotherapy. There are a number of scores from the Rorschach using the Exner system

that indicate ADD-like symptoms, and these are currently being examined at Reiss-Davis.

Such "emotional patterns" of ADD help in understanding the child and in formulating the treatment plan.

We typically analyze all of these data (history, behavior checklists, psychological evaluation) before recommendation for a psychiatric evaluation is made. Issues of confirmation of diagnosis, medication, and multiple diagnoses are finalized during the psychiatric evaluation.

TREATMENT

The proper treatment for AD/HD must cover a number of areas to be effective. The following issues should be considered:

1. *Medical*—a consultation/evaluation by a child psychiatrist or a pediatric neurologist for the purpose of establishing whether or not medication may be necessary. In our experience at Reiss-Davis, some parents will not accept medication for their children. There are two other options that parents may wish to evaluate:

   a. EEG Biofeedback—Some interesting work is being done in this area, which is addressed in other chapters of this book.

   b. Diet—There exists some controversial research on the correction of diet and digestive tract ecology.

2. *Educational*—Learning disabilities or learning problems often coexist with AD/HD and an individualized educational plan (IEP) through the public school should be sought in order to qualify the LD student for special education assistance. Some children or adolescents may also need the one-to-one remedial help provided by an educational therapist. Such practitioners are trained to address learning style and perceptual problems, and to teach students how to use their strengths in learning.

3. *Parent education*—Parents often need information about the disorder so that they can better understand their child. AD/

HD children can be difficult to parent and many family issues, such as discipline and structure, need to be addressed. The National Organization of Children and Adults with Attention-Deficit Disorder (CHADD) sponsors helpful, informative, and supportive groups for parents. Some parents and families may need more than this, such as family therapy or more individualized treatment for the parents.

4. *Social skills training*—The problems that AD/HD children have with peer interaction are well documented and the subject is addressed thoroughly later in this book.

5. *Therapy*—When comorbid emotional problems are diagnosed and are severe enough to warrant treatment with individual psychotherapy, then this should be discussed with parents. This type of treatment may include a model of psychoeducational psychotherapy also addressed in this book.

A review of the literature of psychotherapy with children diagnosed with AD/HD suggests that as a group they may not respond as favorably to treatment. The differences between ADD + H and ADD–H were not often taken into account, and this important point could well change a treatment plan. As a group, this population may have better outcomes with a more directive form of therapy and other adjunctive services in place.

At Reiss-Davis we have been astonished by the number of referrals over the past four years in which parents have raised the issue of ADD. Often they have been told by teachers that this is the problem. Many times, too, the parents have seen television shows or read newspaper articles in which the symptoms that were listed could fit almost any given child at a particular time.

Our interest at Reiss-Davis has particularly been with the ADD–H individual because so many possibilities exist with symptoms of inattention, forgetting, not following directions, inconsistent performance, processing speed, and many other cognitive, behavioral, and emotional components. While professionals from different training orientations often tend to view these individuals from their own perspective, it is our goal at Reiss-Davis to integrate the information from the fields of psychology, psychiatry, special education, and neurology into a more unified diagnostic and treatment orientation for this population.

REFERENCES

Achenbach, T. M. (1991). *Youth Self-Report Checklist for Ages 11–18.* Burlington, VT: University of Vermont.

American Psychiatric Association. (1994). *Diagnostic and Statistical Manual of Mental Disorders*, 4th ed. *(DSM-IV).* Washington, DC: American Psychiatric Association.

Barkley, R. A. (1990). *Attention Deficit Hyperactivity Disorder: A Handbook for Diagnosis and Treatment.* New York: Guilford.

Biederman, J., Faraone, S., and Lapey, K. (1992). Co-morbidity of diagnosis in attention deficit hyperactivity disorder. *Child and Adolescent Psychiatric Clinics of North America* (2):335–360. Philadelphia: Saunders.

Copeland, E., and Love, V. (1991). *Attention, Please! A Comprehensive Guide for Successfully Parenting Children with Attention-Deficit Disorders and Hyperactivity.* Atlanta, GA: Southeastern Psychological Institute Press.

Erk, R. (1995). The conundrum of attention-deficit disorder. *Journal of Mental Health Counseling* 17:131–145.

Glasser, J. (1995). *The AD/HD Report.* New York: Russell Barkley.

Kane, R., Milalac, C., Benjamin, S., et al. (1990). Assessment and treatment of adults with AD/HD. *In Attention Deficit Hyperactivity Disorder: A Handbook for Diagnosis and Treatment*, ed. R. Barkley, pp. 613–655. New York: Guilford.

Kinsbourne, M. (1992). Overfocusing: attending to a different drummer. CHADDER Newsletter, Spring–Winter, pp. 23–33.

Lahey, B., and Carlson, C. (1992). Validity of the diagnostic category of attention-deficit disorder without hyperactivity: a review of the literature. In *Attention-Deficit Disorder Comes of Age: Toward the Twenty-First Century*, ed. S. E. Shaywitz and B. A. Shaywitz, pp. 119–144. Austin, TX: Pro-Ed.

Lahey, B., Pelham, W. E., Schaughency, E. A., et al. (1988). Dimensions and types of attention-deficit disorder. *Journal of the American Academy of Child and Adolescent Psychiatry* 27:330.

Lahey, B., Schaughency, E. A., Hind, G., et al. (1987). Attention deficit disorder with and without hyperactivity: comparison of behavioral characteristics of clinic-refused children. *Journal of the American Academy of Child and Adolescent Psychiatry* 26:718–723.

Loney, J., Kramer, J., and Milich, R. S. (1981). The hyperactive child grows up: predictors of symptoms, delinquency and achievement at follow-up. In *Psychosocial Aspects of Drug Treatment for Hyperactivity*, ed. K. D. Jadow and J. Loney, p. 381. Boulder, CO: Westview.

Neiman, G., and DeLong, R. (1987). Use of the personality inventory for children as an aid in differentiating children with mania from children with attention-deficit disorder with hyperactivity. *Journal of the American Academy of Child and Adolescent Psychiatry* 26:381–388.

Popper, C. (1989). Diagnosing bipolar versus AD/HD. *Newsletter of the American Academy of Child and Adolescent Psychiatry* Summer:5–6.

Ross, D. M., and Ross, S. A. (1976). *Hyperactivity: Research, Theory, and Action*. New York: Wiley.

Silver, L., (1992). Longitudinal studies of AD/HD and adult outcomes. *Child and Adolescent Psychiatric Clinics of North America* 1(2):325–332. Philadelphia: Saunders.

Wechsler Intelligence Scale for Children–III. (1991). San Antonio, TX: Psychological Corporation.

Werry, J. (1992). Long term follow-up of AD/HD children. *Child and Adolescent Psychiatric Clinics of North America* 1(2):297–325. Philadelphia: Saunders.

5

Overfocusing: An Apparent Subtype of Attention Deficit/Hyperactivity Disorder

Marcel Kinsbourne

Key to the construct of overfocusing, a disordered pattern of attention and personality, is the concept of an instability of brain arousal mechanisms (Kinsbourne and Caplan 1979). The hypothesized instability exposes the individual to excessive arousal swings when stimulated, and these engender dysphoria. Overfocused behavior can be construed as in defense of a stable arousal level (Kinsbourne 1980). It is adaptive with respect to stability of internal state, and the patients appear to give this objective precedence over adaptation to constraints of the environment.

This chapter first appeared in *Pediatric Neurology*, vol. 1, pp. 18–35, copyright © 1991 by S. Karger AG, Basel, and is reprinted by permission.

OVERFOCUSING AS A PERSONALITY
DISORDER

Overfocusing involves a narrow focus of attention and social withdrawal. Constricted attention limits the amount of experienced stimulation. But a corollary drawback is that it reduces the individual's ability to detect and monitor unexpected change in the environment. If attention is very focused, then when change outside that focus finally obtrudes upon attention, it appears to come from out of nowhere, and is correspondingly experienced as disruptive. Notably, people bobbing up in the overfocuser's personal space are an irritation. He/she resents novelty because of the lack of enough spread of attention to anticipate and adapt to the arrival of unexpected stimuli. Avoiding social interaction is an additional safeguard against overstimulation. Integral to social interactions is empathy, picking up the other person's affective state. To recognize someone else's affective state, it is thought, is to some extent to model it. The individual as "psychologist" (Humphrey 1986) identifies the other's feeling by simulating how it would feel were he/she in the other's situation, looking and acting like the other person (Ekman et al. 1983). So social interaction calls for empathy, and empathy elicits an imitative arousal, and this is unwelcome to someone whose arousal system is unstable. The act of empathizing with other people triggers just that surge of arousal that the overfocuser tries to avoid. Anomalous styles in attention and in social interaction address the same issue. So whether one emphasizes the attentional disorder or the restricted social interaction, overfocusing is a personality disorder.

Of the two major complementary domains of human higher mental function—intellect and personality—intellect encompasses the efficiency with which one is able to control the outside world by controlling one's behavior relative to it. Intellect is orthogonal to overfocusing, and overfocusers are found at all levels of intellect. Personality represents a set of individual variables that describe how one goes about protecting one's own internal states, makes individualized choices in how to behave, and seeks settings that are conducive to maximize personal comfort. Personality designates enduring behavior patterns, or trait characteristics of the individual. Insofar as these are innate, reflecting brain organization, they are expressions of temperament. A major component of internal regulation is maintaining one's arousal systems at congenial settings. Some people's arousal systems are set lower than they would like, and by their actions they attempt to enhance arousal. They are "sensation-seeking" (Zentall and Zentall 1983) or "novelty-seeking" (Cloninger 1987) and are often hyperactive. Others have arousal systems that continually threaten to overshoot, and so they strive to dampen down arousal, so as to keep it under control. To do so they avoid situations and interactions that might be too arousing. The latter personality type includes the type of individual that I call overfocused.

Within a wide normal range the diverse expressions of personality are not maladaptive. Personality traits need not militate against the individual's own interest. A person may be very sociable or rather quiet, bold and risk-taking or hesitant and careful, but not to a detrimental extent. Diverse personality types find their individual niches in our complex society. But an expression of personality that is sufficiently extreme will necessarily impede the individual's efforts to meet his own external goals (Cloninger 1987). If protecting one's own internal well-being is so exacting that one has to resort to extremes of behavior, one may then exhibit deviant personality patterns and a clinically significant personality disorder. Many overfocused children are at the borderline between an unusual personality and psychopathology. Whether such a child is regarded as essentially normal although a little odd or different, or as having psychopathology, can be as much a matter of social context as of the child's inherent characteristics. Whether such marginal behavior patterns are adaptive or maladaptive depends on their interaction with social setting and societal expectations.

The discussion that follows approaches overfocusing from the perspective of attention. Overfocused children almost uniformly present with attentional disorders. This may be because of our society's emphasis on school achievement. When children fail in school or at least underachieve relative to their manifest potential on account of deviant personalities, they often present clinically on this account. That they are socially inept, get on badly with peers, and are sad about it, may come up only incidentally, although it is by no means less important. Some children with attention deficit/hyperactivity disorder (AD/HD) are of the overfocused type. Conversely, most overfocusers meet criteria for attention deficit (ADD+H): *DSM-III* (*Diagnostic and Statistical Manual of Mental Disorders*, 3rd ed.) or AD/HD (*DSM-III-R*). I first consider how overfocusers differ from the more commonly recognized "typical" hyperactives, here called "underfocusers," on some standard test instruments, and then present the items of a symptom rating scale designed to capture more of what they are like.

UNDERFOCUSED VERSUS OVERFOCUSED ATTENTION DEFICIT

The conventionally recognized underfocused child with AD/HD and the overfocused child appear to occupy opposite extremes of a general dimension of personality. The well-known impulsive and sensation-seeking temperament that is typical in AD/HD is diametrically opposed to the guarded hesitancy of overfocusers. Nonetheless, overfocusers are routinely mistaken for typical AD/HD. Both are inattentive to ongoing instruction, the former in favor of flitting displacement and attention to diverse extraneous matters, the latter in favor of persisting concentration on some earlier topic of interest. Overfocusers do at times behave impulsively, namely when overaroused, and they are restless, especially when stressed or intensely concentrating. Their restlessness, however, does not take the usual form of unpredictable large amplitude motions, but of repetitive movements of small amplitude. The above differences can readily be extracted from parents' responses to appropriately constituted questionnaires. We begin with the standard *DSM-III* criteria for ADDH.

The *DSM-III* symptom list for ADDH is subdivided to exemplify inattentiveness, impulsivity, and hyperactivity. On discriminant analysis, one can distinguish overfocusers from the more typical underfocused hyperactives. This analysis, and all comparisons that are subsequently mentioned, are references against my clinical diagnosis based on a comprehensive history and examination. Several *DSM-III* items, cited below and rated according to the SNAP rating scale, distinguish the overfocuser.

The attention-deficient individual who is overfocused will not, like the more usually underfocusers, fail to finish things that he starts. On the contrary he/she will still be doing it tomorrow. The overfocuser exhibits a sticky perseveration of mental set and task orientation, which is the reverse of how the underfocused children behave. Nor does the overfocuser often act before thinking. On the contrary he/she will think extensively and perhaps not act at all. Overfocusers act impulsively only when trapped in situations in which they cannot avoid becoming overstimulated. Overfocusers do not have difficulty waiting for [their] turn in games or group situation. On the contrary, they will hang around the fringes and wait longer than necessary. Overfocusers do not frequently interrupt other children's activities. Rather they stay on the fringes. Only after the other children take the initiative to admit the overfocuser into their company will the overfocuser launch into a personal tirade, which then seems to continue indefinitely. There is no particular difficulty staying seated, nor do they fidget excessively when sitting. They do not excessively run and climb. They have no particular difficulty sustaining attention. Indeed they sustain it to excess.

OVERFOCUSERS ON THE KINSBOURNE FOCUS OF ATTENTION RATING SCALE: CASE ILLUSTRATIONS

The Kinsbourne Focus of Attention Rating Scale (K-FARS) is used to identify the overfocused child. Ratings span a 0- to 3-point range ("never" to "very often"). The examples that follow illustrate how the particular items describe these children. They are concrete instances cited verbatim from testimony recorded in my case records. The subheadings (a, b, c, etc.) designate different individuals.

(1) Prefers sameness, upset by sudden changes in routine

   (a) He has a number of "rituals." He has to sleep with socks on and likes tight-fitting leggings. He likes soft clothes and has a hatred for pockets. When he plays he has to be absolutely alone. No one must be in his field of vision.

(b) He will eat only five different foods and wear two different pairs of trousers.

(c) He likes sameness and no surprises. When he comes home with a star he cautions his mother, "Don't get all excited."

(d) He helped stack his diapers so that the baby portrayed on each box faced left.

(2) Socially withdrawn and unskilled, especially with strangers

Overfocusers are not basically unsociable. They like to interact with others, but on their own terms, about their own topics, in a monologue. They will hesitate to interact with a stranger who may insist on discussing a topic of his own choice. So "withdrawn and unskilled" applies to the initial checking-out and 'get-acquainted' period.

(a) He avoids interaction and eye contact upon meeting new people, then warms up over time.

(b) He is not streetwise, does not understand other children, lacks sensitivity. His mother might be totally engaged with demands from the rest of the family, but he will shout above the ruckus about his comparative analysis of ski runs. He keeps talking long after people have stopped listening. He does not seem to understand about hurting other people's feelings. For instance he will make critical comments about his 3-year-old brother in his presence.

(c) He does not like crowds and prefers to see other children one-on-one. He is embarrassed if he is the center of attention and will never open any presents in public. Any parties for him he prefers to have just within the family.

(d) At birthday parties he gets overcharged and behaves in a silly way. His mother is always present to get him out of the situation when necessary.

(e) He "will say anything" in public, "the truth, no matter how much it hurts." He has no concept of any discomfort he might be inflicting. He calls another child "fatty," although he himself suffers from being teased.

(f) He is oblivious, has no idea whether anyone is listening to him, does not attend to physical objects.

(g) He does not pick up signs that tell children they have reached the end of joking or fooling.

(h) His speech used to be excessively loud, something of which he was not aware. He still laughs inappropriately and keeps talking when the listener has walked out of the room.

(3) Works slowly and may be compulsive

On psychometric and neuropsychological tests, these children do badly whenever time is an issue. Regardless of time limits, they perform slowly. They hate to be wrong, and would rather not do a thing at all than risk doing it incorrectly.

(a) In arithmetic he never passed any timed test and yet he was early to learn to multiply. He has "writer's block."

(b) He was unable to finish school assignments on time because he did not like to leave a task unfinished once begun.

(4) Resists being hurried or told to do more than one thing at one time

Told to do two things, an overfocuser will do neither. If you tell the child to put on his shoes as well as his socks, neither shoes nor socks will go on. Parents learn to ready these children for change step by step with very structured feedback. "Put on your sock. Now put on that one. Now put on this shoe." No other way succeeds.

(a) It is horrendous to get him dressed. He pulls a sock on, then pulls it off, and the same applies to any hope of having him wash his face. One hour later he comes out of the bathroom with a toy and a dirty face.

(b) He has to be gotten dressed piece by piece.

(c) When given several things to do, he does none of them. Even when given one task only, he will talk instead.

(d) He has difficulty following verbal instructions and would lose the gist if he was told more than one thing at a time.

Told "Go and wash and when you come upstairs again please bring X," he panics at having to do so much.

(e) To get ready he has to be walked through every detail for about one hour.

(f) His room is in chaos and one can just about tiptoe through it. When asked to clean up he does not, and when forced to do so he pushes his stuff under the bed and crams it into his underwear drawer. His Lego is in ten plastic dishes all over his room.

(5) Organization is difficult, especially at the beginning tasks

Whereas the underfocused child often starts well but then deteriorates, overfocusers begin the school year poorly and improve as they settle into a routine.

(a) He asked to face the wall in school to avoid distractions. If, when getting dressed, he sees a book within three feet he will start reading, even though he wants to be on time. Nevertheless, he is lost in the book.

(b) He was always willing to do something when he was 100 percent in command and ready.

(6) Often seems preoccupied with his own thoughts

Once embarked on a train of thought, the overfocuser cannot stop. This is often seen by teachers as rejections of their efforts. It is not meant to be. The child is still pondering what happened a minute or half an hour or a day ago.

(a) He describes himself as thinking more than other people.

(b) When excited he wriggles and talks nonstop. He mostly gets excited "in his head."

(c) He knows a lot. His mind is always busy and he is eager to share his knowledge. He tends to get stuck on one idea and cannot stop talking or thinking about it.

(d) He could always concentrate intently on certain things. When he was only 3 months old he would play for hours with his fingers. He hated to be picked up or disturbed in any way during these times.

(7) Is bothered by loud noises

  (a) He did particularly badly when timed because of attending to the ticking of the clock.

Because they do not check out the environment, it continually takes them by surprise. Therefore, they may overreact and overstartle to what others expect and have made allowance for.

(8) Has unusually sensitive hearing

  (a) He can hear a bell that is covered in snow.

(9) Has a narrow scope of interest

A bright overfocuser's narrow field of interest may be astrophysics. Many of the older ones go into computer science. Selections for play and hobbies seem to reflect the need for stability. One example is expertise in dinosaurs (even before it became fashionable). The reason is perhaps twofold. There is a finite number of dinosaurs to know about. So you know what you are up against. Also they are dead, so they cannot get you. They are eminently manipulable in one's mind. Another example is preoccupation with Lego. When at risk of becoming overstimulated, at transitions particularly, overfocusers will retreat to playing Lego, which will calm them down. Going to school and coming home from school are both difficult times, because both involve transitions. One of my patients on coming home marches through the house up to his room, noticing nobody. After half an hour of Lego he comes downstairs, perfectly pleasant, ready to assume the new persona of being at home.

  (a) He gets "stuck on things." He may have a project on dinosaurs and then spend two or three weeks getting every book out of the library, talking incessantly about them, reading and making up dinosaur stories. Then he drops the topic totally and goes onto antique cars, planes, Charlie Brown, Garfield. He likes to read those stories to his mother over and over again.

(b) He loved to wake early and draw for an hour. He was into sharks and had a period of dinosaurs. He would trace them and be very hard on himself; the rendition had to be perfect.

(c) He used to be fascinated by gadgets such as microwave ovens. He now enjoys computers.

(d) At 2½ years he was an expert on dinosaurs. At 3 years he made complex models for ages 14 years and up. He also had phases during which he was very interested in plants, rocks, and coins. At 10 years, he memorized a 400-page book on coins.

(e) He tends to fall asleep at 7:30 in the evening, and at 3:00 or 4:00 in the morning he is up and reading encyclopedias. He can spend six hours on a computer with continuous complete attention, not stopping to eat or for anything.

(f) He is a specialist. He is particularly well informed about ski jumps and has recently taken on Australia as a special interest. He knows all the best places to ski in Australia.

(g) He draws constantly, drawings of a single Ambo-like figure placed in the middle, upper half of the page. The finished figure is then stuffed under his desk and he reaches for another sheet.

(h) He draws a profusion of battle scenes, guns firing, and curious creatures equipped with military uniform and paraphernalia.

(10) Prefers to focus on one thing at a time

(11) Explores topics of own choosing in depth

(a) The first-grade teacher thought he was deaf because he usually left tasks unfinished as if he had not understood her directions. She then realized that he was overwhelmed by the amount of work, as he could concentrate on only one thing at a time. His performance improved once this was taken into consideration.

(b) His style is to be totally focused on one activity at a time, his perseverance being to the exclusion of anyone else's needs.

(12) Resists shifting attention or changing activities on somebody else's timetable

This is a problem in the classroom. The child is doing something different from the class because he is still doing what the class did earlier. He simply does not see the need to change topics. Teachers need to understand this. It is not intended to be personally insulting and aggravating to the teacher, although it turns out often to be.

(a) He will explore topics of his own choosing indefinitely. He will write the same letters over and over. He has watched *South Pacific* and *The Wizard of Oz* so often that he knows every line. As a child he played with bricks and made the same tower over and over. He has difficulty changing from his chosen activity.

(b) Before the school bus picks him up, he swings his legs nervously; when he comes home from school, he rushes and locks himself in his room. When he emerges, he is his "sweet self."

(c) He can get stuck on a certain subject and seems unable to stop thinking and talking about it, much to the annoyance of his family.

(d) He is generally furious if interrupted, but mostly he is oblivious.

(13) Worried and anxious

(a) He has the worst difficulty in making decisions such as what to eat. This is for fear of making an incorrect decision. He is highly anxious.

(b) He was very fearful and worried in anticipation.

(c) He becomes very anxious when problems are to be solved if he feels he has not got complete mastery over doing so.

(14) Overly sensitive to negative feedback

In contrast to underfocusers, the overfocusers are very sensitive and hate to be judged, either positively or negatively. They prefer neutral, detached, impersonal interactions, and the adult who does best around the overfocuser is understated.

(a) He is short-tempered, easily upset, and very sensitive to criticism. He tends to think everyone is his enemy.

(15) May interpret a parent's frown as indicating anger or a teacher's scolding to the class as directed specifically to him

(a) He takes thing literally and personally.

(16) Has trouble remembering more than one thing at a time (classroom assignments and chores)

Many overfocusers forget their homework, or do it but forget to turn it in. They may make poor grades, although they have good knowledge, because they do not conform to the classroom structure.

(a) He is very forgetful, does not know where he put his shoes, keeps losing his watch or having it stolen. Additionally, he does not learn from such experience.

(b) His room is a disorganized disaster area, although he likes things neat.

(c) Graded papers with comments to help improve the next assignment were very often lost. Even with an assignment pad, he would forget to have me sign it, or forget to turn in the work that he had done.

(17) Is quietly oppositional and stubborn

(a) He is described as a very willful child. He does what he likes and in his own way. If he does not want to do something, he says he cannot do it and refuses to do it. His mother describes how he refused to say his allegiance to the flag and stood in the corner for hours while his teacher waited for him.

(18) May have explosive outbursts and take a considerable time to cool off

If the world intrudes upon overfocusers, and they cannot shut out this interference or otherwise reduce their arousal, then they go out of control and become every upset. Typical is the overfocuser at a birthday party: he hangs around the fringes as a wallflower, watches what is going on and hopes to be left alone. But if he fails to separate himself from the action, he goes out of control. Stimulation overload translates into aimless wild activity. Embarrassed parents flutter anxiously in the background.

(a) He stays upset or angry for a long time and cannot let go of his anger.

(b) He can get very mad and stay mad for a very long time, out of proportion to the precipitating cause.

(c) When he is angry he tends to go to bed angry and rejects attempts at reconciliation.

(19) Performs better on tasks and in situations after getting used to them

(a) At the beginning of each school year she does extremely badly, cannot settle down to tasks. It takes until March each year for her to make some academic progress.

(20) May keep the same posture or facial expression for unusually long time periods

This reflects the invariance of mental set. Particularly in young children, posture and expression reflect thought process.

(21) Is frightened of anticipated new or intense experiences

They threaten to engender overarousal.

(a) He is very overwhelmed by how many questions there are that he will have to address.

(b) In anticipation of the resumption of school in the fall he couldn't sleep for several nights. Similarly whenever he has trouble sleeping, it is because something is about to happen, or happen again, like the resumption of swimming lessons.

(c) He gets uptight, for instance about going on field trips; he worries he might get lost.

(22) Becomes preoccupied with impending, anticipated events

Anticipatory anxiety is much in evidence ahead of holidays like Christmas and pending family visits. For days or weeks the child is out of joint. Uncle John is coming. Will Aunt Jane come, too? Will they bring presents? Where will they sleep? What will they wear? What will we do with them when they come? Overfocusers drive people berserk with obsessive questioning.

(a) When anticipating events, he has difficulty falling asleep because he is "thinking too much."

(23) Engages in repetitive movements

Repetitive movements of overfocusers are easily distinguishable from the more usual unpredictable restlessness of the underfocused hyperactive (although they are often mistaken for the latter). Small-amplitude repetitive movements appear at moments of intense concentration, or when novelty is experienced. Though variable in form, they usually involve bisymmetrical rotation or pronation-supination at the wrists, sometimes also including the forearms. Finger and foot tapping also occur.

People regard these movements not so much as abnormal as peculiar, and parents are embarrassed when the child makes them in social situations. Repetitive movements are de-arousing devices (Kinsbourne 1980). They help the child calm himself down.

(a) When excited he would flap both hands and stare at one of his hands fixedly, accompanied by soft vocalizations, like whispers.

(b) He does a lot of hand wringing, especially when overtired.

He has rubbed his hands so much that they look like they were hit by a hammer and were ten years older. When sitting he bends down and touches his hands to the floor. From time to time he makes large-amplitude bilateral flailing movements of the limbs. After a period of mannerisms he falls asleep.

(c) He makes repetitive hand movements and is always walking around.

(d) When overwhelmed he makes rapid repetitive, rotary movements of his forearms from his elbows.

(e) When overwhelmed with input from other people, he spins. Otherwise he lies flat on the floor and makes specific finger movements such that the fingers of the two hands demarcate patterns.

(f) He may work on a computer then take time off to jump up and down in his chair repetitively and repeatedly swing his head from side to side. He then resumes work.

(g) He walks in circles, exclusively counterclockwise.

(24) Often sits hunched over when working

(a) He hunches over his work, pulling his face close to the paper.

(25) Is shy

(a) In preschool he was very shy especially with adults, with the exception of ones he liked.

Based on these criteria, the K-FARS is intended to discriminate between under- and overfocusers. Discriminant function analysis identifies ten of these twenty-five criteria which discriminated twenty-three overfocusers from eighteen underfocusers with 100 percent accuracy. Those were, in order, 22, 20, 17, 25, 5, 10, 23, 1, 16, 6 (5 higher in underfocusers). A factor analysis of the data from this scale features a first factor interpretable as social anxiety/social withdrawal. A second factor represents a narrow focus of attentional interests. A recently completed data set for 199 normal schoolchildren ages 6 to 13 features a comparable first factor and a second factor indicating defensive/oppositional tendencies.

OVERFOCUSERS ON ADDITIONAL TEST INSTRUMENTS

On the Diagnostic Interview for Children and Adolescents–Parent Form (DICA-P), a structured psychiatric interview, the underfocusers, the typical hyperactives, are more oppositional and exhibit more conduct disorder, whereas the overfocusers are more apt to exhibit dysphoria or major affective disorder. Enuresis and encopresis are more common in the overfocuser, as is overanxiety.

On the Personality Inventory for Children (PIC) the factors of withdrawal and social incompetence differentiated 90 percent of the subjects correctly into under- and overfocused categories. Also discriminating were depression, anxiety, problems with social skills, and somatic concerns.

On the Wechsler Intelligence Scale for Children (WISC), the overfocusers did significantly better than underfocusers on Similarities, that is, on verbal reasoning. They were relatively poor on Arithmetic and Coding. Disproportionate difficulty in arithmetic is a common correlate of overfocused behavior. Effective coding requires one to work quickly and not continually check back, but these children feel they have to check back constantly. Consequently they lose time credits and thus score poorly. In other neuropsychological testing we found a deficit for the overfocusers in Rapid Automatic Naming and in the Stroop test. Shifting rapidly from response to response and overcoming response competition (between a color name and a different color word) is a weak point with overfocusers. Also discriminating was the Rey Osterreith test, which involves copying a complex figure that lacks obvious organization. Overfocusers had trouble constructing the necessary organization for purposes of their copy. They had no particular trouble remembering the gist of their rendering of the figure subsequently, however, and are not inferior to underfocusers on the memory section of the test.

DEVELOPMENTAL ASPECTS

The information on overfocusers presented to this point refers to the school-age child. Within that range, our cross-sectional normative data indicate no age-related trend of change in K-FARS ratings. Less is known about other phases in the life span.

Some cases of overfocusing emerge from a preschool syndrome more akin to the customary presentation of underfocused attention deficit. More commonly, however the young child is neither restless nor impulsive, but even quiet, placid, and passive to an unusual degree. Occasionally, a mild degree of interpersonal reserve and gaze avoidance is present. But, in contrast to autistic individuals, overfocusers unequivocally demonstrate a normal potential for emotional responsivity and affectionate relating, notably with their parents, as well as imaginative play.

After apparently normal infancies and even preschool periods, the onset of overfocusing is sometimes clearly related to an outstandingly stressful event, such as a death or separation in the family, or relocation of the family to a new and strange environment. The overfocusing that results does not, however, recede when the stress has waned, but seems to attain functioning autonomy.

The special interests that characterize overfocusers usually do not arise from parental initiative or even relate to parental areas of interest. Idiosyncratic though they are, they hold out a prospect of intellectual achievement in an otherwise inexplicably self-limiting individual. In time, however, the essentially nonadaptive, irrelevant, and nonprogressive nature of the preoccupation becomes apparent.

This quality of irrelevance of the focus of mental effort may become troublesome in adult years. Whereas the overfocuser's preference for lengthy, circumscribed, and repetitive tasks is conducive to success in certain contemporary fields, notably computer sciences, this option is only open to the more intellectually gifted individuals. Even among them, in severe instances the overfocuser will attend preferentially to some minor aspect of the task, or even be diverted from the task by some intriguing though task-irrelevant observation. This may delay completion, or even lead to an unwanted product. Comparable biases in selective attention impair domestic functioning.

OVERFOCUSING VERSUS PERVASIVE
DEVELOPMENTAL DISORDER

The preceding description of overfocusing has emphasized its differentiation from typical AD/HD (although underfocused AD/HD features can also occur in combination with overfocusing). Is there a *DSM-III-R* category under which overfocusing could be subsumed? We next consider a possible continuity between overfocusing and entities on the "continuum of autistic characteristics" (Wing 1988).

Robinson and Vitale (1954) presented case vignettes of children with "circumscribed interest patterns." Although "of average or better intelligence," they had come to clinical notice because "they had not established friendships or engaged in group activities" (p. 760). Discussing their presentation at the 1953 orthopsychiatric meeting, Kanner, who first described autism, agreed that these children differed from cases of early infantile autism. But, as Kanner pointed out, children with several different psychopathologies can exhibit rigidly circumscribed interests. The children so described may not all have been overfocusers.

Qualitatively, many overfocusing characteristics find their counterparts in descriptions of pervasive developmental disorder, not otherwise specified [PDD (NOS)] with respect to pragmatics of speech, ability to converse, stereotyped movements, disturbance on account of environmental change, and restricted interests. However, language disorder is the most frequent presenting complaint in PDD (NOS) (Levine and Demb 1987). Language disorder is not a characteristic of overfocusing. More generally, PDD (NOS) children, and even their mildest subset, multiplex developmental disorder (Cohen et al. 1987), are more severely functionally handicapped than overfocused children, though there is presumably overlap between mild instances of the former and severe instances of the latter. The same applies to Allen's (1988) subtyping of "autistic spectrum disorders," with respect to its mildest manifestation, subtype V. The overfocusing concept is also distinctive in its overlapping applicability to children regarded as truly deviant and children regarded as merely distinctive in style. Except for the characteristic style described above, these children are normal. Overfocusers represent a much larger group of children that appears to come more readily to pediatric than to psychiatric attention, and overlaps the normal range of variation in personality. Overfocusing constitutes persuasive support for conceptualizing a dimension of personality that extends the continuum of autistic behavior (Wing 1988) into normality. Subtyping in PDD is in general problematic (Fein et al. 1985). Whether overfocusing can be defined as a separate subtype of PDD is an as yet unresolved empirical issue.

NEUROCHEMICAL BASIS OF OVERFOCUSING

Direct information about the neurotransmitter status of overfocusers is unavailable. However, catecholamine overactivity can be hypothesized, based on animal models. Amphetamine treatment augments responses high in the animal's repertoire (Robbins 1975). Perseveration (Anisman and Kokkinidis 1975) and social withdrawal (Gambil and Kornetsky 1976) can be induced in rodents by dopamine agonists. Restless locomotion and stereotypic behaviors arise from excess dopaminergic activity in mesolimbic (Kelly and Iverson 1976) and nigrostriatal (Creese and Iverson 1974) circuitry, respectively. Selective attention can be enhanced by excess norepinephrinergic activity (Kokkinidis and Anisman 1980). Thus a provisional attribution of excessive catecholamine activity to overfocusing offers heuristic promise. Our specific hypothesis incriminates excessive or disinhibited nigrostriatal activity, which produces perseverative and stereotypic responding to a single incentive (Robbins and Everett 1982).

IS OVERFOCUSING A RIGHT HEMISPHERE LEARNING DISABILITY?

The social withdrawal of the overfocuser gives scope for misinterpretation, both in terms of the supposed entity of social or nonverbal learning disability (Myklebust 1975), and of nonspecific emotional consequences of academic and interpersonal setbacks. If the child presents with an apparent school problem to an educational testing facility, the pattern of academic failure across subject areas may be overemphasized, and the attentional abnormality ignored or misunderstood, because both psychoeducational and neuropsychological test batteries currently make little provision for attentional disorder. In the absence of explicit language or reading disability, it is currently fashionable to invoke right hemisphere deficits (Badian 1983, Rourke 1989, Weintraub and Mesulam 1983).

Descriptions of individuals allegedly impaired in right hemisphere development have repeatedly been offered since the initial report by Rudel and colleagues (1974). The children are typically poorly characterized with respect to their attentional characteristics, so that overfocused attention might have been overlooked. Coexisting depression could complicate the diagnosis, as it itself is capable of causing deficient arithmetic and visuospatial performance (Kinsbourne 1988) in children (Brumback and Staton 1982), these allegedly being characteristics of the right hemisphere–disordered individual (Weintraub and Mesulam 1983). Indeed, depressed children are also, like right-hemisphere cases (Rourke 1989, Tranell et al. 1987, Voeller 1986), described as subject to left-sided sensorimotor impairment, and the whole syndrome can apparently be reversed by antidepressant therapy (Brumback et al. 1984). We have not found a predominance of visuospatial or left sensorimotor deficit in overfocusers. Insofar as overfocusers resemble high-functioning autistoid individuals, we note that autism also cannot be accounted for by simply incriminating underdevelopment of one hemisphere (Fein et al. 1984).

REFERENCES

Allen, D. A. (1988). Autistic spectrum disorders: clinical presentation in preschool children. *Journal of Child Neurology* 4(suppl):48–56.

Anisman, H., and Kokkinidis, L. (1975). Effects of scopolamine, d-amphetamine and other drugs affecting catecholamines on spontaneous alternation and locomotor activity in mice. *Psychopharmacologia* 45:55–63.

Badian, N. A. (1983). Personal–social characteristics of children with poor mathematical computation skills. *Journal of Learning Disabilities* 16(3):154–157.

Brumback, R. A., and Staton, R. D. (1982). A hypothesis regarding the commonality of right hemisphere involvement in learning disability, attentional disorder, and childhood major depressive disorder. *Perceptual and Motor Skills* 55:1091–1097.

Brumback, R. A., Staton, R. D., and Wilson, H. (1984). Right cerebral hemisphere dysfunction (letter). *Archives of Neurology* 41:248–249.

Cloninger, C. R. (1987). A systematic method for clinical description and classification of personality variants. *Archives of General Psychiatry* 44:573–588.

Cohen, D. J., Paul, R., and Volkmar, F. R. (1987). Issues in the classification of developmental disorders and associated conditions. In *Handbook of Autism and Pervasive Developmental Disorders*, ed. D. J. Cohen and A. M. Donellan, pp. 20–40. New York: Wiley.

Creese, I., and Iverson, S. D. (1974). The role of forebrain dopamine systems in amphetamine-induced stereotyped behavior in the rat. *Psychopharmacologia* 39:345–357.

Ekman, P., Levenson, R. W., and Friesen, A. (1983). Autonomic nervous system activity distinguishes among emotions. *Science* 221:1208–1210.

Fein, D., Humes, M., Kaplan, E., et al. (1984). The question of left hemisphere dysfunction in infantile autism. *Psychological Bulletin* 95:258–281.

Fein, D., Waterhouse, L., Lucci, D., and Snyder, D. (1985). Cognitive subtypes in developmentally disabled children: a pilot study. *Journal of Autism and Developmental Disorders* 15:77–95.

Gambill, J. D., and Kornetsky, C. (1976). Effects of chronic d-amphetamine on social behavior of the rat: implications for an animal model of paranoid schizophrenia. *Psychopharmacology* 50:215–223.

Humphrey, N. (1986). *The Inner Eye*. London: Faber & Faber.

Kelly, P. H., and Iverson, S. D. (1976). Selective 6-OHDA-induced destruction of mesolimbic dopamine neurons: abolition of psychostimulant-induced locomotor activity in rats. *European Journal of Pharmacology* 40:450–460.

Kinsbourne, M. (1980). Do repetitive movement patterns in children and animals serve a dearousing function? *Journal of Developmental and Behavioral Pediatrics* 1:39–42.

——— (1988). *Hemisphere Function in Depression*. Washington, DC: American Psychiatric Association.

Kinsbourne, M., and Caplan, P. J. (1979). *Children's Learning and Attention Problems*. Boston: Little, Brown.

Kokkinidis, L., and Anisman, H. (1980). Amphetamine models of paranoid schizophrenia: an overview and elaboration of animal experimentation. *Psychological Bulletin* 88:551–579.

Levine, J. M., and Demb, H. B. (1987). Characteristics of preschool children diagnosed as having an atypical pervasive developmental disorder. *Journal of Developmental and Behavioral Pediatrics* 8:77–82.

Myklebust, H. R. (1975). Nonverbal learning disabilities: assessment and intervention. In *Progress in Learning Disabilities*, vol. 3, ed. H. R. Myklebust. New York: Grune & Stratton.

Robbins, T. W. (1975). The potentiation of conditioned reinforcement by psychomotor stimulant drugs: a test of Hill's hypothesis. *Psychopharmacologia* 45:103–114.

Robbins, T. W., and Everett, B. J. (1982). Functional studies of the central catecholamines. In *International Review of Neuropsychology*, vol. 123, ed. J. R. Smythies and R. J. Bradley, p. 1010. New York: Academic Press.

Robinson, J. F., and Vitale, L. J. (1954). Children with circumscribed interest patterns. *American Journal of Orthopsychiatry* 24:755–767.

Rourke, B. F. (1989). *Nonverbal Learning Disabilities. The Syndrome and the Model.* New York: Guilford.

Rudel, R. G., Teuber, H. L., and Twitchell, T. E. (1974). Levels of impairment of sensorimotor functions in children with early brain damage. *Neuropsychologia* 12:95–108.

Tranell, D., Hall, L. E., Olson, S., and Tranell, N. N. (1987). Evidence for a right-hemisphere developmental learning disability. *Developmental Neuropsychology* 3:113–127.

Voeller, K. K. S. (1986). Right hemisphere deficit syndrome in children. *American Journal of Psychiatry* 143:1004–1009.

Weintraub, S., and Mesulam, M. M. (1983). Developmental learning disabilities of the right hemisphere: emotional, interpersonal, and cognitive components. *Archives of Neurology* 40:463–468.

Wing, L. (1988). The continuum of autistic characteristics. In *Diagnosis and Assessment of Autism*, ed. E. Schopler and G. Mesibov, pp. 125–151. New York: Plenum.

Zentall, J. S., and Zentall, T. R. (1983). Optimal stimulation: a model of disordered activity and performance in normal and deviant children. *Psychological Bulletin* 94:446–471.

6

Using the T.O.V.A. in the Diagnosis and Treatment of Attention Disorders

Lawrence Greenberg

The Tests of Variables of Attention (T.O.V.A.) are continuous performance tests (CPTs) that directly assess attention variables. These computer tests provide clinicians with information about attention that is necessary in the diagnosis of disorders of attention, to predict response to treatment, to titrate dosage, and to monitor treatment over time. The T.O.V.A. is the visual version, and the T.O.V.A.-A is the auditory version. In this chapter I present an overview of the T.O.V.A.s and their clinical use.

BACKGROUND

In the past, clinicians have had to rely on subjective and often unreliable histories to make a diagnosis of Attention deficit/hyperactivity disorder (AD/HD). While the development of symptom checklists and behavior ratings have been helpful, the diagnosis remains problematic, particularly since reliable measures of attention have only recently become available.

CPTs, introduced by Rosvold and his colleagues in the mid-1950s, are increasingly being used by researchers and clinicians to delineate attention processes and deficits and to measure the effects of treatment. Most CPTs are visual and language based, using a variant of the original "A–X" task in which the subject responds whenever they see an "A" followed by a "X", which occurs infrequently. As a result, most CPTs measure errors of attention in the course of a boring and usually very short task.

To avoid confounding attention characteristics with learning disorders (LD), and to avoid the more complex processing skills needed to recognize alphanumeric and sequential stimuli, we created a nonlanguage based, nonsequential CPT in 1966 (McMahon et al. 1970). It used two easily discriminated geometric figures—a circle with smaller circle near the top margin (the target) or near the bottom margin (the nontarget). Left-right discrimination was not involved, and there were no appreciable practice or LD effects.

We also introduced a new test condition: the frequent presentation of the target (measuring what is now called "disinhibition"), which was paired with the traditional infrequent presentation of the target (measuring vigilance). The test measured attention in both boring and highly stimulating conditions. Each subtest was designed to be long enough (11.5 minutes) to catch most persons with attention problems.

Our first study, a clinical comparison of the effects of three medications, illustrated two basic principles that have governed all of our subsequent research and test development: (1) accurately define the targeted symptom(s), and (2) measure changes with accurate, symptom specific, and reliable instruments (Greenberg et al. 1972). In this study we found what appeared to be mutually contradictory results. Hyperactive children treated with a psychostimulant (dextroamphetamine) dramatically improved (as documented by teachers' classroom behavior ratings and our CPT), while mothers' behavior ratings clearly indicated that a tranquilizer (chlorpromazine) was significantly better than the psychostimulant. Although the teachers and mothers used the same behavior rating form, they based their ratings on two different criteria. The teachers were focusing on the attention behaviors, which worsened with the tranquilizer and improved with the psychostimulant. However, the mothers focused on the disrupting behaviors, which often did not change with the psychostimulant but did "improve" with the tranquilizer because the children were too sedated to be disruptive. Our CPT results, even with an accuracy of only ±100 msec, documented the efficacy of the psychostimulant and the deleterious effects of the tranquilizer on attention. Perhaps the most important outcome of this initial study was the recognition that attention and hyperactivity needed to be targeted separately and that we needed appropriate tools to measure each.

With the availability of the Apple IIe computer in the 1980s, we were able to design our CPT so that other researchers and clinicians could use it. The new software program and the specially designed microswitch significantly enhanced the sensitivity of the Minnesota Computer Assessment (MCA), as it was then named, by reducing the error of measurement to ±1 msec. The stimuli became squares, which were more easily constructed than circles, and each subtest became 10.8 minutes long. Similar to our original CPT, stimuli were presented every 2 seconds for 100 msec in fixed random fashion in both the infrequent and frequent test conditions.

The MCA was renamed the Test of Variables of Attention (T.O.V.A.) when a potential copyright conflict arose. The T.O.V.A. was normed (Greenberg and Waldman 1993) and used in a number of clinical trials before its release in the late 1980s when the software was developed for PCs. In the early 1990s the self-contained, immediately available analysis program was created, and the T.O.V.A.-specific technical and clinical support services were developed.

Since then, the T.O.V.A. has continued to be upgraded and made more user friendly. Ongoing test research and clinical experience have enabled us to make frequent improvements in the interpretation program, establish year-by-year norms for children, and add signal detection indices and the comparison AD/HD score. Version 7, including the School and Home Intervention Reports and the T.O.V.A.-A., was completed in 1996 (Greenberg and Kindschi 1996). Clinicians can now assess and compare visual and auditory information processing. The T.O.V.A.-A. uses two tones: G above middle C (392.0 Hz) is the target, and middle C (261.6 Hz) is the nontarget.

SELECTION GUIDELINES

While both T.O.V.A.s are used when conducting a neuropsychological assessment, the visual T.O.V.A. is generally used for diagnosis and monitoring treatment effects since most people have reasonably similar auditory and visual information processing skills. Of course, a significant visual or hearing impairment would influence the selection. If someone's vision were compromised or unusually well developed, the auditory T.O.V.A.-A would be the test of choice.

While many people favor one or the other, their performances on the auditory and visual T.O.V.A.s are reasonably similar. It is estimated, however, that 10 to 15 percent of the population have sufficiently uneven processing skills that their visual T.O.V.A. performance is significantly different than their T.O.V.A.-A performance. Accordingly, when taking the history, the clinician needs to determine whether there is a particular processing problem. The patient is asked whether there are more problems with reading and visually tracking or when trying to follow a particular conversation in a noisy setting. If the history indicates an auditory processing problem, the auditory T.O.V.A.-A should be administered.

> As a case illustration, an adult with a graduate degree reported that he performed well on his job until he was moved from a private office to a large room that was shared by six others. He became very distracted, and his job performance deteriorated quickly. He had the same problem all of his life but had been successful in keeping auditory distractions to a minimum when he needed to concentrate. His visual T.O.V.A. was within normal limits. However, the auditory T.O.V.A.-A was significantly deviant from the norm but normalized with a psychostimulant. (See Case Illustration, below.)

The T.O.V.A.-A should be considered when the T.O.V.A. is normal, but the clinical picture is strongly indicative of an attention deficit. Individuals with considerable computer-game experience, high intelligence, and excellent visual tracking skills (like pilots) and highly trained athletes can perform well on the visual T.O.V.A. even with AD/HD.

DESCRIPTION

The T.O.V.A. measures the following variables:

1. Errors of omission are a measure of inattention (vigilance). They occur if the subject does not press the microswitch when a target appears. These errors are frequently seen in children with attention problems and/or Central Nervous System (CNS) problems.

2. Errors of commission are a measure of impulsivity and/or disinhibition. They occur when the subject incorrectly responds to the nontarget. These errors are seen in children and adults with attention problems and disorders of impulsivity.

3. Correct response time is the processing time (in milliseconds) that it takes to respond correctly to a target. Response time is usually slower than normal in individuals with AD/HD.

4. Variability is a measure of inconsistency of correct response times. Individuals with AD/HD are inconsistent—they may be able to perform within normal limits for a while, but they "lose it" much sooner than the non-AD/HD. Variability is the most important T.O.V.A. measure, accounting for 80 percent of the variance.

5. Anticipatory responses are a measure of guessing. An anticipatory response is any response to a stimulus (target or nontarget) that occurs within the 200 msec of the appearance of the stimulus (that is, before one could distinguish target from nontarget).

6. Postcommission response time is the response time immediately following a commission error (mistakenly pressing the button when a nontarget appears). Clinical observations indi-

cate that while most people (including individuals with AD/
HD) slow down for the next response, conduct-disordered
youngsters often do not.

7. Multiple responses are a reflection of neurological status. Excessive multiple responses may indicate nonspecific neurological immaturity or dysfunction.

8. d' or response sensitivity (the ratio of hit rate to false-alarm
   rate) is a measure derived from signal detection theory. It is
   considered to be a measure of performance decrement.

The first half is a more traditional, boring vigilance task (in which
the target appears infrequently), while the second half is a high response demand mode (in which the target appears frequently) to
measure disinhibition. There is a 10.8 minute standardized T.O.V.A.
version of 4 to 5-year-olds.

Norms

The T.O.V.A. and T.O.V.A.-A were normed with 2,000 and 2,550
normal children, respectively, to control for age and gender
(Greenberg and Crosby 1992). Provisional norms are available for
adults.

USE OF THE T.O.V.A. IN THE DIAGNOSIS OF DISORDERS OF ATTENTION

Although the emphasis in this chapter is on AD/HD, tests like
the T.O.V.A. are equally valuable in the assessment of attention in a
number of conditions, including sleep disorders, epilepsy, brain damage, and side effects of medications. However, the most frequent use
of CPTs is in the diagnosis and treatment of AD/HD.

The sensitivity and specificity of the T.O.V.A. are critical considerations since the older, first-and-second-generation CPTs had very
low "hit" rates. The sensitivity (ability to correctly identify AD/HD
cases) and its specificity (ability to correctly identify normal individuals) have been generally determined by means of discriminant analy-

sis. Using this method, the T.O.V.A. overall correctly identifies 86 percent or more of AD/HD and normal subjects (Greenberg and Crosby 1992b). However, the use of discriminant analysis is predicated on having a sample that is generalizable to other samples. This assumption does not apply to any of the currently available CPTs.

Use of the more conservative technique, receiver operator characteristic analysis, is more appropriate. With this technique, the T.O.V.A. has a sensitivity and specificity of 80 percent. Thus, there is an 80 percent chance that a T.O.V.A. (with no other information about the individual) is correct. Of course, with additional relevant data (such as history, behavior ratings, and IQ), the "hit" rate improves significantly.

Test-retest reliability is another critical consideration that affects sensitivity and specificity. Test-retest results for thirty-three randomly selected normal children, forty children with AD/HD, and the twenty-four normal adults revealed no significant differences (paired t-test) in T.O.V.A. variables. There was a nonsignificant tendency for commission errors to increase (worsen) during the first half of the test from first test to second test but not for subsequent tests.

These computerized tests are easy to administer in the office setting, and the report is computer generated and immediately available. However, no CPT makes a diagnosis of AD/HD—only a clinician makes the diagnosis after obtaining a history, behavior ratings, and other relevant information, including a test like the T.O.V.A.

In the illustration from the T.O.V.A. of a 9-year-old boy with AD/HD (Table 6–1) inattention, response time, and variability are all significantly deviant from normal (matched for age and gender) and would be interpreted as compatible with an attention disorder. (The normal ranges are -1 to +1 standard deviations and 90 to 110 standard scores. The more negative the standard deviation and the lower the standard score, the more deviant the results.)

In clinical practice, the child and parents or the adult (and spouse, if applicable) are interviewed, and behavior ratings and a symptom checklist are completed. As indicated, a general physical and screening neurological examination, educational, and/or psychological assessments are obtained. For children, behavior ratings are obtained from the classroom teacher. The T.O.V.A. is administered in the

Table 6–1.
Baseline T.O.V.A. Results for a 9-Year-Old with AD/HD

Total omission errors (inattention)	
Standard deviation	-1.8*
Standard score	73*
Total commission errors (impulsivity/disinhibition)	
Standard deviation	0.3
Standard score	105
Total response time	
Standard deviation	-1.7*
Standard score	75*
Total variability	
Standard deviation	-2.1*
Standard score	69*

*Significantly deviant from the norm.

morning (to avoid diurnal attention effects) with the tester present. All of this information is used to determine the diagnosis and a treatment intervention. Acceptance and understanding of the diagnosis and treatment recommendations are enhanced when the interpretations of the behavior ratings and the results of the T.O.V.A. are shared with the patient and family.

USE OF THE T.O.V.A. TO PREDICT RESPONSE TO PSYCHOSTIMULANTS

If a psychostimulant is being considered, a medication challenge test is conducted to determine whether the medication will be efficacious and the best dosage level. Until the use of CPTs, clinicians had to rely on the subjective reports of the patient and family activity-level biased behavior ratings to determine the outcome of a two- to four-week clinical trial of medication. This is no longer necessary. The clinician can now compare the baseline (no medication) T.O.V.A. obtained during the diagnostic workup with a T.O.V.A. obtained 1.5

hours after a single low dose of a psychostimulant (5 mg methylphenidate of 2.5 mg of dextroamphetamine or Adderall). The challenge dose needs to be small to avoid "shocking" the child and causing upsetting side effects, leading to resistance and noncompliance.

Noting the medication effects on attention variables, a clinician can successfully predict response to medication and determine a good therapeutic dosage. (It is not possible to predict response to antidepressants in the same way, since they can take three to four weeks to stabilize.)

A challenge test is often very useful when the family or patient are reluctant to undergo a clinical trial of medication. However, they will often consent to a single dose. If the attention variables show the usually dramatic improvement with the single dose, there is more cooperation with a medication trial. In the illustration from the T.O.V.A. of the 9-year-old boy with AD/HD (Table 6–2), inatten-

Table 6–2.
Challenge T.O.V.A. Results for a 9-Year-Old with AD/HD

	No Medication	5 mg Ritalin
Total omission errors (inattention)		
Standard deviation	-1.8*	0.9
Standard score	73*	114
Total commission errors (impulsivity/disinhibition)		
Standard deviation	0.3	0.5
Standard score	105	108
Total response time		
Standard deviation	-1.7*	1.5
Standard score	75*	123
Total variability		
Standard deviation	-2.1*	2.2
Standard score	69*	133

*Significantly deviant from the norm.

tion, response time, and variability, which were all originally significantly deviant from normal, were within normal limits on medication. These results are actually much better than average and are indicative of an excellent medication response.

DOSAGE CONSIDERATIONS: CHILDREN VERSUS TEENAGERS AND ADULTS

Clinicians are often surprised by our low challenge dose recommendations. We have been accustomed to following the recommendation of 0.3 to 0.6 mg/kg/dose for methylphenidate and accepting a higher than necessary failure rate and incidence of side effects. The recommendation for a milligram per kilogram dosage, while it may be applicable for the treatment of a systemic illness, does not seem particularly wise in the treatment of a CNS disorder.

Over the years, we have become accustomed to using much higher dosages for treatment, reflecting our reliance on global clinical judgment and behavior ratings, both of which emphasized hyperactivity and impulsivity at the expense of attention problems. Now with the availability of T.O.V.A.s, the dosage can be very accurately titrated to obtain the best effects on attention. Use of T.O.V.A.s has resulted in a dramatic increase in efficacy, decrease in dosage levels, lower incidence of side effects, and higher compliance.

The decrease in dosage reflects our experience that low doses of psychostimulants affect attention, that high doses affect behavior, and that there is either little overlap between the two effects, or that attention actually worsens with high doses. In the illustration from the T.O.V.A. of a 13-year-old boy with AD/HD (Table 6–3), baseline (no medication) response time and variability were significantly deviant from normal and compatible with an attention deficit. With a 5-mg challenge dose of Ritalin, inattention, impulsivity, and variability significantly improved and fell within normal limits. However, response time significantly worsened. When some variables improve and some worsen, it generally means that the challenge dose was too high. The guideline is that the dosage should be reduced. In this case, all variables improved and were within normal limits with 2.5 mg of Ritalin, which would be dosage level for a clinical trial of medication.

Table 6–3.
T.O.V.A. Results for a 13-Year-Old with ADHD

	No Medication	5 mg Ritalin	2.5 mg Ritalin
Total omission errors (inattention)			
Standard deviation	-0.03	0.05	1.1
Standard score	100	101	117
Total commission errors (impulsivity/disinhibition)			
Standard deviation	-0.01	1.1	0.9
Standard score	100	117	114
Total response time			
Standard deviation	-1.7*	2.9*	-0.1
Standard score	75*	57*	99
Total variability			
Standard deviation	-1.5*	-0.3	0.2
Standard score	78*	96	103

*Significantly deviant from the norm.

It is best to begin with low dosages to minimize side effects and maximize compliance.

ASSESSING AND MONITORING PHARMACOTHERAPY

We recommend obtaining an interim history (including side effects) and behavior ratings in addition to baseline (before taking the morning dose) and on-medication T.O.V.A.s every six to twelve months to determine when the dose needs to be adjusted. In general, dosage increases with age until the early teen years, when it decreases until the late teens and early twenties. (It's still not well recognized that teenagers and adults need less medication than children.) If the patient has "outgrown" the AD/HD, the medication can usually be discontinued in the early teen years. If, however, the AD/HD per-

164   Lawrence Greenberg

sists into adulthood, the dosage remains steady until the late sixties, when it often drops even further. Many teenagers and adults need surprisingly small doses (1–5 mg methylphenidate) and show "no improvement" or even get worse with the more commonly prescribed higher doses.

THE T.O.V.A. REPORT

The computerized interpretation report contains of seven forms and the cover page (see Appendix).

The Cover Page

This page contains a brief description of the T.O.V.A. and the table of contents.

Form 1

The T.O.V.A. interpretation compares the subject's performance with normals of average IQ, matched for age and gender. If the performance is significantly deviant from the norm, it means that this person performed as though there were an attention problem. They were significantly off-task, impulsive, slow to respond and/or variable, but there is no etiologic specificity to this interpretation. A poor performance could be the result of many very different factors.

In the case illustration in the appendix, the T.O.V.A. interpretation was compatible with an attention deficit.

Form 2

The AD/HD score is a comparison between the performance of this person and the performance of individuals with AD/HD. Unlike the T.O.V.A. interpretation, which compares the subject to normals and tells how deviant the subject's performance is from the norm, the AD/HD score tells us how similar the performance is to be performance of someone with AD/HD.

If the interpretation (Form 1) is not within normal limits (that is, is deviant from the norm) and AD/HD score is not within normal limits, there is a high probability that the person has an attention problem.

If the interpretation and the AD/HD score are within normal limits, there is a high probability that the person does not have an attention disorder.

If the interpretation is that the performance was deviant from the norm, but the AD/HD score was not significant, there is a high probability that the person has an attention disorder.

If the interpretation is that the performance was within normal limits, but the AD/HD score was significant, there is a high probability that the T.O.V.A. interpretation represents a false negative, and that the person does have an attention problem. There are many reasons for a false-negative result, including high intelligence (see below) or the presence of an auditory rather than a visual attention problem and vice versa.

In the case example in the appendix, the AD/HD score was compatible with AD/HD and concordant with the T.O.V.A. interpretation.

Form 3

The analysis graph presents T.O.V.A. results using standard scores and percentiles for omissions, commissions, response time, and variability.

In the case example in the appendix, omissions (inattention) are too deviant (too low) to be represented on the graph. All of response times and variabilities are also significantly deviant and are displayed below the standard score cutoff of 80. (The normal range for standard score is 85 to 115. Any result below 80, indicated by the dotted line, is considered significant, assuming average intelligence.)

Form 4

The analyzed data, organized by quarters, halves, and total, using standard scores and standard deviations, are coded for validity and significance.

Reading the analysis table, the totals are examined. In the case example in the appendix, total omissions (inattention), response time, and variability are all significantly deviant from the norm and compatible with an attention deficit.

The halves are then examined first. Half 1 is the boring task when the target appears infrequently. "Underaroused" individuals have difficulty maintaining attention and control in boring situations. If this half is symptomatic, consider increasing toward-task stimulation, decreasing time on-task, introducing activity, and so on. Half 2 is the active or high response demand task in which the target appears frequently and the tendency to respond must be inhibited. "Overstimulated" individuals become disinhibited and make excessive errors. If this half is symptomatic, consider decreasing distractions and pace. In the case example in the appendix, there are significant findings in both halves that would suggest that both intervention strategies are needed.

Quarters within a across halves are then examined. If there is a significant change (worsening) within a half, consider the possibility of a short (5- to 6-minute) attention span in that kind of task or possibly a 12- to 15-minute attention span overall if the change is between quarters 3 and 4. In the case example in the appendix, the results are too inconsistent to interpret in terms of attention span.

Form 5

The data for signal detection and AD/HD score results for Form 2 are presented.

Form 6

The raw data and test information are presented.

Form 7

Notes to the clinician help the clinician understand the findings and implications for treatment.

The School and Home Intervention Reports

Suggestions for the classroom teacher and for the family can be edited and expanded to fit the needs of a particular case. The reports address five categories of behavior—increasing focus on tasks (decreasing distractibility), improving social skills (managing social deficits), increasing thinking before action (decreasing impulsivity), effective behavioral interventions, and promoting consistency in performance (decreasing variability).

THE EFFECTS OF INTELLIGENCE

Many clinicians have observed that individuals with high intelligence perform better on the T.O.V.A. than those with average intelligence. (Similarly, individuals with low intelligence appear to perform less well.) However, the T.O.V.A. interpretation program assumes average intelligence. Patients with AD/HD *and* a high intelligence often are able to perform within normal limits on the T.O.V.A. even though they are performing significantly below their own ability. This would result in a false-negative T.O.V.A. and would be at variance with other clinical data. High intelligence can account for over half of the false-negative T.O.V.A.s. The second most common reason for a false negative is an auditory (rather than a visual) information processing problem. In these cases an auditory T.O.V.A.-A should be administered.

Using an adjustment for intelligence is very helpful, especially when trying to understand a discrepancy between T.O.V.A. results and the other clinical findings when formulating the diagnosis, or when explaining to a patient, parent, or to another clinician why a particular T.O.V.A. performance should be considered deviant when the printout says that it's within normal limits. An adjustment for intelligence is particularly helpful when trying to find the optimal treatment results, especially the best dosage level of medication.

In previous versions, there was an optional adjustment that could be used when encountering this situation in a person with AD/HD and a high (or low) intelligence. The norms could be adjusted up or down by one or two age groups. This correction soon proved to be inadequate, particularly with teenagers and adults, and was deleted.

With a patient with a high intelligence, subtract fifteen points from the IQ and consider that value to be cutoff point between normal and deviant for the standard score of the response time and variability. If someone has an IQ of 125, consider any response time or variability score below 110 (125 - 15) to be significantly deviant for that individual. (Similarly, for someone with an IQ of 75, any response time or variability score above 60 (75 - 15) would be within normal limits for that individual.) To be cautious, restrict the adjustment to not exceed 125 or be less than 65, regardless of IQ.

A line can be drawn across the graphs on Form 3 (or on comparison graphs) for response time and variability at the level of the standard score representing the adjustment, and this graph can be used to illustrate the adjusted results.

In titrating the effects of medication or monitoring the effects of treatment with the T.O.V.A., the response time and variability should normalize. In a case of high (or low) intelligence, the response time and variability should improve toward or into the corrected range.

Although the usual T.O.V.A. profile for a teenager or an adult with AD/HD consists of deviant response times and/or variability, only impulsivity is deviant in approximately 30 percent of these cases, even though they are not particularly clinically impulsive. In these case, adjustments for intelligence would be applied to the impulsivity score since the other variables are not deviant.

CASE ILLUSTRATION 1

The case below was described above (see Selection Guidelines). His visual T.O.V.A. performance was interpreted as within normal limits, assuming average intelligence, although the clinical picture was compatible with AD/HD. He had an advanced science degree and an IQ >120. (If the IQ adjustment had been applied, the variability of 103 would be deviant from his expectable performance and would have been interpreted as compatible with AD/HD.) Because he reported encountering significant difficulty when trying to work in a noisy environment, a T.O.V.A.-A was administered (Table 6–4).

Table 6–4.
T.O.V.A. Results for an Adult with AD/HD

| | T.O.V.A. (Visual): | T.O.V.A.-A (Auditory): | |
	No Medication	No Medication	5mg Ritalin
Total omission errors (inattention)			
Standard deviation	0.48	0.05	0.49
Standard score	107	108	107
Total commission errors (impulsivity/disinhibition)			
Standard deviation	0	-2.4*	0.5
Standard score	100	64*	108
Total response time			
Standard deviation	1.6	-1.1[a]	1.6
Standard score	124	83[a]	124
Total variability			
Standard deviation	0.23	-1.9*	1.1
Standard score	103	72*	116

*Significantly deviant from the norm.
[a]Borderline.

In contrast to the visual T.O.V.A., the baseline (no medication) commissions and variability of the T.O.V.A.-A were significantly deviant from the norm and compatible with an attention deficit. (This case is a good illustration of a discrepancy between visual and auditory processing skills.) His performance normalizes with medication.

CASE ILLUSTRATION 2

An 11-year-old boy was tested in 1988 as part of our norming study. At that time behavior ratings were clearly within normal limits. He was referred for a clinical evaluation in 1990 following a serious auto accident and a long period of unconsciousness. Since the accident his behavior changed dramatically, and he then met criteria for ADD with hyperactivity. Neuropsychological assessment revealed a mild memory impairment but was otherwise within normal limits. The T.O.V.A. results shown in Table 6–5 were obtained.

Table 6–5. T.O.V.A. Results for a Head Injury Case			
	1988	1990	1990 5mg Ritalin
Total omission errors (inattention)			
Standard deviation	0	-1.8*	0.45
Standard score	100	73*	107
Total commission errors (impulsivity/disinhibition)			
Standard deviation	0.7	0.3	0.1
Standard score	111	105	101
Total response time			
Standard deviation	0.3	-1.7*	0.4
Standard score	105	75*	106
Total variability			
Standard deviation	-0.1	-2.1	1.1
Standard score	101	69*	110

*Significantly deviant from the norm.

In this case, omissions, response time, and variability, all of which were within normal limits in 1988, are significantly deviant from the norm and compatible with an attention deficit in 1990. After a 5-mg challenge dose of Ritalin was administered, his T.O.V.A. performance normalized. Subsequent follow-up has revealed a stable condition that continues to respond well to medication.

CASE ILLUSTRATION 3

A 10-year-old boy with the clinical diagnosis of AD/HD was referred for a medication trial. The baseline (no medication) results are shown in Table 6–6.

Table 6–6.
T.O.V.A. Results for a 10-Year-Old with Epilepsy

	Quarter			
	1	2	3	4
Omission errors				
Standard deviation	-2.2*	-3.6*	-0.77	≥4*
Standard score	66*	46*	88	< 40*
Commission errors				
Standard deviation	0.16	-2.5*	0.03	0.8
Standard score	102	60*	100	112
Response time				
Standard deviation	-2.8*	-3.3*	-2.5*	-2.9*
Standard score	58*	50*	62*	56*
Variability				
Standard deviation	-0.94	-2.7*	-3.4*	-3*
Standard score	85	58*	48*	55*

*Significantly deviant from the norm.

All four of the variables are significantly deviant from the norm in one or more quarters and are compatible with an attention deficit. However, the deviant omission errors (inattention) merit further examination. While young children (4- to 8-year-olds) with AD/HD make many omission errors, older children and adults do not because of ceiling effects. When a high number of omission errors are encountered, the interpretation program will prompt the clinician to consider the possibility of an underlying neurological condition, such as epilepsy or a sleep disorder. The clinician can review the protocol response by determining the distribution of the omission errors. In general, individuals with AD/HD have scattered errors, but clusters of omission errors are the general rule in the neurologically impaired. In this particular case, there were clusters of errors, and a subsequent neurological examination and electroencephalogram (EEG) confirmed lapse seizures.

CASE ILLUSTRATION 4

This 12-year-old girl was diagnosed as having AD/HD, inattentive type, with no significant impulsivity or hyperactivity. In school she had done acceptably but not at her expected level. Although she was inattentive and distractible in school and at home, she was not a management problem.

The youngster had significant problems (response time and variability were deviant from the norm) in the first half of the test but not the second half (Table 6–7). In the first half of the test, one becomes easily bored while waiting for the infrequent target. In contrast, in the second half, when the targets appear frequently, a subject has to be alert and inhibit the expectation to respond. A discrepancy between halves is seen in many AD/HD cases, although many have difficulties with both test conditions. That is, they get too bored in the first half and too overstimulated in the second half and do poorly in both. In her case, she has difficulties with maintaining attention during boring tasks, such as reading to herself and in long, repetitive tasks. Characterized as "underaroused," she would respond to toward-task stimulation (a nod, a touch on the shoulder, or tapping the page she is supposed to be reading) and a more stimulating environment (like having a chatty and bouncy teacher rather than a quite one). Boring tasks and long in-seat work should be minimized. If someone had problems with the second but not the first half, it would be helpful to reduce or mask environmental noise, visual and auditory. There are a number of helpful suggestions for managing this problem in the school and home intervention reports.

In addition, her performance in quarter 2 was much worse than in quarter 1. This may indicate that her attention span or tolerance

Table 6–7.
T.O.V.A. Results for a 12-Year-Old with AD/HD

	Quarter				Half	
	1	2	3	4	1	2
Omission errors						
Standard deviation	0.2	-1.3[a]	0.4	0	-0.4	0.5
Standard score	103	81[a]	106	100	94	108
Commission errors						
Standard deviation	0.21	-0.6	0.2	0.3	0.3	0.6
Standard score	103	91	103	105	105	109
Response time						
Standard deviation	-1.7*	-3.4*	-0.1	0.9	-3.0*	0.8
Standard score	75*	49*	99	114	55*	112
Variability						
Standard deviation	-2.6*	-3.8*	0.7	0.4	-3.1*	0.6
Standard score	61*	43*	111	106	54*	109

*Significantly deviant from the norm.
[a]Borderline.

of boring tasks is between 5 and 10 minutes. If this were so, boring and in-seat tasks should be brief.

CASE ILLUSTRATION 5

A 33-year-old man was referred with multiple obsessive-compulsive (O-C) traits and a history of inattention, distractibility, academic underachievement, and impulsivity since childhood. He was treated with Prozac (40 mg) for several months with little change in his clinical picture, although he reported feeling significantly better. Self behavior ratings revealed some but not dramatic improvement in the O-C symptoms and little or no improvement in his AD/HD symptoms. The T.O.V.A. results shown in Table 6–8 were obtained.

Table 6–8.
T.O.V.A. Results

	Medication		
	40 mg Prozac	5 mg Ritalin and 40 mg Prozac	None
Total omission errors (inattention)			
Standard deviation	0	0	0
Standard score	100	100	100
Total commission errors (impulsivity/disinhibition)			
Standard deviation	≥4*	0.7	≥4*
Standard score	<40*	110	<40*
Total response time			
Standard deviation	0.4	0.2	0.6
Standard score	106	103	109
Total variability			
Standard deviation	-1.1[a]	1.1	-1
Standard score	84[a]	117	85

*Significantly deviant from the norm.
[a]Borderline.

The commission errors (impulsivity/disinhibition) in the first test with Prozac were clearly deviant from the norm. The finding of deviant commission, often without a history of noteworthy impulsivity, is seen in a third of adults and teenagers with AD/HD. Variability was within normal limits but low. Impulsivity and variability improved significantly and normalized with the addition of 5 mg of Ritalin. Four weeks after discontinuing the Prozac, a baseline (no medication) T.O.V.A. was essentially the same as when administered Prozac alone. Interestingly, the severity of his O-C symptoms lessened appreciably with Ritalin.

APPENDIX

T.O.V.A. Visual Continuous Performance Test Report (Screening Version)[1]

The T.O.V.A. (Test of Variables of Attention) test is a computerised visual continuous performance test for the diagnosis and treatment of children and adults with attentional disorders. This highly reliable test provides relevant screening and diagnostic information about attention that is not otherwise available. The T.O.V.A. is used to accurately predict treatment effectiveness, determine optimal dosage, and monitor the course of treatment.

Several factors may result in a false negative or false positive, including IQ, computer game experience, and the possibility that an attentional problem may be secondary to auditory (not visual) processing difficulties. In the latter case, T.O.V.A.-A (auditory) test can be performed. Since a percentage of false negatives and positives occur with all tests, only a clinician can make a diagnosis, relying on all of the relevant information, including the T.O.V.A.

This screening version of the T.O.V.A. is not to be used for clinical evaluations of treatment. For a free referral to a T.O.V.A. clinician in your area, call (800) REF-TOVA [(800) 733-8682].

Table of Contents

---

1. T.O.V.A. results are confidential. We recommend use of a release of information form when sharing T.O.V.A. results with others.

Universal Attention Disorders, Inc.
4281 Katella Ave, Suite 215, Los Alamitos, CA 90720
Phone: 1.800.PAY.ATTN / Fax: 714.229.8782 / Email: info@uad.com

T.O.V.A. Interpretation (Form 1)

Name:	Subject #: 0023 Session #: 01

Gender: Female   Test Date: 10/05/95   Test Format   : 1 (Std)
DOB: 12/06/84   Test Time: 06:32 AM   Test Version #: 6.0.08
Age: 11.0 yrs   Tester: MCT   Test Serial   #: 0

T.O.V.A. Interpretation

The results of this protocol are not within normal limits and are suggestive of an attentional disorder.

The T.O.V.A. Interpretation evaluates attention in comparison to the norms (see Form 4). It indicates whether this T.O.V.A. is within or not within normal limits, regardless of the diagnosis. A deviant performance only means that the results are not within normal limits regardless of cause.

T.O.V.A. Analysis Graph (Form 3)

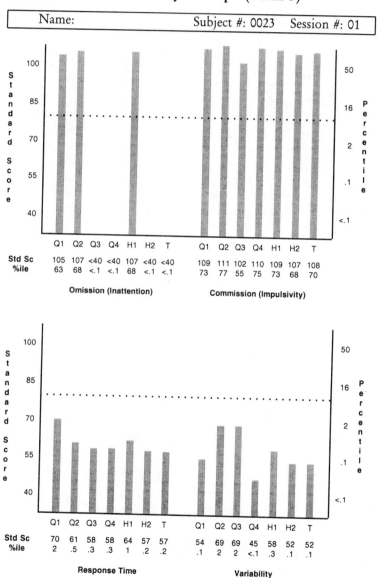

| | | Name: | | | | | Subject #: 0023   Session #: 01 |

Omission (Inattention)

| Std Sc | 105 | 107 | <40 | <40 | 107 | <40 | <40 |
| %ile | 63 | 68 | <.1 | <.1 | 68 | <.1 | <.1 |

Commission (Impulsivity)

| Std Sc | 109 | 111 | 102 | 110 | 109 | 107 | 108 |
| %ile | 73 | 77 | 55 | 75 | 73 | 68 | 70 |

Response Time

| Std Sc | 70 | 61 | 58 | 58 | 64 | 57 | 57 |
| %ile | 2 | .5 | .3 | .3 | 1 | .2 | .2 |

Variability

| Std Sc | 54 | 69 | 69 | 45 | 58 | 52 | 52 |
| %ile | .1 | 2 | 2 | <.1 | .3 | .1 | .1 |

T.O.V.A. Analysis Data (Form 4)

Name:	Subject #: 0023	Session #: 01
Gender: Female DOB: 12/06/84 Age: 11.0 yrs	Test Date: 10/05/95 Test Time: 06:32 AM Tester: MCT	Test Format : 1 (Std) Test Version #: 6.0.08 Test Serial #: 0

These results, compared to the normal same-gender, same-age, and average IQ group, are reported as standard deviations (std dev) and standard scores (std scores). A standard deviation indicates the extent of a problem (or deviance from the norm). The more negative the std dev, the greater the problem. Conversely, a more positive std dev indicates a better than average performance. Normal range is -1.00 to +1.00. The std score (1 std dev = 15 std score points) also compares these results to the norm. Normal range is 85 to 115. Scores above 115 are better than average, and scores below 85 are less than average.

Analysis Table	Quarter				Half		Total
	1	2	3	4	1	2	
Omission errors %	0.00%	0.00%	11.11%*	16.67%*	0.00%	13.89%*	10.80%*
Std deviation (Z)	0.36	0.50	<-4*	<-4*	0.45	<-4*	<-4*
Standard score	105	107	<40*	<40*	107	<40*	<40*
Commission errors %	0.79%	0.00%	19.44%	16.67%	0.40%	18.06%	4.32%
Std deviation (Z)	0.58	0.76	0.15	0.68	0.59	0.46	0.56
Standard score	109	111	102	110	109	107	108
Response time msec	586*	677*	618*	607*	631*	613*	618*
Std deviation (Z)	-2.03*	-2.58*	-2.78*	-2.80*	-2.37*	-2.87*	-2.89*
Standard score	70*	61*	58*	58*	64*	57*	57*
RT variability msec	207*	195*	196*	298*	206*	250*	240*
Std deviation (Z)	-3.05*	-2.07*	-2.05*	-3.66*	-2.80*	-3.17*	-3.17*
Standard score	54*	69*	69*	45*	58*	52*	52*

[ ] = Invalid quarter   * = Significantly deviant result
! ! = Excessive commission quarter   b = Borderline result

Analysis Validation Notes

There are no invalid quarters.

T.O.V.A. Signal Detection Data (Form 5)

Name: Subject #: 0023   Session #: 01

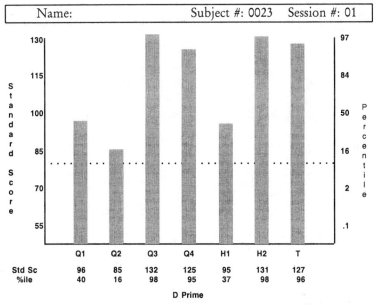

	Q1	Q2	Q3	Q4	H1	H2	T
Std Sc	96	85	132	125	95	131	127
%ile	40	16	98	95	37	98	96

D Prime

Signal Detection Table	Quarter				Half		Total
	1	2	3	4	1	2	
D prime	6.68	8.53b	2.08	1.93	6.92	2.00	2.95
Std deviation (Z)	-0.24	-1.01b	2.11	1.66	-0.33	2.08	1.80
Standard score	96	85b	132	125	95	131	127

[ ] = Invalid quarter   * = Significantly deviant result
! ! = Excessive commission quarter   b = Borderline result

An AD/HD Score of -1.80 or less is suggestive of AD/HD,
while a score more than -1.80 is not.

Response Time (Half 1)	-2.37
Revised D Prime (Half 2)	2.08
Variability (Total)	3.17
AD/HD Score	-3.46

T.O.V.A. Information and Results (Form 6)

Name:	Subject #: 0023 Session #: 01

Gender: Female   Test Date: 10/05/95   Test Format   : 1 (Std)
DOB: 12/06/84   Test Time: 06:32 AM   Test Version #: 6.0.08
Age: 11.0 yrs   Tester: MCT   Test Serial   #: 0

ISI: Ontime: Anticipatory: Offtime:
02000 msec   00200 msec   00200 msec   00300 msec

Medication	Dosage	Med-Test Interval
Challenge:	0.00 mg	0.0 hours
Med. #2:	0.00 mg	0.0 hours
Med. #3:	0.00 mg	0.0. hours

Weight: 0.0 kg   Height: 0 cm

Results Table (Tabulated Raw data)	Quarter				Half		Total
	1	2	3	4	1	2	
Omission errors %	0.00%	0.00%	11.11%	16.67%	0.00%	13.89%	10.80%
(inattention) #	0	0	14	21	0	35	35
Commission errors %	0.79%	0.00%	19.44%	16.67%	0.40%	18.06%	4.32%
(impulsivity) #	1	0	7	6	1	13	14
Response time msec	586	677	618	607	631	613	618
RT variability msec	207	195	196	298	206	250	240
Correct responses #	36	36	111	101	72	212	284
Correct nonresp.s #	125	126	29	30	251	59	310
Anticipatory resp.s #	0.00%	0.00%	0.62%	2.47%	0.00%	1.54%	0.77%
Nontargets #	0	0	0	0	0	0	0
Targets #	0	0	1	4	0	5	5
Multiple responses #	0	0	0	1	0	1	1
User interrupts	0	0	0	0	0	0	0
Hardware errors	0	0	0	0	0	0	0
Postcommissions #	1	0	7	6	1	13	14
Response time msec	611	0	855	602	611	738	729
Variability msec	0	0	236	234	0	267	259
D prime	6.68	8.53	2.08	1.93	6.92	2.00	2.95

T.O.V.A. Notes to the Clinician (Form 7)

Name:	Subject #: 0023 Session #: 01

The T.O.V.A. test can be administered after a single challenge dose of medication to reliably predict response to treatment. The T.O.V.A test can also be used to titrate the dose of medication in terms of the attentional variables and to monitor medication efficacy over time. (Please see the T.O.V.A. Manual.)

In quarter 1, quarter 2, quarter 3, and quarter 4, errors of commission (impulsivity/disinhibition) were low and the response time was slow. The subject may have adopted a cautious response strategy to minimize errors, resulting in slow time. Consider retesting after instructing the subject to equally balance accuracy and speed.

The omission errors (inattention) in this protocol are excessive (≤2.0 std dev/quarter) in quarter 3 and quarter 4. Excessive omission errors can be associated with neurological and/or neuropsychological impairment, including sleep disorders.

REFERENCES

Greenberg, L. M., and Crosby, R. D. (1992a). *A summary of developmental normative data on the T.O.V.A. Ages 4 to 80+.* Manuscript. Universal Attention Disorders, 4281 Katella Avenue, Suite 215, Los Alamitos, CA 90720.

———— (1992b). *Specificity and sensitivity of the test of variables of attention (T.O.V.A.).* Manuscript. Universal Attention Disorders, 4281 Katella Avenue, Suite 215, Los Alamitos, CA 90720.

Greenberg. L. M., Deem, M. A., and McMahon, S. A. (1972). Effects of dextroamphetamine, chlorpromazine and hydroxyzine on behavior and performance in hyperactive children. *American Journal of Psychiatry* 129: 532–559.

Greenberg, L. M., and Kindschi, C. L. (1996). *T.O.V.A. Clinical Guide.* Universal Attention Disorders, 4281 Katella Avenue, Suite 215, Los Alamitos, CA 90720.

Greenberg, L. M., and Waldman, I. D. (1993). Developmental normative data on the test of variables of attention (T.O.V.A.). *Journal of Child and Adolescent Psychiatry* 36:1019–1030.

McMahon, S. A., Deem, M. A., and Greenberg, L. M. (1970). The hyperactive child. *Clinical Proceedings of the Children's Hospital of D.C.* 26:295–316.

7

Brain SPECT Imaging and ADD

Daniel G. Amen

Beginning in 1990, my colleagues and I began doing single photon emission computed tomography (SPECT) brain imaging studies on patients who met the criteria for attention deficit/hyperactivity disorder (AD/HD) and attention deficit disorder (ADD) without hyperactivity. Brain SPECT is a nuclear medicine study, in which the patient is injected with a very small amount of a radioactive compound (the level of radiation from the study is similar to an abdominal x-ray). The compound is taken up by receptor sites in the brain and provides an intricate picture of brain blood flow, which is an indirect measurement of brain metabolism. We began our SPECT studies based on the work of Alan Zametkin and Joel Lubar.

In 1990, Alan Zametkin, M.D., of the National Institutes of Health, published an article in the *New England Journal of Medicine* (Zametkin et al. 1990) on the use of positron emission tomography (PET) studies, also a nuclear imaging study, in ADD. He demonstrated that adults with ADD had decreased brain activity in their frontal lobes in response to an intellectual challenge, rather than the expected increase in activity that was seen in normal "control" adults.

This information was consistent with Dr. Lubar's (1991) work with computerized electroencephalogram (EEG) brain wave studies on children and adolescent patients with AD/HD. His studies found that when these patients performed a concentration task, such as reading or copying figures, there was an increase in frontal lobe theta activity (slow brain wave activity) rather than the expected decrease in frontal lobe slow wave activity that is found in normal controls.

Both of these findings are consistent with frontal lobe deactivation in response to an intellectual stress in children, adolescents, and adults with ADD. The more these people try to concentrate, it appears, the worse thinking and concentrating becomes for them. This is a particularly interesting finding in light of the clinical fact that ADD children are often very "stimulation seeking." It is not unusual at all in the history gathered from the parents to find that these children are continually getting other people angry or upset with them. Could this be their attempt to try to stimulate their own brains, or to treat themselves and to feel more normal?

Sally, age 40, was the first person for whom I ordered a brain SPECT study. She was hospitalized for depression and anxiety in the psychiatric facility where I worked. In my clinical interview with her, I discovered that she had problems with a short attention span, distractibility, restlessness, and impulse control. In college, she never wrote the assigned term papers, she often spaced out in class, and many of her teachers told her that she was performing far below her potential. She dropped out of college after two years. In addition, she had a son who had ADD. I ordered psychological testing to help rule out the presence of a learning disability. I was surprised to learn that she had an IQ of 140. She had the potential to be anything she wanted, but was underemployed as a laboratory technician.

At the time Sally was in the hospital, Zametkin's study in the *New England Journal of Medicine* of PET findings in ADD adults was published. It was shortly after I read Zametkin's paper that

Dr. Jack Paldi (my nuclear medicine mentor) gave grand rounds at the hospital on the use of brain SPECT studies in psychiatry. Given Sally's clinical presentation I decided to order a SPECT study on her. I called the University of Wisconsin, known for its research in brain SPECT studies, and inquired about performing the scans on ADD adults. The Wisconsin protocol consisted of a resting study with the patient doing nothing, followed two days later by a study in which the subject performed a series of random math problems. Sally's studies were abnormal. At rest, she had good activity in her brain, especially in the prefrontal cortex. When she tried to concentrate, she had markedly decreased activity across her whole brain, especially in the prefrontal cortex! With that information I placed her on a low dose of methylphenidate (Ritalin), a brain stimulant used to treat ADD children. She responded well. Her mood was better, she was less anxious, and she could concentrate for longer periods of time. She eventually went back to school and finished her degree. No longer does she think of herself as an underachiever, but rather as someone who needs treatment for a medical problem. She says, "Having ADD is like needing glasses. When someone needs glasses it is not because they are dumb, crazy, or stupid. It is just that their eyes are shaped funny. The glasses help them see properly. With ADD, I'm not dumb, crazy, or stupid, I just need the medication to help me feel calm and to be able to concentrate." The scan and her response to medication changed her perception about herself.

SPECT brain imaging has the potential to be clinically more useful than both PET studies and computerized EEG. It has helped to shed light on the various subtypes of ADD, and it has been helpful in very difficult cases, often demonstrating that there were two or three different problems occurring at once. Also, family SPECT studies provide another piece of evidence that ADD has genetic underpinnings. Unlike computerized EEG, SPECT gives a three-dimensional picture of the cortex of the brain as well as the deeper structures of the brain. Computerized EEG depends solely on scalp readings.

PET, which is a direct measure of metabolic activity, would seem to be the most sensitive study of cerebral metabolism. However, with the expense being approximately twice that of a SPECT study, the limited availability of PET equipment (SPECT equipment is found in most community hospitals), and the requirement for an intra-arterial line for the procedure (as opposed to an intravenous line for SPECT), I believe research with SPECT has the greatest potential for everyday clinical utility. With advances in technology, SPECT resolution is becoming comparable to that of PET studies.

In studying psychiatric patients with SPECT brain imaging, researchers have found brain blood flow patterns for different psychiatric conditions. Some clinicians have reservations about the use of SPECT in children, feeling it may be unsafe. But nuclear medicine has been doing studies on children for over thirty years without untoward effects. Having an unresponsive or poorly responsive psychiatric condition has many more risks than the risk of low-dose radiation exposure engendered by a SPECT scan.

In 1993 and 1996, I presented our findings at the annual meeting of the American Psychiatric Association. Our work on SPECT was then published in the *Annals of Clinical Psychiatry* (Amen and Carmichael 1997). The Discovery Channel also did a feature on our work.

In performing SPECT studies on hundreds of children, teenagers, and adults with ADD, I have seen the same frontal lobe "turnoff" that has been reported by Zametkin and Lubar. When people with ADD try to concentrate, the frontal lobes of their brain (which controls attention span, judgment, impulse control, and motivation) decrease in activity. When normal control groups do concentration tasks, there is increased activity in this part of the brain. So the harder individuals with ADD try, the worse it gets for them. When I explain this phenomenon to children, I use this illustration: "When you have ADD, it is like putting your foot on the gas pedal in a car; you expect the car to go faster but it doesn't. It actually goes slower! This is a very important point to remember." ADD is a physical, neurobiological disorder.

It must be emphasized that SPECT brain imaging in most clinical settings is still considered a research tool. To utilize the technology effectively, it is important to use a sophisticated camera (we used a triple-headed camera; most SPECT cameras are still single headed and provide lower resolution). The results should be read by a nuclear medicine physician skilled in interpreting brain studies for psychiatric or functional reasons. The treating psychiatrist should understand how to properly utilize the results of this technology. This expertise is still uncommon.

From the research with SPECT brain studies, my colleagues and I have seen five different brain patterns associated with ADD. I report the results of two studies on each person: a resting study (done while the person was in a resting state) and an intellectual stress study (done while the person was doing a series of concentration tasks, such as random math problems). In evaluating ADD, it is essential to look at a working brain.

CASE REPORTS

Attention Deficit Disorder with Frontal Lobe "Turnoff"

In this category there are no other findings. This is classic ADD, which often responds to stimulant medications alone, as seen in Sandy's case, above.

History

Joe was a 7-year-old boy with a history of increased activity level, short attention span, impulsiveness, failure to finish schoolwork, intrusiveness with other children, and oppositional behavior. The parents had Joe evaluated by a developmental pediatrician, who thought Joe had mild ADD. The parents then brought him to me for a second opinion. I concurred with the ADD diagnosis, but the parents refused my recommendation of medication.

The parents attended a parenting group that I led, which helped Joe's behavior at home. At school the next year, however, the teacher reported his behavior was difficult and disruptive. Joe did not finish assignments, and he bothered other children. The parents and the teacher had a poor relationship. The parents were upset that the teacher could not keep Joe under better control. At that point a brain

SPECT was ordered to document if there was an underlying biological problem that would further suggest the use of appropriate medication.

SPECT Results

The SPECT brain study was normal at rest. When Joe performed a concentration task, there was a marked decrease in activity across the whole brain, especially in the prefrontal cortex.

Follow-up

The SPECT brain scan result convinced the parents of the biological basis of Joe's problems and they agreed to a trial of Ritalin. The child had a marked, positive response. He was more on task at school, finished more of his work, and got along better with other children. The parents and teacher had an improved relationship with him, which has been sustained for six years.

Attention Deficit Disorder with Temporal Lobe Dysfunction

Temporal lobe problems often coincide with reading problems, aggression, mild paranoia (where things are taken as negative when they are not), periods of spaciness or confusion, periods of unwarranted panic or fear, visual illusions (such as shadows or seeing objects change shape), or intense suicidal behavior (especially with left-sided temporal lobe problems). This category of ADD often responds best to anticonvulsant medication.

History

Kris was a 12 year-old boy with a long history of oppositional behavior, emotional outbursts, increased activity level, short attention span, impulsiveness, school problems, frequent lying, and aggressive behavior.

At age 6 Kris was placed on Ritalin for hyperactivity, but he became more aggressive, so the medication was discontinued. He was admitted to a psychiatric hospital at age 8, given the diagnosis of depression, and started on the antidepressant desipramine (Norpramin). By the age of 12, he had been seen for several years of psychotherapy by a psychiatrist, who also had sessions with the parents, to help them be more effective in handling Kris's behavior.

The psychiatrist frequently blamed the mother as the "biggest part of Kris's problem." He told her that if only she would get into psychotherapy and deal with her own childhood issues, then Kris's problems would go away. Kris's behavior escalated to the point where he was aggressive and uncontrollable at home. He was rehospitalized.

I was on call the weekend Kris was admitted to the hospital. To connect with the kids, I often played football with them. Kris was on my team. On every single play he cheated. When we were on defense, in between plays, he would move the ball three steps back and look at me with an expression that said, "Are you going to yell at me like my mother does?" I decided not to yell at him, and refused to play his ADD game of "get the adult angry."

SPECT Results

Kris's SPECT brain study was abnormal at rest, showing marked decreased activity in the left temporal lobe. It was 40 percent less active than his right temporal lobe. When Kris performed the concentration task, there was marked decreased activity in the prefrontal cortex.

Follow-Up

Kris was placed on the anticonvulsant medication carbamazepine (Tegretol) as a way to normalize his temporal lobe. Within a month he was a dramatically different child. He was more compliant, more social, and much more pleasant to be around. Due to the fact that he had two problems (the left temporal lobe disorder and frontal lobe turnoff), I added the stimulant medication magnesium pemoline (Cylert). This helped his attention span, and his schoolwork dramatically improved. His mother no longer seemed to be the problem. The positive response to treatment has held for the past seven years. He recently graduated from high school.

If Kris's temporal lobe problem had not been diagnosed and treated, it is likely that he would have found himself in a juvenile detention center, a residential treatment facility, or multiple psychiatric facilities. His mother would have continued to feel that she was the cause of his problems. Many of these children are erroneously labeled as bad, willful, and defiant, not as children with medical problems that need treatment.

Attention Deficit Disorder with Decreased Activity across the Whole Brain Surface

This category is often accompanied by increased activity in the limbic system, and it typically responds best to antidepressants.

History

William was a 12-year-old boy with a history of oppositional behavior, emotional outbursts, fire setting, erratic school behavior, short attention span, impulsiveness, negativity, and irritability. William had been seen in psychotherapy for a year by a child psychiatrist. He was tried on Ritalin and magnesium pemoline (Cylert) with little response. After a fire-setting episode he was hospitalized.

SPECT Results

William's resting scan showed marked overall decreased activity that worsened during the concentration task.

Follow-Up

William was placed on the antidepressant desipramine (Norpramin). Five years later he remains markedly improved. There have been no fire-setting incidents. He is much more compliant and less emotional. His school performance is better than ever before.

Attention Deficit Disorder with Increased Activity in the Top Middle Portion of the Frontal Lobes

This pattern is reported in the scientific literature in patients who have obsessive-compulsive disorders and problems shifting attention.

History

Bob, a 17-year-old boy, was admitted to a psychiatric hospital after he became withdrawn and depressed. Bob had a long history of emotional outbursts, erratic school performance, periods of social withdrawal, and getting thoughts "stuck" in his brain. His parents reported that once Bob got a thought in his head he was unable to let it go. In fact, his mother said that he would follow her around the house for hours asking her the same questions. Additionally, he was restless, had a short attention span, and was impulsive and very distractible. His mother was also hospitalized for depression with obsessive features.

SPECT Results

Bob's baseline study showed increased activity in the top middle portion of the frontal lobes (also referred to as the cingulate part of the brain), which intensified during the concentration task.

Follow-Up

Bob was placed on the antiobsessive medication clomipramine (Anafranil). Clomipramine has been shown in a number of SPECT studies to decrease activity in the cingulate by raising brain serotonin levels. After several weeks Bob was happier, more social, and doing better in school than he had in several years. He reported being able to sit down and do his homework in "half the time it used to take." After two years of being on this medication in combination with psychotherapy, he was able to discontinue his medication without his symptoms returning.

Attention Deficit Disorder with Areas of Decreased Frontal Lobe Activity Secondary to Head Trauma on the Right or Left Side

This category is often helped by stimulant medications, low doses of anticonvulsant medications such as valproic acid or phenytoin, or brainwave biofeedback over the damaged area.

History

At the age of 3, Brent fell out of a slow-moving car onto his head. He was briefly dazed, threw up, and complained of a bad headache. The emergency room doctor told the parents to watch him for 24 hours. "Not to worry," said the doctor, "if he is fine after that." From that time on his parents noticed a different child. At the age of 16 Brent was brought for evaluation. He had problems with restlessness, hyperactivity, distractibility, and impassivity. Many of his teachers said that he frequently "spaced out" and he was often off-task in school. Brent also had significant periods of irritability. He often became upset for little or no reason. His distractibility caused him many problems at school and home. He would mean to work on his homework or start a long-term project, but he frequently got distracted by whatever was happening at the moment. He tended to leave most things to the last minute and he functioned far below his potential.

SPECT Results

Brent's SPECT studies showed marked decreased activity in the left prefrontal cortex. The studies showed that he had had a significant head trauma at some point in the past.

Follow-Up

Brent was placed on low-dose Adderall, and was treated with thirty sessions of brainwave biofeedback to enhance the functioning over his left prefrontal cortex. Within several weeks of starting his medication he was better able to focus, and he was more thoughtful and more organized. Subsequent to the biofeedback session he was able to lower the dosage of his medication and he continues to do very well four years later.

SPECT Family Study: Depression, ADD, and Obsessive-Compulsive Disorder

History

Before she came to see me, Celina, a 36-year-old woman, had been depressed for ten years, following the birth of her first child. Her symptoms included significant irritability, crying spells, sleeplessness, and weight loss. She also had problems concentrating, and she was unable to manage her two children. Her condition was brought to a crisis when she attempted suicide after separating from her husband. She was initially seen by a psychiatrist who started her on medication for depression, but this had little effect on her. She then came to see me. I treated her with psychotherapy and a different antidepressant. The treatment helped her feel more positive and less irritable. Several months later, she decided that she "should be stronger than the depression" and took herself off the medication. Within several days her depression worsened, but she was resistant to restarting her medication. She told me, "I don't want to have to rely on medication to feel well."

In an effort to demonstrate to Celina that her depression was, at least in part, biological and that her medication was an important part of treatment, I ordered a brain SPECT study. Celina's SPECT study revealed marked decreased frontal lobe activity and increased activity in her limbic system, which fit with her underlying depression. In addition, it showed striking overactivity in the top middle portion of her frontal lobes. This finding is often seen in people with obsessive-compulsive disorder.

With this information I asked her more directly about obsessive thoughts and compulsive symptoms. In fact, Celina was perfectionistic at home and had obsessive negative thoughts. She tearfully remarked, "You mean my husband was right when he said it was strange that I had to have all the shirts buttoned a certain way and put just so in the drawer?"

She then told me about her 8-year-old daughter, Laura, who had rituals. Before Laura would enter a new room she would run a finger under her nose and lick her lips. She also became obsessed with locking doors and would frequently lock her brother and sister out of the house.

Another psychiatrist had been seeing Celina's 10-year-old son, Samuel, for school and behavior problems. He had been diagnosed with attention deficit disorder and was taking a stimulant medication, but it had little effect on him. One of Celina's concerns about Samuel was that once he got a thought in his mind he would be unable to let it go. He would follow her around the house for over two hours asking her the same questions she had already answered.

SPECT Results

Celina's SPECT study showed increased activity in the top middle portion of her frontal lobes. Laura's and Samuel's studies showed the same findings as well, suggesting an obsessive-compulsive component to their problems. Celina deactivated her frontal lobes when she tried to concentrate, as did Samuel. As a child, Celina was labeled an underachiever in school and also had difficulty completing projects. Laura, on the other hand, activated her frontal lobes and was not noted to have any school or concentration problems.

Follow-Up

Based on this information, Celina was placed on the antidepressant fluoxetine (Prozac) to decrease her depression and help lessen her obsessive thinking and compulsive behaviors. Prozac is a very effective treatment for obsessive-compulsive disorder. She had a dramatically positive response and reported that she was not bothered when things weren't "just so." She also said that it was the first time in ten years that she felt "herself." The SPECT study also convinced her that her condition was at least in part biological and not her fault or the result of weak will, which allowed her to take her medication for a longer period of time.

With this information, Samuel's psychiatrist stopped the stimulant medication and started him on Prozac as well. Within several weeks, his behavior normalized and he had a remarkable improvement in school, making the honor roll for the first time. Several months later, Laura was also prescribed Prozac.

Initially, she refused to take the medication and her ritualistic behaviors continued. Approximately eight months later, she agreed to start Prozac and her compulsive behaviors significantly diminished.

Certainly, the family dynamics in his family operated on many levels. The mother's depression contributed to the anxiety and behavior problems in her children and the abnormal brain metabolism in the children probably added to their difficult behavior, which further stressed the mother. The family dynamics improved significantly after the mother and the children were treated with the appropriate medication and psychotherapy.

When I first submitted this family's case study to a medical journal, one of the reviewers said that it was absurd for me to correlate family dynamics to brain studies. I think it is absurd not to. The patterns in our brain have a dramatic effect on how we feel and how we interact with the world.

SPECT brain studies can be very helpful in the diagnosis and treatment of obsessive-compulsive disorder because of the secretive nature of many compulsive behaviors. As this case illustrates, Celina was being treated for depression and it wasn't until the SPECT findings were reviewed that a history of her obsessive thoughts and compulsive tendencies was discovered.

REFERENCES

Amen, D. G., and Carmichael, B. D. (1997). High resolution brain SPECT imaging in AD/HD. *Annals of Clinical Psychiatry* 9(2):81–86.

Lubar, J. F. (1991). Discourse on the development of EEG diagnostics and biofeedback for attention deficit-hyperactivity disorders. *Biofeedback and Self-Regulation* 16:201–225.

Zametkin, A. J., Nordahl, T. E., Gross, M., et al. (1990). Cerebral glucose metabolism in adults with hyperactivity of childhood onset. *New England Journal of Medicine* 323(20):1361–1366.

8

Executive Functions in Children with Learning Disabilities and Attention Deficit Disorder

Leah Ellenberg

Executive functions are those aspects of cognition relating to focused attention, working memory, allocation of cognitive resources, planning, response inhibition, problem solving, and self-regulation. Some of these cognitive operations are referred to as metacognition and higher order thinking processes. Based primarily on studies involving adults with disorders of the brain, executive functions have been assumed to be dependent on the frontal lobes of the cerebral cortex, and the term *frontal lobe functions* is often used to refer to them.

Anatomically, the frontal lobes are the last brain region to fully develop. Myelinization of these cortical areas is not complete until adolescence and it is generally felt that maturity of executive functions does not occur until late adolescence. However, as studies of metacognition have shown, children as young as 4 use some aspects of executive functioning in their approach to tasks. Studies of children at different ages have charted the longitudinal course of development of these functions. Recent research has also focused on appropriate ways to operationalize aspects of executive functions and develop proper assessment tools to investigate them.

Along with interest in the developmental course of executive functions in normal children has come an investigation of possible disorders of executive functioning in childhood. There has been interest in the disruption of normal development caused by trauma or brain disorders such as tumors or hydrocephalus. In addition, the notion that deficits in executive functioning underlie several developmental disorders has been advanced. Particularly, there is much theoretical and research interest recently in the notion that attention deficit/hyperactivity disorder (AD/HD) has, at its root, a disorder of executive functioning. In addition, various learning disabilities sometimes include deficits in areas of metacognition related to the specific learning disorder. This is particularly true in children who have a dual diagnosis of AD/HD and learning disability.

Understanding the contribution of disorder in one or more aspects of executive functioning to an individual child's disability profile is crucial in planning appropriate treatment programs. It is futile to treat a specific learning or behavioral problem if children have a disorder of executive functioning that will not allow them to retain the information presented or generalize what is taught to other circumstances. This chapter explores the concept of executive functioning in normal child development and in disorders of child development as an aid to comprehensive treatment planning.

The field of clinical neuropsychology sought, by investigating individuals with various brain disorders, to localize cognitive functions to various brain areas. Alexander Luria (1966), a Russian psychologist, conceived of the cerebral cortex as mapped into a series of hierarchically organized systems. Strips of cortical neurons called primary areas are responsible for direct analysis of sensory input and execution of motor output. These areas are bordered by secondary areas that analyze the perceptual input and plan output in more complex ways. These secondary areas, in turn, are bordered by tertiary association areas that are responsible for combining input from several modalities for higher order analysis. In this system, the prefrontal lobes of the cortex are felt to be the master control center, responsible for evaluating all information to which the brain has access, including posterior cortical association areas evaluating perceptual input, the medial temporal lobe and limbic system structures serving emotional content and memory, as well as those structures involved with arousal. Decisions are made by the prefrontal lobes as to how brain resources will be allocated in terms of focusing attention, keeping information in working memory, using appropriate strategies, and prioritizing to meet immediate and long-term goals.

A more sophisticated model has been proposed by Stuss (1992). He conceived a hierarchical feedback–feed-forward model that begins with sensations and basic knowledge at the lowest level, executive functions in the middle level, and self-reflectiveness (metacognition) at the highest level. Executive functions and self-reflectiveness are considered part of the frontal lobe systems.

NORMAL DEVELOPMENT OF EXECUTIVE FUNCTIONS

Anatomically, the frontal lobes have been shown to be connected with the limbic system, reticular activating system, and posterior cortex, which allows for analysis of data necessary to perform executive functions. The connections are bidirectional so that control functions can be modified with changes in data and can in turn modify further input by controlling which data are attended to and analyzed (Barbas and Mesulam 1981, Porrino and Goldman-Rakic 1982).

The frontal lobes are not fully functional at birth. Morphological maturity of the prefrontal cortex is not reached until puberty (Orzhekhovskaya 1981). Myelination of the prefrontal cortex is not complete until that time (Yakovlev and Lecours 1967). In addition, electroencephalogram (EEG) studies suggest development of EEG coherence between the frontal cortex and posterior cortical systems develops between 18 months and 11 years of age (Thatcher 1992).

The development of the anatomical substrate for executive functions mirrors the development of corresponding cognitive processes. Piaget (1957) discussed child development in a series of stages involving progressively more complex methods of analyzing data and culminating in the stage of "formal operations" achieved at puberty. Each subsequent stage relies on increasing ability to use executive functions. Kohlberg (1963) identified a similar series of states in moral development, also culminating at puberty.

Behavioral investigations of executive functioning in primates and infants have employed delayed alternation tasks (Goldman-Rakic 1987). The experimental paradigm involves presenting the subject with two objects, under one of which is hidden a reward. After the subject correctly identifies the hiding place. The subject must wait before being allowed to search for the reward again. Goldman-Rakic showed that after a delay, monkeys with dorsolateral prefrontal lesions invariably chose the hiding place that had contained the reward on the previous trial. She suggested that the prefrontal lobe lesion caused a deficit in the ability to retain information in working memory to modify a response. Piaget (1957) and others have noted a similar deficit in human infants below 1 year of age, but not subsequent to that age.

Studies of executive functions in toddlers have focused on the issue of self-control, which Vaughn and colleagues (1984) found as early as 18 months of age on a task involving inhibiting responses to a desired object.

In school-age children, development of executive functions have been investigated by tests involving working memory, use of strategies in problem solving, and research on metacognition and self-reflection. There are clear developmental trends in all these areas that correspond to the anatomical and physiological development of the frontal lobes (Case 1992).

Working memory refers to that aspect of the memory system that acts as a mental scratch pad, temporarily storing information while other cognitive tasks are performed and allowing that information to be used as necessary to complete the cognitive process. It is the brain's rapid-access memory (RAM). This aspect of memory increases steadily throughout childhood (Case 1992), whereas other aspects of memory do not show a similar developmental trend. For example, Morrison and colleagues (1974) report that pre-school-age children can code as much information from briefly presented visual arrays as adults do. However, they cannot use strategies to keep the information available for problem solving.

Along with increases in working memory capacity, there seems to be a developmental improvement in the quality of strategies used for deciding which information is relevant and how best to represent it for problem solving. This results from an increase in mental flexibility, the ability to maintain and shift set, the use of abstract concepts, and planning skills.

Research on metacognition and self-awareness has focused on the development of the ability to judge the quality of one's work and to change responses based on feedback about prior responses.

Spiker and colleagues (1985) assessed young children and found some ability to modify response on a hypothesis testing task based on feedback. However, they showed deficits in appropriate planning and a tendency toward perseveration, focusing on an irrelevant or erroneous aspect of the task and not modifying this erroneous response based on feedback. The ability to modify responses based on feedback and effectively utilize the changes for future planning is still not developed by age 12 (Pea 1982).

Young children routinely overestimate their ability to perform a proposed task. This may be adaptive in allowing them the confidence to attempt to solve novel problems, which is necessary for growth and learning. Flavell and colleagues (1981) investigated the development of this self-monitoring executive function. Children become increasingly more accurate through puberty in being able to evaluate their own competence at performing an activity and gathering relevant information.

TESTS OF EXECUTIVE FUNCTIONS

The concept of executive functions generally assume that these functions are not modality or content specific. They are utilized for the acquisition for new information and sets rather than retrieval of previously acquired knowledge. As such, executive functions are not adequately measured by currently existing tests of intelligence or achievement. It is well documented that adults with acquired frontal lobe dysfunction may show intact IQ scores accompanied by significant deficits in effective self-regulation on both emotional and cognitive levels (Weinstein and Teuber 1957).

To effectively assess executive functions, psychologists have been searching for measures that would differentiate patients with deficits in these areas from other individuals. Stuss and Benson (1986) investigated schizophrenic patients who had undergone prefrontal lobotomy. These individuals had great difficulty functioning outside of institutions. Traditional intelligence tests used could not separate lobotomized schizophrenics from controls. One measure that was found to be quite sensitive was the Wisconsin Card Sorting Test (WCST). This test utilizes four stimulus cards to which an individual must match 128 additional cards. The cards can match the stimulus cards by color, form, or number. The subject is not given rules in advance but told to sort the cards one at a time, after which the examiner indicates whether the response was correct or incorrect. Based on examiner feedback, the subject must modify responses to try to achieve a correct response on the next trial. The trick is that after the subject correctly identifies the first sorting principle (color) and sorts ten cards correctly using this principle, the examiner shifts the correct response set to "form" without informing the subject. The individual must comprehend that the rules of the game have changed and be able to modify behavior to again sort correctly. Patients with prefrontal lesions showed considerable perseveration to earlier response sets even though they were no longer correct. This task continues to be used a great deal in neuropsychology for the investigation of deficits in executive functions. While originally considered a "frontal lobe" task, subsequent research has shown that brain damage involving extrafrontal as well as frontal lobes can cause deficits on this task. The WCST has been used with children, and norms currently exist for individuals from the age of 6 (Heaton et al. 1993).

Another task designed to assess strategies in problem solving is the "Tower of London." Here, the individual must move a series of colored rings into various positions using a set of rules to limit how the rings may be moved. The task involves a successively more difficult series of steps that entail more planning and forethought in moving the rings in the fewest possible steps. This task has been modified for use with children as the "Tower of Hanoi" (Welsh et al. 1991).

The Halstead-Reitan Neuropsychological Battery contains several tests that assess executive functioning. The Category Test exists in adult and child versions. Like the Wisconsin Card Sort Test, it involves using strategies to achieve a correct response on a sequential set of trials. Despite the similarity of the two tasks, a number of studies have suggested performance on them do not necessarily co-vary in individuals with frontal lobe brain damage, and they may, in fact, test different aspects of executive functioning.

The Halstead-Reitan Trail Making Test is another task that assesses mental flexibility. Trails A is a simple dot-to-dot task involving numbers that basically assesses visual tracking and psychomotor speed. Trails B, however, involves making a trail that alternates between letters and numbers, moving 1–A–2–B, and so on. There is a clear developmental trend in the ability to shift set in this manner, and this task is significantly affected by brain damage of various sorts, including frontal lobe damage.

Another task designed to assess ability to shift set is the Stroop Color Word Test (Golden 1978). Here, the individual is first asked to rapidly read a series of color words printed in black ink. Next, the individual is asked to say the colors in which a series of X's are printed (red, green, or blue). On the third page, the "interference" task is presented. Here, there are color names printed in incompatible colors. For example, the word *red* might be printed in green ink. The individual is asked to quickly report the color of ink, ignoring the word. This task is quite difficult for adults, whose automatic response is to read the word. The initial response must be inhibited in order to say the ink color and performance is slowed considerably. The degree of slowing, or the interference effect, is affected by brain damage. Norms for this task have been extended to children, but there is little research documenting the effectiveness of the Stroop for differentiating groups of children with various disorders.

The Rey-Osterrieth Complex Figure was designed to investigate the use of planning and strategies in a drawing task. The subject is asked to copy a complex design. He/she is sequentially given a series of colored pencils as the design is drawn, either when each element has been completed or every 30 seconds. By evaluating the individual's approach to completing the design, the investigator assesses the effectiveness of the metacognitive approach to the task. Adults with frontal lobe brain dysfunction as well as young children tend to show a piecemeal, line-by-line strategy rather than the more effective holistic approach. Norms have been developed for qualitative analysis in children (Waber and Holmes 1985). Children with brain dysfunction related to cranial radiation for leukemia show more piecemeal strategies than controls of comparable age and intelligence. The task has recently been used successfully to differentiate children with AD/HD from controls (Cahn et al. 1996).

Another task often used to assess executive or frontal lobe functioning is a verbal fluency task, the most common of which is the Controlled Word Association task of Spreen and Benton (1977). In this task, the individual is required to verbalize as many words as possible in one minute that begin with the letters F, A, and S. Other verbal fluency tasks involve categories, such as animals. Writing fluency tasks are similar to verbal fluency tasks, except that the response is written rather than spoken. The Controlled Word Association task has norms for adults and children. The task is considered to assess executive functions because it involves set maintenance and self-initiation of responses without examiner input, feedback, or questioning. It is sensitive to damage in frontal and prefrontal lobes (Benton 1968) and in children with language and attentional problems (Grodzinsky and Diamond 1922, Koviol and Stout 1992).

Working memory is an important aspect of executive functioning to assess. Tests such as the Wechsler Adult Intelligence Scale–Revised and Wechsler Intelligence Scale for Children–III Digit Span subtests have been investigated for this purpose. In children, the ability to recall digits presented and repeat them backward has been correlated with deficits in working memory. This skill may not be correlated with working memory in adults.

Several verbal memory tasks assess aspects of working memory. The Selective Reminding Test (Bushke and Fuld 1974) is a complex verbal list learning task. The individual is given a list of twelve words—animal names in the version for children 12 years and younger and random nouns for individuals over 12. Once the list has been presented, the individual recalls as many as possible. He/she is then reminded by the examiner of those words not spontaneously recalled and the individual tries to recall the entire list again. Several measures may be taken and are normed. The primary measures are long-term storage, which assesses the ability of the individual to repeat the word on two successive trials without having been reminded (the assumption being that the item has been stored in working memory), and consistent long-term retrieval, a measure of the individual's ability to continue to recall the word through all subsequent trials of the task. The discrepancy between storage and retrieval scores may be an assessment of the adequacy of working memory. The California Verbal Learning Test in its adult (Delis et al. 1985) and child (Delis et al. 1989) versions yields several scores that assess aspects of working memory including categorization, rate of information acquisition, and interference effects.

Tests of vigilance, often called continuous performance tests, are useful in assessing the ability to maintain attention, one important aspect of executive functioning. Several tests are currently in use including the Continuous Performance Test, the Test of Variables of Attention, the Conners Continuous Performance Test, and the Gordon Diagnostic System. These measures have in common the instruction to maintain visual attention to a screen where a signal is occasionally presented to which the individual must make a rapid response. Different tests assess different aspects of attentional functioning including omission of signals (inattention), responding to nontarget signals (impulsivity), reaction time, and the variability of reaction time across trials. Continuous performance tests have been repeatedly shown to differentiate groups of children with AD/HD from unaffected controls.

In assessing executive functioning, it is important to consider task modality (Denckla 1996). For example, the Rey-Osterrieth Complex Figure Drawing requires the ability to analyze the design visuospatially and proceed with visual motor and constructional skills. It is necessary to ascertain that an individual's deficit on the task presented is because of executive function difficulty rather than modality-specific processing or performance deficits.

Robert and Pennington (1996) suggest that tasks that assess prefrontal lobe cognitive functioning, specifically executive functioning, tap into two major dimensions. First, they tap working memory, defined as the ability to maintain and manipulate short-term information that may be needed to generate action. Second, the tasks require inhibition of inappropriate action. The authors suggest an interactive framework in that working memory allows for the processing of incoming information to determine the best response, and inhibition prevents the execution of an incorrect, competing response. Tasks sensitive to executive dysfunction strengthen an incorrect, competing response, forcing greater demands on both working memory and inhibition in order to produce a correct response.

The search for reliable and valid tests of executive functions continues. By their nature, these functions are difficult to measure in the structured assessment setting since the examiner may provide the subject with many of the tools necessary to bypass executive functions because of the structure inherent in the testing paradigm. For this reason, careful history and reliable observations by individuals involved in a child's environment are crucial in determining the presence and nature of any executive function deficits the child may have. Age and developmental level are also crucial factors to consider.

EXECUTIVE FUNCTIONING IN CHILDREN WITH BRAIN DYSFUNCTION

Executive functions have been examined in children with various brain insults including congenital abnormalities, disease, and head injury.

It has been shown that children who survive severe head injuries are frequently left with brain damage. A high incidence, perhaps 50 percent, show frontal and/or temporal contusions (Levin et al. 1993, Mendelsohn et al. 1992). Recent studies have recognized significant deficits in aspects of executive functioning such as narrative discourse (Chapman et al. 1992) and attention (Dennis et al. 1996) following significant head injury in children. Recent work has focused on delineating these differences. Levin and colleagues (1996) correlated a battery of tests assessing frontal lobe functioning with volume of frontal lobe lesion as seen on magnetic resonance imaging (MRI). The battery loaded on five factors. Volume of frontal lobe lesion contributed significantly to predicting two of the factors labeled conceptual-productivity and planning. Dennis and colleagues (1995) examined metacognition after childhood head injury. They identified two aspects of metacognitive skills that they called knowledge appraisal and knowledge management. Appraisal skills are presumed to involve fact-based knowledge stored in long-term memory and acquired through experience. Knowledge management skills involve monitoring of behavior and regulating performance based on analysis of information gained as a task is performed. They found that younger children with head injury had deficits in both areas of metacognitive skills, but that the problem appeared to arise less from lack of knowledge than from difficulty with sustained application of appraisal skills.

Deficits in executive functioning have been found in children with several types of diffuse brain damage including hydrocephalus (Fletcher et al. 1996), meningitis (Taylor et al. 1996), and cranial irradiation for control of acute lymphoblastic leukemia (Waber et al. 1994). Welsh and Pennington (1988) report on a study of children with phenylketonuria (PKU), which is thought to involve a neurochemical disruption in dopamine, an important neurotransmitter in frontal lobe systems involved in executive functioning. Children with early treated PKU were found to exhibit average or above average IQ and memory performance, but were selectively impaired on tasks requiring executive functioning including planning and mental flexibility. The authors found these deficits to be related to the level of phenylaline in the blood at the time of testing.

Over the last several years, researchers have begun to investigate frontal lobe dysfunction in childhood autism. An investigation by Zilbovicius and colleagues (1995) examined regional cerebral blood flow in autistic children using a single photon emission computed tomography (SPECT) scan. They found frontal hypoperfusion in younger autistic children and suggested delayed frontal maturation in childhood autism. Prior and Hoffmann (1990) found significant deficits on the Wisconsin Card Sort, Rey-Osterrieth Complex Figure, and Milner Maze Test in autistic children compared to both a chronological age control group and a mental age control group. Autistic children show significant perseveration and difficulty with abstracting ability consistent with executive function deficit.

EXECUTIVE FUNCTIONS IN ATTENTION
DEFICIT DISORDER

The notion that a disorder to executive functions is present in AD/
HD has been posited for many years (Pontius 1973, Rosenthal and
Allen 1978). In AD/HD, the hallmark symptoms are impulsivity,
distractability, and hyperactivity. A failure of response inhibition and
poor rule-governed behavior have been posited as the central aspects
of the disorder, which underlies most of the symptoms seen (Barkley
1990). It has been noted that the type of dysfunction seen in AD/
HD is similar to that seen in patients with frontal lobe deficits
(Tromner et al. 1988), which has led several theorists to postulate a
disorder in the frontal lobes, particularly the prefrontal lobes and the
frontal-striatal system as underlying AD/HD (Benson 1991, Heilman
et al. 1991).

Recent studies of brain functioning using positron emission
tomography (PET) to measure cerebral glucose metabolism in adults
who have been hyperactive since childhood indicate that during an
auditory attention task, they show lower metabolism in many brain
regions than do normal control adults. The brain regions with greatest reductions in glucose metabolism were in the frontal lobe, the
premotor cortex, and the superior prefrontal cortex (Zametkin et al.
1990). Many of the prefrontal systems that modulate executive functions are noradrenergic, that is they use dopamine and norepinephrine as neurotransmitters. It may be for this reason that stimulants,
which affect the functioning of these neurotransmitters, are effective
in control of AD/HD.

One of the early attempts to assess children with attention deficit
disorder on tasks that were either empirically or theoretically considered to assess prefrontal lobe functioning was by Gorenstein and
colleagues (1989). They found that twenty-one children with inattentive-overactive behavior problems showed deficits relative to controls
on the WCST (specifically perseverative errors), the Matching
Memory task, the Necker Cube, Trails, the Stroop Color Word Test,
and a sequential memory task for children.

Several other investigators have attempted to utilize tasks assessing executive functions and/or known to be affected by damage to

the frontal lobe in evaluating individuals with AD/HD. Grodzinsky and Diamond (1992) found that boys with AD/HD were inferior to controls on the Stroop Color Word Test, Controlled Word Association Test, Rey-Osterrieth Complex Figure, Porteus Mazes, and a vigilance task. They did not differ on Trail Making or some measures of the WCST, although trials to first category and failure to maintain set were significantly different on the WCST.

A study by Shue and Douglas (1992) used three batteries of tasks to compare twenty-four AD/HD and twenty-four control children. The batteries were sensitive to frontal lobe deficit in motor control, frontal lobe deficits in problem solving, and temporal lobe dysfunctions. Children with AD/HD were significantly different from controls on the two batteries sensitive to frontal lobe dysfunction but not on the battery sensitive to temporal lobe dysfunction, which mainly consisted of memory tasks.

Garcia-Sanchez and colleagues (1996) found that a group of twenty-five teenagers with AD/HD performed more poorly than thirty-five control teenagers on tasks measuring premotor and visual spatial functions with declarative memory relatively preserved. They feel the results are consistent with frontal striatal dysfunction in the AD/HD group.

Reader and colleagues (1994) compared a group of forty-eight boys with AD/HD and above average IQs (median = 117.5) to standardized norms on a number of measures. In their study, children with AD/HD showed significant deficits when compared to the standardization samples on the WCST score for loss of set and on several variables of the Test of Variables of Attention (T.O.V.A.), a continuous performance test, specifically errors of omission, reaction time, and variability of reaction time. Reader and colleagues note that, although most studies in the area show some correlations between AD/HD and deficits in executive functioning, not all studies find deficits on the same measures. They note there is some difficulty with the current measures of executive functions employed since they are often modality specific and may co-vary with an individual's competence in the kind of task employed. For example, performance on the Rey-Osterrieth Complex Figure task is correlated with Wechsler Intelligence Scale for Children (WISC-III) Performance IQ score. Therefore, an individual with a higher Performance IQ score might be expected to do better on the Rey-Osterrieth Complex Figure. An executive function deficit might thus be masked unless Performance IQ was controlled for.

While it has been repeatedly demonstrated that groups of children with AD/HD are deficient on some tasks of executive functions, there is still debate as to whether the discrepancies are large enough and reliable enough to be used for individual diagnosis of AD/HD. Primary diagnosis is still often made by use of history and behavioral observations, sometimes standardized in terms of responses to such checklists as the Achenbach Child Behavior Checklist (Achenbach 1991) and the Conners Parent Symptom Questionnaire (Conners 1989), which also have corresponding versions for teachers, and the Brown ADD Scales (Brown 1996).

A recent study by Barkley and Grodzinsky (1994) reported a positive predictive power level for diagnosing AD/HD, which was acceptable for several tasks, especially a continuous performance task and the controlled oral word association test. However, negative scores on these tests did not necessarily indicate the absence of AD/HD.

Caution must be used in considering any single test as a screening for AD/HD. However, since executive function deficits are so prevalent in children with AD/HD, the examination of the presence and severity of such deficits may be crucial for treating an individual child with AD/HD. Many clinicians employ batteries of tests that include tests of executive functioning as a prominent feature for the complete diagnosis and treatment of children with AD/HD.

EXECUTIVE FUNCTIONS IN CHILDREN WITH LEARNING DISABILITIES

While it is well documented and generally accepted that children with AD/HD and some brain disorders show deficits in executive functions, the literature is less voluminous and less clear for children with learning disabilities. One complicating factor is that learning disabilities are diverse and the criteria used in different studies vary. In addition, since AD/HD, brain disorders, and learning disabilities are often comorbid conditions, it is necessary to carefully control for these factors in group selection.

An elegant study by Pennington and colleagues (1993) evaluated four groups of children: reading disabled (RD) only, AD/HD only, comorbid RD plus AD/HD, and controls. Tasks administered were divided into two cognitive domains—phonological processes (PP) and executive functions (EF). This study addressed the question of whether attention deficits seen in children with RD were the same as those seen in children with AD/HD only or were a phenotypic manifestation of an underlying problem related to the RD. Results showed a double-dissociation wherein the RD-only group showed significant deficits in PP and no deficits in EF, whereas the AD/HD only group showed the opposite pattern with significant EF deficits and no PP deficits. Of interest in this study, the RD plus AD/HD group resembled the RD-only group, suggesting that the AD/HD seen in this group was secondary to the RD and different in quality from the symptoms seen in the AD/HD-only group. Other studies (Kataria et al. 1992, McGee et al. 1989) failed to find such clear-cut differences, since both learning-disabled and AD/HD children showed deficits in aspects of executive functioning and working memory.

Hall and colleagues (1997) evaluated executive and behavioral functioning in four groups of children separated by presence or absence of AD/HD and reading disability (RD): AD/HD-,RD- (controls); AD/HD-,RD+; AD/HD+,RD-; AD/HD+,RD+. They found that children with AD/HD showed more impulsivity, higher activity level, and difficulty with response inhibition whether or not they had a comorbid RD. RD alone did not result in deficits relative to controls on any of the measures used.

It is probable that children with learning disabilities show deficits in executive functioning related to their area of disability. Siegel and Ryan (1989) conducted a study assessing working memory for sentences and counting in four groups of children: a group with AD/HD, a group with reading disability, a group with arithmetic disability, and a normally achieving group. Subjects were tested at three different ages. Results indicated that children with AD/HD were impaired only on the most difficult task, memory for sentences, and only at the youngest age group. Children with reading disabilities were impaired on both tasks across age groups and those with arithmetic disabilities were impaired only on the counting task. The authors concluded that attentional problems will cause deficits in any complex working memory task, while reading disability or arithmetic disability are associated with more modality-specific deficits in working memory.

Kelly and colleagues (1989) examined 12-year-old reading-disabled and nondisabled boys using a variety of tasks that they grouped into tests of posterior brain function and tests of prefrontal brain function. They found that a discriminant function analysis based on three tests of prefrontal functions—Controlled Oral Word Association Test, Wisconsin Card Sort Test, and Stroop Color Word Test—correctly classified 88 percent of the children into reading disabled or control group. Prefrontal tests were generally more effective than posterior measures in separating the groups. This study did not control for children who may have shown AD/HD in addition to reading disorders, however.

Several studies have focused on the relationship of learning disabilities to metacognition, which refers to an individual's awareness of his or her cognitive actions in regard to learning and the ability to monitor and regulate them. Executive functions are one aspect of metacognition, but it also involves examining long-term memory for access to information about past experience, task difficulty, and effective strategies. Metacognition is related to general intelligence to some extent, but also appears to have a distinct set of characteristics. A study by Swanson and colleagues (1993) examined metacognition and analogical reasoning in mentally retarded, learning-disabled, average, and gifted children. They suggested that while mentally retarded children showed a central-processing deficiency across all areas assessed, children with learning disabilities showed specific deficits in some components of metacognition, specifically those relating to planning of strategies. Other studies (e.g., Short 1992) failed to find a difference in metacognition between learning disabled and normally achieving students, finding only language differences to be consistent. However, they defined metacognition as awareness of cognitive competence rather than analysis of strategies for performing at task.

It seems that individuals with learning disabilities show deficits in some aspects of executive functioning related to the modality of their learning disability, such as verbal working memory for children with reading disabilities and working memory for numerical information in children with arithmetic disabilities. In addition, individuals with learning disabilities may show some more generalized deficits in such areas of metacognition as use of appropriate strategies and mental flexibility, although the research in this area is as yet inconclusive.

SUMMARY AND CONCLUSIONS

Executive functions can be conceptualized as a constellation of cognitive functions mediated by a prefrontal lobe system that is a relatively independent factor in learning and behavior. Executive functions include aspects of attention, working memory, planning, problem solving, sustained focus, and response inhibition. Metacognition, a broader concept, includes these functions as well as skills of allocation of cognitive resources, self-monitoring and self-regulation, and the use of effective strategies based on analysis of incoming information and experience stored in long-term memory. These functions have been studied in the laboratory and tests have been devised to assess them experimentally and clinically.

Deficits in executive functioning are considered by many to be the hallmark of AD/HD. The presence of these disorders in the learning-disability syndromes is more complex and less certain. When examining groups of individuals with learning disabilities in the absence of AD/HD, there appear to be modality-specific deficits in attention, working memory, and use of appropriate strategies. Some authors suggest a more generalized executive dysfunction in students with learning disabilities, and this certainly requires more research with very specifically defined groups of children.

In clinical practice, children are frequently seen who have AD/HD combined with LD. This morbidity is extremely common, so that many children seen will have some form of deficit in executive functioning.

Treatment of these deficits has been addressed in several ways. For children with AD/HD, the use of medication, primarily stimulants, is widely recognized as the most effective treatment. However, it is clear that even successful treatment with medication often does not eliminate all deficits in executive functioning or, in those patients with comorbid learning disabilities, necessarily result in academic improvement (Conners and Wells 1986). Direct treatment of deficits in self-regulation has been attempted using cognitive behavioral therapy (Lockman 1992). Such techniques as "thought stopping" can be beneficial. For younger children, this may involve the image of a stop sign before action is initiated, for example. Games such as Stop, Relax, and Think (Bridges 1990), and role-playing games modeling planning and response control have been used successfully. Coaches to help adolescents and adults plan, organize, and follow through on long-term tasks can be extremely useful.

Educational therapy can be helpful for children with AD/HD as well as those with learning disabilities in overcoming executive function deficits in working memory and planning. Emphasis on organizational techniques and study skills is crucial since children with executive function deficits often fail to generalize or develop appropriate strategies for novel situations. An interesting study by Feitler and Hellekson (1993) examined the use of overt strategies in helping first graders who were behind in reading. Groups exposed to these strategies for a semester improved significantly compared to the control group given additional help in reading without the use of specific strategies in paraphrasing and verbally expressing techniques used for identifying words.

Other techniques for increasing the effective use of strategies in older students are currently being explored in the learning-disabilities literature (Durlak et al. 1994, Vogel and Adelman 1992). Most techniques stress training in self-monitoring and planning using real-life situations of importance to the individual client and then encouraging generalization of self-regulation skills.

Conceptualizing executive functions and metacognition as factors separate from intelligence, motivation, psychological issues, and abilities in specific areas of learning can lead to more focused and effective treatments for children with AD/HD and learning disabilities.

REFERENCES

Achenbach, T. M. (1991). *Child Behavior Checklist for Ages 4–18*. Burlington, VT: University of Vermont.

Barbes, H., and Mesulam, M. M. (1981). Organization of afferent input to subdivisions of area 8 in the rhesus monkey. *Journal of Comparative Neurology* 200:407–431.

Barkley, R. A. (1990). *Attention Deficit Hyperactivity Disorder*. New York: Guilford.

Barkley, R. A., and Grodzinsky, G. M. (1994). Tests of frontal lobe functions useful in the diagnosis of attention deficit disorders? *Clinical Neuropsychologist* 9:121–139.

Benson, D. F. (1991). The role of frontal dysfunction in attention deficit/hyperactivity disorder. *Journal of Child Neurology* 6:S9–S12.

Benton, A. L. (1968). Differential behavioral effects in frontal lobe disease. *Neuropsychology* 6:53–60.

Bridges, B. (1990). *Stop, Relax, and Think*. Arlington, TX: Fourth Street Company.

Brown, T. E. (1996). *Brown ADD Scales*. San Antonio, TX: Psychological Corporation.

Bushke, H., and Fuld, P. A. (1974). Evaluating storage, retention and retrieval in disordered memory and learning. *Neurology* 24:1019–1025.

Cahn, D. A., Marcotte, A. C., Stern, R. A., et al. (1996). The Boston qualitative system for the Rey-Osterrieth Complex Figure: a study of children with Attention Deficit/Hyperactivity Disorder. *Clinical Neuropsychologist* 10:397–406.

Case, R. (1992). The role of the frontal lobes in the regulation of cognitive development. *Brain and Cognition* 20:51–73.

Chapman, S. B., Culhane, K. A., Levin, H. S., et al. (1992). Narrative discourse after closed head injury in children and adolescents. *Brain and Language* 43:42–65.

Conners, C. K. (1989). *Conners Rating Scales*. North Tonowanda, NY: Multi-Health Systems.

Conners, C. K., and Wells, K. C. (1986). *Hyperkinetic Children: A Neuropsychosocial Approach*. Beverly Hills, CA: Sage.

Delis, D. C., Kramer, J. H., Kaplan, E., and Ober, B. A. (1985). *The California Verbal Learning Test*. San Antonio, TX: Psychological Corporation.
——— (1989). *The California Verbal Learning Test: Children's Version*. San Antonio, TX: Psychological Corporation.

Denckla, M. B. (1996). Research of executive function in a neurodevelopmental context: application of clinical measures. *Developmental Neuropsychology* 12:5–16.

Dennis, M., Barnes, M. A., Donnelly, R. E., et al. (1996). Appraising and managing knowledge: metacognitive skills after childhood head injury. *Developmental Neuropsychology* 12:77–104.

Durlak, C. M., Rose, E., and Bursuck, W. D. (1994). Preparing high school students with learning disabilities for the transition to postsecondary education: teaching the skills of self-determination. *Journal of Learning Disabilities* 27:51–59.

Feitler, F. C., and Hellekson, L. E. (1993). Active verbalization plus metacognitive awareness yields positive achievement gains in at-risk 1st graders. *Reading Research and Instruction* 33:1–11.

Flavell, J. H., Speer, J. R., Green, F. L., and August, D. L. (1981). The development of comprehension monitoring and knowledge about communication. *Monographs of the Society for Research in Child Development*, serial No. 192, p. 46.

Fletcher, J. M., Brookshire, B. L., Landry, S. H., et al. (1996). Attentional skills and executive functions in children with early hydrocephalus. *Developmental Neuropsychology* 12:53–76.

Garcia-Sanchez, C., Estwvez-Gonzalez, A., Suarez-Romero, E., et al. (1996). Frontal striatal dysfunction in attention deficit disorder. *Journal of the International Neuropsychological Society* 2:183.

Golden, C. J. (1978). *Stroop Color and Word Test*. Chicago: Stoelting.

Goldman-Rakic, P. S. (1987). Circuitry of primate prefrontal cortex and regulation of behavior by representational knowledge. In *Handbook of Physiology, Sec. 1. The Nervous System, Vol. 5: Higher Functions of the Brain* ed. F. Plum, pp. 373–417. New York: Oxford University Press.

Gorenstein, E. E., Mamato, C. A., and Sandy, J. M. (1989). Performance of inattentive-overactive children as selected measures of pre-frontal-type function. *Journal of Clinical Psychology* 45:619–632.

Grodzinsky, G. M., and Diamond, R. (1992). Frontal lobe functioning in boys with attention deficit/hyperactivity disorder. *Developmental Neuropsychology* 8:427–445.

Hall, S. J., Halperin, M., Schwartz, S. T., and Newcorn, J. T. (1997). Behavioral and executive functions in children with attention deficit/hyperactivity disorder and reading disability. *Journal of Attention Disorders* 1:235–247.

Heaton, R. K., Chelune, G. J., Talley, J. L., et al. (1993). Wisconsin Card Sorting Test Manual. Revised and Expanded. Psychological Assessment Resources.

Heilman, K. M., Voeller, K. F., and Nadeau, S. E. (1991). A possible pathophysiologic substrate of attention deficit/hyperactivity disorder. *Journal of Child Neurology* 6:S76–S81.

Kataria, S., Hall, C. W., Wong, M., and Keys, G. F. (1992). Learning styles of LD and NLD AD/HD children. *Journal of Clinical Psychology* 48:371–378.

Kelly, M. S., Best, C. T., and Kirk, U. (1989). Cognitive processing deficits in reading disabilities: a prefrontal cortical hypothesis. *Brain and Cognition* 11:275–293.

Kohlberg, L. (1963). The development of children's orientation toward a moral order: 1. Sequence in the development of moral thought. *Vita Humana* 6:11–33.

Koviol, L. F., and Stout, C. E. (1992). Use of a verbal fluency measure in understanding and evaluating AD/HD as an executive function disorder. *Perceptual and Motor Skills* 75:1187–1192.

Levin, H. S., Culhane, K. A., Mendelsohn, D., et al. (1993). Cognition in relation to magnetic resonance imaging in head injured children and adolescents. *Archives of Neurology* 50:897.

Levin, H. S., Fletcher, J. M., Kusera, J. A., et al. (1996). Dimensions of cognition measured by the Tower of London and other cognitive tasks in head-injured children and adolescents. *Developmental Neuropsychology* 12:17–34.

Lochman, J. E. (1992). Cognitive-behavioral intervention with aggressive boys: three year follow-up and preventive effects. *Journal of Consulting and Clinical Psychology* 60:426–432.

Luria, A. R. (1966). *Higher Cortical Functions in Man.* New York: Basic Books.

McGee, R., Williams, F., Moffitt, T., and Anderson, J. (1989). A comparison of 13 year old boys with attention deficit and/or reading disorder on neuropsychological measures. *Journal of Abnormal Child Psychology* 17:37–53.

Mendelsohn, D., Levin, H. S., Bruce, D., et al. (1992). Late MRI after head injury in children: relationship to clinical features and outcome. *Child's Nervous System* 8:445.

Morrison, F. J., Holmes, D. L., and Haith, M. M. (1974). A developmental study of the effect of familiarity on short-term visual memory. *Journal of Experimental Child Psychology* 18:412–425.

Orzhekhovskaya, N. S. (1981). Fronto-striatal relationships in primate ontogeny. *Neuroscience and Behavioral Physiology* 11:379–385.

Pea, R. (1982). What is planning development the development of? *New Directions for Child Development* 18:5–27.

Pennington, B. F., Groiffer, D., Welsh, M. C. (1993). Contrasting cognitive deficits in attention deficit/hyperactivity disorder versus reading disability. *Developmental Psychology* 29:511–523.

Piaget, J. (1957). *Logic and Psychology.* New York: Basic Books.

Pontius, A. A. (1973). Dysfunction patterns analogous to frontal lobe system and caudate nucleus syndromes in some groups of minimal brain dysfunction. *American Medical Women's Association* 28:285–292.

Porrino, L. J., and Goldman-Rakic, P. S. (1982). Brainstem innervation of prefrontal and anterior cingulate cortex in the rhesus monkey revealed by retrograde transport of HRP. *Journal of Comparative Neurology* 205, 63–76.

Prior, M., and Hoffmann, W. (1990). Brief report: neuropsychological testing of autistic children through an exploration with frontal lobe tests. *Journal of Autism and Developmental Disorders* 20:581–590.

Reader, M. J., Harris, E. L., Schuerholz, L. J., and Denckla, M. B. (1994). Attention deficit/hyperactivity disorder and executive dysfunction. *Developmental Neuropsychology* 10:493–512.

Robert, R. J., and Pennington, B. F. (1996). An interactive framework for examining pre-frontal cognitive processes. *Developmental Neuropsychology* 12:105–126.

Rosenthal, R. H., and Allen, T. W. (1978). An examination of attention, arousal and learning dysfunctions of hyperkinetic children. *Psychological Bulletin* 85:689–715.

Short, E. J. (1992). Cognitive, metacognitive, motivational, and affective differences among normally achieving, learning-disabled, and developmentally handicapped students: How much do they affect school achievement? *Journal of Clinical Child Psychology* 21:229–239.

Shue, K. L., and Douglas, V. I. (1992). Attention deficit/hyperactivity disorder and the frontal lobe syndrome. *Brain and Cognition* 20:104–124.

Spiker, C. C., Cantor, J. H., and Klouda, G. V. (1985). The effect of pretraining and feedback on the reasoning of young children. *Journal of Experimental Child Psychology* 39:381–395.

Spreen, O., and Benton, A. L. (1977). *Neurosensory Center Comprehensive Examination for Aphasia (NCCEA)*, rev. ed.

Stuss, D. T. (1992). Biological and psychological development of executive functions. *Brain and Cognition* 20:8–23.

Stuss, D. T., and Benson, D. F. (1986). *The Frontal Lobes*. New York: Raven.

Swanson, H. L., Christie, L., and Rubadeau, R. J. (1993). The relationship between metacognition and analogical reasoning in mentally retarded, learning disabled, average and gifted children. *Learning Disabilities Research and Practice* 8:70–81.

Taylor, H. G., Schatschbeider, C., Petrill, S., et al. (1996). Executive dysfunction in children with early brain disease: outcome post *Haemophilus influenzae* meningitis. *Development Neuropsychology* 12:35–52.

Thatcher, R. W. (1992). Cyclic cortical reorganization during early childhood. *Brain and Cognition* 20:24–50.

Vaughn, B. C., Kopp, C. B., and Krakow, J. B. (1984). The emergence and consolidation of self-control from eighteen to thirty months of age: normative trends and individual differences. *Child Development* 55:990–1004.

Vogel, S. A., and Adelman, P. B. (1992). The success of college students with learning disabilities: factors related to educational attainment. *Journal of Learning Disabilities* 25:430–441.

Waber, D. P., and Holmes, J. M. (1985). Assessing children's copy productions of the Rey-Osterrieth Complex Figure. *Journal of Clinical and Experimental Neuropsychology* 7:264–280.

Waber, D. P., Isquith, P. K., Kahn, C. M., et al. (1994). Metacognitive factors in the visual spatial skills of long-term survivors of acute lymphoblastic leukemia: an experimental approach to the Rey-Osterrieth Complex Figure Test. *Developmental Neuropsychology* 10:349–357.

Weinstein, B., and Teuber, H. L. (1957). Effects of penetrating brain injury on intelligence test scores. *Science* 125:1036–1037.

Welsh, M. C., and Pennington, B. F. (1988). Assessing frontal lobe functioning in children: views from developmental psychology. *Developmental Neuropsychology* 4:199–230.

Welsh, M. C., Pennington, B. F., and Grossier, D. B. (1991). A normative-developmental study of executive function: A window on prefrontal function in children. *Developmental Neuropsychology* 7:131–149.

Yakovlev, P. I., and Lecours, A. R. (1967). The myologenetic cycles of regional maturation of the brain. *Regional Development of the Brain in Early Life*, ed. A. Minkowski, pp. 3–70. Oxford and Edinburgh: Blackwell Scientific.

Zametkin, A. J., Nordahl, T. E., Gross, M., et al. (1990). Cerebral glucose metabolism in adults with hyperactivity of childhood onset. *New England and Journal of Medicine* 323(20):1361–1366.

Zilbovicius, M., Garreau, B., Samson, Y., et al. (1995). Delayed maturation of the frontal cortex in childhood autism. *American Journal of Psychiatry* 152:248–252.

PART III

Treatment of AD/HD in Children and Adolescents

INTRODUCTION TO PART III

In this section, a number of different treatment approaches are discussed, many of which can be used together in treating the AD/HD child or adolescent. These approaches are presented because we feel that it is important for clinicians to know that treatment need not be limited solely to stimulant medication. As previously noted in the section on assessment, certain subtypes of AD/HD require specific types of pharmacological agents. But other methods can work when medication is not desired or is proscribed. Most importantly, however, many of the treatment approaches discussed in this section can and should be considered in developing a more integrated treatment plan to work with AD/HD children and adolescents.

In Chapter 9, Lance Steinberg, M.D., presents a more traditional but comprehensive look at the various medication options available for treating the young AD/HD patient. He cites a number of different levels of medication to fit the various subtypes of AD/HD as well as its comorbid disorders. In Chapter 10, Siegfried Othmer, Ph.D., Susan F. Othmer, B.A., and David A. Kaiser, Ph.D., present an alternative approach to treating AD/HD in one of the most comprehensive theoretical articles in the field of neurofeedback. In Chapter 11, Thomas M. Brod, M.D., begins with a brief but interesting historical overview of EEG biofeedback and then focuses on the clinical application of neurofeedback in the therapeutic work with AD/HD youth. In Chapter 12, Sebastiano Santostefano, Ph.D., observes that current treatment approaches seem to ignore the inner world of the AD/HD child, and he suggests a more active, integrative approach that appreciates and addresses the child's inner life in psychotherapeuic work. In Chapter 13, Dani Levine, Ph.D., and Persila Conversano, Psy.D., look at an important adjunctive treatment approach to working with AD/HD children and adolescents—the development of appropriate social skills.

9

ADD or AD/HD Medication Treatment

Lance Steinberg

Medications help the great majority of people with attention deficit disorder or attention deficit/hyperactivity disorder (ADD/AD/HD), stimulants being the cornerstone of therapy. Prior to starting medicine, it is important to verify the diagnosis by clinical history to assure *DSM-IV* criteria are met.

DIAGNOSTICS

Parent/teacher questionnaires, old report cards, and continuous performance tasks all serve to further substantiate the diagnosis and can serve as a baseline before medication intervention. Comorbid conditions on Axis I and Axis II are especially critical to delineate, since they can masquerade or coexist with ADD/AD/HD. Once again, the comprehensive clinical history is key. Broad-based standardized psychological measures, as well as educational batteries, are often helpful in clarifying vague emotional disorders and any underlying learning disabilities. All medical problems that can mimic or exacerbate ADD/AD/HD symptomatology should be ruled out by an experienced clinician through a thorough physical examination and appropriate laboratory tests. The most effective and safe medicine for a given individual can be greatly influenced by the person's medical status. Pregnancy, substance abuse, drug-drug interaction, hypertension, neurological state, metabolism, and excretion difficulties affect the choice of medication.

TARGET SYMPTOMS

All caregivers of an individual with ADD/AD/HD should be made aware of a symptom hierarchy that is used in assessing the effects of the medication. Evidence exists that certain medications may affect cognitive difficulties at lower doses than for social/behavioral difficulties. Target symptoms anchor the use of medication and guide later approaches that may either increase the medication at the risk of increased side effects or prompt a change to another medication.

The patient, family, and school greatly benefit by knowing the goals of pharmacology by developing proper expectations of the outcome. This is an excellent opportunity to further dispel any myths about the use of medications, as well as to obtain any further needed baseline information. Concepts to be conveyed to all people involved with an individual's treatment include the fact that medication is merely one aspect of a multimodal team approach, and that it is extremely important that all team members report both benefits and side effects of the medication trial. The medication trial can only be enhanced by such nonpharmacological interventions as more one-to-one attention in the classroom, positive reinforcement of all good behaviors, consistency and limit-setting in all spheres of the individual's life, and increasing an individual's self-esteem by use of hobbies and achievement of responsibilities. The phrase *medication trial* informs all team members that not only may an individual medication need to be titrated slowly upward, but that sometimes several medications may need to be tried to find the right fit between an individual and a given medication.

STIMULANT MEDICATION

Stimulant medications have proved to be the most effective and safe group of medicines in the great majority of individuals with ADD/AD/HD. Central nervous system (CNS) stimulants are the baseline treatment for almost any individual with ADD/AD/HD, except for such special circumstances as an individual with addiction problems, significant hypertension, and so on.

First-line stimulants include methylphenidate (Ritalin) as well as dextroamphetamine (Dexedrine, Adderall) (Table 9–1). Short-acting methylphenidate tablets and short-acting dextroamphetamine tablets are usually used initially, and later their respective longer-acting forms may be used following titration of their short-acting tablet forms. The second-line stimulant medications include methamphetamine (Desoxyn) or pemoline (Cylert). Methylphenidate or dextroamphetamine are normally started at approximately 2.5 mg per dose, with a dose giv-

Table 9–1.
Stimulant Doses

		Average Calculated Maximum by Weight[1]	Do *Not* Exceed	Doses Per Day
Methylphenidate	(Ritalin)	1.0 to 2.0 mg/kg/day	60+ mg/day	SA[2] (2–4), LA[3] (2–3)
Dextroamphetamine	(Dexedrine)	0.5 to 1.0 mg/kg/day	40+ mg/day	SA (2–4), LA (2–3)
Dextroamphetamine salts	(Adderall)	Not specified	40+ mg/day	1–3
Methamphetamine	(Desoxyn)	Not specified	? 15–25 mg/day	SA (2–4), LA (1–2)
Pemoline	(Cylert)	Up to 3.0 mg/kg/day	112.5 mg/day	1–2

[1]Estimates only. Consult PDR, latest literature.
[2]Short-acting.
[3]Long-acting.

en after breakfast, a dose given after lunch, and a dose given just prior to homework at approximately 2:30 to 3:30 P.M. Each dose can be increased in approximately one week by another 2.5 mg until the desired benefit is obtained. The calculated maximum amount of methylphenidate by weight is commonly a total of 1.0 to 2.0 mg per kilogram per day, but not to exceed approximately 60 mg per day. With dextroamphetamine, the average calculated maximum amount by weight is 0.5 mg to 1.0 mg per kilogram per day, but not to exceed approximately 40 mg per day. The most commonly used medication now seems to be methylphenidate. Methylphenidate is effective, but there is some feeling that the long-acting (sustained release) form may not be as effective and as smoothly acting as anticipated. Additionally, it only comes in a 20-mg size sustained-release form. Dextroamphetamine is a very well respected medication that can be titrated at 2.5-mg increments just like methylphenidate, and it has a longer-acting form that comes in various-sized spansules, even as low as 5 mg. Dextroamphetamine now also comes in a form of four dextroamphetamine salts in one medication: Adderall. Adderall is relatively new to the treatment of ADD/AD/HD, but can be broken in small portions, either from a 10-mg or a 20-mg tablet. Adderall appears to exhibit a smooth action similar to dextroamphetamine spansules. There also seems to be a slightly longer duration of action from both the dextroamphetamine spansules and the Adderall. Ultimately, it may be possible to dispense long-acting forms of Ritalin at breakfast and lunch or in the afternoon, so as to require only two doses. Dextroamphetamine spansules and Adderall potentially can also be stretched to a twice a day (breakfast and lunch/afternoon) dosage schedule. All dosage schedules greatly depend on the metabolism of the individual and thus vary greatly from person to person.

"Second-line" stimulants, such as methamphetamine (Desoxyn) or pemoline (Cylert), are very effective medications and have advantages and disadvantages; however, some physicians use pemoline as a first-line medication. Methamphetamine has a "meth" stigma attached to it and is frequently hard to obtain, and rather expensive in comparison to the other medications. It has a short-acting form that can be used three times a day, but also has a longer-acting form (Desoxyn Gradumet) that comes in 5-mg tablets that may be given in the morn-

ing and just after school or lunch. Pemoline is an excellent medication for many individuals and is frequently used on a twice-a-day
dosage or sometimes even once-a-day dosage, but it requires liver
function tests, both as a baseline as well as several months later, because of the reported, but rare, hepatic irritation associated with its
use. Some physicians choose to use pemoline as a first-line stimulant
because it requires no special triplicate prescription and can be dispensed by phone.

Most physicians choose either dextroamphetamine or
methylphenidate and, if the initial medication of choice does not
work, they then try the other. If neither methylphenidate nor
dextroamphetamine works, then one of the second-line stimulants is
tried, and, if that does not work, the other second-line medication is
tried. Monotherapy with one specific stimulant is currently the approach most commonly used by clinicians in the United States. The
second-line medications have a different set of calculated maximum
amounts by weight: methamphetamine has no absolute specifications
other than generally not exceeding 15 to 25 mg per day, while
pemoline is generally given up to a calculated maximum dosage by
weight of 3 mg per kilogram per day, with a total maximum of 112.5
mg per day.

The optimal dosage regime offers the most effective use of medication at the specific time it is needed, while ultimately decreasing
the total amount of medication used in 24 hours and greatly decreasing the side effects. Regardless of the specific preparation, if more than
one dose per day is necessary, sculpting the regime usually entails an
increased amount of medication in the morning immediately following breakfast, with the same or slightly lowered dose at noontime
immediately after lunch, and a slightly lower amount of medication
following school but just prior to homework. Combinations of both
the short-acting and long-acting formulation of a given medicine are
quite frequently used in order to avoid taking medication at lunch-
time at school, because of the stigma, as well as using a small amount
of short-acting medication prior to getting out of bed in the morning in order to facilitate a more focused and clear approach to getting dressed and prepared for school. Many clinicians prefer to start
with short-acting preparations in order to calculate the amount of

long-acting preparation needed for a given individual, but at decreased frequencies. Some physicians are so comfortable with dispensing stimulants that they may accurately ascertain an approximate dosage schedule using long-acting preparations and can gently titrate according to the individual's needs. Well-made long-acting preparations include methamphetamine (Desoxyn Gradumet) and pemoline (Cylert). Once- or twice-a-day dosage is often sufficient. Adderall may offer a longer lasting form of dextroamphetamine, at least equivalent to the spansule form and possibly longer in duration of action.

"Third-line" medications include an unusual antidepressant known as bupropion (Wellbutrin). Adult and pediatric studies seem to validate this medication as a relatively effective treatment for ADD/AD/HD; however, it may also exacerbate an underlying tic disorder, as many stimulants do, and is contraindicated in individuals with anorexia nervosa, bulimia, or epilepsy. It is used initially in low doses of 37.5 mg with breakfast and approximately 37.5 mg 6 hours later, and potentially another 37.5 mg 6 hours after that. Some individuals may benefit from a slightly increased dose of 75 mg either at breakfast or at breakfast as well as lunch. There is great individual variation with this medication and its effects on concentration and focusing. Open trials with fluoxetine (Prozac) and venlafaxine (Effexor) seem promising but potentially not as effective as stimulants. These two medicines, fluoxetine and venlafaxine, are newer antidepressant medications.

The next line of medications includes alpha-adrenergic medicines, both clonidine (Catapres), patch or pill form, and guanfacine (Tenex). These medications may be effective in certain individuals, especially for hyperactivity and impulsivity. Their effectiveness with attention and concentration is less substantiated at this point in time. These medications do have the advantage of not being likely to increase any preexisting tics in a given individual. These medications require careful monitoring from start to finish, as well as very careful titration during discontinuation, because they are both antihypertensive medications. These medications, as well as bupropion, fluoxetine, and venlafaxine, have not been fully evaluated to the same extent as stimulants in children and adolescents, and are usually not as efficacious as standard stimulants.

The next line of medications includes the heterocyclic antidepressants. Because of several sudden deaths occurring in young children over the past several years, there has been a reconsideration of their use. However, many physicians are quite confident of their safety and use them as the "third line" prior to bupropion, venlafaxine, fluoxetine, and alpha-adrenergics. Many studies show good to excellent efficacy. The use of heterocyclic antidepressants require a complete cardiac examination prior to initiation of a medication trial, and cardiac status must be reevaluated at frequent intervals. Briefly, medications in this category include desipramine and imipramine, both of which have shown substantial efficacy in several studies. Nortriptyline for ADD/AD/HD has been studied and shows efficacy. Clomipramine, although not as fully researched, has its advocates. If a physician chooses a heterocyclic antidepressant, then extremely close monitoring of the electrocardiogram (ECG) and medication blood levels is clearly a prudent approach.

Monoamine oxidase inhibitors have been shown to be effective in several studies; tranylcypromine, clorgyline, and l-deprenyl have been studied. Clorgyline and tranylcypromine seem to show good response. Meclondomide, a reversible monoamine oxidase inhibitor that is in use in Canada, shows some potential. The major drawback for using these kinds of medications centers around difficulties with particular restrictions on diet, several over-the-counter medications, and prescribed medicines. Although the severity of the reaction is less with the reversible monoamine oxidase inhibitors, hypertensive crisis can result and, thus, these medications must be used with extraordinary caution in both children and adolescents.

MANAGEMENT OF ADVERSE STIMULANT EFFECTS

Decreased appetite secondary to anorexia or nausea may occur following stimulant administration. Subsequent weight loss may ensue. By reducing the dosage of the medication and administering the medication immediately after a meal, these problems usually decrease. On rare occasions, a high-caloric food supplement may be necessary, with emphasis on eating large but balanced meals at breakfast and dinner that can be monitored by the parent. Headaches may occur and the treatment may be simply a decrement in dosage or the use of an appropriate nonsteroidal anti-inflammatory medication. Often headaches are transient, but a blood pressure check might be advised. A blood sugar check may also be helpful and, if problems continue, an evaluation of the headache may be deemed necessary, or the headache may necessitate change to another medication. Insomnia may also occur and can be treated by administering the last dose of medication earlier, changing to a short-acting preparation at the last dose, possibly decreasing or discontinuing the last dose, and sometimes even adding a small dose just prior to bedtime. Sometimes an antihistamine such as diphenhydramine may be suitable. On rare occasions, the use of an alpha-adrenergic medicine, such as clonidine or guanfacine, may be a helpful adjunct, but needs very careful monitoring because of its cardiovascular effects.

Irritability may arise directly when the medication is at moderate levels in the bloodstream, thus necessitating a change in medication or a reevaluation of a coexisting type of depression or anxiety. Irritability occurs most often after the medication has left the system and is termed "rebound," which can be treated by changing the timing of the dose so as to have overlapping doses or by an additional small dose just prior to the rebound irritability.

The issue of growth impairment has been discussed for many years in the literature; however, most reports show very little evidence. Monitoring of height and weight should be done at least several times per year. Some physicians choose to reduce the dosage of a given medication or use a "drug holiday" if it is feasible for a given individual. The mandatory use of medication cessation on weekends does not seem to be logical unless there are significant concerns over the growth of an individual, or an individual does not gain benefit from the medication at all (including social interaction).

COMORBID/COEXISTING SPECIAL CONDITIONS

Individuals with a personal or family history of tics or Tourette's syndrome are frequently placed on stimulants as the first-line medi-

cation for ADD/AD/HD. This seems to be consistent with literature, but conflictual with the *Physician's Desk Reference* (PDR). An
explanation for usage of stimulants in this situation should be part
of the informed consent process. Multicenter evaluations are now
being undertaken to elucidate the ideal medication treatment for individuals with these difficulties. Many physicians still opt for the use
of an alpha-adrenergic medication prior to stimulants in this population. Some physicians prescribe antidepressants prior to the use of
stimulants for these individuals. Should stimulants be used and an
underlying tic disorder manifests itself, or a preexisting tic condition
becomes exacerbated, a decrease in the dosage of stimulant or change
of stimulant often proves helpful. Adjunctive medication specifically
for the use and control of tics (alpha-adrenergics, neuroleptics) may
prove useful if used cautiously.

When ADD/AD/HD is associated with depression, the use of selective serotonin reuptake inhibitors (SSRIs) or bupropion may be
especially beneficial. The dosage of medications in the SSRI class or
bupropion must be adjusted for age and metabolism. The clinician
should always consult the latest literature in the treatment of
comorbid depression in order to find the most current and effective
medications. Bipolar depression seems to be more prevalent than
previously thought, even in prepubertal individuals. An accurate history and family history should alert the physician to the possibility
of this entity, and the potential likelihood of being "flipped" into a
manic phase must always be kept in mind when using stimulants as
well as antidepressants.

Anxiety may also accompany ADD/AD/HD. The SSRIs are often very helpful for anxiety. Many individuals may opt for other medication adjuncts to the stimulants. These include alpha-adrenergics and
possibly buspirone. Heterocyclic antidepressants should be used with
great caution.

Obsessive-compulsive disorder often coexists with ADD/AD/HD.
The addition of SSRIs, such as fluoxetine, sertraline, paroxetine, and
fluvoxamine, is very beneficial. Should one SSRI not be beneficial,
changing to another one in the same category may prove fruitful.
There are various augmentation strategies should a given medication
only be partially effective. The latest literature should be consulted.

ADD/AD/HD may be associated with extreme impulse control problems beyond the impulsivity that may be a part of the ADD/AD/HD spectrum. Sometimes the use of alpha-adrenergics may curb impulsivity, and sometimes an SSRI may also serve the same function. The use of buspirone needs to be further elucidated. Should bipolar or episodic dyscontrol disorder be suspect, one would consider lithium or other mood stabilizers (carbamazepine or valproate). One should not hesitate to reexamine the nervous system and strongly consider an electroencephalogram (EEG). Should Tourette's syndrome be a likely possibility, a neuroleptic may be of particular help. In people with mental retardation with accompanying self-injurious behavior, neuroleptics should be considered as well.

Substance abuse can be a comorbid condition. Whether an individual is sober or "unstable," many physicians find it prudent to use medications other than stimulants. Bupropion has been very helpful. Alpha-adrenergics in conjunction with bupropion may also help. Although the absolute efficacy of SSRIs and venlafaxine remain to be confirmed, they should be considered upon further accumulation of literature. Many physicians might try pemoline as a last-line medication in this population.

CONCLUSION

Medication should only be prescribed by physicians who are thoroughly familiar with the extensive and ever-changing literature, and who can accurately assess emotional, environmental, and medical difficulties. Following parameters such as height, weight, blood pressure, pulse, medication effectiveness, and side effects should be done at frequent intervals during the year. These, in addition to blood chemistries/panels, must be prudently evaluated according to current literature and the patient's medical status. Data from teachers, educational therapists, psychotherapists, the patient, and family can be used to pinpoint the periods of maximum and minimum cognitive, behavioral, and social performance, which can alert the physician to times during which a patient's medication may need to be altered. If changes cannot be promptly made during the school year, summer vacation may be an excellent time to test alternative medications or to attempt a decrease in dosage. Summer school, an educational therapist, or use of continuous performance tasks can serve as a general gauge with which to measure the new medication approach.

Medication should be considered as an adjunct to an individual's own natural abilities and efforts, thus enhancing self-empowerment and self-esteem. Although psychopharmacologic intervention is the mainstay of treatment in ADD/AD/HD, medication should only be used in the context of a multimodal treatment approach.

BIBLIOGRAPHY

Alderton, H. R. (1995). Tricyclic medication in children and the QT interval: case report and discussion. *Canadian Journal of Psychiatry* 40:325–329.

Biederman, J., Thisted, R. A., Greenhill, L. L., et al. (1995). Estimation of association between desipramine and the risk for sudden death in 5 to 14 year old children. *Journal of Clinical Psychiatry* 56:87–93.

Cantwell, D. P. (1996). Attention deficit disorder: a review of the past years. *Journal of the American Academy of Child and Adolescent Psychiatry* 35:978–987.

Chappell, P. B., Riddle, M. A., Seahill, L., et al. (1995). Guanfacine treatment of comorbid AD/HD and Tourette's syndrome: preliminary clinical experience. *Journal of the American Academy of Child and Adolescent Psychiatry* 34:1140–1146.

Connors, C. K., Casat, C. D., Gualtieri, D. T., et al. (1996). Bupropion hydrochloride in attention deficit disorder with hyperactivity. *Journal of the American Academy of Child and Adolescent Psychiatry* 35:1314–1321.

Fenichel, R. R. (1995). Combining methylphenidate and clonidine: the role of post-marketing surveillance. *Journal of Child and Adolescent Psychopharmacology* 5:155–156.

Gadow, K. D., Suerd, J., Spratkin, J., et al. (1995). Efficacy of methylphenidate for attention deficit hyperactivity disorder in children with tic disorder. *Archives of General Psychiatry* 52:444–455.

Green, W. H. (1995). *Childhood Adolescent Clinical Psychopharmacology*, 2nd ed. Baltimore: Williams & Wilkins.

Kutcher, S. (1996). Mini review venlafaxine. *Child and Adolescent Psychopharmacology* 4:1–3.

Leonard, H. L., Meyer, M. D., Swedo, S. E., et al. (1995). Electrocardiographic changes during desipramine and clomipramine treatment in children and adolescents. *Journal of the American Academy of Child and Adolescent Psychiatry* 34:1460–1468.

Prince, J. B., Wilens, T. E., Biederman, J., et al. (1996). Clonidine for sleep disturbances associated with attention-deficit hyperactivity disorder: A systematic chart review of 62 cases. *Journal of the American Academy of Child and Adolescent Psychiatry* 35:599–605.

Popper, C. W. (1995). Combining methylphenidate and clonidine: pharmacologic questions and news reports about sudden death. *Journal of Child and Adolescent Psychopharmacology* 5:157–166.

Popper, C. W., and Zimnitzky, B. (1995). Sudden death putatively related to desipramine treatment in youth: a fifth case and review of speculative mechanisms. *Journal of Child and Adolescent Psychopharmacology* 5:283–300.

Riggs, P. D., Thompson, L. L., Mikolich, S. K., et al. (1996). An open trial of pemoline in drug-dependent delinquents with attention-deficit hyperactivity disorder. *Journal of the American Academy of Child and Adolescent Psychiatry* 35:1018–1023.

Swanson, J. M., Flockhart, D., Vdrea, D., et al. (1995). Clonidine in the treatment of AD/HD: questions about safety and efficacy [Letter]. *Journal of Child and Adolescent Psychopharmacology* 5:301–304.

Wender, P. H., and Shader, R. I. (1994). Diagnosis and treatment of attention-deficit hyperactivity disorder in children and adults. In *Manual of Psychiatric Therapeutics*, ed. R. I. Shader, 2nd ed. Boston: Little, Brown.

Werry, J. S., Biederman, J., Thisted, R., et al. (1995). Resolved: cardiac arrhythmias make desipramine an unacceptable choice in children. *Journal of the American Academy of Child and Adolescent Psychiatry* 34:1239–1248.

10

EEG Biofeedback: Training for AD/HD and Related Disruptive Behavior Disorders

Siegfried Othmer, Susan F. Othmer, and David A. Kaiser

OVERVIEW

This chapter presents a model in which AD/HD is seen as a deficit in fundamental cerebral regulatory function relative to physiological arousal, attention, and affect. This regulatory function must be accomplished not only in the neurochemical domain but also in the bioelectrical domain. Organization of global as well as localized cortical function is deemed to occur in the electrical domain through collective, periodic neuronal activity that requires explicit organization and management by rhythmic mechanisms that initiate and maintain task-appropriate activation of neuronal groups. The state of such collective activity may be observed in the electroencephalogram (EEG).

Operant conditioning of the rhythmic mechanisms by means of EEG biofeedback is found to yield long-term normalization of regulatory function, by analogy to long-term alteration in neuromodulator function through psychopharmacology. The therapeutic potential of EEG biofeedback was discovered serendipitously, and has a long—but unfortunately neglected—research history for epilepsy and for AD/HD. It has recently found favor among clinicians primarily for addressing AD/HD and affective disorders. The technique has evolved with use, along with various schema for clinical decision making.

The conceptual model that has emerged out of this work is based on established principles of neurophysiology, which are described herein. The model is then examined in light of the striking results that have been obtained over the past several years. On the basis of such results it is expected that in the future EEG biofeedback will complement other behavioral interventions as well as pharmacology in addressing the attention, behavior, learning, and affective disorders of children.

It is always difficult to introduce radically new concepts into a field that has already reached a certain level of scientific and clinical maturity. The existing models have already been honed to a certain self-consistency and completeness. Experts have spent their entire careers on it. The very success of existing models may bar the claims of the new. Thus it is with AD/HD. Despite a colorful history throughout the *DSM* series that includes several identity changes, a defensible model has now emerged, the core of which has found general acceptance. Thus it is unlikely that a new model will entirely displace the old. Therefore, our purpose here is to reframe the existing data so that current models are seen in a new light, and to allow new data to be properly appraised.

In the 1990s, the decade of the brain, there have been numerous developments that will have fundamental import for our understanding of brain function. From the present perspective, they are as follows:

1. *Brain plasticity.* The brain has been found to be much more adaptable than once thought, and this has profound implications for remediation of a variety of disorders. This is also bringing about a reconsideration of certain disorders in terms of functional rather than structural deficits.

2. *Brain imaging.* The ability to see the brain at work through positron emission tomography (PET), single photon emission computed tomography (SPECT), and functional magnetic resonance imaging (fMRI) is refocusing attention among neuroscientists to the level

of integrated brain function. These tests contrast with the earlier computed axial tomography (CAT) scans and standard MRIs, in that they are indicators of function rather than structure. These new techniques complement the recent preoccupation with the building blocks at the receptor, membrane, and cellular levels.

3. *The neural code.* New insights, along with advances in mathematical modeling, have led to an appreciation of how the brain manages to integrate individual neuronal activity into ensembles that represent either information, units of processing, or states of the system. It is found that tight temporal correlation of large ensembles of neurons exists, and probably defines what "belongs together" functionally in cortex. It is also found that periodic (that is to say, rhythmic) activity—ubiquitous in cortex—can organize such tight temporal coupling.

4. *Neuroregulation.* The discovery of the mechanisms by which collective neuronal activity is organized draws attention to the bioelectrical domain of neuroregulation, to complement the prevailing focus on chemical means of neuroregulation.

5. *The disregulation model.* Models have emerged that regard disorders of attention and affect from the standpoint of regulatory dysfunction. Such disorders could arise from problems either in the neurochemical or the bioelectrical domains. Most likely both domains are involved, and the two may ultimately not be separable.

6. *Operant conditioning (EEG biofeedback).* Finally, there has been the recognition among clinicians that operant conditioning on the mechanisms of bioelectrical neuroregulation can effect normalization of function in a manner that is complementary to pharmacological means of reregulation. These findings could not be readily appreciated, however, until the other developments mentioned above were understood and integrated as well.

STRAINS IN THE PARADIGM

The current consensus view of AD/HD is based on phenomenological models. Certain patterns of behavior, if seen in combination, serve to identify AD/HD of either the inattentive type, the impulsive/hyperactive type, or the combined type (*DSM-IV*). However, it is acknowledged that many additional behaviors can be seen in concert with the specific ones called out as defining characteristics. If some of these other behaviors exceed certain bounds, then the child may also be labeled oppositional-defiant disordered (ODD), conduct disordered (CD), Tourette's syndrome (TS), anxious, dysthymic, depressed, dysphoric, manic, or bipolar. A thorough study of the prevalence of these comorbidities by Biederman and colleagues (1991, 1996) shows that such comorbidities are more the rule than the exception. Considering only anxiety, depression, and conduct disorder, less than half of AD/HD children manifest without these comorbidities. ODD all by itself has 60 percent overlap with AD/HD. Bipolar disorder was recently shown to have a prevalence of greater than 20 percent within the AD/HD population (Biederman et al. 1996).

In the above survey, Biederman and colleagues abided by the strict diagnostic criteria. If one now admits to the discussion subclinical manifestations of anxiety, depression, dysphoria, conduct disorder, ODD, obsessive behavior, and tic disorders in the children labeled AD/HD, it is clear that the vast majority have a broad mix of symptoms, in addition to the defining ones. If one includes sleep disorders, chronic pain syndromes, certain learning disorders, and elimination disorders, one finds that the children generally have a multitude of symptoms, all of which can be considered within the panoply of AD/HD phenomenology. That is, their incidence is greater, or the symptoms exacerbated, in the population identified as AD/HD than it is in the population at large.

One could also take the opposite perspective, and look at those identified with disorders such as depression, anxiety, substance-related disorders, and Tourette's syndrome, and find problems of attention to be ubiquitous in these populations. In the appendix of the *DSM-IIIR* is a long list of conditions for which attention problems are prevalently comorbid. With attention problems so thoroughly mixed with other symptom patterns, one wonders if we are not reaching the end of the road of ever-more refined differential diagnosis as a basis for our understanding (it may continue to be useful for therapeutic intervention, of course). It may be more fruitful to regard many of these symptoms as being the behavioral manifestation of a few characteristic failure modes of our nervous system, and that these can play out variously in different constitutions.

Both the physicist Freeman Dyson and the psychiatrist Peter Kramer (1993) have pointed out that science tends to move cyclically between the poles of a *splitting* or a *lumping* perspective. We may now be in a phase in psychiatry and psychology where further refinements of the *DSM-IV* are no longer that earth-shaking or illuminating. After all, the categorizations of the *DSM-IV* don't really line up with physiologically based models of these disorders, or even with pharmacological efficacy. In a salient study, Suffin and Emory (1995) demonstrated that several subtypes of AD/HD could be identified from the quantitative EEG, and that these were closely matched with pharmacological efficacy. Thus, one subtype was found to respond to stimulants, another to antidepressants, and a third to anticonvulsants. Even more revealing was the fact that these same three subtypes were identified as well among children referred for affective disorders as opposed to attentional disorders, and that pharmacological efficacy tracked the EEG subtype rather than the diagnosis. Finally, it was found that the same EEG subtypes were not restricted to attentional or affective disorders, but rather were found scattered among a variety of other clinical categories (Suffin and Emory 1996).

Once it is realized that many AD/HD children should be treated with antidepressants rather than stimulants, and that many depressed children are more responsive to stimulants or even to anticonvulsants than to antidepressants, it is clear that the *DSM-IV* categories are not a good guide either to pharmacological intervention or to mechanisms of dysfunction. We are driven to look elsewhere for the basic neurophysiological mechanisms that are responsible for these patterns of behavior. In this search, it is noteworthy that little progress has been made over the years in pinning down the central issue in AD/HD at the neurophysiological level. All attempts to find a discernible structural basis for the disorder to date have failed. Even attempts to discern a unitary functional basis for the disorder have come to naught. The finding by Zametkin and colleagues (1990) that there was reduced perfusion in frontal cortex associated with AD/HD (which finding made it all the way to the cover of *Time*) was later withdrawn and found not to be a fruitful area of inquiry (Zametkin et al. 1993). Not only was there no tight correlation between low perfusion and symptomatology, but low frontal perfusion could also be found in a range of other disorders, such as schizophrenia and dementia.

Restating the Problem

As is often the case, the evidence for a new formulation of a problem is ubiquitous, but is not seen because of the constraints of the dominant paradigm. In the following, it is suggested that the primary issue in AD/HD is neither hyperactivity nor attention, but rather *disorder*, and that AD/HD is traceable to functional, as opposed to primarily structural, deficits in the way the brain organizes the management of arousal, attention, and affect. The organization of these functions involves the bioelectrical domain as well as the neurochemical. Thus, the deficits may not manifest primarily in the neurochemical domain. Moreover, these functions are managed by all of the neuromodulator systems, and any deficits may not be restricted to one or even two such systems, but may exhibit a general disregulation. While the use of pharmacological agents that impinge upon neuromodulator systems may serve to change "set points" of functioning, this does not preclude the possibility of intervention at the bioelectrical level with means that alter the bioelectrical regulation of the neuromodulator systems.

This proposition has testable implications. First of all, one would not expect to see such disregulation manifest only in a narrow set of behavioral sequelae. That is, if the model is valid, then it can be drawn upon to explain not only AD/HD but its principal comorbidities as well. Thus, one would expect a successful intervention addressing itself to the issue of disregulation to manifest efficacy not only for AD/HD but also for the other behavioral sequelae traceable to such a functional disorder. Additionally, one would expect a successful nonpharmacological remediation addressing itself to the core issue of disorder to largely displace the need for pharmacological intervention for AD/HD and its comorbidities. Thus, just as successful pharmacological intervention for AD/HD has served to underpin the assumption of a structural deficit (e.g., the insulin-replacement model of pharmacology), a successful behavioral intervention would make the case for a functional basis.

What may be called the disregulation model of AD/HD actually has already surfaced in the literature. Virginia Douglas proposed as far back as 1988 that AD/HD children are characterized by a generalized self-regulatory deficit that affects information processing, the process of attention throughout information processing, as well as deficits in behavioral inhibition. The self-regulatory deficit is seen to cross visual, auditory, and perceptual motor modalities (Douglas 1988). "Organization of information processing encompasses planning, executive function, metacognition, optimum set maintenance, regulation of arousal and alertness, and self-monitoring" (Pennington 1991, p. 93). Such complex functions are not the burden of any single regulatory system in the brain, nor of any single neuromodulator substance.

Weinberg has made the case that AD/HD may be intrinsically a composite disorder, with variable contributions from an affective (anxiety) dimension, from a primary disorder of vigilance, and from learning disabilities (Weinberg and Brumback 1992, Weinberg and Harper 1993). This view is valuable particularly for its highlighting of the affective dimension of these disorders. Certainly if we include the disruptive behavioral disorders within the AD/HD spectrum, then the affective dimension is paramount. And if we acknowledge the role of motivation in guiding attentional faculties, then it appears that the primary disregulation underlying even "pure" AD/HD may involve the affective realm as well. The implicit message is that AD/HD phenomenology involves a rather global disregulation, as opposed to being a narrowly based disorder.

The need for a systems perspective also comes from the world of special education. According to Cherkes-Julkowski (1996),

> Information processing models have emphasized separate processes such as attention, memory, and executive function. In practice, this conceptual splitting has contributed to painful debates at planning and placement team meetings to decide whether a child's problems are due to motivation or attention, motivation or a learning disability, memory or executive function, attention or working memory, whether a child has a neurological impairment such as attention deficit disorder, or whether learning problems are related to emotional disturbance. From a systems perspective, these issues are more interconnected than they are discrete. [p. 20]

On the basis of the above, the case can be made for consideration of AD/HD as a spectrum disorder that breaches the accepted boundaries of diagnostic categories. It is grounded in varied but diffuse functional disregulations in a number of interactive systems that subserve the functions of modulation of physiological arousal, management of attention, affect regulation, and information processing.

BACKGROUND FOR THE MODEL

In the largest possible sense, it may be said that the business of the brain is handling information. In this we include information respecting its own function as well as information relating to other bodily functions and to the outside world. The principal agency of communication is the action potential, which does not encode information in its magnitude, but rather solely in its timing. It is now known that "rate coding," in which information is encoded in the firing repetition rate, is insufficient to convey all the data that the brain must have available to it in order to function. Hence, information must be contained in the subtle timing of action potentials. Such timing cannot be meaningful in isolation, but rather only in the context of other firing events. Thus it follows that much of what constitutes information in the brain is represented by ensembles of firing events. Such collective activity requires explicit mechanisms to coordinate it, and such mechanisms of course need to be self-organizing.

In recent years, the importance of such mechanisms has come to be appreciated. It has been postulated that simultaneity in firing may be the criterion that distinguishes one entity or representation in the brain from another. That is, it belongs together as a functional entity. This hypothesis is known as *time binding* (von der Malsburg 1995). If the simultaneous firing is repeated, then the entity or gestalt can be maintained in a manner similar to the refresh cycle of a dynamic random-access memory (RAM). Periodic (or rhythmic) activity is required to orchestrate such repetitions. It is therefore reasonable to propose that rhythmic activity defines the context in which highly correlated timing events occur in the brain in a manner that allows information to be held in working memory, to be processed and refined to higher levels, to be communicated from one part of the cortex to another and received, and to coordinate the execution of motor acts.

A recent report explicitly demonstrates both the importance of relative timing and the effect of activation on such timing mechanisms (Munk et al. 1996). It was observed that when a visual image (a red square) was moved across a cat's visual field, the response in visual cortex was mildly temporally correlated between the two hemispheres. When the brain stem was electrically stimulated, to simulate sudden activation and arousal of the animal, the temporal correlation suddenly strengthened significantly.

When the red square was subsequently divided into two squares moving in opposite directions, those neurons "illuminated" by one square were correlated with their fellows in the opposite hemisphere, but not with those representing the other square! This elegant experiment shows that temporal correlation may be the means by which the brain accomplishes figure-ground separation, that this control mechanism is a continuous function, and that explicit arousal of the organism can heighten the contrast in the scene and rivet attention to the object of interest. Since these mechanisms are effective across the hemispheric fissure, subcortical mechanisms must be involved in orchestrating this temporal correlation. Moreover, since the brain stem knows nothing about whether there are two squares or only one, there must be local cortical mechanisms that organize the ensembles into collective correlated activity. Hence, the phenomena of image processing and activation are linked in a symphony of both cortical and subcortical rhythmic activity—the music of the brain.

One more significant piece of information can be extracted from this work. The authors found that if the resulting EEG was separated into different regions of frequency, activation resulted in an enhancement of activity at the higher frequencies, around 40 to 50 Hz, and a reduction at frequencies below 30 Hz. This implies that binding of the phenomenon of "red square" may take place around 40 Hz and above, and it suggests that activation involves the frequencies below 30 Hz. Paradoxically, increased activation is correlated with decreases in the lower frequency amplitudes. (More on this later.) It is almost as if the lower frequencies were like the conductor of an orchestra who sets the overall pace of things, and the "tone" of the nervous system. Upon this basic coordinating rhythm, the piece plays itself out at higher frequencies.

It should be noted that we have not said anything about neurochemistry. One could describe all of the above in terms of neurochemical events, including the action potential, but it would be exceedingly cumbersome. The fact is that there must be a description of brain function in the bioelectrical domain that complements the description in the neurochemical domain. Different languages are suitable to different aspects of brain function. Further, it is true that if the above mechanisms are not ultimately the correct explanation for the phenomena described, then some other such mechanism will be found responsible that also must be discussed in the bioelectrical domain. Ineluctably, the issues we will find important in arousal and attention cannot be fully appreciated without treatment of the bioelectrical domain. And it is highly likely that rhythmic activity will be found to be central to the orchestration of brain timing. At this point, the best we can hope for is to present a hypothesis that is both internally self-consistent and comprehensive.

A MODEL FOR EEG BIOFEEDBACK

On the basis of the above understandings, AD/HD is ascribed to functional disregulation in the mechanisms by which arousal, attention, and affect are managed. These mechanisms cannot be fully understood until disregulation in the bioelectrical domain is considered and included. The activation and arousal of the central nervous system are governed in the bioelectrical domain by explicit rhythmic activity in neuronal firing patterns. Activation and arousal are functions of the frequency of these rhythms, and of the amplitude. Because synchronous neuronal activity leads to periodic modulation of the ambient postsynaptic potential, the instantaneous state of arousal of the organism can be seen in the spectral distribution of the EEG. At any point on the scalp, the EEG reflects both global (general) organismic arousal and local cortical excitability and activation.

Higher frequencies in the EEG are associated with higher arousal, and a shift from parasympathetic nervous system dominance to sympathetic dominance. By means of electrical stimulation of the thalamus and hypothalamus, W. R. Hess (1954) established that shifts in autonomic nervous system balance were coupled with changes in the voluntary or somatic nervous system as well. A sympathetic shift was accompanied by increased vigilance, an orientation toward external stimuli, heightened visual acuity, narrowing of focus of attention, and increased motoric tone. A parasympathetic shift, by contrast, would be accompanied by a shift toward internal focus of attention, reduced visual acuity, broad and inclusive focus of attention, and reduced motor tone. In the extreme, electrical stimulation of a single site could even evoke somnolence, torpor, or sleep. Hess called the former an ergotropic shift, and the latter a trophotropic shift. The two were complementary, in that promotion of one would entail suppression of the other. The fact that such consistent patterns of arousal could be identified suggests that they were managed either by a hierarchical control system or by mutual interaction.

EEG biofeedback is a technique of operant conditioning of the EEG, in particular its rhythmic properties. In current practice, the subject is rewarded for a selective increase in the instantaneous amplitude of the EEG in certain limited frequency regimes. It is empirically observed that if the reinforcement frequency is just above 15 Hz, then an ergotropic shift is elicited in most human subjects. Thus it is no longer necessary to plunge a microelectrode into the thalamus to achieve this objective (as Hess was compelled to do). Conversely, reinforcement frequencies less than 15 Hz lead to a trophotropic shift in most subjects. The reinforcement is seen most parsimoniously as an exercise of the regulatory mechanisms by which the rhythms are maintained. And such exercise is deemed to eventuate in improved self-regulation.

Differential response to different reward frequencies is demonstration of the specific efficacy of the conditioning. Different mechanisms are active at different arousal levels. Hence in actual practice it may not be sufficient to exercise the system at only one frequency. In any event, with such exercise the brain augments its ability to manage these rhythms autonomously. The mechanisms are clearly already operative in any individual who is not in a coma or in a persistent vegetative state. In AD/HD we are not dealing with gross malfunction. It is a matter of refining the regulatory instrumentalities and extending their dynamic range through direct and repeated minor challenges that take them out of the then-prevailing equilibrium. The brain, thus challenged, will attempt to return to equilibrium. This backing-and-forthing can be seen by analogy to stair-steppers for exercising the body. The more one pushes, the more the instrument pushes back. And thus with the brain. The long-term consequence for the brain is improved self-regulation of arousal, attention, and affect, as will be shown below in the review of the data.

The Brain as Control System

Because this is the core of the model, it is useful to consider it again from a slightly different perspective—that of control system theory. If it is true that the instantaneous degree of rhythmicity of the EEG over a certain frequency range reflects not only the state of the brain (as happenstance) but also the deliberate state of the control system, then an alteration of that state through introduction of a new, external feedback loop may constitute a challenge to that control system. The new state of the system will not correspond to what was determined to be appropriate out of the internal milieu alone. The internal control loops will thus experience a change of state, and hence move to restore the levels appropriate to the previously intended internal state. Introduction of the external feedback loop constitutes a challenge to all the internal control loops that collectively manage organismic arousal and activation. If such a challenge is sufficiently subtle (i.e., continuing to exercise the mechanisms of homeostatic balance without radically altering state), it will result in the strengthening and heightened interaction of the internal control loops. Such strengthening of internal control should manifest itself in amelioration of the principal failure modes of control systems. These include the failure to maintain the proper set point in the steady state, inappropriate transient response, and reduced dynamic range. We therefore refer to this as the regulatory challenge model of EEG biofeedback.

In the case of AD/HD, steady-state set point errors include inappropriate states of activation for the circumstances. This may mean an inability to maintain vigilance on the underactivation side, and it may mean anxiety, perseveration, obsessiveness, and an incapacity for divided attention on the overactivation side. Overarousal may manifest as an exaggerated startle response, distractibility, and impulsivity; underarousal might be reflected in a lack of engagement, inattentiveness, irritability, and thrill-seeking (self-stimulating) behavior. Inappropriate transient response can be seen as an inability to shift attentional states, as impulsivity, as motor and vocal tics, and in terms of low threshold for temper tantrums. Limited dynamic range may show itself in chronic pain patterns (head pain and stomach pain), and in poor sleep patterns. One can take issue with one or more of these identifications (they are clearly oversimplifications). However, the key point is that the brain is a multidimensional control system, and what is known about the standard failure modes of control systems should apply. If the disregulation model is applicable, an identification should be possible between the phenomenology of AD/HD and the ways in which control systems are known to fall short.

If there is one overriding issue in AD/HD it is that of variability. The AD/HD brain is not able to maintain state consistently, and hence it fails to respond properly to the demands put upon it by the environment, or to the demands of internal processing. Thus the problem in AD/HD is not usually one of underarousal specifically, or overarousal, or any other such state. The problem lies more generally in the maintenance and transient response of states under a particular challenge. In the AD/HD child, the prevailing state is somewhat unmoored from the demands of the moment. This is an issue of control itself. Thus all of the phenomenology of AD/HD must map into some identifiable flaw in the control mechanisms. It is quite sufficient that these flaws be predominantly in the functional domain, without an obtrusive structural basis. This implies that AD/HD can be largely a learned response, which in turn holds out the hope that it can also be unlearned. And even if AD/HD is ultimately traceable to some discrete anatomical defect in some receptor property (e.g., Comings et al. 1991), the brain's multifaceted control mechanisms appear to manifest sufficient plasticity that the normal range of function can be acquired through behavioral means in the general case, as we shall show.

Determining the Reinforcement Protocol

According to the model, EEG biofeedback exercises the rhythmic mechanisms by which states are maintained, and thus enhances the brain's capacity to maintain states. As it happens, improved control of states also entails better management of the transient response and improved dynamic range. The clinical burden, then, is to determine which frequency range is in particular need of exercise, in order to move the individual toward a wider range of performance, and a better capacity for maintaining homeostasis. These choices are based on empirically derived patterns that then need to be confirmed with each individual on the basis of his or her response to the training. In this procedure, the client serves as his own control in the ongoing training. The training must therefore be accompanied by continuing assessment of movement according to the relevant dimensions of control.

This is not as problematic as it seems. Since the effect of the training is so global, the individual can be globally assessed. Thus, the training should effect a remediation of sleep problems, pain syndromes, and mood disregulation, in addition to the reported attentional and behavioral difficulties, if the protocol has been appropriately selected and titrated. In the usual cases referred for EEG biofeedback training—which tend toward the more intractable end of the spectrum—there are usually a host of indicators that the training is proceeding either in the proper direction or in one that requires adjustment. In practice, then, the parent and/ or the child are queried on each visit with respect to all the areas in which disregulation is being manifested. The child may also be tested on each occasion for reaction time and variability in reaction time, in a manner that he or she may regard more as a game (even a reward!) than as a test. Finally, the child is monitored as the training is ongoing, with respect to his or her ability to manage the task of training.

In addition to choice of frequency band for reinforcement, there is the need to select a site on the cortex for the EEG training. This choice is heavily based on the research history of this field, which is reviewed below. It has been refined over the years on an empirical basis, guided by insights from neurophysiology regarding localization of function. Most recently, however, these empirically derived approaches have found support in more theoretical models of AD/HD. Malone and colleagues (1994) have proposed a model of AD/HD based on the original work of Tucker and Williamson (1984). This model describes a bilateral control system in which the left hemisphere bears the primary burden for sequential processing and motor planning, and the right hemisphere bears a primary burden for simultaneous appraisal of the environment via parallel processing. This implies a special relationship between the left hemisphere and the frontal lobe, which is in charge of intention and executive function, and a special relationship between the right hemisphere and the parietal lobe, which is in charge of the associational processing of the different primary sensory modalities. The left hemisphere interaction is primarily mediated by dopamine, and to a lesser extent acetylcholine, and the right hemisphere interaction is primarily mediated by norepinephrine, and secondarily by serotonin. Malone and colleagues have proposed that "AD/HD is a bi-hemispheric dysfunction characterized by reduced dopaminergic and excessive noradrenergic functioning" (p. 181). The effect of stimulants in general, and methylphenidate (Ritalin) in particular, is ascribed to up-regulation of dopamine function as well as down-regulation of norepinephrine function, leading to "increased control over the allocation of attentional resources between hemispheres" (p. 181).

This hypothesis is very congenial to what we are proposing as a mechanism for EEG biofeedback. The stimulant medications do not supply a missing neurotransmitter, as is often falsely represented to a naive public (i.e., Ritalin as vitamin R). They alter set points of functioning (i.e., general level of activation or arousal) to effect improved control. The same is true of EEG biofeedback, except that in this case the brain responds to the operant conditioning challenge by learning a new operating capability (increased stability as well as improved transient response and dynamic range). Because the process is learned, the brain can continue to draw on its new capacity (and to reinforce it through use) over the longer term.

Cerebral Failure Modes

The Tucker and Williamson model has implications for the failure modes of the left and right hemispheres. Being in charge of sequential processing, the left hemisphere manages tonic activation, vigilance, and the set point of motor system poise. The right hemisphere, oriented toward appraisal of new inputs, is in charge of phasic arousal, startle response, and habituation. The left hemisphere is forward-looking in time, and hence is in charge of maintaining vigilance, such as we measure in continuous performance tests. It fails by becoming inattentive, or hyperfocused and perseverative. It is also subject to anxiety (worry) and depression (in the traditional cognitive sense of helplessness and hopelessness). When sequential processing is not well managed, the whole chain of events leading from intention to action may not run smoothly, leading to behavioral disinhibition, as in hyperactivity, as well as motor and vocal tics. (There can also be failures of integration of function, leading to stuttering and dyslexia.) In other situations, the subject may experience chronic effort in processing and may persistently hover near the threshold of cognitive fatigue, or ultimately collapse into fatigue.

The right hemisphere, on the other hand, may fail by being impulsive and distractible. It may manifest a lack of continuity in state. Whereas the left hemisphere fails by "collapsing inward" and blaming itself, the right hemisphere fails outwardly, blaming the world. Thus it is the right hemisphere that tantrums and manifests explosive behavior. The right hemisphere owns mania and hysteria. In terms of anxiety, it responds with fear and dread. In terms of depression, the right hemisphere manifests agitation, and it may turn outwardly violent or suicidal. There are also right-side cognitive deficits (such as difficulty with spatial relationships, geometry, word problems, and appraisal of facial expressions) that can be indicators of right-side dysfunction.

It must be admitted that although there is merit to the use of neurophysiological models to determine training protocols, these still represent gross simplifications at the present state of maturity of the field. We see much more evidence for hemispheric specificity when things don't work well. In a well-tempered brain, the functions to be addressed in the training are so well integrated that it is much more difficult to categorize the separate roles of each hemisphere. Additionally, physiological arousal and activation are not independent, but are in fact closely coupled. Thus, appealing to one hemisphere with the training also involves the other. Additionally, after the specific deficits in hemispheric function have been addressed, the remaining challenge is to train interhemispheric communication.

In any event, the Malone model serves as a guide for selecting initial training sites that have been graced with clinical success. Using this model, problems of underactivation, depression, and inattention are primarily addressed with left-side training at the higher frequencies (above nominally 15 Hz) in order to shift the subject to external focus of attention and to appropriate levels of activation and arousal. Correspondingly, the problem of impulsivity, thrill-seeking behavior, as well as many of the more severe behavioral problems associated with AD/HD are primarily addressed with right-side training at the lower frequencies (below nominally 15 Hz), which are seen to be more calming and stabilizing. Ultimately, as behavior and range of function normalize, training will commonly be done on both sides to bring the brain into better bihemispheric communication.

A Review of the Literature

The field of EEG biofeedback has had a remarkable history, and it is therefore appropriate to review the literature in order to reconstruct some of the discoveries that relate to the model presented here, and to promote a deeper level of understanding. The original research in this field related to the study of sleep. Initially, it was thought that sleep was simply a matter of the passive withdrawal of wakefulness. Later, it was recognized that there was active management by the brain not only of entry into sleep, but of the various sleep stages. Pavlov had found originally that sleep could be behaviorally induced by means of an operant conditioning paradigm. That proved it was subject to an active process, which he referred to as *internal inhibition* (see Wyrwicka et al. 1962).

In an extension of this work many years later, Sterman and colleagues set about to study the process of internal inhibition of the motor system, again with an operant conditioning design (Roth et al. 1967, Sterman and Wyrwicka 1967, Sterman et al. 1969b, Wyrwicka and Sterman 1968). After cats were trained to obtain food through a bar press, they were then taught to inhibit the bar press upon presentation of a high-frequency tone. During the presentation of the tone, cats were not rewarded for a bar press, but were forced to wait until the tone ceased. Pressing the bar during the tone resulted in extension of the duration of the tone. During periods of resulting motor stillness, as the cats awaited cessation of the tone and their ultimate reward, bursts of rhythmic activity were observed on the sensorimotor area of cortex. Accordingly, this was referred to as the sensorimotor rhythm (SMR). An analogy can be drawn to the alpha rhythm, which is seen in the visual cortex when the visual system is not being stimulated (Andersen and Andersson 1968). Thus, the SMR appeared to be another manifestation of an idling system, only in this case the dominant frequency was higher, in the range of 12 to 15Hz (versus 8 to 12 Hz for alpha).

In the next phase of the work, the attempt was made to train the EEG rather than the behavior (Sterman and Wyrwicka 1967, Wyrwicka and Sterman 1968). Not only was this graced with success, but it was found to be even easier to train the EEG than it was to train the behavior. Of course, the EEG phenomenon of SMR bursts required the cats to be motorically idle (see also Chase and Harper 1971). Thus, the EEG and the behavior were always co-occurring. Here was the first reported instance of behavior being altered by means of EEG training. And it was happening in cats, which were undoubtedly unaware of the subterfuge being perpetrated on them. Additionally, it became clear that voluntary behavior was not the only thing being altered. Sleep was affected as well (Sterman et al. 1970). And surely the cats could not have voluntarily altered their sleep patterns as a result of the training.

At this point, serendipity intervened. The National Aeronautics and Space Administration (NASA) was having difficulty in the Apollo program with its astronauts, who were episodically exhibiting symptoms of mental disorientation in space (a well-kept secret at the time). The service module rocket fuel, a hydrazine compound known to be toxic, was thought to be responsible. Sterman was asked to evaluate the subconvulsive effects of the substance in his cats. In mapping out the dose-response curve, it was found in the midst of the series of experiments that the original dose-response curve bifurcated into two. There were clearly now two populations of cats in terms of their response to this substance where there previously had been only one. Upon checking records, it became clear that a subgroup of cats that were more resistant to seizures from the hydrazine challenge had been previously trained to produce the SMR (Sterman 1976, Sterman et al. 1969a). Thus, unequivocally, heightened seizure threshold could be trained by means of a behavioral technique. Again, note must be taken of the fact that the cats had no biased interest in this experiment, that the experiment inadvertently turned out to be a completely controlled design, and that the researcher was truly blinded in this case.

This discovery was followed by replications, first in cats (Sterman et al. 1977), then in primates (Sterman et al. 1978), and finally in man (Sterman and Friar 1972, Sterman et al. 1974). Controlled studies followed, with small subject populations (Lubar et al. 1981, Sterman and MacDonald 1978). The results were also replicated in other research centers (Cabral and Scott 1976, Ellertson and Klove 1976, Finley 1976, Finley et al. 1975, Kott et al. 1979, Kuhlman 1978, Kuhlman and Allison 1977, Lubar and Bahler 1976, Seifert and Lubar 1975, Tansey 1985, Tozzo et al. 1988). The latest controlled study on seizures was published by Lantz and Sterman in 1988. (A review of this history can be found in Sterman [1996].)

Already early on during the work on seizures, it was recognized that the effect on motor inhibition in seizure disorders could have implications for hyperactivity, and it was observed that if the epileptic subject also exhibited hyperactivity, then the latter remediated with the training as well. Lubar and Shouse (1976) conducted the first systematic study of EEG biofeedback with hyperactivity in the absence of seizure history. A reversal design was used as a control. Behaviors responded to the contingent training. The effect of the training was found to be greater than that of Ritalin alone. This work was followed by a more comprehensive study (Shouse and Lubar 1979). Four subjects were monitored for classroom behavior as a measure. Three out of the four children responded to the training. Combining the drugs with the biofeedback showed greater effects than had been achieved with the drugs alone, and withdrawal of the medications showed that behaviors could be sustained. A subsequent study focused on left-hemisphere learning disabilities and attentional deficits (Lubar and Lubar 1984). Six boys were trained long-term with SMR training (12 to 14 Hz) following the earlier work, and with beta training (16 to 20 Hz) for increased arousal and focused attention. There was concurrent inhibition of excessive EEG amplitude in the 4- to 7-Hz regime. This was motivated by the observation that hyperactivity, learning disabilities, and seizures would often manifest with elevated low-frequency amplitudes. The explicit down-training of such amplitudes was undertaken in an effort to normalize function through normalizing the EEG. The study was compromised by the fact that the children were obtaining concurrent remedial academic training. However, it should be noted that the academic training had been ongoing, and the effect of adding the biofeedback was striking in several of the cases.

There were replications of this work by Tansey and Bruner (1983) and by Tansey (1985, 1990). The first of these was a single case study of a child with both hyperactivity and learning disabilities, and it used both conventional electromyogram (EMG) (muscle relaxation) and EEG biofeedback training. The second study was based on four subjects. However, the focus here was on learning disabilities rather than attentional deficits. This was the first study in which IQ improvements were documented with the EEG training. The third report was on twenty four subjects, of whom eleven had been diagnosed as neurologically impaired, eleven were judged perceptually impaired, and only two were diagnosed with ADD. The average Wechsler Intelligence Scale for Children (WISC-R) full-scale IQ score improved by nineteen points, with comparable improvements in performance IQ (+19) and verbal IQ (+16). The improvements were biased toward those areas in largest deficit at the outset.

Unfortunately, the mid-1980s were the time when the National Institutes of Health (NIH) turned away from funding behavioral interventions in order to promote more research on basic biochemistry of neural systems. The field of EEG biofeedback also suffered from a self-inflicted wound. It was expected that if the EEG amplitude is reinforced in training, then enhanced EEG amplitudes should eventuate. A changed EEG in response to the training had indeed been found in the cats (in which the incidence, though not necessarily the amplitude, of SMR bursts increased with reinforcement), and that set the expectations for human subjects. Thus, the expectation of increased EEG amplitude in the steady state among trained subjects became a litmus test for whether EEG training had actually taken place. This turned out to have been a mistake. Alas, the normal human EEG does not show the dramatic SMR spindles seen in the waking cat EEG. Thus, they should hardly have been expected to emerge with the training. (Actually, they do show up at night during stage II sleep, where they are called sleep spindles. These indeed did show increased incidence with the training! [Sterman and Shouse 1980].)

Moreover, human work was with subjects who came in with (medically uncontrolled) epilepsy. It wasn't chemically induced. These people showed the typical EEG phenomena we associate with epilepsy, namely an EEG that is elevated in amplitude, particularly at the lower frequencies (less than 10 Hz). If the training is truly efficacious, one would expect the EEG to normalize, which means that all the frequency components should come down in amplitude. This would mean principally the lower frequencies that are most significantly elevated, but the argument applies to the whole frequency range (because the irregular low frequency activity is accompanied by higher Fourier components). This is indeed what was observed in many instances (Wyler et al. 1976), whereas in others the EEG amplitude in the training band increased as expected by researchers at the time. The failure to observe EEG changes with consistency unfortunately relegated the work to temporary oblivion, and the dramatic effects of the training were written off to "nonspecific" effects that were not further specified (Quy et al. 1979). The shifting tides of research interest helped to make sure that this promising work would remain buried for a time as a relic of modern science.

Absent funding, the work continued only in a few clinical settings, with the exception of Lubar at the University of Tennessee, who continued despite an adverse funding climate. Lubar published a long-term follow-up on his early work on ADD, which demonstrated that the training had long-term favorable effects (Lubar 1995). Starting in about

1989, with the development of a new generation of instrumentation for clinical use, there was a rekindling of interest among a new group of clinicians. Linden and colleagues (1996) reported on an earlier controlled study in which a significant increase in IQ score of nine points was found for an experimental group of nine children versus a control group of nine (p <.05). The experimental group also showed significant improvement in inattentiveness according to parental ratings. For his Ph.D. dissertation, Cartozzo and colleagues (1995) performed a controlled study with fifteen AD/HD children (eight experimentals and seven controls) using the Arithmetic, Coding, and Digit Span subtests of the WISC-R, the T.O.V.A. continuous performance test (CPT, see below), the AD/HD Rating Scale, and the Child Attention Profile (CAP) as measures. The controls were exposed to a normal video game as an attention control. Significant improvements were seen in the inattention scale of the CAP. Improvements in the overactivity scale were negated by the fact that the control group improved as well! The same was true of the AD/HD Rating Scale, in which the control group improved in stellar fashion (p <.001!), thus neutralizing the (likewise significant) improvement in the treatment group. The attention score of the T.O.V.A., and the WISC subtests improved significantly only in the treatment group. These results will be discussed further below.

Rossiter and LaVaque (1995) performed a controlled study in which EEG biofeedback was compared to stimulant medication (discussed below). Alhambra and colleagues (1995) performed an outcome study with numerous measures in which broad efficacy of the training was documented. And finally, Thorpe (1997) reviewed data from a number of clinical settings all using the same protocols, and all using the T.O.V.A. CPT as a measure. Significant improvements were documented in the inattention and impulsivity scores. The momentum in the field clearly does not come from these few formal studies that have been done, many of which could be critiqued on various methodological grounds, as well as on group size. Rather, the momentum comes from clinicians communicating with one another about the results that they are achieving with this technique. There are now an estimated 2,000 professionals active in this field around the world. Our own involvement began in 1985 with development of a suitable EEG biofeedback instrument. We began our clinical work in 1988. This work by now encompasses several thousand case histories at our home office, and many tens of thousands in other practices employing identical protocols.

The Protocols

Historically, EEG biofeedback was initially restricted to training of the 12- to 15-Hz region of frequencies at sensorimotor cortex, with bipolar placement at C3-T3. (This will be referred to as SMR training in the following.) Subsequently, Sterman also evaluated the higher frequency regime of 15 to 18 Hz (called beta training, below) (Sterman and MacDonald 1978). Lubar initially adopted the same scheme, and found the higher frequency training useful for focused attention, whereas the SMR training was used for control of hyperactivity. Tansey adopted training on the midline, with a large-area electrode reaching forward and aft of Cz, the central midline placement, in order to train the supplementary motor area, and he centered his training band on 14 Hz. In time, Lubar (1991) found with quantitative EEG evaluations that the disregulations seen in the EEGs of AD/HD children appeared to reach an extremum on the center line, so he adopted this placement as well.

The protocols used in the work to be reviewed here evolved from the above. Training with bipolar placements at C3-T3 was in time replaced with referential placement at C3 with ear reference. Our initial work was largely with the beta band of 15 to 18 Hz. For behavioral control we added training in the SMR band at Cz, following Tansey. Later, we observed that for the benefits we sought from training at Cz, stronger effects could be elicited with training at C4. Then it emerged that the left hemisphere and the right responded in certain characteristic ways to this challenge. Hence, hemispheric specificity became a central organizing principle for protocol selection in our work. Training became a matter of deciding which hemisphere most needed attention. The pattern of training the left hemisphere at the higher band, and the right hemisphere at the lower, was almost invariably observed. Eventually, both hemispheres were trained in most subjects either because the issues were bilateral, or in order to help with hemispheric balance. Training was still concentrated on the sensorimotor strip, which seemed to yield the minimum of unpredictable and untoward effects.

Two further refinements bring us up to the present. The training was leaving out the frontal lobe, which clearly plays a role in AD/HD, and might therefore play a role in the training as well. Following Malone, the first refinement was to train the frontal lobe in bipolar placement with the sensorimotor strip (C3-Fp1). Similarly, the right hemisphere was trained with bipolar placement involving the parietal lobe (C4-Pz). These placements sometimes yielded stronger effects than training on the sensorimotor strip alone. By training both sites simultaneously, one is presumably challenging the cortical communication loops between those sites, thus exercising the critical relationships between frontal and left side, and between parietal and right side. Finally, training the communications loop between the right sensorimotor strip and prefrontal has also been fruitful (C4-Fp1), thus training the communication between frontal and right side.

A second refinement was to tailor the reward frequency band in small steps (0.5-Hz) until it was optimized for each individual. In such optimization, it is almost invariably found that the left-side training requires higher frequencies than the right, confirming the pattern that had become established during all the years when fixed reinforcement bands were employed. This may be due to the fact that left hemisphere function is more localized, and hence tends to get organized at higher (spatial and temporal) frequencies. It may also have to do with the postulated failure modes, namely that the left hemisphere needs up-training to address its failures, and the right needs down-training for stabilization and control. Localized injury, such as in traumatic brain injury or pediatric stroke, or a focal seizure does, of course, also have specific implications for training sites. Similarly, a presumptively localized dysfunction, such as an articulation disorder, would prompt training on the appropriate site (Broca's area, in this instance). Such choices generally lead to rapid empirical confirmation (or else the effort would be abandoned).

In addition to the reward frequency band, there are also two inhibit bands, so that the reward is inhibited if the EEG amplitude exceeds some threshold in the other bands. Subjects are inhibited for excessive amplitudes in the low-frequency regime of 4 to 7 Hz or 2 to 7 Hz, where excesses are often seen in epilepsy, in AD/HD, and in cases of learning disabilities. Rewards are also inhibited for elevated amplitudes in the high frequency regime of 22 to 30 Hz, where muscle tension, anxiety, dietary sensitivities, and drug dependence may manifest. The use of inhibits goes back to the early days of Sterman's work, where they were used in order to keep from rewarding the subject for interictal activity (Sterman et al. 1974). Such irregular interictal or paroxysmal EEGs contain a broad range of frequencies, including in particular the training band, which could lead to inadvertent rewards for such inappropriate activity. Since in Sterman's approach only extreme excursions in SMR amplitude were rewarded, the reward rate was low, making false rewards a significant issue. In the AD/HD child, the elevated low-frequency activity may be always present in the waking EEG, as opposed to being episodic, as in epilepsy. Such elevated low-frequency amplitude could be the signature of a chronic underarousal condition, or simply of sleep debt, but it can also follow from birth injury or even from emotional trauma. In any event, by alerting the child to its magnitude, control may be achieved over time in a kind of EEG-shaping paradigm.

In fact, the EEG-shaping model of EEG biofeedback has dominated this field from the early days. There are problems with this, however. A review of the literature reveals that changes in the EEG that track the specific protocol are not consistently observed with the EEG training. It was already pointed out that this inconsistency helped to derail the field in its earlier struggle for recognition. That dismal history notwithstanding, even today insufficient formal attention is being paid to this disagreeable inconsistency by enthusiastic clinicians and researchers. If the EEG is manifestly abnormal, as in elevated low-frequency amplitudes, then normalization to at least some degree is usually observed. But the amplitude in the SMR or beta regime of training frequencies may not track the protocol. We have already suggested a way out of this dilemma. The EEG tends to normalize with the training, wherever that may lie (Kuhlman 1978). Also, the beta and SMR training are intended to train mechanisms, not specifically to normalize the EEG. Hence, the EEG does not have to be clearly abnormal to justify this intervention. The information necessary for accomplishing the EEG biofeedback challenge is always present in the EEG, irrespective of any pathology that may prevail. The information being processed from the reward bands is a concomitant of function, not of dysfunction.

The reward signal is usually recovered with a digital filter or fast Fourier transform technique. The filtered signal is rectified and smoothed, and then mapped into some kind of visual display and/or auditory signals. Typically, both continuous representations of the reward and inhibit waveforms are presented, as well as discrete rewards for additional reinforcement. The information in the reward band may also be presented as a continuous tactile stimulus, or as a continuous auditory signal, in both cases with a linear transfer function. The auditory reward has to be translated up in frequency to be audible. In our implementation, an 80-Hz carrier is modulated with the waveform in the reward band. In this manner, the individual can track his EEG with minimum delay. With such prompt feedback of an information-rich signal, an individual's physiology may respond in a frequency-specific manner within mere minutes. Effects traceable to changes in state induced by the training are often reported by the end of a single 30-minute session. Training is conducted from one to ten times per week, with three sessions per week the most common. Comprehensive reassessment is done at twenty-session intervals and at completion of the training.

CONFIRMING CLINICAL AND RESEARCH DATA

Outcome Study, 1991

A formal evaluation of this clinical approach was undertaken at our center in 1990 and 1991. The study was undertaken to be representative of what was actually being done in the clinical setting. And it used paying clients. Objectivity was sought by having all evaluations done by an independent clinical psychologist (Clifford Marks) who had no stake in our operation. Only the key findings are reviewed here. The full report on the study is available on the Internet (Othmer et al. 1992), or as a monograph from EEG Spectrum, a center for neurofeedback services and research. No attempt was made to publish these results in a refereed journal. Consultation with various authorities in the field of AD/HD research at that time persuaded us that publication of such startling results would not be countenanced by journal editors unless they were the outcome of a fully controlled experimental design. Nevertheless, the confirmation of these findings in numerous clinical settings and in controlled studies performed by others in subsequent years retrospectively justifies a careful review of this early study.

Marks determined at his sole discretion what measures were to be used in the assessment. Objectivity was sought by using only quantifiable performance measures, which meant that no behavioral rating scales were employed. Marks chose the WISC-R, Wide Range Achievement Test (WRAT), Benton Visual Retention Test, the Tapping Subtest of the Harris Tests of Lateral Dominance, and the Peabody Picture Vocabulary Test.

The children accepted into the study were those whose insurance was willing to cover the cost of assessments. The training was done on a reduced-fee basis whenever necessary. Age range was 6 to 16. Eighteen subjects were accepted into the study, but three dropped out early in the training. Fifteen completed the training, and were retested. Of these, fourteen were referred for AD/HD, and one for learning difficulties and dysthymia traceable to birth injury. Seven of the fourteen were hyperactive. Of the fifteen, seven also had learning disabilities; six also met criteria for oppositional-defiant disorder (ODD), and two for conduct disorder (CD). Thirteen of the fifteen reported sleep difficulties of various kinds, including four cases of sleepwalking and sleep talking, two of sleep anxiety, and three of nocturnal enuresis. Five of the children reported chronic headaches. There were three cases of chronic anxiety, and four of dysthymia or childhood depression; one child had obvious motor tics. Two of the children were on Ritalin at the outset, and one on imipramine. One child was on the Feingold diet, and two children were in concurrent psychotherapy or educational therapy.

Results of pre-post testing on the WISC-R are shown in Figure 10–1. Retesting took place typically nine months after the pretest, but at minimum the test-retest interval was six months. The pretest average full-scale IQ score was 107, showing the group to be generally intellectually competent. The common ADD pattern is observed, with the "ACID test" categories scoring low: Arithmetic, Coding, Information, and Digit Span. The essential character of the curve is still reflected in the posttest. However, the overall level of performance has been significantly enhanced, with the average posttest IQ score now at 130, for an average increase of twenty three points. If one considers only the subtest scores that started out in deficit, which is perhaps more relevant to our interests, one obtains the results shown in Figure 10–2. The number of data points involved in each subtest is indicated. Thus, for example, six subjects were in deficit at the outset in terms of arithmetic score, and these improved by an average of six points. The improve-

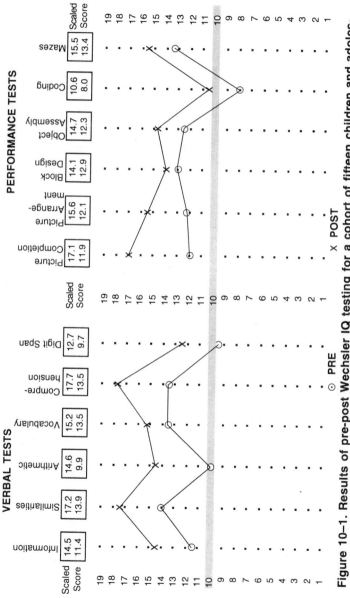

Figure 10–1. Results of pre-post Wechsler IQ testing for a cohort of fifteen children and adolescents. Pretest data show the expected AD/HD pattern. Posttesting shows function to be globally elevated. Average IQ score improvement was twenty-three points, from 107 to 130.

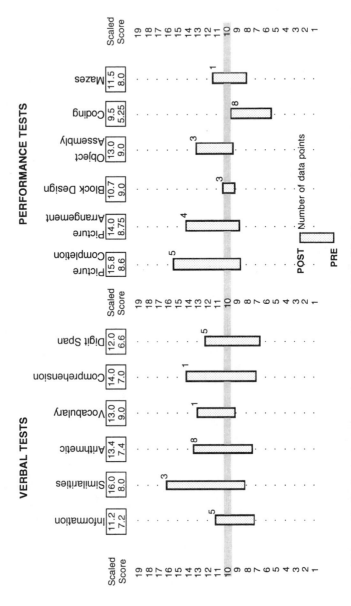

Figure 10–2. Average pre-post change in WISC-R subtest scores for all those who initially tested in deficit. The number of data points making up each average is indicated.

ment cannot be written off to test-retest effects, since the trial is stopped after three errors. To improve by six points, the child has to be into new ground in the test. We attribute the improvement to an enhanced ability for the child to maintain state in general, and to increased working memory in particular. This is also the implication of the improved Digit Span performance, where those in deficit improved by 5.4 units. Test-retest issues cannot be involved here. If a child cannot remember strings of numbers for 20 seconds, he is not going to remember them for six months.

A comparison of verbal and performance WISC-R IQ is shown in Figure 10–3, in which one is plotted against the other. Change along a 45-degree line would mean that the performance and the verbal improvements were equal. Surprisingly, most subjects did in fact show comparable change in both areas. This was unexpected in view of the fact that nearly all of the training was done on the left side. Thus we have evidence that training even on one side in fact impinges on function in both hemispheres. This is an important finding, one that is unlikely to be replicated in our office. Now that we know how to train both hemispheres to get better results, it would be unethical to return to the use of a single protocol for purposes merely of research.

Results of IQ improvements as a function of starting value in IQ show the expected dependence that the lowest starting scores exhibit the largest gains. This is shown in Figure 10–4. At the high end, the results may be affected by the fact that the WISC has a headroom limit of 165 in IQ. Significantly, the curve has not shown any tendency to turn over at the low end of IQ. One wonders what this technique might offer for even lower starting IQs. We are not aware of any systematic study. However, we know of one case of 70 IQ that was remeasured after a year of training at 112. One is certainly encouraged by these data to consider an evaluation even with mildly mentally retarded children.

The WRAT yielded more variable outcomes than the WISC.

Only ten of the fifteen children were evaluated with the WRAT. In the reading test, only one child scored below grade level at the outset. That child improved more than three grade levels with the training, and reached age-appropriate norms. Five other children significantly advanced their reading performance above grade level, in rank order by 5.6 years, 4.5 years, 4.2 years, 3.5 years, and 2 years. In arithmetic, nine out of the

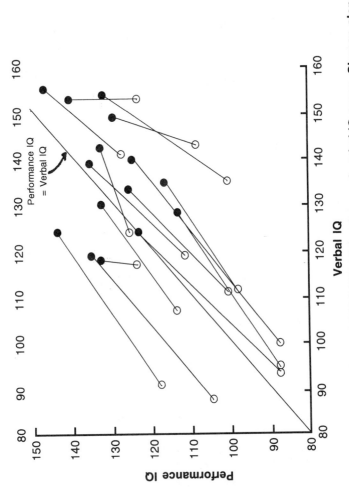

Figure 10–3. Comparison of WISC-R performance and verbal IQ score. Change along the 45-degree line would indicate comparable change in both. Such is seen to be the pattern for most of the subjects, even though left-side training strongly predominated.

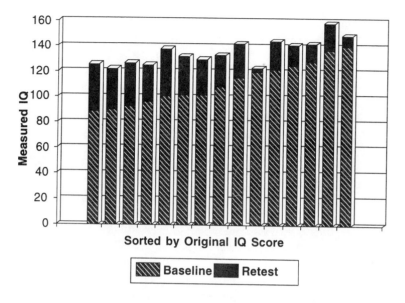

Figure 10–4. WISC-R changes for all the subjects, ordered by initial value of IQ score. The largest gains are shown for those with the lowest starting values. At the highest values, results may be compromised by the headroom limit of the WISC.

ten scored in deficit at the outset. After training, five had shown significant improvement: 7.6 years, 2.7 years, 2.3 years, 2 years, and 1.6 years. Two more treaded water, with gains of one year.

The Peabody Picture Vocabulary Test yielded mixed results. Five subjects were at the maximum Peabody IQ of 145, where the test lost discrimination. Four subjects showed a general trend similar to that of the WISC, as would be expected. However, five subjects actually showed declines in IQ, in contrast to the WISC. All but three showed a higher WISC IQ than Peabody IQ. No explanation for these results is offered. However, the fact that some scores declined in the face of a general improvement in test scores is taken to be significant. It is conceivable that some right-hemisphere function was compromised with a nearly exclusive focus on left hemisphere training.

Results for the Benton Visual Retention Test are shown in Figure 10–5. The contrast to the WISC-R is striking, in that this group manifests a significant deficit in visual retention. As with IQ score, however, the observed improvement was significant. Six subjects testing at average or below at the outset ended up testing superior. This is perhaps another indicator that the training is helpful with maintenance of state, thus improving short-term memory. Only fourteen subjects were given the pretest. For the record, the fifteenth tested at very superior on the retest. And for the record also, the child who only improved from defective to borderline on this test nevertheless went on to thrive academically. More training was recommended to this family on the basis of this result, but the parents did not see the need.

The Tapping Subtest of the Harris Tests of Lateral Dominance was most revealing. The results are shown in Figure 10–6. The average improvement in tapping performance was 20 percent. The median improvement, however, was 40 percent, and three subjects showed improvements of more than 100 percent. Even more revealing, however, was the trend in laterality implied by these changes. The Harris criterion for laterality is that one hand exceeds the other by 20 percent or more in tapping score. The criterion lines are also indicated in the figure. It appears that laterality normalizes. This is more readily seen in Figure 10–7, where the same data are replotted in terms of right-hand to left-hand ratio. Whereas before the training there is a broad distribution of ratios, after the training the distribution collapses. The outliers are gone, and there is a depletion of mixed dominance. Most became more confirmed right-handers, with a peak in the range of 20 to 40 percent better right-hand performance. Presumably, the residual left-handers are the "true" left-handers.

This test is perhaps the most robust in terms of providing evidence for change at the control system level. The other tests could all have been affected favorably by factors such as motivation and compliance, which manifestly also improved with the training. However, it is difficult to argue that the ratio of right-hand to left-hand performance could be altered by motivational and compliance issues. These results may be understandable on the basis of the first behavioral indicators we have of nascent laterality: fetal thumbsucking. In a study using ultrasound, Hepper and colleagues (1990) found that some 95 percent of fetuses prefer their right thumb prior to birth, but only 85 percent do so afterward. The

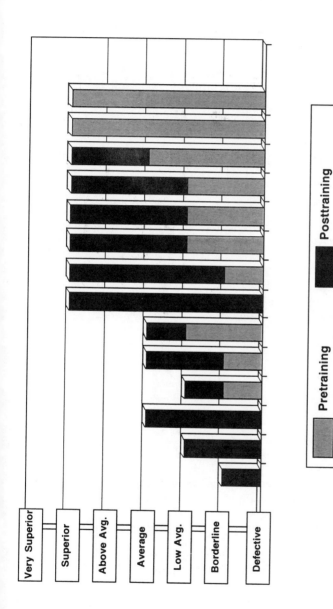

Figure 10–5. Results are shown for the Benton Visual Retention Test, where the subject population showed significant deficits at the outset.

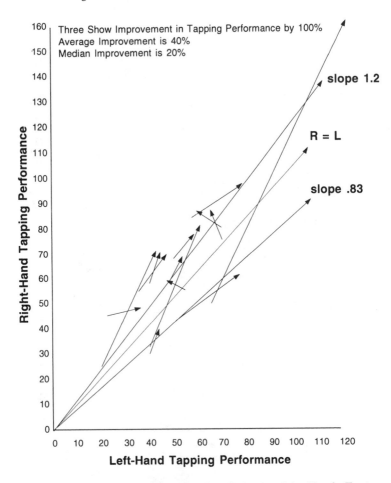

Figure 10–6. Results of the Tapping Subtest of the Harris Tests of Lateral Dominance. Right and left dominance are indicated if the dominant hand exceeds the other by 20%. A trend toward right-hand dominance with the training is indicated.

difference may be attributable to minor head injury or anoxia from the birth process. If the dominant hemisphere is injured, the other may take over, leading either to mixed or to opposite laterality. It is congenial to propose that the functional deficit resulting from birth

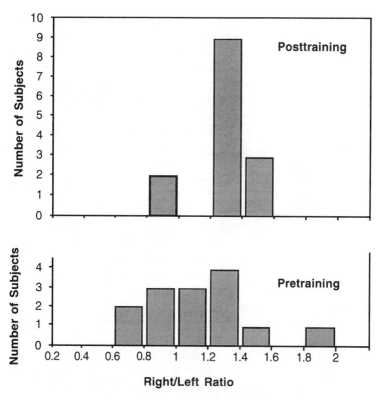

Figure 10–7. Ratio of right-to-left hand performance in the Tapping Test before and after EEG training. Normalization of laterality is indicated.

trauma is remediated by the EEG training, restoring the capacity for resumption of native dominance. The latter is already revealed by such simple challenges as the tapping test. In more complicated tasks such as writing, the shift in laterality may not be as evident, since matters are biased by the extensive practice that must have occurred in the process of learning to write.

The absence of behavioral measures has already been alluded to. An attempt was made, however, to get feedback from the families after about a year. This was done in a manner so as to elicit the parents' own reactions, with a minimum of prompting with questions. Out of this came the finding that the most significant improvement was in terms of self-esteem of the child. The overall results are shown in Figure 10–8. In each category, a plus was given for a favorable parental rating; two pluses for a rave review, and a minus for things that were still problem areas. A given child could therefore receive both a plus and a minus in the same category.

The data of Figure 10–8 are arbitrarily divided into two categories: those in which significant benefit was seen and little residual problem, and those in which a significant difficulty still remained. The positive ratings are of course gratifying. In connection with the category of school grades it should be observed that five of the fifteen children were in ungraded environments. In fact these five children did well academically after the training also, thus making improved school performance a nearly universal finding for this group. The residual issues were those related to behavior, to stability of mood, to reading performance, and to math performance. In retrospect, this is not surprising, given the limited protocol employed in this study. The refinements added to the EEG training subsequent to this study have yielded better outcomes in the behavioral domain, in mood management, and in more global functioning. With respect to reading and math, it must be kept in mind that improving the child's functionality does not by itself address the problem of the child lagging academically. Other interventions must also be brought to bear.

Subsequent to this formal follow-up, some parents have gotten in touch with us regarding the continuing progress of their children. This is, of course, a biased sample, but these parents by and large recognize the EEG biofeedback training to have been a turning point in their children's lives.

Continuous Performance Test Results

A neurophysiologically based technique such as EEG biofeedback should be assessed with a neurophysiological measure. The standard continuous performance test, already commonly used for titration of stimulant medication in AD/HD children, is an appropriate test vehicle in that it assesses inattention (vigilance), impulsivity, response time, and variability in a manner that is highly repeatable, manifests no practice effect, and is entirely computer-administered and scored. We have been

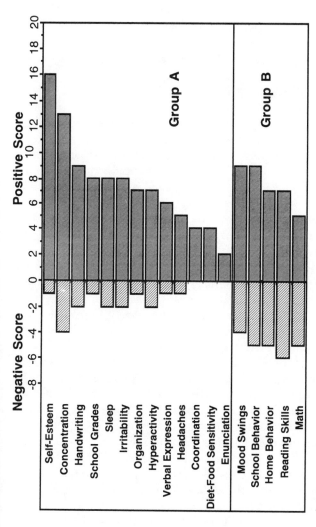

Figure 10–8. Results of informal follow-up with parents nominally one year after the training was completed. Indications of significant positive change were given a plus (major improvements were given ++), and residual problem areas were given a minus. The categories divided into those in which few problems remained, and those which were still issues to be addressed.

using the Test of Variables of Attention (T.O.V.A.) (Greenberg 1987) since 1991 to monitor the effects of the training. This is somewhat different from the standard usage in helping to diagnose AD/HD. In application to EEG biofeedback, one is not concerned with the binary choice of whether to medicate or not. Rather, the issue is in the analog rather than the digital domain: How does one make a particular nervous system function better? Hence, it is a matter first of characterizing the strengths and weaknesses of a particular nervous constitution. In broad brush, the technique allows us to determine whether a subject tends to be fast and impulsive, or slow and inattentive. These basic functional styles of the nervous system have direct implications for training protocol. The slow and inattentive subtype will tend to be given the higher-frequency training on the left side, whereas the fast and impulsive type will more likely respond to the lower frequency training on the right. This is consistent with the Malone model.

Beyond these obvious distinctions, more subtle issues can also be determined. The test is a good measure of variability, and it even gives clues to conduct disorder, to anxiety, and to a pattern of response that could be called "hyperfocus." If the test always confirmed one's clinical impressions through interview and other testing, then one would clinical not need it. However, the T.O.V.A. often yields clues that may have been missed in other parts of the assessment. When that is the case, the T.O.V.A. results generally need to be taken seriously. In other words, the overall picture that emerges regarding the client must accommodate the T.O.V.A. data.

Since we have been using the T.O.V.A. routinely in our assessments since 1991, it is a simple experiment of nature to survey the results for children and adults referred for attentional difficulties (though not necessarily having been diagnosed with AD/HD). These results are summarized in Figure 10–9 for the four subscales of the T.O.V.A. Results are presented in terms of standard scores, where the norm is 100, and the standard deviation 15. Data have been arbitrarily truncated at four standard deviations (standard score of 40), and every value less than that has been arbitrarily assigned the value 40. The most consistent results are shown for impulsivity. For those in most severe deficit (four standard deviations), the average improvement is three standard deviations. It is two standard deviations for inattention and variability. Moreover, the entire population benefits, regardless of starting point. That is, the train-

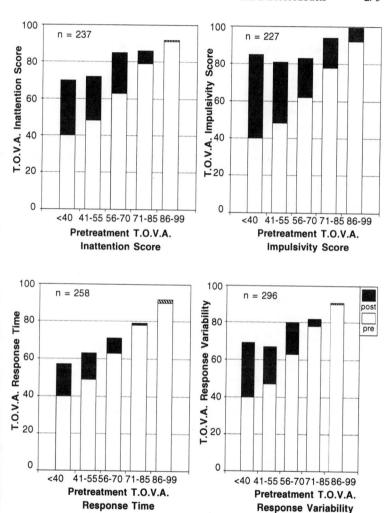

Figure 10–9. Results of pre-post testing with the T.O.V.A., a continuous performance test, for 342 subjects. Results are shown for the four subtests of the T.O.V.A. in terms of standard scores, for which norms are 100, and the standard deviation 15. Results are highly significant, and exhibit substantial effect size for those in significant deficit in any area.

ing is not merely a means of restoring function where it is deficient, but rather a means of enhancing the functionality of most nervous systems.

This can be seen more readily in Figure 10-10, where every subject history comprising the data of Figure 10-9 has been plotted individually for impulsivity. The data are ranked in the order of starting value of impulsivity. Several features are noteworthy. First of all, many subjects end up testing above norms after training, regardless of their starting point. This tends to support the "functional deficit" model of AD/HD. That is, after training there may be no identifiable residual deficit, according to the T.O.V.A., in these subjects. This would not be expected if there were a significant organic flaw underpinning the disorder. Of course, this does not rule out organic problems as causative for AD/HD, which is a condition of heterogeneous etiology. Many other subjects shown in Figure 10-10 do not thrive as well with the training, and organic issues such as traumatic brain injury may be at issue. It is nevertheless significant that AD/HD symptomatology can arise even absent manifest organic injury.

Figure 10-10 also shows some scores declining after training. Some of these are attributable to the vagaries of life, and with special conditions prevailing on retest. A child may be in recovery from an illness, excited about a return trip home after the retest, and so on. The T.O.V.A. also presents us with a difficulty not normally incurred in its application to titration of medication. Since the training often takes months, a child may be bumped into another age bracket for the norms. When the training takes six months or more, this is appropriate, but when the training takes only a month or two, it would be inappropriate to assign a one-year change in maturity. This is particularly an issue with younger children. With adults, age-bracket crossover can also be a problem, since decade-wide norms are used. When all is said and done, however, a number of the declining test scores are probably quite real, indicating that the issue of impulsivity has not been successfully addressed, and even exacerbated, with the training in some cases.

These data illustrate the specificity of the training protocol. In the relevant cases of declining test scores, the primary clinical issue may have been sleep regulation, pain management, anger control, conduct disorder, or depression, rather than the attention or impulsivity problems specifically. Thus, clients or their family may feel that their needs have been addressed even though impulsivity is still an issue on retest. If training

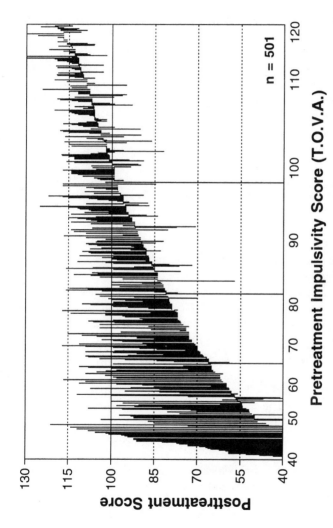

Figure 10–10. Individual results in terms of T.O.V.A. impulsivity are shown as standard scores for 501 subjects. Every subject is shown as a separate line on the graph, ordered by starting value of impulsivity. The graph reveals the individual variation in response to the training, including declines in some scores with training.

were to continue with a focus on impulsivity, it is likely that that too could be successfully redressed in many cases. However, the clinical setting does not usually allow unlimited latitude to seek more satisfactory and globally optimal outcomes. It has also been shown that more extended training can usually succeed in achieving better results, but there are usually economic constraints that limit the duration of training. Many of the data points on Figure 10–10 therefore represent snapshots on the path of progress, rather than ultimate end points of training.

The point should not be lost that the technique is capable of moving someone to a less functional place. It takes clinical acumen to observe that the client is being well served by the training, and that progress in one area is not being purchased at the cost of dysfunction elsewhere. Hence, there is no alternative to employing global assessment with people undergoing training. It is not sufficient to be narrowly focused on a specific symptom or disability. Fortunately, it appears to be generally true that when new protocols are tried, the results are usually additive to what has already been achieved in the prior training.

The continuous performance test has been found very useful in assessing the style of nervous system functioning not only for ADD but also for other disorders. Hence, it is now used generally for guiding the EEG training, irrespective of diagnosis. It has been useful as a measure of progress in training for a variety of conditions, and normalization of the T.O.V.A. is one of the milestones to be achieved in training.

Other Tests of Cognitive Function

A number of additional tests are usually performed in our office with children in the age range of 6 to 14 to assess progress in training. These include the Benton Visual Retention Test (BVRT), the Word Fluency Test, the Symbol Digit Modalities Test (SDMT), the Grooved Pegboard Test, and the Digit Span. These tests were chosen for their variety of coverage, their brevity, their objectivity, and their familiarity in the field of remedial education. Together with the T.O.V.A. the tests can be given in less than an hour.

Statistical results are shown in Figure 10–11 for some sixty-four children who were successively evaluated in our office in 1994–95. This cohort included many children who were not in deficit with

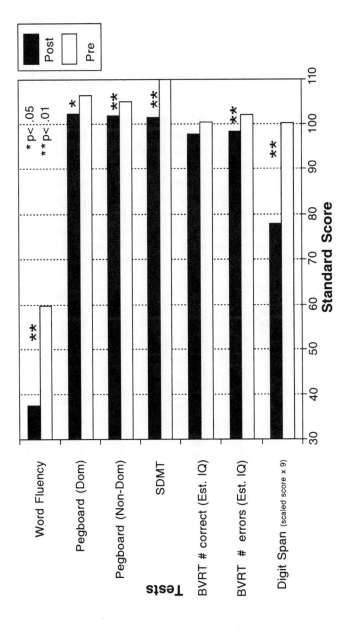

Figure 10–11. Effect of EEG biofeedback on seven cognitive tests for sixty-four children and adolescents. Pre- and posttreatment standard scores are presented (except for the Digit Span, where a scaled score is used). The two categories in deficit show improvement of more than one standard deviation. Three of the tests show improvement beyond naïve norms (Grooved Pegboard and Symbol Digit Modalities Test).

respect to many of these tests. For example, the group average for the Grooved Pegboard and the SDMT were already above 100 in standard score before the training. A statistically significant improvement was nevertheless achieved in these cases. This means that the training is to be seen more in terms of optimization of function as opposed to remediation of deficits.

The subject population was in deficit with respect to word fluency and the Digit Span tests. Here the global improvement was 1.5 standard deviations in both cases, a significant effect size. The average BVRT score was normal for this population, and since the maximum possible standard score is 105, little global improvement could be demonstrated. Since the summary graph includes many children who score in the normal range and therefore dilute the relevant results, it is more revealing to show the individual responses for these tests. These are shown in Figure 10–12 for the Word Fluency Test, first in the order of starting score, and second in the order of gains made.

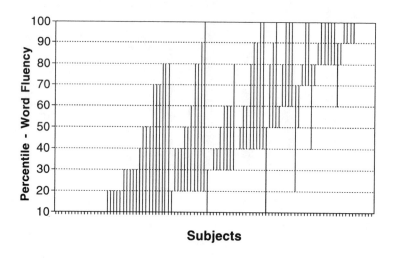

Figure 10–12. Pre-post data on the Word Fluency Test for 100 subjects. Improvement in most cases exceeds the test-retest error. Some children decline in score, suggesting that further optimization of the protocol is needed.

Here the subject population is 100; 90 percent of the scores show an improvement, which is in some cases substantial. This again implies that the typical improvement is larger than the test-retest error. Some of the decreasing scores also show substantial changes, and one has the sense that these represent "negative" responders, rather than nonresponders, just as was found in the T.O.V.A. impulsivity data. If one lumps the positive and the negative responders together, it is apparent that nearly all subjects respond to the training in some significant way. One presumes that protocols exist that would remedy the deficits in those who have shown declines, and that further training would be beneficial. The fact that some of the changes are so significant allows the training to be seen as a kind of bottleneck breaker in word recall. Collectively, these data are persuasive that an active process is involved, and that placebo factors cannot suffice to explain this graph.

Individual data are shown for the Benton in Figure 10–13 in terms of standard score. Scoring on this test is very grainy. However, a significant impact on those in deficit is indicated: 9 percent of subjects decline in score for number correct, and only 4 percent decline in terms of errors. The implication of the data is that visual retention deficits are highly remediable, and that a normal range of function is to be expected for a high percentage of clients with the training.

Individual scores on the Grooved Pegboard are shown in Figure 10–14 in terms of standard score. Those found in deficit are seen to normalize in function in all cases. After training, no subject scored less than 85 in standard score. Above a standard score of 100, the changes with training appear more random.

The individual data for the Wechsler Digit Span are shown in Figure 10–15 in terms of actual scores. The range of scores is from 1 to 19; 78 percent of subjects show an improvement, 10 percent show no change, and 12 percent show declines in scores. The impression one has from the data is that modest improvement in scores is expected with high probability for a typical subject population seen for AD/HD and related disorders. This improvement does not depend strongly on whether a person starts out in deficit. A few outstanding gains in scaled scores were observed: from 6 to 19, from 5 to 12, and from 12 to 18. These too require explanation. An increase in working memory and/or short-term memory is implied by the rather systematic improvements seen in this group of subjects.

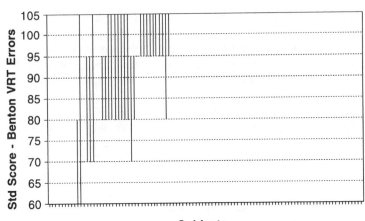

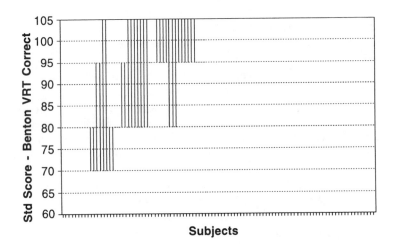

Figure 10–13. Pre-post data on the Benton Visual Retention Test for a subject pool of 100. Significant improvements are shown for many of those in deficit. The data suggest that normalization of performance on the Benton may be a reasonable expectation for children referred for AD/HD or learning disabilities.

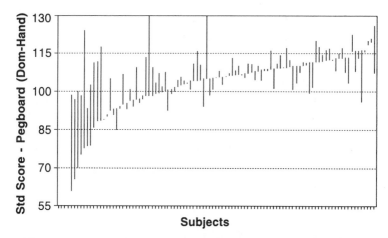

Figure 10–14. Individual test data are shown for the Grooved Pegboard Test for the dominant hand. These data lead one to anticipate that normalization of performance on this test is generally to be expected with the EEG training of AD/HD children.

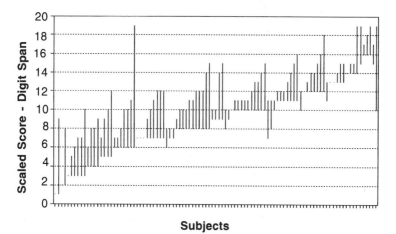

Figure 10–15. Individual test data are shown for the Digit Span of the WISC for the subject pool of 100. Significant improvement in scores, again exceeding the test-retest error, is to be expected for this test in an AD/HD population.

The results for the SDMT are shown in Figure 10–16, in terms of standard score; fifty-nine subjects improved with training, whereas twenty-four subjects saw their score decline. For scores below 100, which are more relevant, the corresponding figures are thirty improvements and twelve declines. A few striking individual improvements are also seen (two and three standard deviations). The overall results are more equivocal than for some of the other tests. This may be due to the fact that the task is much more complex than the other tests. The SDMT is thought to be a measure of frontal lobe function as well, and for the bulk of these results the electrode placement was only on sensorimotor strip, and hence did not involve frontal lobe training directly.

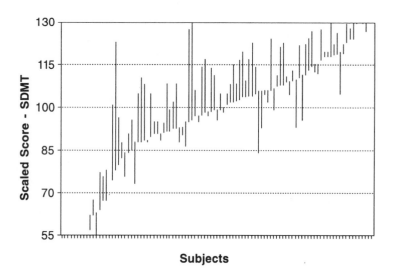

Figure 10–16. Individual test results are shown for the Symbol Digit Modalities Test. Results are more variable here than for any other test performed. This may be a matter of the complexity of the challenge. It may also be due to the fact that this is a more rigorous test of frontal lobe functioning, and that frontal lobe training has not yet been sorted out.

Discussion of the Clinical Results

Collectively, the data on tests of cognitive function indicate a basic responsiveness to training that encompasses nearly all subjects. This finding has led to a rather firm expectation in our office that children with cognitive deficits can be helped with this technique if only the right protocol can be ascertained. The extent to which benefit is derived remains highly variable among individuals, and is also dependent on clinical skills in protocol selection and in assessment. The cumulative benefit in terms of cognitive function is typically worthwhile, particularly if the subject is in significant deficit at the outset.

The training impacts a broad range of cognitive challenges, which by itself would be consistent with a model based on secondary effects of the normalization of basic functions of arousal and attention. However, the very significant gains seen in some of the tests tend to rule that out. Instead, it is proposed that the training impacts on the organization of cortical communication loops either directly or via the thalamocortical regulatory network. The training appears to address the fundamental timing mechanisms by which cognitive functions, as well as functions of arousal, activation, and attention, are organized. To a certain extent, then, the effects of training are nonspecific, with the effects on attention being largely inseparable from the effect on specific cognitive function. That is, if the instrumentalities of control are challenged to work better, they do so in some generality.

If the effects of the EEG biofeedback exercise are to improve self-regulatory function in the general case, how then is this consistent with the observation that occasionally there are negative outcomes? It must be recognized that the EEG biofeedback challenge is fundamentally a constraint upon the brain. The brain is rewarded for a particular brain state, when in fact no single brain state can be thought of as functional. Thus, it is postulated that the remediation does not follow from the brain's progressive approximation of the rewarded state, but rather from the fact that the shift in state brings forth a reaction in the opposite direction. This successive action-reaction cycle at a certain point in multidimensional state space is likely to move the brain gradually toward homeostatic conditions, but it is possible also that the brain may enter regions of instability, or that the brain actually does become somewhat constrained in its operational range. In the latter case, the EEG biofeedback challenge needs to provide a greater variety of protocols.

Already it has emerged that the typical training protocols employed all have "antidotes" that undo the observed constraints. Thus, an excess of left-hemisphere training is compensated for by right-side training, and excessive higher-frequency training is compensated for by lower-frequency training. If one extrapolates from recent history, it is likely that the next few years will see the emergence of more refined protocols and assessment schema that will avoid the appearance of adverse outcomes with greater assurance.

Despite the passage of time, and the increased popularity of the EEG training among clinicians, it remains true to this day that the finding of significant IQ increases with the EEG training invites skepticism. From the outset, at the beginning of the twentieth century, it has been a matter of belief that IQ was essentially invariant and not subject to significant alteration. Thus it is satisfying to observe that every study on EEG biofeedback that has tracked IQ has shown a significant increase. Figure 10–17 compares the results of three studies that used the Wechsler IQ test (revised) and also furnished data on the relevant subtests of Arithmetic, Digit Span, and Coding. The first is the work of Tansey, the second is our own clinical study, already discussed above, and the third is the work of Cartozzo, which also employed controls. It should also be pointed out that comparable changes in Wechsler test scores have also been observed with Ritalin. In a test-retest situation of a boy in first grade (with only a five-day interval), improvements in the Wechsler Arithmetic score were +4, in Digit Span -1, and in Coding +6. Full-scale IQ score improved eighteen points from 118 to 136 (Cherkes-Julkowski et al. 1995).

Even with such consistency among the findings, the question needs to be asked whether emotional and motivational factors, or even improvement in sleep, could account for much of the observed increase in IQ scores, or whether an improvement in intellectual function has in fact been demonstrated. The verbal commentary by Marks that accompanied the pre-post testing in our own study makes it quite clear that motivational factors had been favorably impacted by the training. The initially oppositional child might simply not have cared how he did on the pretest, whereas on the posttest it now mattered to him, and greater effort was exerted. Also, parental reporting was consistent with respect to improvements in sleep.

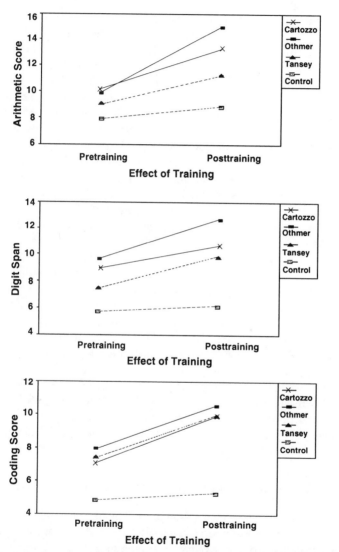

Figure 10–17. Comparison of different studies with respect to relevant WISC-R scores (for Arithmetic, Digit Span, and Coding). The studies are uniform in finding improvement with EEG training. Data for the controls in Cartozzo's study are also indicated.

In the present perspective, improvements in emotional control and in sleep are also considered "specific" effects of the training, as opposed to "nonspecific," or placebo, effects. So the question of whether intellectual function has been directly impacted is not to be seen as one of separating specific from nonspecific effects of the training. The best evidence for an improvement in intellectual functioning lies in the individual test data, which often showed large shifts in very selected areas. Thus, for example, the three largest individual gains seen in the Arithmetic subtest were 8, 7, and 6; in Digit Span, 7, 7, and 7; in Coding, 7, 6, and 4. Outside of these three categories, which have a specific role in ADD, the largest individual improvements were seen in Picture Completion (10, 7, and 7); in Similarities (9, 8, 7); in Comprehension (8, 7, 7); and in Picture Arrangement (8, 7, 6).

The three categories of Arithmetic, Digit Span, and Coding are often taken together as a measure of "freedom from distractibility." One could translate this conceptualization at the behavioral level directly to the neurophysiological level as continuity in mental processing. The most likely explanation for improvement in intellectual functioning is that the biofeedback training enhances the ability of the brain to maintain continuity of states. Such continuity may be the defining issue in working memory, in memory processes in general, and in mental association or word recall tasks. In this view, then, distractibility may be merely the behavioral observable of a disruption of continuity in mental processing resulting from deficient internal control mechanisms. It is interesting in this regard that an early scientist in the field is said to have once defined poor attention in just these terms—as the inability to bring material into consciousness and to retain that material in consciousness for an appropriate length of time.

EEG Biofeedback and Pharmacotherapy for AD/HD

A more thoroughgoing comparison of EEG biofeedback training and stimulant medication was undertaken by Rossiter and LaVaque using a carefully matched group of twenty three subjects in each cohort. The T.O.V.A. was used as a measure. Statistically significant improvement was seen in both groups. Comparison of groups is shown in Figure 10–18. Comparable change with both EEG biofeedback and stimulant medication would show up as a 45-degree line. All four subtests tend to show that pattern. That is, there was no significant difference in T.O.V.A. change scores between the two groups. Further, when data were examined individually, there was no difference between EEG and medications in the number of subjects responding, which was 19/23 in the case of EEG and 20/23 in the case of medications.

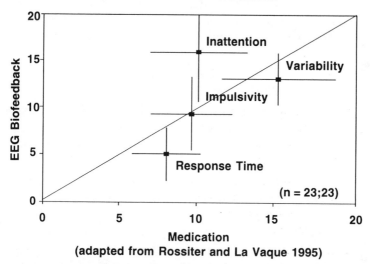

(adapted from Rossiter and La Vaque 1995)

Figure 10–18. Comparison of EEG training cohort and medication cohort using T.O.V.A measures, from the study by Rossiter and La Vaque (1995). Comparable changes are indicated by a general parallelism to the 45-degree line. All four parameters of the T.O.V.A. in fact trend along the line, demonstrating comparable efficacy for EEG biofeedback and stimulant medication.

This similarity in response to very different interventions gives some support to the suggestion that both modalities are appealing to the same mechanisms, but that one does so via the bioelectrical domain, and the other via the neurochemical. The advantages of the EEG training are:

1. the beneficial effects are more global than those of medication; that is, the benefits of stimulant medication are only a subset of those to be anticipated with EEG training;

2. little or no continuing drug administration or careful titration is required;

3. there are no rebound effects, or other effects of varying dosage with time;

4. there are no observed negative side effects; with EEG biofeedback, the side effects tend to be positive, and to yield improved function where none may have been expected (academic skills, sports performance, quality of sleep, anxiety and depression, tics, OCD);

5. there is almost never a need for polypharmacotherapy in conjunction with EEG training;

6. even if complementary medications optimize function beyond that achievable with EEG training alone (which is often the case), the dosage is usually lower than that which would be employed absent the training, hence reducing unwanted side effects;

7. the benefits of training are likely to compound favorably even after the training is completed, through autonomous reinforcement of the self-regulatory mechanisms that have been stimulated by the training;

8. the EEG training can be done at an early age when compliance is not much of an issue, whereas with medication there is a continual issue of compliance;

9. the EEG training can be successfully initiated at a very early age (<2 years) in the case of severe problems; at such ages, medication would not ordinarily be considered;

10. the long-term outcome of EEG training is favorable, whereas a follow-up study on stimulant medication showed no long-term benefit of prior use of such medication;

11. the option of selectively addressing hemispheric dysfunction, of fine-tuning the training frequency band, and of titrating the various protocols in terms of duration of training, yields an operational flexibility not available with medications (except possibly with a level of professional engagement that would be prohibitive in the ordinary case).

Among the benefits cited for EEG training vis-à-vis medication, the one that bears the most discussion is the claim that the beneficial effects of the training are more global than those of medication. This is based on the observation that the training readily remediates the sleep disorders and pain syndromes often seen in AD/HD children; that the training remediates the comorbid disruptive behavior disorders (ODD and CD); and that the training ameliorates the symptoms of Tourette's syndrome and obsessive-compulsive disorder. Perhaps even more significant than all of these is the favorable impact on anxiety and depression. In the proposed disregulation model of AD/HD, which in our view is most congenial to the EEG technique, the affective dimension is considered as part and parcel of the AD/HD spectrum disorder (as urged by Weinberg originally). The training is capable of enhancing self-regulation and normalizing range of function over the entire anxiety-depression-mania continuum. In this context, the technique can also be helpful with behavioral extrema of social withdrawal, explosive rage behavior, suicidality, as well as nascent sociopathy.

Generalization of the Model

In the application to conduct disorder and incipient sociopathy, the essence of the EEG training technique is perhaps made most starkly apparent. As one observes oppositionality melt away with the training, and "cold-bloodedness" change to solicitude, one has the sense that these children and adolescents had simply been disconnected from the wellspring of their own emotions. After all, the training is capable of restoring a full range of appropriate emotional responsiveness. Hence, the capacity for such responsiveness was never lost. The training appears to reestablish functional connections that then allow the appropriate control and modulation of behavior. The most parsimonious view, then, of EEG biofeedback is that the training enhances cortical-cortical, corticothalamic, and limbic-thalamo-cortical functional connectivity. The reinforcement of certain critical frequencies promotes bringing larger regions of the cerebrum, and critical pathways, into temporal coherence so that effective internal communication can take place. Such functional connectivity and internal communication may be the mechanism by which continuity of states is assured.

The breakdown in internal communications leading to emotional disregulation is quite possibly no different qualitatively from that leading to cognitive and attentional deficits. Considered from one vantage point, the deficits in the realm of the emotions, of motivation, intention, and engagement, may be the more fundamental issue in much of the AD/HD spectrum, as already suggested. However, all of the identified deficits may ultimately be reducible to a few simple failure modes in the control mechanisms of a self-organizing system. In this perspective, the attentional, cognitive, and affective manifestations may be seen as the behavioral observables—even the epiphenomena—of a more fundamental disordering of the instrumentalities of internal control. The clinical success of the EEG training technique may hasten a return to a systems perspective on the functionality of the brain, and a return to the consideration of the neurophysiological basis of behavior at higher levels of functional integration. The next frontier in the mental health field may lie in understanding the brain at the network level.

If the focus on control itself as the primary issue is appropriate, and if the resulting organismic behavior is to be regarded first and foremost as an observable concomitant of disregulation, then a continuum in the behavior domain must exist in which this proposition is more or less relevant depending on the severity of the disregulation. That is, the more severe the disregulation, the more behavior must be captive to it. One may take autism, for example, as perhaps one of the most severe manifestations of a right-hemisphere dysfunction. Similarly, one may take Down syndrome as one of the most severe manifestations of a left-hemisphere dysfunction. And one may take attachment disorder as one of the most severe manifestations of emotional disregulation. If control issues are primary, and if EEG biofeedback addresses the control machinery, then one would expect a favorable impact of the EEG training even on these more severe exemplars of disregulation. Initial clinical findings on these conditions, which were undertaken as an outgrowth of the work on AD/HD, are in fact favorable, and suggest that further, more rigorous and comprehensive research be urgently undertaken.

CONCLUSION

A model has been presented in which AD/HD is reframed as a spectrum disorder traceable to deficits in basic cerebral regulatory function relative to arousal, attention, vigilance, and affect. The mechanisms by which these functions are managed depend on dynamical interactions between cortical and subcortical regions that can only be fully described by including the bioelectrical domain of information transfer in the cerebrum. Organization of information in the time domain must be explicitly managed, and this must clearly occur by self-organizing means. Temporal correlation in the activity of neuronal ensembles is seen to underlie the hierarchy of management of cortical electrical activity. Rhythmicity in such activity is the external manifestation (seen in the EEG) of such temporal organization. EEG biofeedback is an operant conditioning technique that impinges on such regulatory activity, which leads generally to an improvement in regulatory function. Such enhanced regulatory function underlies the observed improvement in behavioral control, management of attention, and affect regulation in children manifesting with AD/HD or its clinical cousins, the disruptive behavior disorders, affective disorders, Tourette's, and OCD. Specifically, the improvements are ascribed to increases in continuity of brain states, and to increased functional connectivity of different brain regions.

EEG biofeedback training has consistently led to improvements in measures of intellectual function, in continuous performance tests, in other academic skill measures, and in behavioral assessments in studies going back thirty years. The results are so ubiquitous in impact, and often dramatic in magnitude, that they should lead to a reappraisal of behavior, affective, and attentional disorders in terms of the failure mechanisms of control systems. Such a reformulation will require renewed attention to brain function at higher levels of integration than has been the case in recent decades.

REFERENCES

Alhambra, M. A., Fowler, T. P., and Alhambra, A. A. (1995). EEG biofeedback: a new treatment option for ADD/AD/HD. *Journal of Neurotherapy* 1(2):39–43.

American Psychiatric Association. (1994). *Diagnostic and Statistical Manual of Mental Disorders*, 4th ed. (*DSM-IV*). Washington, DC: American Psychiatric Association.

Andersen, P., and Andersson, S. A. (1968). *Physiological Basis of the Alpha Rhythm*. New York: Appleton Century Crofts.

Biederman, J., Faraone, S., Mick, E., et al. (1996). Attention-deficit hyperactivity disorder and juvenile mania: an overlooked comorbidity? *Journal of the American Academy of Child and Adolescent Psychiatry* 35(8):997–1008.

Biederman, J., Newcorn, J., and Sprich, S. (1991) Comorbidity of attention deficit hyperactivity disorder with conduct, depressive, anxiety, and other disorders. *American Journal of Psychiatry* 148(5):564–577.

Cabral, R. J., and Scott, D. F. (1976). Effects of two desensitization techniques, biofeedback and relaxation, on intractable epliepsy: follow-up study. *Journal of Neurology, Neurosurgery, and Psychiatry* 39:504–507.

Cartozzo, H. A., Jacobs, D., and Gevirtz, R. N. (1995). EEG biofeedback and the remediation of AD/HD symptomatology: a controlled treatment outcome study. Presented at the Annual Conference of the Association for Applied Psychophysiology and Biofeedback, Cincinnati, OH, March.

Chase, M. H., and Harper, R. M. (1971). Somatomotor and visceromotor correlates of operantly conditioned 12-14 c/sec sensorimotor cortical activity. *Electroencephalography and Clinical Neurophysiology* 31:85–92.

Cherkes-Julkowski, M. (1996). The child as a self-organizing system: the case against instruction as we know it. *Learning Disabilities* 7(1):19–27.

Cherkes-Julkowski, M., Stolzenberg, J., Hatzes, N., and Madaus, J. (1995) Methodological issues in assessing the relationship among ADD, medication effects and reading performance. *Journal of Learning Disabilities* 6(2):21.

Comings, D. E., Comings, B. G., Muhleman, D., et al. (1991) The dopamine D2 receptor locus as a modifying gene in neuropsychiatric disorders. *Journal of the American Medical Association* 266:1793–1800.

Douglas, V. I. (1988). Cognitive deficits in children with attention deficit disorder with hyperactivity. In *Attention Deficit Disorder: Criteria, Cognition, Intervention*, ed. L. M. Bloomindale and J. Sergeant, pp. 65–81. A book supplement of the *Journal of Child Psychology and Psychiatry*, no. 5. New York: Pergamon.

Ellertson, B., and Klove, H. (1976). Clinical application of EEG biofeedback training in epilepsy. *Scandinavian Journal of Behavior Therapy* 5:133–144.

Finley, W. W. (1976). Effects of sham feedback following successful SMR training in an epileptic: follow-up study. *Biofeedback and Self-Regulation* 1:227–235.

Finley, W. W., Smith, H. A., and Etherton, M. D. (1975). Reduction of seizures and normalization of the EEG in a severe epileptic following sensorimotor biofeedback training: preliminary study. *Biological Psychology* 2(3):189–203.

Greenberg, L. M. (1987). An objective measure of methylphenidate response. Clinical use of the MCA. *Psychopharmacology Bulletin* 23:279–282.

Hepper, P. G., Shahidullah, S., and White, R. (1990). Origins of fetal handedness. *Nature* 347:431.

Hess, W. R. (1954). Diencephalon, autonomic and extrapyramidal functions. *Monographs in Biology and Medicine*, vol. 3. New York: Grune & Stratton.

Howe, R. C., and Sterman, M. B. (1972). Cortical-subcortical EEG correlates of suppressed motor behavior during sleep and waking in the cat.
Electroencephalography and Clinical Neurophysiology 32:681–695.

Kaplan, B. J. (1975). Biofeedback in epileptics: equivocal relationship of reinforced EEG frequency to seizure reduction. *Epilepsia* 16:477–485.

Kott, A., Pavlofski, R. P., and Black, A. H. (1979). Reducing epileptic seizures
through operant conditioning of central nervous system activity: procedural
variables. *Science* 203:73–75.

Kramer, P. D. (1993). *Listening to Prozac.* New York: Penguin.

Kuhlman, W. N. (1978). EEG feedback training of epileptic patients: clinical
and electroencephalographic analysis. *Electroencephalography and Clinical Neurophysiology* 45(6):699–710.

Kuhlman, W. N., and Allison, T. (1977). EEG feedback training in the treatment of epilepsy: some questions and some answers. *Pavlovian Journal of Biological Sciences* 12:112–122.

Lantz, D. L., and Sterman, M. B. (1988). Neuropsychological assessment of
subjects with uncontrolled epilepsy: effects of EEG feedback training. *Epilepsia*
29(2):163–171.

Linden, M., Habib, T., and Radojevic, V. (1996). A controlled study of the
effects of EEG biofeedback on cognition and behavior of children with
attention deficit disorder and learning disabilities. *Biofeedback and Self-
Regulation* 21:35–49.

Lubar, J. F. (1991). Discourse on the development of EEG diagnostics and
biofeedback for attention deficit/hyperactivity disorders. *Biofeedback and Self-
Regulation* 16:201-225

———— (1995). Neurofeedback for the management of attention-deficit/hy-
peractivity disorder. In *Biofeedback, A Practitioner's Guide*, ed. M. S.
Schwartz et al., pp. 493–522. New York: Guilford.

Lubar, J. F., and Bahler, W. W. (1976). Behavioral management of epileptic seizures following EEG biofeedback training of the sensorimotor rhythm. *Biofeedback and Self-Regulation* 1:77–104.

Lubar, J. F., Shabsin, H. S., Natelsen, S. E., et al. (1981). EEG operant conditioning in intractable epileptics. *Archives of Neurology* 38:70–74.

Lubar, J. F., and Shouse, M. N. (1976). EEG and behavioral changes in a
hyperactive child concurrent with training of the sensorimotor rhythm
(SMR). A preliminary report. *Biofeedback and Self-Regulation* 1:293–306.

Lubar, J. O., and Lubar, J. F. (1984). Electroencephalographic biofeedback
of SMR and beta for treatment of attention deficit disorders in a clinical
setting. *Biofeedback and Self-Regulation* 9(1):1–23.

Malone, M. A, Kershner, J. R, and Swanson, J. M. (1994). Hemispheric processing and methylphenidate effects in attention-deficit hyperactivity
disorder. *Journal of Child Neurology* 9(2):181–189.

Munk, M. H. J., Roelfsema, P. R., Koenig, P., et al. (1996). Role of reticular activation in the modulation of intracortical synchronization. *Science* 272:271–274.

Othmer, S., Othmer, S., and Marks, C. S. (1992). EEG biofeedback training for Attention Deficit Disorder, specific learning disabilities, and associated conduct problems. *Journal of the Biofeedback Society of California* Fall/Winter, pp. 24–27, 21–26.

Quy, R. J., Hutt, S. J., and Forrest, S. (1979). Sensorimotor rhythm feedback training and epilepsy: some methodological and conceptual issues. *Biological Psychology* 9:129–149.

Pennington, B. F. (1991). *Diagnosing Learning Disorders: A Neuropsychological Framework*. New York: Guilford Press.

Rossiter, T. R., and La Vaque, T. J. (1995). A comparison of EEG biofeedback and psychostimulants in treating Attention Deficit/Hyperactivity Disorder. *Journal of Neurotherapy* 1:48–59.

Roth, S. R., Sterman, M. B., and Clemente, C. D. (1967). Comparison of EEG correlates of reinforcement, internal inhibition and sleep. *Electroencephalography and Clinical Neurophysiology* 23(6):509–520.

Seifert, A. R., and Lubar, J. F. (1975). Reduction of epileptic seizures through EEG biofeedback training. *Biological Psychology* 3(3):157–184.

Shouse, M. N., and Lubar, J. F. (1979). Operant conditioning of EEG rhythms and Ritalin in the treatment of hyperkinesis. *Biofeedback and Self-Regulation* 4:299.

Sterman, M. B. (1976). Effects of brain surgery and EEG operant conditioning on seizure latency following monomethylhydrazine intoxication in the cat. *Experimental Neurology* 50(3):757–765.

——— (1977). Sensorimotor EEG operant conditioning: experimental and clinical effects. *Pavlovian Journal of Biological Science* 12(2):63–92.

——— (1996). Physiological origins and functional correlates of EEG rhythmic activities: implications for self-regulations. *Biofeedback and Self-Regulation* 21(1):3–33.

Sterman, M. B., and Friar, L. (1972). Suppression of seizures in epileptic following sensorimotor EEG feedback training. *Electroencephalography and Clinical Neurophysiology* 33:89–95.

Sterman, M. B., Goodman, S. J., and Kovalesky, R. A. (1978). Effects of sensorimotor EEG feedback training on seizure susceptibility in the rhesus monkey. *Experimental Neurology* 62(3):735–747.

Sterman, M. B., Howe, R. D., and MacDonald, L. R. (1970). Facilitation of spindle-burst sleep by conditioning of electroencephalographic activity while awake. *Science* 167:1146–1148.

Sterman, M. B., LoPresti, R. W., and Fairchild, M. D. (1969a). *Electroencephalographic and Behavioral Studies of Monomethylhydrazine Toxicity in the Cat.* Technical Report AMRL-TR-69-3. Wright Patterson Air Force Base, OH: Air Systems Command.

Sterman, M. B., and MacDonald, L. R. (1978). Effects of central cortical EEG feedback training on incidence of poorly controlled seizures. *Epilepsia* 19(3):207–222.

Sterman, M. B., MacDonald, L. R., and Stone, R. K. (1974) Biofeedback training of the sensorimotor electroencephalogram rhythm in man: effects on epilepsy. *Epilepsia* 15(3):395–416.

Sterman, M. B., and Shouse, M. N. (1980). Quantitative analysis of training, sleep EEG and clinical response to EEG operant conditioning in epileptics. *Electroencephalography and Clinical Neurophysiology* 49:558–576.

Sterman, M. B., Shouse, M. N., Lucia, M. B., et al. (1977). Effects of anesthesia and cranial electrode implantation on seizure susceptibility of the cat. *Experimental Neurology* 57:158–166.

Sterman, M. B., and Wyrwicka, W. (1967). EEG correlates of sleep: evidence for separate forebrain substrates. *Brain Research* 6:143–163.

Sterman, M. B., Wyrwicka, W., and Roth, S. R. (1969b) Electrophysiological correlates and neural substrates of alimentary behavior in the cat. *Annals of the New York Academy of Science* 157:723–739.

Suffin, S. C., and Emory, W. H. (1995). Neurometric subgroups in attentional and affective disorders and the association with pharmacologic outcome. *Clinical Encephalography* 26(2):76–83.

——— (1996). *Neurometric EEG classifiers and response to medicine.* Paper presented at the 1996 Annual Meeting of the American Psychiatric Association, Washington, DC.

Tansey, M. A. (1985). The response of a case of petit mal epilepsy to EEG sensorimotor rhythm biofeedback training. *International Journal of Psychophysiology* 3(2): 81–84.

——— (1990). Righting the rhythms of reason. EEG Biofeedback training as a therapeutic modality in a clinical office setting. *Medical Psychotherapy* 3:57–68.

——— (1993). Ten-year stability of EEG biofeedback results for a hyperactive boy who failed fourth grade perceptually impaired class. *Biofeedback and Self-Regulation* 18(1):33–44.

Tansey, M. A., Brainwave Signatures. (1985). An index reflective of the brain's functional neuroanatomy: further findings on the effect of EEG sensorimotor rhythm feedback training on the neurologic precursors of learning disabilities. *International Journal of Psychophysiology* 4:91–97.

Tansey, M. A., and Bruner, R. L. (1983). EMG and EEG biofeedback train-ing in the treatment of a 10-year-old hyperactive boy with a developmen-tal reading disorder. *Biofeedback and Self-Regulation* 8:25–37.

Thorpe, T. (1997). *EEG biofeedback training in a clinical sample of school age children treated for Attention-Deficit/Hyperactivity Disorder.* Unpublished dissertation, California School of Professional Psychology, Los Angeles.

Tozzo, C. A., Elfner, L. F., and May, J. G., Jr. (1988). EEG biofeedback and relaxation training in the control of epileptic seizures. *International Journal of Psychophysiology* 6:185–194.

Tucker, D. M., and Williamson, P. A. (1984). Asymmetric neural control system in human self-regulation. *Psychological Review* 91:185–215.

von der Malsburg, C. (1995). Building in models of perception and brain func-tion. *Current Opinion in Neurobiology* 5:520–526.

Weinberg, W. A., and Brumback, R. A. (1992). The myth of attention deficit-hyperactivity disorder: symptoms resulting from multiple causes. *Journal of Child Neurology* 7(4):431–445.

Weinberg, W. A., and Harper, C. R. (1993). Vigilance and its disorders. *Neurologic Clinic* 11:59–78.

Wyler, A. R., Lockard, J. S., and Ward, A. A. (1976). Conditioned EEG dissynchronization and seizure occurrence in patients. *Electroencephalography and Clinical Neurophysiology* 41:501–512.

Wyrwicka, W., and Sterman, M. B. (1968). Instrumental conditioning of sen-sorimotor cortex EEG spindles in the waking cat. *Physiology and Behavior* 3(5):703–707.

Wyrwicka, W., Sterman, M. B., and Clemente, C. D. (1962) Conditioning of in-duced EEG sleep patterns. *Science* 137:616–618.

Zametkin, A. J., Liebenauer, L. L., Fitzgerald, G. A., et al. (1993). Brain me-tabolism in teenagers with attention-deficit hyperactivity disorder. *Ar-chives of General Psychiatry* 50(5):333–340.

Zametkin, A. J., Nordahl, T. E., Gross, M., et al. (1990). Cerebral glucose me-tabolism in adults with hyperactivity of childhood onset. *New England Journal of Medicine* 323(20):1361–1366.

11

Notes on Brainwave Biofeedback for Young People: AD/HD and Related Issues

Thomas M. Brod

Although the use of brainwave biofeedback (also called electroencephalogram [EEG] biofeedback and neurofeedback) has swept through the world of biofeedback, it is a story that has received relatively little notice in the psychiatric—and general medical—world. The reason must be unfamiliarity: the roots of neurofeedback are in physiological psychology, efficacy and safety studies have so far been published only in peripheral journals, and the mechanisms of action are not "ordinary"—involving brain state modification through cortical-cortical and cortical-subcortical loops. And, of course, there is no marketing muscle to push images into the collective therapeutic belief system. Nonetheless, twenty years of published clinical studies point to immediate and long-term benefits of neurofeedback for the treatment of attention deficit/hyperactivity disorder (AD/HD). Protocols have been developed for inattention as well as hyperactivity, and a cluster of related learning disorders as well. Additionally, a

provocative finding from the research is the consistent emergence of
significant improvement of IQ scores in children and adolescents. All
told, neurofeedback has a legitimate and growing place in AD/HD[1]
treatment, along with medication, skills training, and individual/fam-
ily psychotherapy.

This chapter reviews AD/HD treatment in the history of biofeedback, gives an overview of brain waves, and reviews several component models that explain the efficacy of brain-wave biofeedback for
AD/HD.

AN OVERVIEW OF ATTENTION DEFICIT/ HYPERACTIVITY DISORDER

AD/HD is a behavioral and perceptual-cognitive function disorder, presently diagnosed on clinical grounds alone (see below for
recent studies indicating that we are dealing with multiple neurobiological entities). Primary characteristics of the disorder include hyperactivity, impulsivity, distractibility, and excitability. Affected children
may also demonstrate a short attention span; concentration problems;
clumsy motor movements; inability to perform fine motor tasks;
restlessness; high levels of frustration; impaired spatial perception,
memory, and speech; overreaction to stimulation; and rapid, unpredictable mood swings.

AD/HD children also often experience difficulty in making
friends, and they spend a disproportionate amount of time alone or
with younger children. A common result is lower self-esteem levels
and/or depression. Some children develop antisocial and maladaptive
attention-getting behaviors. Commonly reported is the emotional immaturity of the child, and the lack of ambition and ability to maintain goals.

A different perspective on AD/HD has been developed by Thom
Hartmann (1997), who recognized in the features of the condition

---

1. In line with present standard nomenclature, AD/HD includes
   attentional disorders or the inattentive and hyperperactive/impulsive
   types.

traits that might have survival value to our ancient human forebearers. Hartmann, noticing the cascade of self-esteem problems created in the attention-deficient person by social misfit, miscuing, and misfiring, introduced the reframing metaphor of the hunter/gatherer in a farmer's world. Hartmann makes a reasoned argument that people with AD/HD represent a gene pool surviving from ancient times. A summary of his sharp observations is found in Table 11–1.

Table 11–1.
A New View of ADD, as a Natural Adaptive Trait

Trait as It Appears in the "Disorder" View	How It Appears in the "Hunter" View	Opposite "Farmer" Trait
Distractable	Constantly monitoring their environment	Not easily distracted from the task at hand
Attention span is short, but can become intensely focused for long periods of time	Able to throw themselves into the chase on a moment's notice	Able to sustain a steady, dependable effort
Poor planner: disorganized and impulsive (makes snap decisions)	Flexible; ready to change strategy quickly	Organized, purposeful; they have a long-term strategy and they stick to it
Distorted sense of time: unaware of how long it will take to do something	Tireless: capable of sustained drives, but only when "hot on the trail" of some goal	Conscious of time and timing; they get things done in time, pace themselves, have good "staying power"
Impatient	Result oriented; acutely aware of whether the goal is getting closer now	Patient; aware that good things take time; willing to wait
Doesn't convert words into concepts adeptly, and vice versa; may or may not have a reading disability	Visual/concrete thinker, clearly seeing a tangible goal even if there are no words for it	Much better able to seek goals that aren't easy to see at the moment

Table 11–1. continued
A New View of ADD, as a Natural Adaptive Trait

Trait as It Appears in the "Disorder" View	How It Appears in the "Hunter" View	Opposite "Farmer" Trait
Has difficulty following directions	Independent	Team player
Daydreamer	Bored by mundane tasks; enjoy new ideas, excitement, "the hunt," being hot on the trial	Focused; good at follow-through, tending to details, "taking care of business"
Acts without considering consequences	Willing and able to take risks and face danger	Careful; "look before you leap"
Lacking in the social graces	"No time for niceties when there are decisions to be made!"	Nurturing; creates and supports community values; attuned to whether something will last

Reprinted from Hartmann 1997, copyright © 1993, 1997 by Mythical Intelligence, Inc., and used by permission.

A neuropsychological model of AD/HD as a disorder of self-regulation and executive function has recently become discernible from a growing body of anatomic neuroimaging studies. While the attentional process itself appears to be directed through the right cingulate gyrus located near the back of the frontal cerebral cortex (Casey et al. 1997b), AD/HD involves a complex of abnormalities and circuits looping between the prefrontal cortex (especially on the right) on the underlying subcortical "switching stations" of the basal ganglia (Casey et al. 1997a; see especially the review by Castellanos 1997). The story is even more complex: these circuits are modulated by dopamine secreting fibers from the midbrain, and interact with circuits that connect the rest of the cerebral hemispheres to the right prefrontal cortex (Filipek 1997). Molly Malone and colleagues have been experimentally validating their hypothesis that some or all AD/HD may represent excessive norepinephrine stimulation of the right hemisphere, and reduced dopaminergic stimulation of the left (Campbell et al. 1996, Malone et al. 1994, Sunohara et al. 1997). Thus Shelton and Barkley (Chapter 2) conclude that AD/HD affects various domains of functioning and manifests as defects in behavioral inhibition, working memory, regulation of motivations, and motor control.

The implication of this far-flung neuroanatomical system is that related difficulties may manifest in a variety of forms and, conversely, that similar symptomatology may have root in various neuroanatomical substrates. That is why there is as yet no consensus on the subtypes of AD/HD, and why attentional disorders are still divided into crude clinical categories like inattentive and hyperactive/impulsive types even though there are an array of disturbances in these broad categories.

Consistent with the evidence for an underlying broadly distributed system of executive, self-regulatory function are the streams of comorbidity and genetic studies. Comorbidity with AD/HD and obsessive spectrum disorders, such as obsessive-compulsive disorder (OCD) and Tourette's syndrome, has long been recognized (Biederman et al. 1991). The association with conduct disorder is more intuitive but only recently established by strict diagnostic criteria (Klein et al. 1997). Interestingly, despite the near-universal observation of familial clustering in the 70 to 80 percent range, proof of genetic transmission has not yet been well delineated (Eaves et al. 1997). The genetic picture, in brief, is still blurry. We expect to find—as in many other neuropsychiatric disorders—polymorphic gene-mediated defects expressed through intracellular metabolic function that affect receptor sensitivities of neurotransmitters (such as dopamine and its modulator serotonin) and ion-channel mediated sites (such as inhibitory γ-aminobutyric acid [GABA] and excitatory glutamine). Consistent with that prediction is the preliminary report of a major collaborative study (Blum et al. 1997) following transgenerational transmission of three dopaminergic genes. Eighty percent of all AD/HD subjects carried a DRD2 TaqA1 allele versus 3.3 percent of symptom-free controls.

Closer to clinical neurofeedback are the growing electrophysiological EEG studies that quantify and analyze multiple characteristics of EEG recordings. Quantitative EEG (QEEG) studies have demonstrated statistical group differences between normal control and AD/HD patients (Chabot and Serfontein 1996, Chabot et al. 1996, Mann et al. 1992, Monastra 1997, Suffin and Emory 1995). Initially it appeared that the patterns of excessive slow wave activity (and a related feature known as hypercoherence) indicated merely developmental delay in AD/HD children and adolescents. Then subgroups with different responses to medication emerged. But these statistical measures did not have the power to reliably discriminate from normal any particular individual who might be diagnosed AD/HD. Recently Robert Chabot (1997) reported that his group not only reliably discriminates attention deficit disorder (ADD) children from normal, but can predict which children will respond to methylphenidate, amphetamines, or no drug with 87 percent sensitivity and 91 percent specificity. Thus, a trend is developing toward clinical applications of ever more precise QEEG technologies and alogorhythms. (See Chapter 10, for a discussion of the controversy over whether QEEG adds anything substantive to the treatment of the AD/HD patient.)

Treatment of AD/HD is always multimodal, including work with parents and school, and conventionally entails the use of medication (Jacobvitz et al. 1990, Klein and Wender 1995, Malone and Swanson 1993, Shaywitz et al. 1997). This chapter illustrates the use of brainwave biofeedback—with and without medication—for the treatment of AD/HD in the areas of inattention, hyperactivity, and concomitant learning disorders.

A BRIEF HISTORY OF BIOFEEDBACK

It was brain-wave biofeedback that first excited public interest in biofeedback. However, EEG biofeedback suffered from its popularization; its technology and protocols were not as developed as the expectations it aroused. In recent years, advances in microchip technology have allowed the more technically demanding EEG feedback to emerge anew on the leading edge of the field. Neurofeedback is *not* relaxation or meditation training.

In the beginning was the alpha wave. Barbara Brown popularized brain-wave biofeedback with the 1977 publication of *Stress and the Art of Biofeedback*, in which she described a machine-boosted form of meditation that reinforced alpha waves with sound/light signals. Brown, Joe Kamiya, Elmer and Alyce Green, and other pioneer biofeedbackers studied a *disengaged* but *concentrated* state of mind characterized by synchronized pulses of relatively slow brain waves peaking eight to twelve times per second. Because these pulses were the same frequency as encephalographic waves usually picked up on the back of the head (from the occipital cortex) when the eyes are closed, they were assigned the same name: alpha waves.[2] In fact, because the synchronized (coherent) waves propagate across the entire cortex, not just the rear, they came to be recognized as markers of what became known as the alpha state.

It was observed that people felt better when they learned to achieve alpha states. Anxiety diminished. Mental skills improved (Kamiya 1968, Kamiya and Nowlis 1970). Biofeedback was demonstrated to vastly improve the learning and use of Zen meditation. Stress-related ills of all sorts were reported to clear up when people learned to produce alpha and even slower organized pulses called (on the same historical basis) theta waves (Brown 1977, Green and Green 1977). Researchers Elmer and Alyce Green, working at the Laboratory for Voluntary Control of Internal States at Menninger Foundation, demonstrated that alpha/theta states were integral to the extraordinary bodily control of the Indian Yogis. The teaching of self-regulation with biofeedback became the technological edge of the humanistic psychology/consciousness movement.

Although brain-wave technology was electronically sophisticated for its time, technical limits (and human exuberance) contributed to a backlash of disappointment in alpha-wave training. The public image of biofeedback began to swing into the wacky fringe of pop psychology, somehow akin to the penny biorhythm machines of coffee shop lobbies.[3]

---

2. *Alpha* is a historical term deriving out of its encephalographic origins. This particular wave was the first, therefore the alpha, to be described.

3. Biorhythm itself was a popular corruption of serious academic endeavor, foreshadowing chronobiology, with its study of the cycle of sleep, seasonal light, and ultradian rhythms.

By the mid-1980s, in clinical psychophysiological practice brain-wave biofeedback was also becoming passé because other more elegant and reliable, and less cumbersome, forms of biofeedback (muscle tension; finger skin temperature; and finger skin sweating/conductance, the galvanic skin response [GSR]) were available to practitioners that overlapped most of the benefits of training brain waves for the alpha state. Deep relaxation and the resultant physiological control could be taught in many ways, and researchers demonstrated that under ideal conditions, many kinds of biofeedback (physiological monitoring) could coincidentally produce an alpha state.[4]

However, as most biofeedback clinicians lost interest in brain-wave biofeedback, neurophysiologists continued basic research begun in the late 1960s. One highly esteemed researcher, M. Barry Sterman, Ph.D., made a series of observations of cat motor system brain-wave patterns that ultimately revised the way we think of attention and the body-mind connection (reviewed in Sterman 1996). He discovered a new brain-wave rhythm that appeared when cats motionlessly waited for a reward (analogous to a pre–pounce-on-a-mouse state). He called this the sensory-motor rhythm (SMR) because it was picked up most prominently on the central strip that connects the sensory (parietal lobe) and motor (posterior frontal lobe) cortices. SMR falls in the range of twelve to fifteen cycles per second (the unit is conventionally referred to as Hertz, or Hz). Sterman noted that cats with predominant SMR were less prone to seizures, and later demonstrated that cats trained to enhance the SMR could prevent such seizures. Then, in a series of brilliant experiments (Lantz and Sterman 1988, Sterman 1976, Sterman and Friar 1972, Sterman and MacDonald 1978, Sterman and Shouse 1980, Sterman et al. 1970, 1974), he demonstrated that several types of human seizures could be controlled in patients who were taught to enhance SMR while diminishing a slow wave (called theta[5]) that emerged from the midbrain. Sterman's findings

---

4. To be fair, Barbara Brown (who had ignited the public interest in EEG feedback) had described those correlations in her excellent book.

5. The nomenclature can get confusing. Theta refers to any coherent wave in the 3- to 8-Hz range, regardless of its origin and path. Earlier, we noted that there are synchronous waves in the theta range that connect

were replicated and recognized, as nonpharmacological treatment for epilepsy (Chase and Harper 1971, Ellertsen and Klove 1976, Finley 1976, Finley et al. 1975, Lubar and Bahler 1976, Lubar and Deering 1981, Lubar et al. 1981).

Further research has shown that those seizure patients who were trained with EEG biofeedback developed better skills in attending to difficult material[6] (Lubar and Shouse 1976, 1977, Lubar et al. 1985). Eventually, several protocols were developed for humans who learned to diminish slow rhythm activity while enhancing SMR or certain beta rhythms in the range of 15 to 18 Hz (Lubar 1995, Lubar and Lubar 1984, Lubar and Shouse 1976, Othmer et al. 1991). It is more technically challenging to give proper feedback of SMR and beta[7] than for the slower alpha rhythms, but computerized office-based systems have evolved from Sterman's prototypical research.[8] Later, more clinical variations were added. For instance, training toward the higher beta (15–18 Hz) frequencies on the left side of the head diminishes both hyperactivity and depression. Training on the right side toward the slower SMR helps perceptual learning problems, bipolar extremes, and is generally calming. Over the years, a variety of EEG training protocols have been developed for treating the full range of

---

the occipital and frontal cortex during states of profound mediation and self-healing states. As Sams (1997) has pointed out, there are undoubtedly many sorts of theta. For instance, 6.5 Hz is associated with sustained attention, extroversion, and low anxiety, and 4 Hz is associated with object naming.

6. The initial observations were the hyperactivity diminished; the link to the central component of attention was not made until the 1980s.

7. Historically, beta is the name applied to all waves faster than alpha, 12 to 50 Hz or more. In brain-wave biofeedback, beta denotes the 16- to 23-Hz segment of the beta band.

8. From Sterman's work have come important applications beyond seizure control that, while not well known, have been proving themselves in clinical practice. Important examples include rehabilitation of stroke and closed head trauma (postconcussion syndrome). In fact, Sterman's original experiments on cats utilized analogue equipment; computer power becomes an issue when complex video visual displays are provided in real time.

physical conditions (migraines, irritable bowel, sleep disturbances, pain syndromes, and on and on) with mind-body interactions.

CLINICAL NEUROFEEDBACK FOR AD/HD

Clinical applications of contemporary neurofeedback for the various attentional disorders demonstrate how biofeedback has evolved beyond relaxation training. There are EEG brain-map signatures common to these disorders: generalized slowing over the cortex (compared to age-matched norms) and increased alpha density over the frontal cortex (Etevenon 1986, Jahnzen et al. 1995, Lubar et al. 1985, 1990, 1991, Mann et al. 1992).[9] Whether attention-disordered subgroups can be differentiated is not yet settled (Chabot et al. 1996). What has been demonstrated is that each of the several protocols in use has been shown to improve the EEG brain map of children and young adults with AD/HD in thirty to eighty sessions, and that those improvements are maintained at follow-up one year and longer.

In EEG biofeedback, we first tune into the so-called raw signal[10] (Figure 11–1) obtained by placing a sensor on the scalp, with a refer-

---

9. Initially, it appeared that the EEG signature was correlated with the findings of Zametkin and colleagues that attentional deficits in adults were associated with diminished glucose metabolism (on positron emission tomography [PET] scan) in the prefrontal cortex (Zametkin et al. 1990); recently the finding was continued only in adolescent hyperactivity girls (Ernst et al. 1994, Zametkin 1995, Zametkin et al. 1993). This demonstrates again the importance of good research with distinctive subgroup delineation.

10. What we call brain waves are actually the summed effect of billions of cell contacts communicating (especially axon depolarization ionic shifts), contributing to a net electrochemical shift that we can pick up with surface electrodes when enough events happen at the same frequency (in a brief time frame). All kinds of processes involving different frequencies are going on at the same time, rather like our environment, which holds insensible radio waves whose various frequencies require a radio to tune into the specific frequencies. At the present time, we understand that brain rhythms are the product of multiple midbrain

C3 SMR

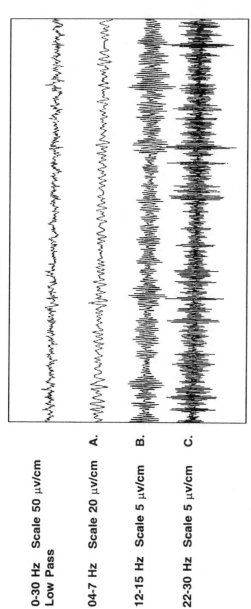

0-30 Hz   Scale 50 μv/cm
Low Pass

04-7 Hz   Scale 20 μv/cm   A.

12-15 Hz   Scale 5 μv/cm   B.

22-30 Hz   Scale 5 μv/cm   C.

Figure 11–1. Fourteen-second "snapshot" of brain wave activity over left frontoparietal area (C3) illustrating display seen on therapist's screen (Neurocybernetics ® system) while patient is working with a game display. Top line: raw EEG (30 Hz). Three of its components are presented in real time, lines A, B, and C. A: Theta band display (4-7 Hz). B: SMR band display (12-15 Hz). C: high beta band display.

ence sensor and ground on the ears. After electronic amplification the seemingly chaotic EEG signal is computer analyzed into component frequencies, which can be selected, monitored in real time, and displayed simply or in game format. In Figure 11-1 we see a raw EEG strip with three of its component brain waves below it. The raw EEG is made up of A + B + C as well as other coherent rhythms that have not been culled for this display.

In clinical work with AD/HD we want to reinforce certain frequencies (SMR or beta) while discouraging slow, subcortical rhythmic pulses that have a disorganizing effect on conscious attention. The reinforcement is built into video game displays. The subjects try to get points, beeps, and other game-type rewards, initially without understanding what they are doing. Generally three conditions are trained: (1) SMR or beta increased, (2) decreased theta, and (3) no major muscular tension (to decrease hyperactivity).

Note this crucial theoretical point: with AD/HD training, we are not looking for a neutral, deeply relaxed state like that sought in alpha/theta training. Similarly, we are not (exactly) training the patient to enter a bodily felt state that can be sensed and returned to at will. We are ultimately training varieties of *attentiveness*, but not by urging the patient to switch into a particular bodily felt state of mind. Rather, the training progresses as the patient approximates the end result we are seeking. For SMR, it is attentive stillness (using images such as "on the starting block," "ready to pounce," "the sniper"); for beta, it is attentive flow (images: freely skating, riding a bike, or canoeing). If the subject is not settled down and paying attention, feedback turns off (no rewards on the display). In other words, subjects first inadvertently shape brain waves by conscious behavior (quiet, attentive), and then are nonconsciously reinforced many times a second, leading to the resetting of brain functional patterns. Thus, neurofeedback is part of a larger feedback system in which the sub-

---

"pacemakers" (thalamic and parathalamic generators), which "receive multiple nonspecific inputs from brainstem cholinergic, adrenergic, and serotonergic pathways" (Sterman 1996, p. 27) as well as resonant loops (local, regional, and global) in the cortex itself (Lubar 1997).

jects are not rewarded until they pay attention, then once attentive they are available to receive training, which makes it easier to attend.

BRAIN WAVE TRAINING IS HYBRID PSYCHOTHERAPY

While EEG feedback is not about behaviorally reinforcing hyperactive kids so they will settle down and pay attention, it does have a cognitive-behavioral component. Neurofeedback is rarely just a straightforward interaction with a machine. After the novelty of training and its fancy video displays has passed, motivation must be maintained. Most patients with AD/HD go through one or more sleepy stages that we understand not only as an AD/HD response to tedium, but as reflecting a change of state; paradoxically, drifting or fraying consciousness reflects more coherent brain-wave activity. These are moments of opportunity for transition into new brain-wave patterning. Technically, the therapist adjusts thresholds for rewards, but effective therapists always bring authority, empathy, and inventiveness into play for motivating the patient/client. See Barabasz and Barabasz (1995) for a discussion of how hypnosis-like alert attention instructions (instantaneous neuronal activation procedure) (INAP) appears to be a valuable supplemental intervention.[11]

As is always the case, the success depends on the quality of the therapeutic relationship. Dynamic interpretations of intrapsychic conflict or relational processes are not usually introduced. Emphasis is task oriented, yet I have found that even long-alienated young people begin to open up about how the symptoms of inattention have become troubling components of pariah or misfit status. Thus a tertiary effect, comparable to other psychotherapy, is that patients are able to attend to social cuing systems, and peer alienation is diminished.

Louise Norris (1995) makes an essential point in reminding us that AD/HD children and young adults who have not attended well in their academic careers are likely to be bereft of cognitive strategies:

---

11. Barabasz and Barabasz believe INAP to be a form of hypnosis. Perhaps its mechanism of effect is more of a trance breaker (i.e., of self-induced protective dissociation).

"They do not know how to organize and encode information in ways that facilitate recall, application, and generalization" (p. 74). And these patients are prone to poor self-calming skills because rather than having developed alternative coping mechanisms, "They shifted their attention to some new attraction,[12] which provided instant stimulation and excitement" (p. 75). As Norris puts it, the wide array of cognitive-behavior strategies are "all valuable instruments in the hand of the clinician orchestrating the tune of 'Improved Performance' " (p. 75), even when neurofeedback is the featured soloist.

BRAIN-WAVE BIOFEEDBACK IS EFFECTIVE TREATMENT

It is twenty years since the first clinical report of neurofeedback for hyperactivity appeared in the biofeedback literature. Even since, there has been a growing stream of studies emerging that go a long way toward establishing that neurofeedback may be as effective as stimulant medication (Alhambra et al. 1995, Barabasz and Barabasz 1995, Cartozzo et al. 1995, Linden et al. 1996, Lubar 1991, 1993, 1995, Othmer et al. 1991, 1995, Rossiter and La Vaque 1995, Tansey 1993). And evidence seems to confirm (depending on one's threshold for accepting confirmation) and long-term benefits of neurofeedback tend to be sustained,[13] unlike stimulant medication. Yet, as of this writing no major United States peer-reviewed journal (outside of the biofeedback field) has published a study on neurofeedback for AD/HD.[14] The

---

12. That is, *attraction toward* their external environment (hyperactivity) or toward their internal world (inattentiveness).

13. Incidentally, such benefit progression, which is typical in biofeedback results, is predicted by systems theory: self-regulation is self-enhancing and restores responsiveness to the effects of contiguous systems. People keep improving after the treatment.

14. In his 1991 review, often quoted by critics, Lee finds "biofeedback," among various treatments for attention deficit disorder, not especially effective. Lee reviewed only three neurofeedback studies (all published before 1984); the rest were the earlier forms of biofeedback (alpha and psychophysiologic feedback), no longer clinically offered for AD/HD.

explanations include the following: (1) ever-stricter selection require-ments, including diagnostic subgroup stratification (cf. Shekim et al. 1990); (2) the difficulty in obtaining large numbers of subjects volun-teering for a six- to nine-month experiment[15]; (3) neurofeedback de-veloped within an explanatory paradigm different from that shared by the academic peer reviewers in the field of AD/HD; and (4) there are a host of technical variables relating to instrumentation and pro-tocol that make multicenter pooling of data difficult.

Another important and controversial area awaiting serious aca-demic study is the consistent finding in clinical studies of statistically significant improvement on IQ scores associated with brain-wave bio-feedback for AD/HD (Barabasz and Barabasz 1995, Cartozzo et al. 1995, Linden et al. 1996, Lubar et al. 1995, Othmer et al. 1995, Rossiter and La Vaque 1995).

THEORIES OF EFFICACY OF NEUROFEEDBACK

Despite the array of clinical protocols used in neurofeedback, there is general agreement that the empirical evidence is that when patients improve with EEG biofeedback, EEG parameters change toward normalcy. Since the typical deviation is to be found in excess theta amplitudes, these are typically at least partially normalized in train-ing. Although not always seen in successful training, generally cen-tral theta activity diminishes in association with increases in SMR or beta. Some clinics tend to train with an emphasis on lowering theta activity since that is felt to represent neurogenic immaturity[16]: slow-

---

15. There is no corporate support for such research as is provided for drug studies; federal grant money for such clinical studies is essentially nil.
16. While the excessive slow wave activity of AD/HD is a product of de-layed maturation, that controlled regression to more "primitive" syn-chronized activity is also associated with a mechanism of adaptation and change: slow wave activity converts relaxation into healing visionary/ mystical states of mind. These states are characterized by high focus, diminished cognition, emotional arousal (perceived as awe, "flow," and sense of conviction) with autonomic—either sympathetic or parasym-pathetic—arousal.

ness of the cortex to become less responsive to the parareticular pace-making of the midbrain. Other schools emphasize training up the rhythms of focused attention, noting that theta attenuates subse-quently. My observation is that individual patients respond better to one type of training or the other. Additionally, Siegfried Othmer has emphasized that whereas the training rewards increased synchronous activity (larger EEG amplitudes) in the moment, the training gener-alizes in life to the observation of appropriately desynchronized (re-duced coherence, lower amplitude) waveforms typical of the alert, attentive, and engaged brain. It is significant that the empirical ob-servation that SMR training is best for the right hemisphere, and beta training for the left, corroborates Malone's work that AD/HD is treated by either quieting the right hemisphere or "heating up" the left hemisphere. More generally, it may be said that the training ex-ercises the mechanisms by which the brain governs itself, which then allows the brain to function better in a variety of states, ranging all the way from sleep to hypervigilance. Thus performance is enhanced beyond the state in which the actual training took place.

Abarbanel,[17] in an excellent review (Abarbanel 1995), explicates a functional model of the brain physiology underlying improvement with neurofeedback treatment in attentional disorders. In specific detail, he indicates the likely mechanisms by which the patient learns to exert neuromodulatory control over the circuitry mediating the attentional process, and how, over time, practice automatizes the improved attentional capacity. He then goes on to explain how theta/beta ratios and attentional competence are mediated and how they relate to each other. Mechanisms include generation of cortical po-tentials in the brain stem–thalmus-cortex axis; neuromodulator con-trol of each of the four major brain-stem systems (noradrenergic, cholinergic, serotonergic, and dopaminergic) that interact with tha-lamic and limbic circuitry to optimize attention shifting; the switch-ing of brain centers between different states; and the process of long-

---

17. Abarbanel is a former theoretical physicist who went on to get an M.D. degree and psychiatric training at Harvard's Mt. Auburn and McLean Hospitals.

term potentiation, which is a stable and relatively long-lasting increase of synaptic response in circuits connecting the prefrontal cortex and the hippocampus.

CONCLUSION

Neurofeedback for AD/HD is a rapidly evolving field being pressed forward by practitioners, most of whom are outside the academic environment. In this chapter we have reviewed the uses of brainwave biofeedback, and its promise in the treatment of AD/HD. In the future we look forward to more rigorous studies of well-delineated subgroups that will further assess the effectiveness and durability of neurotherapy, and the surprising ancillary findings like change in IQ scores, improvement of miscellaneous learning disabilities, and treatment of depression.

ACKNOWLEDGMENTS

The author gratefully acknowledges the input of Siegfried Othmer, Ph.D., and Julian Issacs, Ph.D., who reviewed earlier drafts of this chapter.

REFERENCES

Abarbanel, A. (1995). Gates, states, rhythms, and resonances: the scientific basis of neurofeedback training. *Journal of Neurotherapy* 1(2):15-38.

Alhambra, M. A., Fowler, T. P., and Alhambra, A. A. (1995). EEG biofeedback: a new treatment option for ADD/AD/HD. *Journal of Neurotherapy* 1(2):39-43.

Barabasz, A., and Barabasz, M. (1995). Attention deficit hyperactivity disorder: neurological basis and treatment alternatives. *Journal of Neurotherapy* 1(1):1-10.

Biederman, J., Newcorn, J., and Sprich S. E. (1991). Co-morbidity of attention-deficit hyperactivity disorder. *American Journal of Psychiatry* 138:564-577.

Blum, K., Lubar J. O., Lubar, J. F., et al. (1997). Generational association and linkage studies of dopaminergic genes in AD/HD probans and multiple family member up to four generations. *Journal of Neurotherapy* 2(3):62–63.

Brown, B. B. (1977). *Stress and the Art of Biofeedback*. New York: Harper & Row.

Campbell, L., Malone, M. A., Kershner, J. R., et al. (1996). Methylphenidate slows right hemisphere processing in children with attention-deficit/ hyperactivity disorder. *Journal of Child and Adolescent Psychopharmacology* 6(4):229–239.

Cartozzo, H. A., Jacobs, D., and Gevirtz, R. N. (1995). EEG biofeedback and the remediation of AD/HD symptomatology: a controlled treatment outcome study. *Proceedings of the 26th Annual Meeting of the Association for Applied Psychophysiology and Biofeedback*, pp. 21–25. Wheatridge, CO: AAPB.

Casey, B. J., Castellanos, F. X., Giedd, J. N., et al. (1997a). Implications of right frontostriatial circuitry in response inhibition and attention deficit/hyperactivity disorder. *Journal of the American Academy of Child and Adolescent Psychiatry* 86(3):379–383.

Casey, B. J., Trainor, R., Giedd, J. N., et al. (1997b). The role of the anterior cingulate in autonomic and controlled processes: a developmental study. *Developmental Psychobiology* 30(1):61–69.

Castellanos, F. X. (1997). Toward a pathophysiology of attention-deficit/ hyperactivity disorder. *Clinical Pediatrics* (Phila.) 36(7):381–383.

Chabot, R. J. (1997). Quantitative EEG profiles of children with attention and learning disorders and the role of QEEG in predicting medication response and outcome. *Journal of Neurotherapy* 2(3):61–62.

Chabot, R. J., Merkin, H., Wood, L. M., et al. (1996). Sensitivity and specificity of QEEG in children with attention deficit or specific developmental learning disorders. *Clinical Electroencephalography* 27(1):26–33.

Chabot, R. J., and Serfontein, G. (1996). Quantitative EEG profiles of children with attention deficit disorder. *Biological Psychiatry* 40:951–963.

Chase, R. J., and Harper, R. M. (1971). Somatomotor and visceromotor correlates of operantly conditioned 12-14 c/sec sensorimotor cortical activity. *Electroencephalography and Clinical Neurophysiology* 31:504–507.

Eaves, L. J., Silver, J. L., Meyer, J. M., et al. (1997). Genetics and developmental psychopathology: 2. The main affects of genes and environment on behavioral problems on the Virginia Twin Study of adolescent behavioral development. *Journal of Child Psychology and Psychiatry* 38(8):965–980.

Ellertsen, B., and Klove, H. (1976). Clinical application of biofeedback training in epilepsy. *Scandinavian Journal of Behavior Therapy* 5:133–144.

Ernst, M., Liebenauer, L. L., King, A. C., et al. (1994). Reduced brain metabolism in hyperactive girls. *Journal of the American Academy of Child and Adolescent Psychiatry* 33(6):858–868.

Etevenon, P. (1986). Application and perspectives of EEG cartography. In *Topographic Mapping of Brain Electrical Activity*, ed. F. H. Duffy, pp. 113–141. Boston: Butterworth.

Filipek, P. A., Semrad-Clikean, M., Steingard, R. J., et al. (1997). Volumetric MRI analysis comparing subjects having attention-deficit hyperactivity disorder with normal controls. *Neurology* 48(3):589–601.

Finley, W. W. (1976). Effects of sham feedback following successful SMR training in an epileptic: a follow-up study. *Biofeedback and Self-Regulation* 1:227–235.

Finley, W. W., Smith, H. A., and Etherton, M. D. (1975). Reduction of seizures and normalization of the EEG in a severe epileptic following sensorimotor biofeedback training: preliminary study. *Biological Psychology* 2:189–203.

Green, A., and Green, E. (1977). *Beyond Biofeedback*. New York: Dell.

Hartmann, T. (1997). *Attention Deficit Disorder: A Different Perception*. Grass Valley, CA: Underwood.

Jacobvitz, S., Srofe, L. A., Steward, M., and Leffert, N. (1990). Treatment of attentional and hyperactivity problems in children with sympathomimetic drugs: a comprehensive review. *Journal of the American Academy of Child and Adolescent Psychiatry* 29:677–688.

Jahnzen, T., Graap, K., Stephan, S., et al. (1995). Differences in baseline EEG measures for AD/HD and normally achieving preadolescent males. *Biofeedback and Self-Regulation* 20(1):65–82.

Kamiya, J. (1968). Conscious control of brain waves. *Psychology Today* 6:86–91.

Kamiya, J., and Nowlis, D. (1970). The control of electroencephalographic alpha rhythms through auditory feedback and the associated mental activity. *Psychophysiology* 6:476.

Klein, R. G., Abikoff, H., Klass, E., et al. (1997). Clinical efficacy of methylphenidate in conduct disorder with and without attention-deficit hyperactivity disorder. *Archives of General Psychiatry* 54:1073–1080.

Klein, R. G., and Wender, P. (1995). The role of methylphenidate in psychiatry. *Archives of General Psychiatry* 52:429–433.

Lantz, D. L., and Sterman, M. B. (1988). Neuropsychological assessment of subjects with uncontrolled epilepsy: effects of EEG feedback training. *Epilepsia* 29(2):163–171.

Lee, S. W. (1991). Biofeedback as a treatment for childhood hyperactivity: a critical review of the literature. *Psychological Reports* 68:163–192.

Linden, M., Habib, T., and Radojevic, V. (1996). A controlled study of EEG biofeedback effects on cognitive and behavioral measures with attention-deficit disorder and learning disabled children. *Biofeedback and Self-Regulation* 21:35–49.

Lubar, J. F. (1991). Discourse on the development of EEG diagnostics and biofeedback for attention-deficit/hyperactivity disorders. *Biofeedback and Self-Regulation* 16:201–225.

——— (1993). Innovation or inquisition: the struggle for ascent in the court of science: neurofeedback and AD/HD. *Biofeedback* 21(1):23–30.

——— (1995). Neurofeedback for the management of attention-deficit/hyperactivity disorder. In *Biofeedback: A Practitioner's Guide*, ed. M. S. Schwartz et al., 2nd ed., pp. 493–522. New York: Guilford.

——— (1977). Neocortical dynamics: implications for understanding the role of neurofeedback and related techniques for the enhancement of attention. *Applied Psychophysiology and Biofeedback* 22:2111–2125.

Lubar, J. F., and Bahler, W. W. (1976). Behavioral management of epileptic seizures following EEG biofeedback training of the sensorimotor rhythm. *Biofeedback and Self-Regulation* 7:77–104.

Lubar, J. F., Bianchini, K. J., Calhoun, W. H., et al. (1985). Spectral analysis of EEG differences between children with and without learning disabilities. *Journal of Learning Disabilities* 18:403–408.

Lubar, J. F., and Deering, W. M. (1981). *Behavioral Approaches to Neurology.* New York: Academic Press.

Lubar, J. F., Gross, D. M., Shively, M. S., and Mann C. A. (1990). Differences between normal, learning disabled, and gifted children based upon an auditory evoked potential task. *Journal of Psychophysiology* 4:470–481.

Lubar, J. F., Shabsin, H. S., Natelson, S. E., et al. (1981). EEG operant conditioning in intractable epileptics. *Archives of Neurology* 38:700–704.

Lubar, J. F., and Shouse, M. N. (1976). EEG and behavioral changes in a hyperkinetic child concurrent with training of the sensorimotor rhythm (SMR): a preliminary report. *Biofeedback and Self-Regulation* 3:293–306.

——— (1977). Use of biofeedback and the treatment of seizure disorders and hyperactivity. *Advances in Childhood Clinical Psychology* 1:204–251.

Lubar, J. F., Swartwood, M. O., Swartwood, J. N., and O'Donnell, P. H. (1995). Evaluation of the effectiveness of EEG neurofeedback training for AD/HD in a clinical setting as measured by changes in T.O.V.A. scores, behavioral ratings, and WISC-R performance. *Biofeedback and Self-Regulation* 20(1):83–99.

Lubar, J. O., and Lubar, J. F. (1984). Electroencephalographic biofeedback of SMR and beta for treatment of attention deficit disorders in a clinical setting. *Biofeedback and Self-Regulation* 9:1–25.

Malone, M. A., Kershner, J. R., and Swanson, J. M. (1994). Hemispheric processing and methylphenidate effects in attention-deficit hyperactivity disorder. *Journal of Child Neurology* 9(2):181–189.

Malone, M. A., and Swanson, J. M. (1993). Effects of methylphenidate on impulsive responding in children with attention-deficit hyperactivity disorder. *Journal of Child Neurology* 8(2):157–63.

Mann, C. A., Lubar, J. F., Zimmerman, A. W., et al. (1992). Quantitative analysis of EEG in boys with attention deficit hyperactivity disorder: controlled study with clinical implications. *Pediatric Neurology* 8:30–36.

Monastra, V. J. (1997). Neurometrics and attention-deficit/hyperactivity disorder: a status report. *Biofeedback* 25(4):13–16.

Norris, S. L. (1995). Neurofeedback: one instrument in the orchestra. *Journal of Neurotherapy* 1(2):74–76.

Othmer, S., Kaiser, D., and Othmer, S. F. (1995). EEG biofeedback training for attention deficit disorder: a review of recent controlled studies and clinical findings. *California Biofeedback* 11(4):5–8.

Othmer, S., Othmer, S. F., and Marks, C. S. (1991). EEG biofeedback training for attention deficit disorder, specific learning disability, and associated conduct problems. (Available from EEG Spectrum, Inc., 16100 Ventura Blvd., Suite 10, Encino, CA 91436.)

Rossiter, T. R., and La Vaque, T. J. (1995). A comparison of EEG biofeedback and psychostimulants in treating attention deficit/hyperactivity disorders. *Journal of Neurotherapy* 1(1):48–59.

Sams, M. (1997). Theta: don't tread on me. *Journal of Neurotherapy* 2(3):67.

Shaywitz, B. A., Fletcher, J. M., and Shaywitz, S. E. (1997). Attention-deficit/hyperactivity disorder. *Advances in Pediatrics* 44:331–367.

Shekim, W. O., Asarnow, R. F., Hess, E., et al. (1990). A clinical and demographic profile of a sample of adults with attention deficit hyperactivity disorder, residual state. *Comprehensive Psychiatry* 31(5):416–425.

Sterman, M. B. (1976). Effects of brain surgery and EEG operant conditioning on seizure latency following MMH intoxication in the cat. *Experimental Neurology* 50:757–765.

——— (1996). Physiological origins and functional correlates of EEG rhythmic activities: implications for self-regulation. *Biofeedback and Self-Regulation* 21(1):3–34.

Sterman, M. B., and Friar, L. (1972). Suppression of seizures in an epileptic following sensorimotor EEG feedback training. *Electroencephalography and Clinical Neuropsychology* 33:89–95.

Sterman, M. B., Howe, R. C., and MacDonald, L. R. (1970). Facilitation of spindle-burst sleep by conditioning of electroencephalographic activity while awake. *Science* 167:1146–1148.

318   Thomas M. Brod

Sterman, M. B., and MacDonald, L. R. (1978). Effects of central cortical EEG feedback training on seizure incidence in poorly controlled epileptics. *Epilepsia* 19:207–222.
Sterman, M. B., MacDonald, L. R., and Stone, R. K. (1974). Biofeedback training of the sensorimotor electroencephalographic rhythm in man: effects on epilepsy. *Epilepsia* 15:395–416.
Sterman, M. B., and Shouse, M. N. (1980). Sensorimotor mechanisms underlying a possible common pathology in epilepsy and associated sleep disturbances. In *Sleep and Epilepsy*, ed. M. B. Sterman, M. N. Shouse, and P. Passouant, pp. 19–42. New York: Academic.
Suffin, S. C., and Emory, W. H. (1995). Neurometric subgroups in attentional and affective disorders. *Clinical Encephalography* 26(2):76–83.
Sunohara, G. A., Voros, J. G., Malone, M. A., and Taylor, M. J. (1997). Effects of methylphenidate in children with attention deficit hyperactivity disorder: a comparison of event-related potentials between medication responders and non-responders. *International Journal of Psychophysiology* 27(1):9–14.
Tansey, M. A. (1993). Ten year stability of EEG biofeedback results for a hyperactive boy who failed fourth grade perceptually impaired class. *Biofeedback and Self-Regulation* 18(1):33–44.
Zametkin, A. J. (1995). Attention-deficit disorder. Born to be hyperactive? *Journal of the American Medical Association* 273(23):1871–1874.
Zametkin, A. J., Liebenauer L. L., Fitzgerald, G. A., et al. (1993). Brain metabolism in teenagers with attention-deficit hyperactivity disorder. *Archives of General Psychiatry* 50(5):333–340.
Zametkin, A. J., Nordahl, T. E., Gross, M., et al. (1990). Cerebral glucose metabolism in adults with hyperactivity of childhood onset. *New England Journal of Medicine* 323(20):1361–1366.

12

A Psychodynamic Approach to Treating Attention Deficit/Hyperactivity Disorder: Recent Developments in Theory and Technique

Sebastiano Santostefano

For decades children and adolescents, who are now labeled AD/HD, had been recognized as needing assistance because, in spite of average intelligence, they showed short attention spans, distractibility, excessive daydreaming, poor retention of details, boredom, hyperactivity, and occasional outbursts of physical and/or verbal aggression. A committee attributed these behaviors to functional deviations in the central nervous system and labeled the cluster "minimal brain dysfunction" (Clements 1966). But the first *Diagnostic and Statistical Manual of Mental Disorders* (*DSM-I*), published in 1952 by the American Psychiatric Association, and its second edition (*DSM-II*) published in 1968, did not offer a diagnostic category for these children, primarily because, at that time, the diagnosis of children was essentially ignored.

The attention deficit disorder diagnosis created was in 1980 when *DSM-III* was published. The disorder included two subtypes: with hyperactivity and without. Now familiar to all clinicians, the essential features of the hyperactive type included signs of developmentally in-appropriate inattention, impulsivity, and hyperactivity. In the class-room these children do not complete a task, shift from task to task, have difficulty organizing work, give the impression that they are not listening or have not heard what they have been told, produce sloppy work, misinterpret easy items, and are excessively restless, and some-times aggressive. Symptoms worsen in situations that lack intrinsic appeal. In addition, it is usually rare for a child with this disorder to display these symptoms in all settings or even in the same setting at all times. As for the subtype without hyperactivity, the features are the same except for the absence of restlessness. These symptoms emerge by the age of 3, although the disorder may not come to the attention of professionals until the child enters grade school.

Seven years later, the revision of the third edition (*DSM-III-R*) in 1987 relabeled this constellation of symptoms attention deficit hyper-active disorder (AD/HD), and in the fourth edition (*DSM-IV*) in 1994 the label was modified slightly, now termed attention deficit/hyper-activity disorder (AD/HD). While the description of AD/HD has remained essentially unchanged since 1980, the *DSM-IV* notes that al-though children with AD/HD show poorer performance than con-trols on tests that require "effortful mental processing . . . it is not yet entirely clear what fundamental cognitive deficit is responsible for this" (p. 81).

When I and other psychodynamically oriented clinicians consider the description of AD/HD, we become concerned and raise several questions that are relevant for treatment. (1) What do we mean by "developmentally inappropriate inattention," and how do we revise attention so that it is developmentally appropriate? (2) What are the fundamental cognitive deficits, structured during the first three to four years of life, that are responsible for inattention, and what are their implications for treatment? (3) If a child tends not to hear what she/he has been told, misinterprets information, and becomes distracted by irrelevant stimuli, is there something else, other than homework, a teacher's instructions, and parental directions, that is receiving the child's attention, and should that something else also be a target for therapy? (4) If it is rare for a child to display these behaviors in the same setting at all times, and if symptoms worsen in situations that lack intrinsic appeal, is it possible that how the child construes a situation changes from time to time, and can we include the child's interpretations of environments in treatment? (5) If hyperactivity-impulsivity and/or aggressive behaviors accompany a child's inattention, are there treatment techniques that integrate regulation of the body with cognitive functioning, on the one hand, and emotion with cognition, on the other?

The following clinical vignette illustrates these questions.

From marginal school performance during the first grade, Sally's academic productivity now in the second grade slipped well below grade expectation. Since the first grade, she was observed to be inattentive, hyperactive, easily distracted, and she disliked engaging classroom tasks. In addition, when in the playground, she sometimes impulsively pinched the buttocks of peers. Another behavior recently appeared that made teachers and parents quite anxious. On several occasions, children witnessed Sally urinating on the floor of the school bathroom and ran to the teacher to report the disaster.

During the evaluation, Sally was surely hyperactive as she coped with cognitive and intellectual tests. The results showed a short attention span and a tendency to misinterpret test items. During testing she was distracted by pictures on the wall and voices from outside the office. In addition, when telling a story to Card 10, for example, of the Children Apperception Test–Animals (a bathroom scene), she anxiously shared that when sitting over "the hole of the toilet" she became frightened by the fantasy that "a giant lobster" would reach up; "it tears you all up with humongous claws." She also associated to her father, who frequently yelled at her while favoring her brother. The school psychologist diagnosed Sally as afflicted by AD/HD, Combined Type.

Should a therapist treat Sally's inattentiveness by training her to use self-instruction, or treat her impulsively pinching the buttocks of peers with behavior modification techniques? Or should a therapist treat her frightening fantasy with the technique of systematic desensitization by training her to relax and imagine less frightening and gradually more frightening scenes? Or should a therapist help Sally gain conscious insight into the unconscious dynamic that the lobster reaching up from the toilet bowl is a symbol of her father punishing her for being a bad girl, and the mental force prescribing that she pinch the buttocks of peers.

My thesis is that a therapist does not have to choose among Sally's symptoms of inattention, frightening fantasy, impulsive actions, and unconscious symbols. Stimulated by revisions in psychodynamic concepts and technique, I have developed a treatment approach that addresses the needs of AD/HD children holistically, in Sally's case integrating as one her cognition, emotions, hyperactive/impulsive actions, and conscious and unconscious fantasies.

Before describing these revisions and the treatment model, a preliminary discussion addresses how revisions in psychodynamic concepts and techniques suggest heuristic ways to diagnosis and treat AD/HD children holistically.

HOW THE VIEWPOINT OF NOSOLOGY PRODUCED THE CATEGORY OF AD/HD

The model of nosology (or diagnostic categories) has a long and successful history in medical science, dating back at least to the ancient Egyptians (Temkin 1965). This point of view proposes that to understand pathology it is necessary to locate diseases in separate, independent classifications. These classifications help clinicians and researchers order the morass of phenomena presented by patients, communicate with each other about their patients, and plan investigations. Given the success of the nosological model in medical science, it is not surprising that the viewpoint was gradually adopted by psychological practitioners.

What are the steps the model of nosology follows when applied to human behavior? (1) Qualitatively different and relatively stable behavioral traits that patients exhibit are described in as much detail as possible. (2) Whenever behaviors are observed to occur together, the cluster of traits define a category of psychopathology. (3) The categories formed by clusters of traits are viewed as mutually exclusive. Thus, not listening and running about excessively, which signify AD/HD, are viewed as different from ignoring parental prohibitions and running away, which signify a conduct disorder. The main goal of nosology, then, is to construct stable pictures of typical patients whose behavioral traits represent the category.

Was the model of nosology always accepted without criticism in behavioral science? Although gaining rapid popularity from the start, the viewpoint of diagnostic categories was in fact the subject of intense debate in a conference held soon after the first diagnostic manual was published. These deliberations appear not to have influenced the construction of subsequent manuals, nor the approach most clinicians apply when formulating diagnoses.

In 1965, three years before the second edition of *DSM* was released, the National Institute of Mental Health (NIMH) invited professionals from various disciplines to discuss the role and methodology of classification in the mental health field (Katz and Cole 1965). The invited guests did more than discuss; they vigorously debated the advantages and disadvantages of diagnostic categories, including the following: (1) Do the virtues of categorizing people outweigh the resulting loss of information about their individuality? (2) Could the mental health field advance more effectively if characteristics of people are viewed as interacting in a complex manner rather than as fixed diagnostic entities? (3) Why do some clinical conditions look relatively different at different points in time? (4) What are the limitations inherent in establishing diagnostic types on the basis of behaviors observed by others, self-description, interviewing, and questionnaires?

At this conference, David Shakow (1965) cautioned that classifying mental disorders and locating them into fixed categories could result in (1) *reification*—the danger of reifying a diagnostic category (which I believe has occurred with AD/HD); (2) *compartmentalization*—taking only a part of the picture and locating a person in a category on the basis of a few pieces of behavior; and (3) *simplification*—taking a simpler, more easily understood explanation of a complex phenomenon that may be difficult to grasp in all its intricacies. He also questioned the principle of forming diagnoses by clustering traits that are observed to occur together and assuming the cluster has meaning. He illustrated by pointing out that while pencils of yellow-painted wood are common, the color yellow is not essential to the function of pencils.

George Kelly (1965) proposed that clinicians who reify diagnoses suffered from a condition he termed "hardening of the categories" (p. 158) (an affliction that I believe can still be observed affecting some clinicians using the diagnosis of AD/HD) and offered a remedy we consider below.

In their summary remarks of this conference, Katz and Cole (1965) asked questions we might still raise today. "Are mental disorders really made up of these particular configurations of symptoms and characteristics? And why is it that when we think of diagnosis it is difficult not to think of types?" (p. 563).

Two issues discussed in the section of *DSM-IV* titled "Limitations of the Categorical Approach" relate to the deliberations of the NIMH conference that took place thirty years earlier, and converge with the position I am taking here with regard to AD/HD. The clinician is cautioned not to assume "that each category of mental disorder is a completely discrete entity with absolute boundaries dividing it from the other mental disorders [and that individuals] described as having the same mental disorder are alike in all important ways" (p. xxii). It seems to me these precautions are not usually taken into account by clinicians dealing with AD/HD. Research reports commonly compare the test performance of children who "have" AD/HD with those who do not (e.g., Cahn et al. 1996).

With the second issue, *DSM-IV* authors acknowledged that classification could be organized following "a dimensional model rather than a categorical model" (p. xxii) and that dimensional models convey more information because, unlike categorical models, they consider "clinical attributes that are subthreshold," that is, deep (unconscious) as well as surface (conscious) behaviors. But a dimensional model was proposed thirty years earlier by Kelly (1965) at the NIMH conference as a way of preventing "hardening of the categories" among clinicians. He argued that constructing diagnostic categories "proves itself to be almost completely sterile in suggesting something new to be looked for" (p. 158) and that behaviors should be plotted along each of several dimensions, which he termed "universal reference axes."

The heuristic value of a dimensional model did not originate with Kelly, since Freud, and later Piaget, made the same recommendation. In his early writings, Freud (1916) noted, "We seek not merely to describe and to classify phenomena, but to understand them as *signs* or an interplay of forces [dimensions or axes] of the mind, as a manifestation of purposeful intentions working concurrently or in mutual opposition. We are concerned with a dynamic view of mental phenomena" (p. 67, my italics).

Years later Piaget (1975) expressed reservations over the fact that "psychiatry is largely based on the principle of 'syndromes' " (i.e., categories) (p. viii). As an alternative, he proposed "an analytic approach" by which he meant that the clinician become immersed "in the 'ensemble' of elements that are involved at different levels of functioning" (i.e., conscious and unconscious) (p. vii). In proposing that we go beyond compartmentalizing and classifying diseases, then, Freud and Piaget suggested we look at behaviors as symbols, revealing an active interplay of mental activities and constellations of behaviors that operate at different levels. Applied to AD/HD, treatment should address holistically a child's actions, fantasies, and thoughts that are organized at conscious and unconscious levels.

BOUNDARIES THAT INTERFERE WITH A TREATMENT MODEL OF MULTIPLE DIMENSIONS[1]

When asking what we should observe and understand, students of behavior have drawn many boundaries (e.g., between conscious and unconscious, and verbal and nonverbal), with one member of the polarized pair viewed as true and more worthy. Drawing such boundaries, Ken Wilber (1977, 1979) argued, is a characteristic of Western thinking that splits off what is construed as unacceptable and pursues what is construed as pleasurable. These boundaries have segregated human psychology, and eventually psychotherapy, into domains, obscuring from view "ensembles" of behaviors that are interrelated, although occurring at different levels.

In the early years of American psychology, while the Western tradition of constructing boundaries was already exerting considerable influence, a few workers were critical of this tendency. Surveying what

---

1. For a more detailed discussion of this topic, see Santostefano 1998.

students of human behavior of that day were doing, Sir Francis Galton (1884) stated, "there are two sorts of [investigators] . . . those who habitually dwell on pleasanter circumstances . . . and those who have an eye out for the unpleasing ones" (p. 180). A few years later, Frederick Lyman Wells (1912, 1914), reviewing studies of the word association method, noticed a trend that disturbed him. He believed that too many investigators had been avoiding the unpleasant task of learning about a person's emotional life by "hiding themselves" in pleasanter studies of lexical and intellectual connections between the stimulus word spoken by the investigator and the associated response spoken by the subject.

Since the work of Galton and Wells, American psychology has continued to draw boundaries dividing issues into opposing camps. Three of these boundaries have relevance for treating AD/HD. One boundary segregates "real" and "subjective" knowledge, another body and mind, and another cognition and emotion.

THE BOUNDARY DIVIDING THE BASIS OF KNOWLEDGE: OBJECTIVE/REAL VERSUS SUBJECTIVE

If we accept the view that all children gather and experience knowledge, whether or not a child is inattentive, distractible, and hyperactive, we are faced with the question, What is knowledge and how does a child revise knowledge and her/his understanding of experiences? There have been two responses to this question reflecting a boundary dividing two opposing camps (Overton 1994, 1997, 1998, Overton and Horowitz 1991). One camp is usually referred to as objectivism and the other as interpretationism.

Objectivism

This position holds that the external world contains knowledge that already exists, and the person or knower is separate from this knowledge. Neutral, well-controlled observations discover that knowledge and permit inferences. To discover knowledge that already exists, a boundary is set between the clinician and the patient, another between the patient and the environment (in order to observe how the patient and the environment each respond when one acts on the other), and a third between "real" phenomena, perceived by the clinician, and the "subjective" (i.e., what the patient reports). It is assumed the patient is inherently passive and responds only when stimulation occurs.

The assumptions of objectivism have been characterized by the metaphor of a person as a "machine" (e.g., most recently the digital computer) that guides what a clinician sees: (1) Behavior can be separated into parts; with AD/HD, for example, these parts include "does not listen," "fails to finish schoolwork and chores," "is often forgetful," "fidgets," and so on. (2) The whole can be defined by adding these parts. (3) The "machine" receives inputs (stimuli or information) and delivers outputs (responses, behaviors) that produce positive or negative consequences in the environment that determine whether the behavior will occur again.

The machine metaphor views interpersonal relationships in terms of whether and how each person exerts an independent, direct, and causal influence on the other. Relationships are acquired and determined by a schedule of reinforcements provided by the environment and the availability of others serving as models. In terms of what happens within an individual, the machine metaphor presents an image of an interior containing discrete stimuli and responses snapped together in a linear fashion to form chains called "mediators" that derive from learning and imitation and that express feelings, attitudes, and expectations. Each mediator, or "cognitive representation," is evaluated in terms of how well it fits the real event that was experienced.

For objectivism, change and development take place as a person adds (accumulates) or subtracts (eliminates or replaces) behaviors and cognitive representations in terms of whether they correspond with what the real world requires.

Interpretationism

This position holds that knowledge does not exist in the environment independent of the knower but is constructed by a person's cognition and actions. Therefore, it is assumed that all observations, including those experimentally controlled, are influenced by what the observer already thinks. If the clinician participates in, and in part determines, what is observed, how does she/he construct explanations and understanding? The observer searches for patterns or "ensembles" displayed by phenomena, as suggested by Freud and Piaget, using a metaphor to explain them (e.g., mental schemas, mechanisms of defense).

The assumptions of interpretationism have been characterized by various organic metaphors, symbolizing a person as a plant, embryo, or cell, that guide what a clinician sees: (1) The cell (person) along with other cells (persons) and the atmosphere (environment) that surrounds them form a holistic system. (2) Each person is in a reciprocal, dialectical relationship with others. (3) A person is inherently active, self-organizing, and directional, moving from one level of functioning that is global to levels that are increasingly articulated, differentiated, and integrated.

Relations between persons involve dialectical exchanges, with each actively approaching, avoiding, and selecting stimulation from the other. As the paradox between two persons is negotiated, elements of each are integrated, and the relationship spirals to a new level where another paradox is articulated and negotiated, and so on. Developments within a person, such as, for example, the relationship between what a person fantasizes about others, and how the person acts with them, involve the same processes (holism, dialectics, differentiation, and integration) that result in a person's internal relationships. In Stern's (1985) model, for example, these internal relationships are termed *representations of interactions generalized*, mental organizations that represent actions a person has taken with others, what a person expects from interactions with others, and guide actions the person takes in the present.

For interpretationism, change and development take place as a person, participating in a dialectical process, revises and renders more flexible (differentiation-integration), subjective meanings (cognitive/affective understanding) assigned to experiences constructed with others, and that guide actions. Earlier meanings are not replaced but are integrated within new ones.

AD/HD and the Boundary between Objective and Subjective

The position of objectivism can be seen operating in many clinicians when they approach AD/HD through the lens of *DSM-IV*. This manual asks clinicians to collect neutral observations of a child, especially those reported by teachers and parents, and establish whether the child displays the designated number of criterion behaviors. To collect these observations a boundary is located between the child, on the one hand, and teachers, parents, and clinician, on the other, with the views of the latter held as "true" (Searight et al. 1995). When a child is treated from the objectivist position, the child's overt behaviors and conscious thoughts, viewed as resulting from consequences that occurred in the environment, become the target of treatment. The child is asked to engage in tasks designed to modify the problem behavior directly, or use self-talk to guide attention, or change the environment by correcting the ways in which the child's cognition is misrepresenting it. The child gains control over the problem behavior by accumulating skills. Moreover, unconscious meanings tend to be ignored. The interpretationist approach to viewing and treating AD/HD children is quite different and is illustrated by the methods discussed below.

THE BOUNDARY DIVIDING BODY AND MIND

A boundary between body and mind has been maintained in Western thinking since the writings of ancient Greek philosophers (Fisher 1990), resulting in the dualism of soul (mind) and body that, as a source of passion and pain, was usually segregated as undesirable. Adapting this view, American psychology split off the body as a psychological concept and held it in the shadows until the 1980s (Cash and Pruzinsky 1990).

This has not been the case, however, in psychodynamic therapy. After the neurologist Henry Head proposed, in 1926, an unconscious "body schema" to conceptualize how body perceptions are integrated to form a picture of the self, Paul Shilder (1935) elaborated Freud's notion that the first ego is a "body ego," which integrated body experiences with personality, and conceptualized that a "body image" emerges from early interactions with others, is ever changing, and gains expression in everything from one's clothing to experiencing empathy and anger. Following these early studies, other psychoanalysts gradually elaborated Schilder's holistic, dialectical concept of body image (Grand 1977, Kramer and Akhtar 1992, Mahl 1987).

Receiving isolated attention within mainstream psychology, the concepts of embodied experiences and body image eventually entered through the doorway of cognition. For example, Wapner and Werner (1965) demonstrated that body attitudes influence perceptions of one's position in space, and Fisher and Cleveland (1958) illustrated that a person's body image boundaries correlate with personality. But after these programs peaked in the 1960s, interest in body image research declined (Tiemersma 1989).

More recently body image research has resurfaced, focusing mainly on eating disorders (Cash and Pruzinsky 1990). However, the conceptualizations of these investigators differ from that of Schilder's holistic, dialectical view and reflect the zeitgeist of objectivism. The subjective body image of a person is viewed as reflecting distortions of the real image that exists independent of the knower. Moreover, methods used by investigators (Thompson et al. 1990) to assess body image typically ask a person to respond to questionnaires, or to rate satisfaction with a series of silhouettes that vary in size/weight, procedures that gather conscious knowledge about body image rather than symbolic representations as emphasized by Schilder. And from their review of body image studies, Cash and Pruzinsky (1990) argued that most forms of psychotherapy portray the patient as a "disembodied entity."

AD/HD and the Boundary between Body and Mind

The boundary between body and mind can be seen influencing techniques commonly used to treat AD/HD children that require restriction of body activity (Alexander-Roberts 1994, Braswell 1993, Fraser et al. 1992, Goldstein and Goldstein 1995, Gordon et al. 1991); for example, (1) *time out*—the child is asked to sit in the corner of a room or in a separate room, as an opportunity for the child to get control of herself/himself; (2) *token system*—whenever a child stops inappropriate actions, she/he receives a token that can be used to buy a desired object; (3) *grounding*—if the child breaks a major rule at home, or school, or the treatment situation, he/she loses privileges; (4) *timer*—a timer is set that regulates a child's speed in performing some task; (5) *quiet corner*—the child is provided with an area that is free of external distractions; (6) *self-instruction training and modeling*—while completing a task, the child is taught to imitate verbal statements and questions by an adult, intended to "teach children to slow down and cognitively examine their behavioral alternatives before acting" (Kendall and Braswell 1985, p. 1).

Rather than segregate body and mind, the psychodynamic approach described below interrelates body images and body activities with the mind's conscious and unconscious fantasies.

THE BOUNDARY BETWEEN COGNITION AND EMOTION

A boundary has also been drawn between cognition and emotion since the early Greek philosophers (Kagan 1978) in order to preserve thought as right and rational and to protect it from passion and the irrational (Bruner 1986). In the first decades of this century, orthodox behaviorism, which dominated American psychology, split off the mind and its emotions as taboo and declared that only overt behaviors were the legitimate topic of study.

Then along came the studies of Piaget, which provided one way of understanding the forbidden mind. American psychology quickly embraced his view, cast aside the boundary between mind and behavior, and produced a flood of studies resulting in the development of a sophisticated cognitive science (Gardner 1985). As the mind's new science grew, the boundary between cognition and emotion, dormant during behaviorism's suppression of the mind, was established. Investigators began to locate themselves either on the side of cognition or on the side of emotion (Santostefano 1986).

Curiously, Piaget, who is credited with freeing American psychology from orthodox behaviorism, was also held responsible for the division that developed between cognition and emotion and the emphasis he gave to the former (Bearison and Zimiles 1986). However, Piaget recognized that the boundary between cognition and emotion was not real but served as a conceptual convenience and noted, "Freud focused on emotion, I chose intelligence" (Decarie 1978, p. 183) because (referring to his mother's poor mental health), "I have always . . . preferred the study of normalcy and the workings of the intellect over that of the tricks of the unconscious (Campbell 1977, p. 116). Although drawing a boundary, still used by many, that equates normalcy with intellect and emotions with the tricks of the unconscious, Piaget (1973) made significant contributions to our understanding of unconscious mental activity to which I return later.

AD/HD and the Boundary between Cognition and Emotion

The boundary between cognition and emotion is perhaps revealed most poignantly in the treatment of AD/HD children with self-instruction training, one of the most popular cognitive-behavioral techniques (Baer and Nietzel 1991). Emerging from the writings of the Soviet psychologists Vygotsky and his student Luria, the technique proposes that by internalizing verbal commands spoken by an adult, the child establishes control over her/his attention and behavior. Emotions are not considered an integral part of cognitive activity, and thought (conscious cognition) is presumed to be right and rational and to contain power that guides attention, emotion, and behavior.

DISSOLVING BOUNDARIES: REVISIONS IN PSYCHODYNAMIC CONCEPTS/TECHNIQUES AND THEIR SIGNIFICANCE FOR AD/HD

Until recently psychodynamic clinicians typically peered through a lens that brought into focus several interrelated questions. What are the child's difficulties as observed on the "outside"? What unconscious conflicts on the "inside" are the source of these difficulties? Could psychotherapy translate these unconscious conflicts into conscious awareness and thus revise and reform how the child behaves? During the past two decades this psychodynamic lens has undergone significant changes, three of which hold particular relevance for AD/HD.

Integrating Cognition, Emotion, and Action

During the first cognitive revolution, launched in the 1950s and known as the "New Look" (Santostefano 1991), investigators set out to integrate cognitive functioning and personality. Their studies demonstrated that unconscious cognitive structures determine how a person construes events and influence how a person takes action with her/his environments. George Klein (1951), a psychologist/psychoanalyst who pursued this approach, introduced a method that was relatively unique at the time. While others were asking subjects, for example, to copy geometric designs, or estimate the sizes of circles, Klein asked subjects to engage cognitive tasks that required discrete, cognitive functions and that consisted of neutral stimuli and stimuli that evoked fantasies/emotions. On the basis of his observations, he conceptualized several cognitive mechanisms that coordinate the demands of fantasies, emotions, and wishes with the demands of the environment by selecting, avoiding, integrating, and organizing information from the two worlds. At the heart of Klein's formulation was the proposition that although one could observe either emotion, or cognition, or action, they are one and the same. Klein's methodology provided the groundwork for a diagnostic formulation of developmentally inappropriate inattention we consider below that shaped the psychodynamic treatment for AD/HD children that I propose.

Meanings Given to Experience and the Patient–Therapist Relationship

The meaning given to experiences became one cornerstone of the psychodynamic position from its beginnings. Freud concluded, from his point of view, that memories patients presented were often fantasies expressing unconscious wishes originating from instinctual drives. These wishes/fantasies resulted in meanings that were injected (usually without awareness) into day-to-day experiences, forming a person's psychic reality. More recently psychodynamic investigators, especially those influenced by observations of mother–infant inter-actions (Beebe and Lachmann 1994, Sander 1987, Stern 1985), have proposed that instead of emerging from instinctual drives, the mean-ings a person gives experiences derive from negotiations and interac-tions with others, and integrate a child's cognitive, emotional, mental, and behavioral activities. Moreover, these investigators and others (Bohart 1993, Johnson 1987) emphasized that meanings constructed in the first years of life are embodied, involving perceptions, sensa-tions, and nonverbal interactions with others, and that these early nonverbal meanings are extended throughout later development in-fluencing words and concepts a person uses to label experiences.

This shift in the view of how meanings originate and are con-structed has resulted in a revision of the treatment method formu-lated by the founders of psychodynamic child therapy (Erikson 1964, Anna Freud 1965). The original approach required that the therapist induce a child, by systematic verbal interpretation, to lift unconscious conflicts into conscious awareness where they could be discussed ver-bally. In contrast, more recently, therapists are being asked to em-phasize enactments and interactions instead of verbal, conceptual dis-cussions of problems (Mitchell 1994, Santostefano 1998). As Valenstein (1983) put it, understanding and insight are "driven home" by persis-tent interactions as patient and therapist engage in a prolonged re-petitive process of testing and learning. Weimer (1980) noted that interactions between therapist and patient "taking place over time will create and change the meaning of events for both client and thera-pist" (p. 389).

These developments resulted in a "revolution" (Mitchell 1988, 1994) within psychodynamic theory that gave central importance to dialectical relationships between a person and others, and between a patient and therapist, as the foundation for personality development and change. In Freud's early position, the therapist was to be neu-tral, a "blank screen," enabling a patient to experience the therapist as someone else and thereby learn about her/his difficulties from these distortions of reality. Now the emphasis is on the view that "the therapist's actual behavior strongly affects the patient's actual experi-ence" (Gill and Hoffman 1982, p. 139) and that the therapeutic trans-ference is "codetermined" by patient and therapist (Gill 1984).

A PSYCHODYNAMIC APPROACH TO TREATING AD/HD

Influenced by the holistic view that a child's cognitive activity, emotions, and actions are interrelated, and that the meanings she/he gives to experiences, and revision of these meanings, emerge from prolonged, dialectical interactions with others, I have developed a hierarchy of methods to treat children typically viewed as afflicted with AD/HD. Following a dimensional rather than a categorical model, these methods integrate body/action, cognition, emotion, and meaning, addressing an ensemble of conscious and unconscious behaviors. Moreover, the methods attempt to address key aspects of the definition of AD/HD that I underlined earlier. *Developmentally inappropriate inattention* is defined by operationalizing a set of fundamental, cognitive functions, organized and structured during the first four years of life, which coordinates the demands of information from conscious and unconscious fantasies/meanings and from the environment, and which follow a developmental course. Before treatment begins, the therapist determines which of these fundamental, cognitive functions is developmentally delayed and whether the functions are rigidly centered on the demands of information from personal meanings/fantasies or from the environment, or whether cognition shifts rapidly from one domain to the other, failing to integrate them. Treatment techniques are then designed to promote the development of the delayed function and render cognition more flexible in coordinating inner and outer stimulation. I will first review how inattention is defined developmentally and then present sketches of treatment cases to illustrate the treatment approach.

Defining Sources of Inattention Developmentally

A program of research (Cotugno 1987, Santostefano 1978, 1985, 1986, 1995b, 1998, Santostefano and Moncata 1989, Santostefano and Rieder 1984, Wertlieb 1979) supports the view that five fundamental, distinct, interrelated cognitive processes make up the components of what is globally referred to as attention. Each process, or cognitive control mechanism, defines a developmental range, from global to differentiated organizations, and together they form a developmental hierarchy.

Body-Image–Tempo Regulation

This mechanism concerns the manner in which images/symbols represent and regulate the body and body motility. When asked to move fast and slow, the young child produces nearly the same tempo and represents these with global meanings (e.g., a rocket blasting off). With development, perceptions and representations of the body gradually become more articulated and differentiated (e.g., while balancing on one leg, the child imagines a gymnast performing on parallel bars). Many tempos are refined and regulated, each distinguished from the other.

Focal Attention

This mechanism concerns the manner in which a field of information is surveyed. The young child typically scans information slowly and directs attention only to narrow segments of the available field. With development, the child gradually scans more actively and sweeps attention across larger segments of the field.

Field Articulation

This mechanism defines the manner in which a field of information, containing relevant and irrelevant elements, is managed. The young child attends equally to relevant and irrelevant information. With development, the child gradually directs attention toward what is relevant while actively withholding attention from what is irrelevant.

Leveling-Sharpening

This mechanism concerns the manner in which images of information are constructed of ongoing information, held in memory, and compared with present perceptions. The young child typically constructs fuzzy images of past information and fuses these with present perceptions so that subtle changes in information are not recognized. With development, the child gradually constructs sharper, more differentiated images, and distinguishes them from present perceptions, so that subtle similarities and differences between past and present information are noticed.

Equivalence Range

This mechanism concerns the manner in which information is grouped and categorized in terms of a concept or belief. The young child clusters information in terms of a few narrow, concrete concepts (e.g., "These go together because they are all round"). With age, the child constructs increasingly broader categories conceptualized in terms of more differentiated, abstract concepts (e.g., "These are tools").

These five mechanisms become structured by the third year of life and are viewed as fundamental to attention and all cognitive activity. The process of each remains the same throughout development, but the organization changes. For example, information is surveyed with the focal attention mechanism, whether the child is 3 or 13 years old. But the organization distinguishes these children—one uses narrow, passive, visual sweeps, the other broad, active, visual sweeps. When functioning adequately, the process of one mechanism relies on, and integrates, the processes of other mechanisms lower in the hierarchy. Words, concepts, and beliefs are only part of the process of equivalence range, and all mechanisms usually operate outside of awareness.

In addition to the unique process and developmental course of each mechanism, studies have demonstrated that individual differences are stable over several years. Further, the functioning of these mechanisms is relatively independent of IQ and gender, underlies performance with various academic tasks, predicts learning disabilities, and reorganizes regressively and progressively in response to various personality dispositions, fantasies, and stressful changes in the environment (Santostefano 1978, 1986, 1988, 1995b, 1998, Santostefano and Reider 1984).

Cognitive-Affective Balance in Normal Personality Development

These cognitive mechanisms have been observed (Santostefano 1978, 1986, 1995b) coordinating the demands of information from conscious/unconscious fantasies/emotions with information from the environment. This coordinating process is referred to as maintaining cognitive-affective balance and viewed as fostering adaptation, psychological development, and learning. Research suggests three phases in the coordination maintained throughout normal development. Before the age of 5, cognitive controls are oriented relatively more toward the personal world of fantasy, with external information experienced usually through the lens of private symbols. From ages 5 to 9 these mechanisms steadily become oriented toward environmental stimulation, providing distance from fantasies, and enabling a child to identify with standards of parents and teachers, construct age-appropriate ego mechanisms of defense, and develop work skills that flexibly accommodate to limits and opportunities in the environment. From the ages of 9 to adolescence, cognitive controls become more flexible and mobile, gradually integrating information from both external and internal environments, and elaborating sources of knowledge by including personal meanings when learning.

Cognitive-Affective Imbalance and Psychopathology

Studies of clinical populations (Santostefano 1978, 1995a,b, 1998, Santostefano and Moncata 1989, Santostefano and Rieder 1984) have demonstrated three types of imbalance in cognitive-affective coordination that could distinguish among children typically clustered together as AD/HD, aiding clinicians in individuating treatment programs.

Outer-Oriented Cognitive/Affective Balance

This child maintains a pervasive, rigid cognitive orientation that centers on external stimulation. This orientation limits the accessibility of personal meanings useful in discovering and elaborating new information. Fantasies and personal meanings are split off (uncon-scious) and rarely give meaning to environmental contexts. In terms of AD/HD criteria, this child is typically easily distracted, interrupt-ing a task to attend to external, irrelevant noises, details, and events usually ignored by others (e.g., a classmate sneezes; a picture on the wall is tilted). In addition, because actions and their consequences are segregated from unconscious meanings/fantasies, the latter are not revised as experiences and assimilated. Therefore, the child sometimes suddenly acts impulsively, driven by meanings outside of awareness.

Inner-Oriented Cognitive/Affective Balance

This child maintains a pervasive, rigid, cognitive orientation that centers on personal fantasies/meanings. This orientation limits the ac-cessibility of environmental information, and avoids opportunities and limitations provided by environments for experimental actions. There-fore, actions taken in response to the demands of the environment tend not to be guided by representations of past experiences. In terms of AD/HD criteria, these children are typically tuned out, forgetful, likely to misinterpret items, do not hear what they have been told, and hate tasks that require sustained mental effort on external stimu-lation such as paperwork and reading.

Rapid Shifts in the Orientation of Cognitive/Affective Balance

This child's orientation shifts rapidly back and forth from a de-tail in the environment to an unrelated detail in fantasy, and from a detail in fantasy to an unrelated detail in the environment. Rapid shifting serves to avoid the requirements of both personal meanings and environmental situations by segregating inner and outer infor-mation. In terms of AD/HD criteria, these children typically begin a task, move to another, and then turn to something else, often leav-ing a trail of material carelessly scattered; they frequently shift the content of conversations, interrupt others excessively, and initiate activities and/or conversations at inappropriate times. They also tend to be restless and hyperactive, but not aggressive (e.g., touching or grabbing objects from others, clowning around).

PSYCHODYNAMICALLY ORIENTED PROGRAMS TO TREAT AD/HD[2]

As noted earlier, whatever behaviors a child shows from among those that define AD/HD, the therapist begins by assessing the developmental status of each cognitive control mechanism and the child's cognitive/affective orientation. In addition to relying on history and observation in school and the office, formal tests have been developed that provide developmental, norm-referenced measures (Santostefano 1978, 1988, 1995a,b, 1998).

The goal of treatment is to restructure the cognitive control mechanisms diagnosed as developmentally delayed and to revise a child's pathological cognitive-affective orientation so that cognition eventually flexibly coordinates and integrates the calls for action from the child's personal world of meanings/fantasies/emotions and from various environments, equipping the child to negotiate successful adaptations and efficient learning.

Initially, treatment is structured as therapist and child interact around tasks co-authored by child and therapist. Whether the child is outer-oriented, inner-oriented, or displays rapid shifts in orientation, tasks are designed to join the child's personal meanings/fantasies/emotions with external information, following four progressions: (1) from simple to complex, (2) from neutral to emotionally evocative, (3) from requiring physical actions as responses to requiring cognitive actions, (4) from requiring little delay in responding to requiring more delay. As the child copes with the tasks, during interactions with the therapist, her/his pathological, cognitive orientation is revised, and cognitive functioning is integrated with meanings/emotions/fantasies and action. Gradually the therapist relinquishes directing treatment and passes the initiative to the child, providing the child with opportunities to experience flexibility in coordinating environmental stimulation with her/his personal meanings.

---

2. A more comprehensive discussion of methods, materials, and clinical examples of these treatment programs is available elsewhere (Santostefano 1995a, 1998).

Insight and understanding are viewed as emerging primarily from the interactions, enactments, and negotiations between child and therapist. Verbal interpretations are introduced sparingly, usually in the last phase of treatment, and only if a child's cognitive developmental status and psychological needs indicate that verbal interpretations make a necessary contribution. The vehicle for promoting change in the child's cognitive-affective balance consists of three parts: (1) creative construction of graded tasks by the therapist that uniquely fit the child's cognitive dysfunction and personal world of meanings; (2) carefully regulated interactions between child and therapist that replicate the cognitive/emotional/behavioral processes that take place as child and caregiver interact; and (3) correcting ruptures and interferences that occur in the child–therapist relationship. Sooner or later, a child resists the therapeutic activities because the therapist's cognitive/emotional requirements exceed the child's cognitive/emotional style. Resistance is managed and resolved by following a model of negotiation that replicates a hierarchy of issues (Sander 1962, 1987) the child and caregiver negotiate during the child's first three years of life (e.g., focalizing, initiating, and reciprocating).[3]

When treating AD/HD, therefore, I propose that instead of asking what knowledge can we give a child to help her/him "put on the brakes" or pay attention without tension, we should engage the child in the process of revising how she/he constructs knowledge, revisions intended to promote the integration of cognition, fantasies, emotions, and actions, resulting in efficient learning.

Treating a Child Who Functions with a Rigid, Outer Cognitive-Affective Orientation: Clinical Illustration

After barely managing the first two grades, John seemed almost unable to learn in the third grade. At school he frequently interrupted the task at hand (focusing his attention on minor happenings in the

---

3. See Santostefano 1995a,b, 1998, for a more comprehensive discussion of techniques to manage resistance with children whose cognitive functioning is inflexible.

classroom), rearranged his desk, interrupted his desk work to flip a paperclip across the classroom, and sometimes abruptly pushed a classmate in the playground without provocation. At home, when he was bothered by the laughter and conversation of his siblings, he busied himself lining up, counting, and pasting stickers in a scrapbook. John's therapist referred him because during nearly a year of nondirected play therapy, John had maintained control over the treatment process by initiating games of tic-tac-toe; he seemed impervious to the therapist's interpretations intended to establish trust and help John share the conflicts controlled by his obsessiveness. An evaluation revealed developmental lags in leveling-sharpening and equivalence range and a rigid, outer cognitive orientation. Projective tests indicated that John's outer, cognitive orientation served to avoid unconscious representations of cataclysmic happenings (e.g., with card X of the Rorschach Test, he imaged a volcano exploding with people and animals being hurled in all directions).

Phase I: General Guideline

Because this child's cognitive orientation serves to avoid fantasies/meanings/emotions, the therapist joins this orientation by introducing patterns of information and tasks that are initially simple, ordered, emotionally neutral, static, and delayed. In a stepwise fashion, the tasks gradually include complex, emotionally evocative, changing information that requires more rapid responses.

Illustration

During the first sessions, John initiated games of tic-tac-toe as he had previously. To treat the leveling-sharpening mechanism that had been diagnosed as lagging developmentally, now and then the therapist challenged John to also play a game called "Remember Me." John examined a matrix of four geometric, wooden, colored cutouts for 30 seconds. Then the matrix was covered and a change introduced (i.e., one cutout was replaced by another, or the position of two cutouts were exchanged). The cover was removed; John examined the display, and described any changes he observed. Gradually the complexity of the array to be remembered was increased over sessions by increasing the number, colors, and sizes of cutouts in the matrix, eventually involving a matrix of eight stacks of two cutouts. In addition, time to examine the original display was decreased, and the length of the delay, before the display was reexamined, was increased.

At one point, to relate the Remember Me task to John's interest in tic-tac-toe, the therapist drew a matrix on a large posterboard and suggested that instead of pencil marks, each player locate three cutouts in a row, eventually increasing the number to six. John participated in the Remember Me task and tic-tac-toe with great interest, expressing relief that he had "something to do" and that the therapist was not "bugging" him with questions.

As John showed increasing efficiency holding patterns of twelve cutouts in memory, the therapist eventually elaborated the Remember Me task to develop John's capacity to anticipate and equilibrate changing information. A matrix of four cutouts was located on the tabletop, and John drew a picture of how the cutouts would land when pushed to the floor. The cutouts were then pushed to the floor and John compared the array with his anticipated arrangement.

Middle Phase: General Guideline

As the child and the therapist interact with emotionally neutral stimulation, the therapeutic alliance develops, enabling the child to express, however fleetingly, meanings/fantasies/emotions that are being avoided. At this point the therapist transforms the task used in the first phase to engage the child in the process of symbolizing and elaborating meanings/fantasies/emotions of relevance to the child's personal world.

Illustration

When locating cutouts on the posterboard during a game of tic-tac-toe, John sometimes made a faint growling/snorting sound. Relying on the gains John had made holding more complex patterns of information in memory, the therapist suggested that they "make the cutouts be something," launching a process that would engage John in constructing shared symbols and expressing inner meanings/emotions. John responded by deciding that each cutout was a particular animal (e.g., a large black square was a panther; a yellow diamond, a giraffe). As the game continued, John animated the cutouts more often (e.g., a black square pounced momentarily on a yellow diamond as if a panther attacked a giraffe).

At this point the therapist introduced another elaboration of Remember Me intended to improve John's ability to cognitively anticipate and coordinate sudden surges of fantasies and their emotions. Taking turns, John and the therapist each held three of his "animals" (cutouts) and three that belonged to the other. The cutouts were dropped to the floor. Prior to taking a turn, as was the case previously, each player drew a picture of the pattern the cutouts would form, anticipating and imagining which animals would "pounce" upon which. During these enactments, John occasionally and uncharacteristically showed flashes of intense anger, given his subdued style, when he did not agree with the therapist as to whether a drawing was accurate in anticipating the pattern the cutouts would form.

Final Phase: General Guideline

Elaborate the meanings/fantasies/emotions expressed by the child. Whenever possible relate these elaborations to the child's present and past experiences and join the regulation of action with cognition.

Illustration

As the process unfolded, John's angry tensions became more available to his subjective experience, benefiting from a more flexible cognitive orientation, which was illustrated by his symbolizing and enacting cutouts as fierce animals. Relying on this achievement, the therapist introduced a more elaborate, structured fantasy. He asked John to pretend that a bomb scare had been reported, and he was a member of a special team trained to locate and defuse bombs. John accepted the invitation with enthusiasm. Extending the previously constructed shared symbol, the therapist located stacks of cutouts (two and later three in each stack) throughout the playroom floor and on shelves. With each trial the therapist showed John a stack of cutouts designated as a bomb (e.g., a medium yellow triangle taped to a large blue diamond) that he had to remember. Then John searched for and located bombs, taking them to a "diffusing box" where they were dismantled. With each trial a few of the stacks contained all of the attributes, several contained one or another of the attributes (e.g., a small yellow triangle taped to a large blue diamond), and others contained none of the attributes.

Soon John and therapist competed to determine who required the least amount of time to locate the bombs. If the wrong stack was touched or removed, the player lost points. While engaging in this structured fantasy, John occasionally construed the therapist as furious with him when, for example, John accidentally knocked over a chair while racing about searching for bombs. He also spontaneously associated on these occasions to his father's temper, and spankings received from him (the father acknowledged spankings had occurred several times because of John's unresponsiveness). As another example, John also reported spontaneously that he spent time rearranging his desk at school instead of working, and would jump when someone entered the room, because he imagined that he would be "torn apart" by the teacher after she saw his paperwork, or by the person who suddenly entered the room.

John's rigid, outer cognitive orientation served to avoid its opposite and prevent the construction of representations of rage contained in his personal world. When he entered treatment with the first therapist, his cognition and modes of expression were not equipped to equilibrate and coordinate these meanings/emotions in interactions with the therapist, so that John controlled his aggressive meanings by obsessively playing tic-tac-toe. The tasks introduced by the second therapist enabled John to step into a dialectical circle, reorganize his rigid, outer, cognitive/affective orientation, construct symbols that integrated his repressed rage with available stimulation, and experience and express these meanings/emotions in ways that served the therapeutic process. Toward the end of treatment, John increasingly reported experiences from school and home, and stated that the anger and beatings he anticipated were not forthcoming. At the same time he became more attentive and productive and less obsessional in school as well as more related at home.

Treating a Child Who Functions with a Rigid, Inner Cognitive/Affective Orientation: Clinical Illustration

Jane, a 10-year-old, was described as tuned out, frequently respond-ing with a blank stare when addressed by the teacher, whose instruc-tions she typically misinterpreted. She regularly forgot to take books home, or to turn in homework assignments, and she made it clear that she hated paperwork requiring sustained mental effort. For ex-ample, after sitting for 30 minutes with a math quiz, she had written only a four-letter expletive in the margin. Throughout the first three grades, she steadily became more tuned out and "peculiar." Psycho-logical testing showed that all cognitive control mechanisms were lagging in development and that she was characterized by an inflex-ible, inner, cognitive orientation. In addition, there was no evidence of atypical (psychotic) thinking.

General Guidelines

Because this child's cognitive orientation serves to avoid external information, we begin by participating in the child's personal world and gradually promote differentiation and organization of the main fantasy the child introduces. Aspects of the fantasy are then connected to materials of cognitive tasks used as vehicles to symbolize mean-ings/fantasies. These tasks are gradually modified to provide the child's cognition with opportunities to deal increasingly with environmen-tally relevant information. In the last phase, the child's meanings/fan-tasies/emotions are extended into experiences with complex social situ-ations.

Phase I

Jane arrived with a large two-reel tape recorder. Removing its case with a screwdriver, she ignored the therapist and interacted with the recorder, fingering wires and gears. On occasion she spoke to her dog Cuddles, who, of course, was not present. In an effort to differenti-ate characters and voices in Jane's yet-unknown personal world, the therapist began to peer into the recorder, talk with Cuddles, touch

and inquire about certain parts of the recorder, and engage the recorder in conversation ("What's going on in there? Who's in there?")
Over several sessions Jane identified with and accommodated to this
behavior. She began to imitate the therapist addressing the tape recorder and specified parts of the recorder as particular places. For
example, a gear at one end was Jane's house; a gear at the other end
her school; and a red wire became the road connecting them. As Jane
imposed more differentiated and organized meaning to the inside of
the recorder, the therapist enacted imaginary persons walking to
school, walking home, and shopping in grocery stores by "walking"
her fingers over pathways. Jane soon imitated the therapist. This
imaginary play took place for a number of sessions with child and
therapist sitting quietly and peering into the recorder.

With personal meanings constructed and shared, each referring to
some part of the tape recorder, the therapist introduced an intervention that "bumped into" Jane's rigid, inner orientation, inviting her
to extend the world they had created—"So we can play it better"—
by locating various objects around the recorder and over the surface
of a large tabletop. Wooden geometric cutouts and blocks were used
to designate various buildings, rods to designate telephone poles,
streets were defined with tape, and pictures of stores were cut out of
magazines.

Given that Jane's cognitive mechanisms were identified during the
initial evaluation as lagging developmentally, the therapist, during this
phase, embedded activities within the game of "building a city" to
promote the processes of focal attention and field articulation. To treat
the former, the therapist asked Jane to scan two rods in order to select the larger one (e.g., pencils to be used in school; telephone poles
to be located on streets). The rods were initially set side by side and
gradually placed farther apart. To promote field articulation, Jane
surveyed increasingly longer rows of geometric cutouts strung across
the length of the table, fantasizing that she was inspecting items on a
store counter to select the ones designated.

In addition, Jane and therapist "walked" doll figures on streets and
through stores where items were purchased. Initially these items were
symbolized by Jane in highly personal terms. For example, candy bars
were sometimes represented by paper clips, or a scrap of paper. En-

acting characters who entered the store, the therapist showed confusion over which items were what, and encouraged Jane to fit attributes of items more closely to their meanings. In this way, buttons became hamburgers, pieces of string carefully cut in one-inch lengths became bananas, paper clips became candy bars, and so on. The therapist also introduced various tempos in the actions the characters performed (e.g., one doll, late for school, ran over a pathway; another doll, walking home after school, meandered through stores).

In the next series of meetings the therapist extended the subjective world they had created over the entire floor of the playroom. Cutouts and blocks were stacked to represent a school building, grocery store, home, and a friend's house. To emphasize the process of field articulation when constructing these structures, the therapist carefully designated cutouts of different sizes and colors for each of the structures, and Jane joined in. Once when the therapist was helping to set up their world, she inadvertently placed a large yellow triangle in the center of the school building. Jane immediately noticed the error, "The school is wrong," reflecting that she had been assimilating more articulate fields of relevant and irrelevant information.

Initially Jane revealed that she was centered on the issue of relative size. Later she expressed this issue in terms of highly personal metaphors (e.g., a small blue circle used in a cognitive task was placed in a tiny box and became "a stomach monster eating forever"). The therapist encouraged transformations of this fantasy by, for example, placing the blue cutout in boxes of various sizes (e.g., Jane decided the cutout ate less when in larger boxes). Soon Jane cast the issue in more organized differentiated play (e.g., a stack of cutouts used in a cognitive task was fed to a baby doll as "a mountain of ice cream," while Jane ate from a play cup one inch in diameter). In the course of this play, Jane spontaneously associated to her baby sister (who has it all, while Jane has nothing).

In the last phase, the therapist extended the game to the outdoors. During these sessions, Jane and the therapist walked about the yard surrounding the clinic, designating various bushes and trees as particular places, and enacting a number of the same roles they had played, which now became more elaborated. Then they walked to a nearby shopping area, entered stores, purchased items, and talked to clerks—dealing with information more as it is.

Jane's treatment took place twice weekly over a period of eighteen months. Gradually she became more attentive in school, less tuned out, stuck with paperwork for longer periods of time, and related to peers more appropriately. Treatment concluded when she showed adequate productivity in sixth grade.

Treating a Child Whose Cognitive Affective Orientation Shifts Excessively: Clinical Illustration

Tom, a 14-year-old, fluctuated frequently between wearing stereo headphones and "keeping busy" (e.g., cataloging, again, a collection of CDs). His room, parents noted, epitomized chaos. In school he annoyed peers because he frequently interrupted conversations, and annoyed the teacher because he impulsively blurted out his contribution to an ongoing discussion only to slip away and stare out the window. His psychological evaluation showed an IQ in the superior range, but a significant delay in the development of the equivalent-range cognitive mechanism, as well as a cognitive-affective orientation that shifted constantly. For example, on the Thematic Apperception Test he abruptly interrupted his story to report that he could not concentrate because he was occupied with keeping the fingernail of his left index finger "exactly" in the center of his left thumb. When copying geometric designs he interrupted to give a lengthy, confused account of the movie *Apocalypse Now*.

General Guidelines

Because this child's cognitive orientation shifts rapidly between personal fantasies and external stimulation, the broad course followed first elaborates and categorizes the issue *toward which* cognition leaps, and then the issue *from which* cognition leaps. During the initial phase, the child typically reveals issues in reality and in fantasy that are major sources of stress, resulting in brief but significant bursts of anxiety and agitation. Although this child shifts from one detail to another that is unrelated, gradually he/she returns to a detail a number of times. This perseverative quality suggests that the issue is cast in a category that has "hardened." The issues from which a child's cognition retreats and toward which cognition leaps are slowly integrated with a series of expanding metaphors that gradually increase the emotional intensity the child regulates and that brings new information into view as the child discovers when and why her/his attention leaps away from a detail.

Illustration

In the initial phase of treatment, to foster the development of the mechanism of conceptualizing, which had been diagnosed as lagging developmentally, Tom was asked to examine a series of objects, record each attribute on a card, and categorize the attributes by locating the cards (attributes) into groups that belong together for some reason. Initially the objects were neutral (e.g., a marble cube, a coat hanger) and later more emotionally evocative (e.g., a jackknife, a picture of a young couple walking hand in hand).

While categorizing the attributes of a jackknife, Tom stopped abruptly, seemed agitated, and complained that he could not concentrate because thoughts about biology class were racing through his mind, a topic to which Tom had retreated on other occasions. At this point the therapist asked Tom to list attributes of his biology class. While writing details on cards (e.g., dissecting kit; glass beakers; a report was due; a lab partner was hard to get along with), he paused to report that he frequently looks at frogs immersed in a large jar of formaldehyde, sometimes poking them to see if they are alive or dead. Yesterday the teacher reprimanded him for standing there "dreaming" instead of working.

As Tom elaborated the category "biology class," the therapist returned him to the knife, and to the card on which he had listed the attribute "sharp," from which his cognition had retreated. The therapist asked Tom to recall what was on his mind when he wrote "sharp" and just before his thoughts jumped to the biology class. Tom commented, "Kill! I was going to write 'kill.'" Then he blurted out, "I had a dream about killing."

Tom was asked to list and categorize details of the dream. Over several such analyses, it emerged that Tom experienced a recurring dream in which he repeatedly stabbed some animal or person, and with each stab he lifted the eyelid to see if the "thing" was dead or alive. Initially, while listing details of the dream Tom experienced intense anxiety, vigorously scratching his thighs. Gradually he displayed more cognitive-affective balance while detailing and grouping attributes of the biology class and the dream.

Relying on discussions of several sorting tasks, the therapist pointed out that Tom's attention jumped from the knife (and dream of killing) to the biology class (and jar of dead frogs), that the dream occurs repeatedly, that he repeatedly looks at the jar of frogs, and therefore his mind returns to both details "over and over again." The therapist selected "over and over again" as a relatively neutral and concrete concept joining the two domains. As therapy continued, with Tom categorizing attributes of various objects, he tended to shift his attention less and less and produced other meanings/fantasies he elaborated spontaneously. For example, Tom witnessed a boy playing "Gestapo" by poking his knife at a cat that had been tied up; and while listening to rock music Tom imagined himself as a member of the Hell's Angels.

Eventually Tom anxiously reported that his father had gone to the emergency room to have a cast placed on his ankle after a fall. His thoughts went to a history assignment concerning World War II. With no guidance from the therapist, Tom related aspects of the assignment (describing the invasion of Normandy) with his anger toward father, because, according to Tom, his father was always "on my back" about household chores. In this phase of treatment, Tom showed a cognitive orientation that flexibly related, rather than segregated, external details and fantasy/emotions. Therefore, the therapist assumed a more nondirected posture, encouraging Tom to explore whether and when his anger was appropriate, on the one hand, and, on the other, that his fantasies did not break his father's ankle.

Discussion

To plan treatment for children typically viewed as afflicted by AD/HD, instead of homogenizing them into one category of "inappropriate inattention," they should be distinguished in terms of which one of five fundamental cognitive functions lag in development, and whether a child's inflexible cognitive orientation remains centered on external information (avoiding the contributions of personal meanings/fantasies), or on internal information (avoiding the contributions of environmental stimulation), or shifts back and forth from one domain to the other (avoiding integrating the two). To treat these children, I propose a psychodynamic approach framed within the interpretationist, rather then objectivist position, which accepts that knowledge is constructed as children's cognitive and behavioral activity engages in dialectical interactions with others to form an intersubjective world of shared meanings that includes conscious and unconscious fantasies with their emotions, as well as the demands of external environments.

This treatment approach does not set out to provide the child with instructions or knowledge that could help her/him to learn and cope more efficiently. Rather the approach attempts to revise how a child constructs knowledge and learns. If a child attends selectively and learns efficiently, the child's cognition is typically autonomous from the demands of her/his conscious and unconscious meanings/fantasies and from the demands of the environment, flexibly attending to one demand, then the other, and then integrating the two (Rapaport, in Gill 1967).

Piaget's (1977) definition of learning captures the main steps of the treatment programs described above: "To know [to learn] . . . is to . . . reproduce the object [information] dynamically; but to reproduce, it is necessary to know how to produce [copy information]" (p. 30). The first step in the learning process formulated by Piaget, then, involves copying and producing information. In the proposed treatment approach, this step relates to tasks the child and therapist devise that provide the child with repeated opportunities to produce information, emphasizing one of five cognitive mechanisms: body-image-tempo regulation; surveying information to register its attributes; focusing attention on attributes relevant to the task at hand; holding patterns of information in memory; and categorizing/conceptualizing information. The second step in Piaget's definition involves reproducing information dynamically, that is, translating it into symbols and meanings. In the proposed treatment, this step relates to using tasks to enable the child with a rigid, outer cognitive-orientation to integrate personal meanings she/he is avoiding; to enable the child with a rigid, inner orientation to integrate environmental information she/he is avoiding; and to enable the child who shifts between inner and outer stimulation to integrate the two domains she/he is struggling to keep segregated.

The proposed developmental-dialectical model, and its holistic view of AD/HD children, assigns primary significance to several psychodynamic issues that are also beginning to receive attention from the cognitive-behavioral camp and its objectivist position.

THE IMPORTANCE OF DEFINING COGNITION AND ATTENTION AS INVOLVING BOTH SURFACE AND DEEP BEHAVIORS

I noted earlier that five decades ago psychodynamically oriented investigators joined a cognitive revolution, known as the "New Look," when they abandoned the search for universal laws of cognition as a self-contained entity, and set out to interrelate cognitive functioning and personality. These investigators defined cognition as involving both surface behaviors, such as conscious thoughts and self statements, and deep behaviors, such as unconscious meanings. The stage was set by Heinz Werner's (1949) introduction to a symposium, "Interrelations Between Perception and Personality," which urged researchers and clinicians to study how "the perceived world pattern mirrors the organized need pattern within" (p. 2). A number of clinicians responded, including Klein, whose work we noted earlier. Along the same line, discussing his studies of perception, Hilgard (1951) noted, "We are trying to discover how perception [attention] may be influenced by the realities outside and by the realities within ourselves" (p. 95). Bronfenbrenner (1951) and Gruber and colleagues (1957) emphasized the need to include unconscious cognitive structures since the environment to which a person adapts consists of cognitive representations or symbols rather than actual things as they are. Robert Holt (1964) urged psychodynamic therapists, who had been focused on unconscious conflicts, to consider how the New Look's emphasis on conscious and unconscious cognitive activity influenced therapy. Since these early writings, therapists have discussed cognition and psychodynamics (Colby and Stoller 1988, Horowitz 1988) and have described forms of cognitively oriented psychodynamic therapy that address surface and deep cognitive activity (Santostefano 1995a, Wachtel 1987, Weiner 1985).

The importance of including surface and deep cognitive activity has been given some attention in the cognitive-behavioral camp. Arnkoff and Glass (1982), pointing out that there has been an over-whelmingly narrow focus on self statements and conscious beliefs, noted that a self statement could have several meanings, different statements could have the same meaning, and that some experiences may be inaccessible to spoken language. Along the same line, Hollon and Kriss (1984) conceptualized two types of cognition in hopes of clarifying the confusion about how to define cognitive activity: (1) cognitive products, that is conscious statements and thoughts; and (2) cognitive structures, or unconscious mechanisms that shape the organization and meaning given to information.

The New Look approach to cognition and the contributions of cognitive-behavioral investigators such as Arnkoff and Hollon appear not to have influenced the treatment of AD/HD children. Currently the most commonly used approaches are designed to control surface symptoms by psychostimulants, behavior modification, attention training, and parental education (Baer and Nietzel 1991, Dulcan and Benson 1997) and neurotherapy (brain-wave feedback) (Barabasz and Barabasz 1996) with no attention given to deep cognitive structures. In terms of psychostimulants, however, it is interesting to note that one investigator (Stine 1994), noting the high rate (20–70%) of children and parents who failed to maintain treatment suggested that clinicians should attempt to learn the underlying fears children and parents have about medication and how they construe it (i.e., deep cognitive structures). And in spite of the predominance of techniques that deal with surface cognitive behaviors, a few voices (Chabrol and Bonnet 1996, Jordy 1996, Nathan 1992) can be heard emphasizing the need to address psychodynamically, as Bronfenbrenner put it, the "realities within" as well as the "realities outside."

The view of cognition as including conscious and unconscious activity brings us to another issue I propose as important in designing treatment for children with AD/HD.

THE IMPORTANCE OF MEANING

Skinner (1974), whose work contributed to the foundation of cognitive-behavioral therapies, argued, "A small part of one's inner world can be felt . . . but it is not an essential part . . . and the role assigned to it has been overrated" (cited in Mahoney 1985, p. 20). At the time Skinner stated this position, psychodynamic therapists, of course, disagreed. Since the early 1900s, they had been maintaining their view that a person's inner world is more essential than her/his overt behavior, or at least as essential.

In contrast to the position initiated by Skinner, cognitive-behavioral therapists are now being reminded of the importance of meaning. For example Mahoney (1985), stated, "Far from being vastly overrated, the inner world is probably the least understood and potentially the most revealing frontier in contemporary science" (p. 20). And ten years later (Mahoney 1995a), he reported that a shift can be observed in cognitive-behavioral methods from information processing to connectionism and most recently to constructivism: "Constructivism [emphasizes] the active . . . nature of all knowing. In contrast to the relatively passive models of the mind proposed by information processing . . . constructivism proposes intrinsic self-organizing activity as fundamental to all knowledge processes" (p. 7). Similarly, Meichenbaum (1995), one of the cognitive-behavioral pioneers, noted that initially cognitive-behavioral therapists followed the metaphor of conditioning, then of information processing, and more recently of "constructive narrative." The latter proposes that "the human mind is a product of constructive, symbolic activity, and that reality is a product of personal meanings that individuals create. . . . The task for the therapist is to help clients become aware of how they create these realities and the consequences of such constructions" (p. 23).

These positions by Mahoney and Meichenbaum represent a complete turnaround from Skinner's position, reflecting a shift from objectivism toward interpretationism, and converging with the treatment approach proposed here. However, this shift has not yet influenced cognitive-behavioral treatment of AD/HD children (Baer and Nietzel 1991, Barabasz and Barabasz 1996, Hall and Kataria 1992), which continues to include self-statement modification, reinforcement contingencies, modeling, problem-solving training, biofeedback (Pope and Bogart 1996), and correspondence training (Paniaqua 1992), with and without medication, while omitting the role meanings play in a child's functioning.

THE IMPORTANCE OF INTEGRATING WHAT A CHILD DOES, IMAGINES, AND SAYS

For decades psychodynamic therapists, while essentially ignoring what a child did, focused on what a child imagined, consciously and unconsciously, viewing what a child said as reflecting unconscious motives. In contrast, cognitive-behavioral therapies have focused on what a child consciously thinks and says, and how the child behaves, ignoring what the child imagines. But winds of change in these views can be felt. As we noted earlier, several psychodynamic therapists have argued that the actions a child takes in treatment, and the interactive metaphors a child co-constructs with a therapist, constitute the child's insight, connecting actions, fantasies, and thought (Mitchell 1994, Santostefano 1995a, 1998, Wachtel 1987, Weimer 1980). At the same time, a few cognitive-behavioral therapists (Mahoney and Freeman 1985) have wondered how thoughts, feelings, and actions are related, with Mahoney (1985) noting, "We are committing a costly error of translation if we equate what our clients say with what they think and how they feel" (p. 21). I would add that the error of translation would be more costly if we equate what a child does with what he/she imagines, consciously and unconsciously, feels, and says. The treatment model I outlined attempts to integrate these domains, while in my opinion, cognitive-behavioral techniques continue to segregate them (Baer and Nietzel 1991).

THE IMPORTANCE OF THE RELATION BETWEEN CONSCIOUS AND UNCONSCIOUS PROCESSES

The notion of unconscious processes, and the importance of relating them to conscious thoughts and behaviors, has been a cornerstone of psychodynamic therapy from its inception. How do unconscious meanings enter a person's awareness? Lear (1990) reminded us that Freud proposed that repression contains mental activity at an unconscious level by preventing this activity from developing into a "fully fledged form." Similarly, Piaget (1973) proposed that the unconscious does not contain fully formed fantasies that come into view once we shine a light on them. Rather "the unconscious is furnished with sensorimotor or operational schemata . . . expressing what the subject can 'do' and not what he thinks" (p. 257), and that becoming conscious consists of "a reconstruction on a higher level something that is already organized but differently on a lower level" (p. 257). Similarly, Lear (1990) proposed that the unconscious consists of "orientations," the "reconstruction" of which is a gradual process following a principle of "progressive development."

In the treatment method I proposed this progressive development takes place within a dialectical process between conscious thoughts/fantasies and unconscious, sensorimotor, and operational schemata that prescribe what a child can do. Recall John, who surely was unaware of his aggressive orientation, which he struggled to avoid by centering on external information. As he joined the therapist in repeated games of Remember Me, this orientation was initially reconstructed in the form of faint growls. When the therapist suggested they make the cutouts be something, John imagined the cutouts were animals. At this point, his unconscious aggressive orientation and sensorimotor schemas became candidates for evolving into a conscious concept. As the Remember Me tasks unfolded, now involving dropping cutouts on the floor, the orientation of aggression (animals pouncing on each other) was reconstructed further, and closer to conscious awareness, which resulted in spontaneous expressions of anger at the therapist. And when the activity included locating and diffusing bombs, the orientation became structured at the conscious level, reflected by John's spontaneously associating to and sharing how his father sometimes became angry and spanked him. This interrelated series of reconstructions gradually transformed an unconscious orientation that prescribed danger (managed by remaining detached from others) to a conscious level.

I propose that efforts to treat AD/HD children must include taking a child's unconscious orientations that are contributing to her/

his inattention and reconstructing them at a conscious level. While this proposal is self-evident to psychodynamic therapists, unconscious processes have been ignored for the most part by cognitive-behavioral therapists. However, Mahoney (1985) stated to his cognitive behavioral readers, "Unconscious processes . . . seem to be increasingly difficult to ignore" (p. 21). More recently, he announced, "One of the more surprising developments in cognitive therapy [because of its criticism of psychodynamics] has been the relatively recent acknowledgment of the importance and extensive role played by unconscious processes in human experience" (1995b, p. 10), especially by those who have joined the movement of constructivism. This acknowledgment of the importance of unconscious processes has not yet reached the shores of cognitive-behavioral treatment of AD/HD children as reflected by summaries of reports (Baer and Nietzel 1991, Dulcan and Benson 1997).

THE IMPORTANCE OF DIALECTICAL ENACTMENTS AND STRUCTURED TASKS INSTEAD OF VERBAL DISCUSSIONS AND INTERPRETATION

The treatment approach I outlined relies heavily on the child and the therapist enacting and interacting around structured tasks. In my view unstructured play is not usually effective in treating an AD/HD child because delays in the development of fundamental, cognitive mechanisms, and especially the child's rigid, cognitive orientation, limit the extent to which she/he can copy information from both the environment and personal world and reproduce it dynamically (i.e., symbolize), critical requirements of the psychodynamic processes. In contrast, a child who is not limited by cognitive dysfunctions is able to make growth-fostering use of the nondirective treatment situation that has been a tradition of psychodynamic therapy. She/he comes to treatment with developmentally appropriate cognitive control mechanisms, and a flexible cognitive orientation. Therefore, this child is equipped to participate in a continuous process of producing and symbolizing information from internal and external experiences and conflicts, gradually shifting into awareness issues that have been unconscious.

The aversion psychodynamic therapists have to introducing tasks and structuring treatment has a long history, beginning with Freud's position that it is wrong to set a patient tasks because the therapist must remain neutral. However, as early as 1919, Sandor Ferenczi, facing considerable criticism, advocated a variation of treatment he termed "active therapy," in which he instructed patients to construct a particular fantasy or perform some behavior. Later, David Rapaport (Gill 1967) discussed why for some patients the stimulus-deprivation characteristic of the traditional, neutral psychodynamic treatment situation is not appropriate. Others (Feather and Rhoads 1972a,b, Weiner 1985) outlined forms of psychodynamic behavior therapy using structured interventions with adults.

My proposal that the child and the therapist negotiate around structured tasks converges with a shift that is occurring in psychodynamic therapy from an emphasis on verbal discussion (classical psychodynamic therapy) to enactments and interactions (relational psychotherapy). The relational approach proposed by Mitchell (1988, 1994) and Spiegel (1989), and others, is not yet accepted by all psychodynamic therapists. For example, an issue of *Psychoanalytic Psychology* (1995) was devoted to debates between the two positions. And after reviewing the literature, Altman (1994) noted that while psychodynamic child therapists have been moving toward a relational approach, "the lingering influence of drive theory and associated analytic technique is evident in a common tendency to ignore the impact on the patient on what the analyst does and says in the analytic interaction" (p. 383).

Cognitive-behavioral therapists have used structured tasks for decades, and psychodynamic therapists can benefit from their experience. However, I would like to emphasize that the tasks I outlined are co-constructed, and individuated, by the child and the therapist, and used to construct and regulate meanings/fantasies. In contrast, the same cognitive-behavioral tasks tend to be administered to all children in generally the same way. More importantly, cognitive-behavioral therapists tend not to pay special attention to the negotiating between the child and the therapist that takes place around the tasks.

CHANGE AS INTEGRATION AND CONSOLIDATION

The treatment approach I propose for AD/HD children, with its roots in the interpretationist view of development, psychodynamics, and dialectics, defines change as a process that assimilates and consolidates previous, rigid, cognitive orientations into emerging, more flexible, cognitive styles. Constructed during interactions with a therapist, these flexible cognitive orientations are extended by the child into day-to-day living. This view of change contrasts with that of the objectivist position, which prescribes that inattention should be replaced with other behaviors.

A CLOSING COMMENT

In 1908 Lightmer Witmer attempted to help a child who was a poor speller by administering cognitive tasks. In 1909 Sigmund Freud supervised a father in helping his son uncover the unconscious conflict that caused his fear of horses. And in 1924 Mary Cover Jones desensitized a child's fear of rabbits by moving a caged rabbit closer and closer while the child ate. Each of these early attempts could be viewed as forecasting the major approaches to child psychotherapy that have emerged: cognitive, psychodynamic, and behavioral. A psychodynamic lens is crucial in understanding how to combine these approaches (Chabrol and Bonnet 1996, Nathan 1992). The model I have described represents one probe illustrating that recent developments in psychodynamic concepts and technique provide a way of integrating aspects of each to treat AD/HD children.

REFERENCES

Alexander-Roberts, C. (1994). *The AD/HD Parenting Handbook*. Dallas, TX: Taylor.

Altman, N. (1994). A perspective on child psychoanalysis 1994: the recognition of relational theory and technique in child treatment. *Psychoanalytic Psychology* 11:383–395.

American Psychiatric Association. (1994). *Diagnostic and Statistical Manual of Mental Disorders*, 4th ed. (*DSM-IV*). Washington, DC: American Psychiatric Association.

Arnkoff, D. B., and Glass, C. R. (1982). Clinical cognitive constructs: examination, evaluation, and elaboration. In *Advances in Cognitive-Behavioral Research and Therapy*, vol. 1, ed. P. C. Kendall, pp. 1–34. New York: Academic Press.

Baer, R. A., and Nietzel, M. T. (1991). Cognitive and behavioral treatment of impulsivity in children: a meta-analytic review of the outcome literature. *Journal of Clinical Child Psychology* 20:400–412.

Barabasz, M., and Barabasz, A. (1996). Attention deficit disorder: diagnosis, etiology and treatment. *Child Study Journal* 26:1–37.

Bearison, D. J., and Zimiles, H. (1986). Developmental perspectives of thought and emotion: an introduction. In *Thought and Emotion: Developmental Perspectives*, ed. D. J. Bearison and H. Zimiles, pp. 1–10. Hillsdale, NJ: Lawrence Erlbaum.

Beebe, B., and Lachmann, F. M. (1994). Representation and internalization in infancy: three principles of salience. *Psychoanalytic Psychology* 11:127–165.

Bohart, A. C. (1993). Experiencing: the basis of psychotherapy. *Journal of Psychotherapy Integration* 3:51–67.

Braswell, L. (1993). Cognitive-behavioral groups for children manifesting AD/HD and other disruptive behavior disorders. *Special-Services-in-the-Schools* 8:91–117.

Bronfenbrenner, U. (1951). Toward an integrated theory of personality. In *Perception: An Approach to Personality*, ed. R. R. Blake and G. V. Ramsey, pp. 206–257. New York: Ronald Press.

Bruner, J. S. (1986). Thought and emotion: Can Humpty Dumpty be put back together again? In *Thought and Emotion: Developmental Perspectives*, ed. D. J. Bearison and H. Zimiles, pp. 11–20. Hillsdale, NJ: Lawrence Erlbaum.

Cahn, D. A., Marcotte, A. C., Stern, R. A., et al. (1996). The Boston qualitative scoring system for the Rey-Osterrieth Complex Figure: a study of children with attention deficit hyperactivity disorder. *Clinical Neuropsychologist* 10:397–406.

Campbell, S. F., ed. (1977). *Piaget Sampler: An Introduction to Jean Piaget Through His Own Work*. New York: Jason Aronson.

Cash, T. F., and Pruzinsky, T., eds. (1990). *Body Images: Development, Deviance and Change*. New York: Guilford.

Chabrol, H., and Bonnet, D. (1996). Multimodal treatment of attention deficit hyperactivity disorder. *American Journal of Psychiatry* 153:967.

Clements, S. D. (1966). *Minimal Brain Dysfunction in Children: Terminology and Identification* (Public Health Service publication no. 1415). Washington, DC: Department of Health, Education, and Welfare.

Colby, K. M., and Stoller, R. J. (1988). *Cognitive Science and Psychoanalysis*. Hillside, NJ: Analytic Press.

Cotugno, A. J. (1987). Cognitive control functioning in hyperactive and nonhyperactive children. *Journal of Learning Disabilities* 20:563–567.

Decarie, T. G. (1978). Affect development and cognition in a Piagetian context. In *The Development of Affect*, ed. M. Lewis and L. A. Rosenblum, pp. 183–230. New York: Plenum.

Dulcan, M. K., and Benson, S. R. (1997). Summary of the practice parameters of the assessment and treatment of children, adolescents, and adults with AD/HD. *Journal of the American Academy of Child and Adolescent Psychiatry* 36:1311–1317.

Erikson, E. H. (1964). Clinical observations of play disruption in young children. In *Child Psychotherapy*, ed. M. Haworth, pp. 246–276. New York: Basic Books.

Feather, B. W., and Rhoads, J. M. (1972a). Psychodynamic behavior therapy: II. Clinical aspects. *Archives of General Psychiatry* 26:503–511.

——— (1972b). Psychodynamic behavior therapy: I. Theoretical aspects. *Archives of General Psychiatry* 26:496–502.

Fisher, S. (1990). The evolution of psychological concepts about the body. In *Body Images: Development, Deviance, and Change*, ed. T. F. Cash and T. Pruzinsky, pp. 3–20. New York: Guilford.

Fisher, S., and Cleveland, S. E. (1958). *Body Image and Personality*. New York: D. Van Nostrand.

Fraser, C., Belzner, R., and Conte, R. (1992). Attention deficit hyperactivity disorder and self control: a single case study in the use of a timing device in the development of self-monitoring. *School Psychology International* 13:339–345.

Freud, A. (1965). *Normality and Pathology in Childhood*. New York: International Universities Press.

Freud, S. (1916). Introductory lectures on psycho-analysis. *Standard Edition* 25:15–239.

Galton, F. (1884). Measurement of character. *Fortnightly Review* 36:179–185.

Gardner, H. (1985). *The Mind's New Science: A History of the Cognitive Revolution*. New York: Basic Books.

Gill, M., ed. (1967). *The Collected Papers of David Rapaport*. New York: Basic Books.

Gill, M. M. (1984). Psychoanalysis and psychotherapy: a revision. *International Review of Psychoanalysis* 11:161–179.

Gill, M. M., and Hoffman, I. Z. (1982). A method for studying the analysis of aspects of the patient's experience of the relationship in psychoanalysis and psychotherapy. *Journal of the American Psychoanalytic Association* 30:137–167.

Goldstein, S., and Goldstein, M. (1995). *Parent's Guide: Attention-Deficit Hyperactivity Disorder in Children*, 3rd ed. Salt Lake City, UT: Neurology, Learning, and Behavior Center.

Gordon, M., Thomason, D., Cooper, S., and Ivers, C. L. (1991). Nonmedical treatment of AD/HD/hyperactivity: the attention training system. *Journal of School Psychology* 29:151–159.

Grand, S. (1977). On hand movements during speech: studies of the role of self-stimulation in communication under conditions of psychopathology, sensory deficit and bilingualism. In *Communicative Structures and Psychic Structures*, ed. N. Freedman and S. Grand, pp. 199–211. New York: Plenum Press.

Gruber, H. E., Hammond, K. R., and Jesser, R., eds. (1957). *Contemporary Approaches to Cognition*. Cambridge, MA: Harvard University Press.

Hall, C. W., and Kataria, S. (1992). The effects of two treatment techniques on delay and vigilance tasks with attention deficit hyperactive disorder (AD/HD) children. *Journal of Psychology* 126:17–25.

Hilgard, E. R. (1951). The role of learning in perception. In *Perception: An Approach to Personality,* ed. R. R. Blake and G. V. Ramsey, pp. 95–120. New York: Ronald Press.

Hollon, S. D., and Kriss, M. R. (1984). Cognitive factors in clinical research and practice. *Clinical Psychology Review* 4:35–76.

Holt, R. R. (1964). The emergence of cognitive psychology. *Journal of the American Psychoanalytic Association* 12:650–665.

Horowitz, M. J., ed. (1988). *Psychodynamics and Cognition*. Chicago: University of Chicago Press.

Johnson, M. (1987). *The Body in the Mind: The Bodily Basis of Meaning, Imagination and Reason*. Chicago: University of Chicago Press.

Jordy, C. F. (1996). The hyperactive child and the body: a clinical study of hyperactivity in children. *Arquivos-de-Neuro-Psiquiatria* 54:628–636.

Kagan, J. (1978). On emotion and its development: a working paper. In *The Development of Affect*, ed. M. Lewis and L. Rosenblum, pp. 11–41. New York: Plenum.

Katz, M. M., and Cole, J. O. (1965). Reflections on the major conference issue. In *The Role and Methodology of Classification in Psychiatry and Psychopathology*, ed. M. M. Katz, J. O. Cole, and W. E. Barton, pp. 563–568. Chevy Chase, MD: United States Department of Health, Education, and Welfare.

Kelly, G. A. (1965). The role of classification in personality theory. In *The Role and Methodology of Classification in Psychiatry and Psychopathology*, ed. M. Katz, J. O. Cole, and W. E. Barton, pp. 155–162. Chevy Chase, MD: United States Department of Health, Education, and Welfare.

Kendall, P. C., and Braswell, L. (1985). *Cognitive-Behavioral Therapy for Impulsive Children*. New York: Guilford.

Klein, G. S. (1951). The personal world through perception. In *Perception: An Approach to Personality*, ed. R. R. Blake and G. V. Ramsey, pp. 328–355. New York: Ronald Press.

Kramer, S., and Akhtar, S., eds. (1992). *When the Body Speaks: Psychological Meanings in Kinetic Clues*. Northvale, NJ: Jason Aronson.

Lear, J. (1990). *Love and Its Place in Nature: A Philosophical Interpretation of Freudian Psychoanalysis*. New York: Farrar, Straus & Giroux.

Mahl, G. F. (1987). *Explorations in Nonverbal and Vocal Behavior*. Hillsdale, NJ: Lawrence Erlbaum.

Mahoney, M. J. (1985). Psychotherapy and human change processes. In *Cognition and Psychotherapy*, ed. M. J. Mahoney and A. Freeman, pp. 3–48. New York: Plenum.

———, ed. (1995a). *Cognitive and Constructive Psychotherapies. Theory, Research, and Practice*. New York: Springer.

Mahoney, M. J. (1995b). Theoretical developments in cognitive psychotherapies. In *Cognitive and Constructive Psychotherapies. Theory, Research, and Practice*, ed. M. J. Mahoney, pp. 3–19. New York: Springer.

Mahoney, M. J., and Freeman, A., eds. (1985). *Cognition and Psychotherapy*. New York: Plenum.

Meichenbaum, D. (1995). Changing conceptions of cognitive behavior modification: retrospect and prospect. In *Cognitive and Constructive Psychotherapies: Theory, Research, and Practice*, ed. M. J. Mahoney, pp. 20–26. New York: Springer.

Mitchell, S. A. (1988). *Relational Concepts in Psychoanalysis: An Integration*. Cambridge, MA: Harvard University Press.

——— (1994). Recent developments in psychoanalytic theorizing. *Journal of Psychotherapy Integration* 4:93–103.

Murphy, V., and Hicks-Stewart, K. (1991). Learning disabilities and attention deficit-hyperactivity disorder: an interactional approach. *Journal of Learning Disabilities* 24:386–388.

Nathan, W. A. (1992). Integrated multimodal therapy with attention deficit hyperactivity disorder. *Bulletin of the Menninger Clinic* 56:283–312.

Overton, W. F. (1994). The arrow of time and the cycle of time: concepts of change, cognition, and embodiment. *Psychological Inquiry* 5:215–237.

——— (1997). Developmental psychology: philosophy, concepts and methodology. In *The Handbook of Child Psychology, vol. 1: Theoretical Models of Human Development*, ed. R. M. Lerner, pp. 107–188. 5th ed. New York: Wiley.

——— (1998). Relational-developmental theory: a psychological perspective. In *Children, Cities and Psychological Theories: Developing Relationships*, ed. D. Gorlitz, H. J. Harloff, J. Valsiner, and G. Mey, pp. 315–335. New York: de Gruyter.

Overton, W. F., and Horowitz, H. A. (1991). Developmental psychopathology: integrations and differentiations. In *Rochester Symposium on Developmental Psychopathology, vol. 3: Models and Integration*, ed. D. Cicchetti and S. L. Toth, pp. 1–42. Rochester, NY: University of Rochester Press.

Paniaqua, F. A. (1992). Verbal-nonverbal correspondence training with AD/HD children. *Behavior Modification* 16:226–252.

Piaget, J. (1973). The affective unconscious and the cognitive unconscious. *Journal of the American Psychoanalytic Association* 21:249–266.

——— (1975). Foreword. In *Explorations in Child Psychiatry*, ed. E. J. Anthony, pp. vii–ix. New York: Plenum Press.

——— (1977). The role of action in the development of thinking. In *Knowledge and Development*, ed. W. F. Overton and J. M. Gallagher, pp. 17–42. New York: Plenum.

Pope, A. T., and Bogart, E. H. (1996). Extended attention span training system: video game neurotherapy for attention deficit disorder. *Child Study Journal* 26:39–50.

Psychoanalytic Psychology. (1995). Special section: contemporary structural psychoanalysis and relational psychoanalysis 12(1).

Sander, L. W. (1962). Issues in early mother–child interaction. *Journal of the American Academy of Child Psychiatry* 3:141–166.

——— (1987). A 25 year follow up: some reflections on personality development over the long term. *Infant Mental Health Journal* 8:210–220.

Santostefano, S. (1978). *A Bidevelopmental Approach to Clinical Child Psychology, Cognitive Controls, and Cognitive Control Therapy.* New York: Wiley.

——— (1985). Metaphor: an integration of action, fantasy, and language in development. *Imagination, Cognition, and Personality* 4:127–146.

——— (1986). Cognitive controls, metaphors and contexts: an approach to cognition and emotion. In *Thought and Emotion*, ed. D. Bearison and H. Zimiles, pp. 175–210. Hillsdale, NJ: Lawrence Erlbaum.

——— (1988). *The Cognitive Control Battery.* Los Angeles: Western Psychological Services.

——— (1991). Cognitive style as process coordinating outer space with inner self: lessons from the past. In *Field Dependence-Independence: Bio-Psycho-Social Factors Across the Lifespan*, ed. S. Wapner and J. Demick, pp. 269–286. Los Angeles: Lawrence Erlbaum.

——— (1995a). *Integrative Psychotherapy for Children and Adolescents with AD/HD*, rev. ed. Northvale, NJ: Jason Aronson.

——— (1995b). Embodied meanings, cognition and emotion: Probing how three are one. In *Rochester Symposium on Developmental Psychopathology, vol. 6. Emotion, Cognition and Representation*, ed. D. Cicchetti and S. L. Toth, pp. 59–132. Rochester, NY: University of Rochester Press.

——— (1998). *A Handbook of Integrative Psychotherapies for Children and Adolescents*. Northvale, NJ: Jason Aronson.

Santostefano, S., and Moncata, S. (1989). A psychoanalytic view of cognition within personality: cognitive dysfunction and educating troubled youth. *Resident Treatment for Children and Youth* 6:41–62.

Santostefano, S., and Rieder, C. (1984). Cognitive controls and aggression in children: the concept of cognitive-affective balance. *Journal of Consulting and Clinical Psychology* 52:46–56.

Searight, H. R., Nahlik, J. E., and Campbell, D. C. (1995). Attention-deficit/hyperactivity disorder: assessment, diagnosis, and management. *Journal of Family Practice* 40:270–279.

Shakow, D. (1965). The role of classification in the development of science of psychopathology. In *The Role and Methodology of Classification in Psychiatry and Psychopathology*, ed. M. M. Katz, J. O. Cole, and W. E. Barton, pp. 116–142. Chevy Chase, MD: United States Department of Health, Education, and Welfare.

Shilder, P. (1935). *The Image and Appearance of the Human Body*. New York: International Universities Press, 1950.

Skinner, B. F. (1974). *About Behaviorism*. New York: Knopf.

Spiegel, S. (1989). *An Interpersonal Approach to Child Therapy: The Treatment of Children and Adolescents from an Interpersonal Point of View*. New York: Columbia University Press.

Stern, D. N. (1985). *The Interpersonal World of the Infant: A View from Psychoanalysis and Developmental Psychology*. New York: Basic Books.

Stine, J. J. (1994). Psychosocial and psychodynamic issues affecting noncompliance with psychostimulant treatment. *Journal of Child and Adolescent Psychopharmacology* 4:75–86.

Temkin, O. (1965). The history of classification in the medical sciences. In *The Role and Methodology of Classification in Psychiatry and Psychopathology* ed. M. M. Katz, J. O. Cole, and W. E. Barton, pp. 11–19. Chevy Chase, MD: United States Department of Health, Education, and Welfare.

Thompson, J. K., Penner, L. A., and Altabe, M. N. (1990). Procedures, problems and progress in the assessment of body images. In *Body Images:*

Development, Deviance and Change, ed. T. F. Cash and T. Pruzinsky, pp. 21–50. New York: Guilford.

Tiemersma, D. (1989). *Body Schema and Body Image*. Amsterdam/Lisse: Swets & Zeitlinger.

Valenstein, A. F. (1983). Working through and resistance to change: insight and the action system. *Journal of the American Psychoanalytic Association* 31:353–373.

Wachtel, P. L. (1987). *Action and Insight*. New York: Guilford.

Wapner, S., and Werner, H., eds. (1965). *The Body Perfect*. New York: Random House.

Weimer, W. B. (1980). Psychotherapy and the philosophy of science. In *Psychotherapy Process: Current Issues and Future Directions*, ed. J. M. Mahoney, pp. 369–393. New York: Plenum.

Weiner, M. L. (1985). *Cognitive-Experiential Therapy: An Integrative Ego Psychotherapy*. New York: Brunner/Mazel.

Wells, F. L. (1912). The association experiment. *Psychological Bulletin* 9:435–438.

——— (1914). Professor Cattell's relation to the association method. *Columbia Contributions to Philosophy and Psychology* 22:46–59.

Werner, H. (1949). Introductory remarks. *Journal of Personality* 18:2–5.

Wertlieb, D. L. (1979). *Cognitive organization, regulations of aggression and learning disorders in boys*. Unpublished doctoral dissertation, Boston University, Boston.

Wilber, K. (1977). *The Spectrum of Consciousness*. London: Theosophical Publishing House.

——— (1979). *No Boundary: Eastern and Western Approaches to Personal Growth*. Boston: Shambhala.

13

Social Skills in Children with Attention Deficit/ Hyperactivity Disorder

Dani Levine and Persila Conversano

Children with attention deficit/hyperactivity disorder (AD/HD) experience a broad range of sociobehavioral problems associated with their conditions, one of the most critical and least understood being poor peer relationships. Only over the past fifteen years have researchers begun to explore the relationship between social skills and attention deficit disorder. Yet, according to Gresham (1983), the ability to successfully interact socially is one of the most salient aspects of a child's development.

AD/HD is associated with inappropriate levels of inattentiveness, impulsivity, and motoric hyperactivity that appear in at least two contexts (at home and at school), have persisted for at least six months, have been present since the age of 7 years or earlier, and have caused clinically significant social and academic impairments (American Psychiatric Association 1994). However, the most significant difficulties AD/HD children encounter are the impediments in social development. Pelham and Bender (1982) estimated that over 50 percent of children with AD/HD have significant problems in social relationships with their peers. Curiously, social difficulties are often overlooked when professionals list the core symptoms; however, when people who are familiar with these youngsters are asked to characterize them, problems in their getting along with others invariably surface.

Negative peer interactions are important not only because of their unsalutary impact on the daily lives of children, but also because they are remarkably predictive of serious problems during adolescence and adulthood. Children with AD/HD experience long-term effects of social adaptation problems. Hinshaw and Melnick (1995) suggest that unmodulated emotional arousal may contribute to the particularly problematic and dysregulated behaviors of highly aggressive AD/HD boys. These boys tend to exhibit a stronger emotional reactivity and less effective emotion regulation to frustration than do low-aggressive or comparison youngsters. Throughout their developing years, they receive negative feedback from teachers, peers, and family, leaving an indelible mark on their self-esteem. Since social difficulties extend into adolescence and adulthood (Weiss et al. 1978), it is crucial to understand the nature of the social disabilities that affect children with attention deficit disorder. Appropriate interventions and treatment plans engineered to find the "best fit" between the child and his/her social environment can then be implemented (Barkley 1990).

Self-esteem is derived from interaction with significant others, including family members, peers, teachers, or others in one's surrounding environment. It is, therefore, reasonable to assume that children with AD/HD who have behavioral problems at home and at school, and thus have difficulties in relationships with family, peers, and teachers, would suffer from poor self-esteem (Hechtman et al. 1980). Furthermore, rejection, likely to have a major impact on a child's self-esteem, is something that may exacerbate social problems (Campbell and Paulauskas 1979). The behavioral profile of rejected children is characterized by inappropriate and disruptive activities, physical aggression, solitary off-task behavior, argumentativeness, and hostile comments (Erhardt and Hinshaw 1994). Thus, peer difficulties in children with AD/HD are of paramount concern, and much needs to be learned about the development of negative peer relations (Hinshaw and Melnick 1995).

In clinical settings, AD/HD boys outnumber girls by a large margin, but by a smaller ratio in the community (Szatmari et al. 1989). In addition, research shows that children with AD/HD combined type and predominantly hyperactive-impulsive type (ADD+H) differ socially from children with AD/HD predominantly inattentive type (ADD-H). ADD+H children have little self-confidence, anticipate failure, avoid social participation, possess limited self-discipline, and are unwilling to face interpersonal demands. Additionally, an acute awareness of unpopularity adversely affects their self-esteem. Although not well documented in the literature, it is predictable that the social disabilities of children with ADD-H are also reflected in their self-esteem.

This chapter provides a profile of the social worlds of children with ADD+H and ADD-H. It should be noted that difficulties in the assessment of social skills deficits confounds the ability to appropriately define and treat this population. The literature reviewed highlights the similarities and differences between these two subgroups. Of primary concern is the lack of research on children with ADD-H. An overview of treatment modalities, a social skills training program with clinical examples, and intervention considerations for both groups are also discussed.

The literature emphasizes meaningful differences in peer relationship problems between ADD+H and ADD-H groups. In particular, ADD-H children may experience more difficulty with social withdrawal (Barkley et al. 1990, Edelbrock and Costello 1984, Pelham et al. 1981), whereas outright peer rejection may be more evident in ADD+H children (Barkley et al. 1990, Cantwell and Baker 1992, Clark et al. 1988). Although children with either AD/HD subtype have problems with self-esteem, the focus of their concerns seems to differ. For example, children with ADD+H show low self-esteem in the areas of popularity and behavior, while the ADD-H subgroup's problems stem from concerns about physical appearance, anxiety, and general unhappiness (Lahey et al. 1984).

Peer relationship problems, which have been well documented in children with ADD+H, also appear to be present in children with

ADD-H. Given the propensity for rule-violating and aggressive behavior, children with ADD+H are more disruptive in the classroom and in the household. Because their negative interactions and behaviors are dramatic, they tend to be brought into treatment and empirically studied more readily than children with ADD-H. Although the research suggests that children with ADD-H have peer relationship problems, findings about the social functioning of this subgroup are scarce.

AD/HD ASSESSMENT TOOLS

There are several ways of identifying children with ADD+H and ADD-H; however, difficulties arise in assessing social skills from imprecise, mixed interpretations. Most commonly, studies exploring these children's social worlds use interviews and standard but subjective behavioral checklists, and they collect systematic behavioral observations. Information sources for these studies are teachers, parents, peers, psychiatrists, pediatricians, and AD/HD children's self-reports. There is some concern, however, about the reliability and validity of these types of resources, specifically the ability to recognize appropriate and discordant behavior.

Many of the studies of children with AD/HD lack standardized outcome measures of social deficits. Ambiguity in the definitional criteria of AD/HD and observational subjectivity have created limitations in many studies and have impeded the accuracy of research findings. It is reasonable to assume that children who receive deviant scores from classroom teachers on behavioral checklists differ from children who are clinically diagnosed. Furthermore, pediatricians' behavioral observations differ from clinical diagnoses in that they are situationally limited to behavior observed in the office. Most commonly utilized measures of social skills are observations and assessments of behavior from parents and peers, unequivocally differing from clinical, standardized measurements. Nevertheless, studies have consistently shown that children with AD/HD can be distinguished from comparison samples across different raters (teacher, parents, and peers) and across most social skills dimensions.

PEER STATUS OF CHILDREN WITH ADD+H

Research findings indicate that children with ADD+H have unsatisfactory peer relationships. These children, compared to control groups, consistently display higher rates of inappropriate and disruptive activities, physical aggression leading to avoidance by peers, solitary off-task behaviors, difficulty with verbal exchanges, failure to modulate their behavior with situational demands, peer rejection, and low self-esteem.

Social communication skills found to be related to social status (Hartup 1983) are compromised for children with ADD+H. For example, their intense emotional reactivity and unmodulated affect may compromise socially appropriate behaviors such as conflict resolution, following rules, and prosociability (Hinshaw and Melnick 1995). Hence, it appears that for children to be liked, they must actively engage in play with their peers, and neglect by their peers results in their social isolation (Coie et al. 1990). Children with ADD+H are at risk of not fully benefiting from social opportunities because they are often rejected by their peers due to the quality of their social interactions. Compared to controls, ADD+H children exhibit higher frequencies of talking (Grenell et al. 1987), negative verbal and nonverbal behavior (Pelham and Bender 1982), aggression (Campbell and Paulauskas 1979), and difficulty adapting to situational demands (Milich and Landau 1989, Whalen and Henker 1985). Hinshaw and colleagues (1997) define noncompliant/disruptive behavior as annoying, rule violating, and intrusive behavior that includes teasing or physical contact; verbal aggression such as taunts, swearing, or harsh words directed at a person; physical aggression such as hits, kicks, shoves; and social isolation such as wandering, bystanding, or lack of participation in peer-related activities that are unrelated to noncompliance.

Landau and Milich (1988) ascertained that ADD+H boys, relative to boys in a control group, consistently failed to modulate their behavior as the role requirements changed, and were less responsive to varying social cues. Additionally, the behavior of ADD+H boys resulted in their normal peers altering their response pattern in order to maintain the equilibrium in the dyadic interaction. The inappropriate verbal communication of children with ADD+H may be partly responsible for the negative reactions of others. This has been referred to as "negative social catalysts," suggesting that ADD+H children elicit maladaptive behaviors from others (Whalen and Henker 1985).

Children with ADD+H seem to hold fast to a specific response strategy and apply it relatively independently of the task demands. Whalen and colleagues (1979) found that ADD+H boys placed in a structured role-playing "Space Flight" game with normal peers were less likely to modulate ongoing or habitual behavior patterns and were less responsive to subtle social learning opportunities. Due to their behavioral impulsivity, children with ADD+H have difficulty considering the long-term consequences of their actions. They may not be able to delay the short-term gratification of getting their own way in favor of a longer-term goal of maintaining positive feelings toward one another.

Children with ADD+H may also experience frustration and exhibit aggression because of deficits in verbal communication. Unsuccessful attempts to communicate may exasperate future attempts to interact socially, consequently leading to peer rejection. According to Clark and colleagues (1988), subtle attentional difficulties may disrupt social interaction between children with ADD+H and their peers; however, difficulty in verbal exchanges is what leads to social rejection. In addition, aggression may, over time, lead to withdrawal by peers from interaction with the initiator of aggressive encounters.

Compared to controls, children with ADD+H have been shown to possess less knowledge concerning appropriate behavior with others (Grenell et al. 1987). However, Whalen and Henker (1992) found that AD/HD youngsters exhibit adequate knowledge of appropriate behavior required in social situations, which suggest that subadequate social skills do not explain peer difficulties. Hinshaw and Melnick (1995) report that impaired social performance stems from sociocognitive deficits and biases, deviant social agendas, or dysfunctional emotional regulation strategies. Barkley (1990) found that normal children perceive ADD+H children as being disruptive, unpredictable, and aggressive, and tended to respond to children with ADD+H with aversion and rejection. Milich and Landau (1989) report that even nonaggressive youngsters with AD/HD are more likely to experience peer rejection than purely aggressive children. However, situational differences have an impact on the quality of attention and, hence, the quality of the interaction.

Alessandri (1992) investigated attention, play, and nonplay behavior in preschool children with ADD + H. Significant findings were that children with ADD + H engaged in more transitional behavior (moving from one work area to another), were less effective with peers, and were less attentive and cooperative during group activities. However, the authors found that children with ADD + H were less attentive only during a storytelling activity. No differences were found in attention during a music activity, again suggesting the importance of situational differences.

PEER STATUS OF CHILDREN WITH ADD-H

The limited number of studies of children with ADD-H has led to less consistent results than the preceding studies of the ADD + H group. While some studies suggest that the social deficits of the ADD-H subgroup may be less severe than the ADD + H group, other studies claim that there are no significant differences on peer ratings between ADD-H and ADD + H children. Methodological problems found in these studies were the low number of identified ADD-H subjects, and the teacher and peer rating scales used to define the criteria for the ADD-H group.

King and Young's (1982) found that ADD + H children were more aggressive and had lower self-esteem than ADD-H children. The authors postulated that although the two groups did not significantly differ on peer perception, they may require different prevention/intervention strategies given the differences in their behavior. Similar to these findings, Pelham and colleagues (1981) found no differences on peer rating scales between ADD + H children and ADD-H children on the likability factor of the Pupil Evaluation Inventory (PEI).

Other studies noted significant differences between the two groups on teacher and peer rating scale factors. Children with ADD + H were perceived as more hyperactive and more impulsive than ADD-H children. Significant gender differences further indicated that ADD-

H girls were rated by teachers as more inattentive/passive and immature, and by peers as significantly more withdrawn than ADD + H girls.

Carlson and colleagues (1987) compared peer sociometric nominations of clinic-referred children with AD/HD. Similarly to the King and Young (1982) study, children were asked to write names of three children they liked the most and three children they liked the least. The results were similar to those of King and Young (1982) and Pelham and colleagues (1981) in that the ADD-H and ADD + H groups both were found to have peer relationship problems. However, Carlson and colleagues (1987) suggested that children with ADD + H are likely to have poorer peer relationships, with more of them nominated as "least liked" than children with ADD-H.

Cantwell and Baker (1992) found no significant differences in the prevalence of peer problems between ADD + H and ADD-H children. Their findings also suggested that there were no significant differences between the two groups on social withdrawal measured by a child interview and a teacher questionnaire. These findings did not support other findings claiming that children with ADD-H appear to be more socially withdrawn (Edelbrock and Costello 1984, Pelham et al. 1981). The authors acknowledge that there may be some bias in their population in that the children were referred not for psychiatric assessment but rather for evaluation of their developmental speech/language difficulties.

In contrast with previously mentioned findings, Edelbrock and Costello (1984) and Lahey and colleagues (1984) suggest that peer problems among children with ADD-H are reflected by social withdrawal. Edelbrock and Costello strongly suggest that ADD-H children may function better socially than the ADD + H group. Discrepancies between their findings and others' findings may be attributed to methodological limitations of the studies. It is possible that peer unpopularity among children with ADD-H was not detected because of the low number of subjects and the use of teacher ratings, with the exclusion of peer ratings.

Lahey and colleagues (1984) found children with ADD-H to be more anxious and withdrawn than ADD + H children. As in the Carlson and colleagues (1987) study, both AD/HD groups received more "least liked" nominations and less "most liked" nominations than controls. In addition, the ADD + H group received significantly more "least liked" nominations than the ADD-H group. Results of the above study were consistent with Edelbrock and Costello's (1981) findings, indicating social withdrawal among the ADD-H group and differences in peer popularity between the two groups.

Clearly, the lack of available research using clinical samples to represent the ADD-H subgroup necessitates further investigation.

EVALUATION OF THE LITERATURE

The literature reports that both ADD + H and ADD-H children suffer from problems in social relations. The majority of the studies previously cited examined the social facets of children with ADD + H: Landau and Milich (1988), Whalen and colleagues (1979), Clark and colleagues (1988), Pelham and Bender (1982), to name a few. There has been less research on social relations in the ADD-H group.

Issues that plagued previous research were present in both the ADD + H and ADD-H studies. A major drawback was that many of the studies utilized primarily white, male AD/HD subjects diagnosed entirely on the basis of teacher ratings. Other crucial weaknesses were evident in methodological problems, including small numbers of subjects, unreliable diagnoses (retrospective or based on behavior rating scales), and the presence of comorbid problems.

Many of the studies reviewed utilized nonclinical samples of children defined as either ADD + H or ADD-H only as a result of relatively high scores on teacher rating scales. These scores would not necessarily be considered clinically deviant. The extent to which results are representative of clinic-referred children with AD/HD is therefore questionable.

In the ADD + H and ADD-H studies, the diagnostic criteria for both groups are compromised by failure to discriminate comorbid conditions, especially oppositional and conduct disorders. Thus, some observed effects might not be due to AD/HD. Clinical data suggest that comorbid conditions are less common among children with ADD-H. However, anxiety and depressive disorders are associated with ADD-H (Cantwell and Baker 1992).

The literature regarding the social concomitants of children with ADD+H and ADD-H was reviewed. Given that children with ADD+H and ADD-H differ behaviorally, it is not surprising that their social functioning differs as well. Treatment strategies should therefore be targeted at their specific deficits to increase the likelihood of successful interventions.

INTERVENTION TARGETS

As evidenced by the literature previously reviewed in both AD/HD groups, stigmatization from peers exacerbates low self-esteem and decreases the opportunity of social support and modeling. Moreover, these thwarted attempts toward socialization result in further interpersonal difficulties. Treatments directed toward optimizing interpersonal functioning in children with AD/HD are therefore imperative.

The etiology and manifestation of social deficiencies affect the nature of the intervention. Acknowledging ADD+H and ADD-H as separate and distinct disorders with disparate social deficits would have a tremendous impact on treatment. Wheeler and Carlson (1994) hypothesize that a difference in social deficiencies between ADD+H and ADD-H characterizes two subtypes of social functioning. They further postulate that children with ADD+H suffering from a performance deficit are socially rejected. The behavioral excesses of children with ADD+H are responsible for their poor social skills. Additionally, in considering treatment goals for children with ADD+H, there must be a clear understanding of their social motivation. Although the quality of their social interactions is poor, their desire for social contact is healthy. Therefore, interventions should focus less on increasing prosocial behavior and more on modifying social interactions.

Children with ADD-H are comparatively more isolated and socially withdrawn than their ADD+H counterparts. Whereas children with ADD+H demonstrate a performance deficit, children with ADD-H exhibit deficiencies in social knowledge (skills). Although it would seem as if the most efficacious treatment for children with ADD-H would be social skills training, the scarcity of research on children with ADD-H does not empirically support this conviction.

MULTIDIMENSIONAL TREATMENT

Multiple goals including the enhancement of accurate social information processing, increasing peer status, and decreasing negative behaviors are necessary in the treatment of children with AD/HD. Different treatment programs use single approaches within this broad context. However, change is contingent upon a multimodal intervention (Hinshaw 1992). Multidimensional treatment approaches encompass an array of educational, cognitive, behavioral, psychodynamic, and pharmacological interventions, because research has shown that each of these treatments by itself has limited effect on social repertoires and fails to normalize peer relations. The necessity of individualized treatment plans is also underscored in the literature. Furthermore, Melnick and Hinshaw (1996) support that notion that children's self-set goals reflect their social status. Through these goals ADD+H children who are rejected are better able to discover a pathway to social acceptance.

In recent years, there has been a surge of social skills training utilizing cognitive/behavioral interventions. This training involves modeling appropriate social skills, shaping the skills through reinforcement, and encouraging the children to practice the acquired skills. Children with AD/HD who have difficulties with problem solving, verbal mediation skills, and reading social cues are theoretically believed to benefit from cognitive/behavioral interventions.

Cognitive training enables children to socially alter their interaction style, to learn new coping skills, and to improve self-monitoring. In combination with cognitive reformulations, children are taught behavioral strategies through role playing, assertiveness training, and internalized verbalizations (self-talk). These interventions are aimed at changing discordant behavior, and offer children the opportunity to practice their newly acquired skills. These cognitive/behavioral techniques with a psychodynamic underpinning are used as short-term interventions. However, longer-term interventions may be needed to ameliorate these children's long-standing social problems.

Interventions for promoting social competence are best facilitated in a group setting. This in vivo training forum provides an arena in which newly learned cognitive and behavioral strategies can be rehearsed. Additionally, group formats offer social support, critical feedback opportunities, and socialization opportunities. Exposure to multiple models in a group is instrumental in the shaping and changing of ineffective behavior patterns. If cognition is altered and behavior is regulated within a group, presumably the changes will be generalized.

Hinshaw and colleagues (1997) found that the family's belief in using firm limits, appropriate confrontation, and reasoning while being warm and supportive lays the foundation for the promotion of social competence. Parental education is crucial in the reformation of the children's deficient social skills. Programs for increasing parental competence use teaching, case examples, and videotapes. Education gives both parents and children information regarding the ramifications of medications, additional symptoms children may be experiencing, compensatory strategies for deficiencies, and available resources provided in the community. Social skills education and training help children and their families develop new patterns of thoughts, feelings, and behaviors (Erk 1995).

Following is an example of a twelve-week social skills training for AD/HD children, in addition to a six-week parents' support group. A licensed clinical psychologist, experienced in working with AD/HD children, and a co-therapist conduct the groups. Each session is an hour long.

This social skills training program provides a forum where the children are invited to play, talk, role play, and gain an understanding of their social motivation, and to experiment with alternate modes of expressing feelings and negotiating relationships. The general focus of the group is to help the children deal with peer provocation, peer rejection, and feelings of frustration and aggression, and to assist them in initiating and maintaining friendships. No rewards or punishments for positive or negative behaviors are implemented by the therapist, so the children can appreciate the intrinsic value of their newly learned social behaviors.

The parents' support group meets every other week during the twelve-week program. This group provides a supportive environment for parents to better understand their feelings about having an AD/HD child, and to understand their child's feelings and behaviors.

Parents are encouraged to explore with their child the nature of his/ her social difficulties, and to explore alternate methods of responding to them.

Initially, each child and parent(s) are interviewed separately to identify problem areas and to establish goals. Children who are developmentally and chronologically close in age and appropriate for the group are placed together. Play materials such as pencils, drawing pad, glue, scissors, toys, popsicle sticks, building blocks, and games are provided for the children. In the first meeting, children are asked by the therapist why they are in the group, and what they want to accomplish. It is important to identify if the child perceives his or her behaviors as problematic and needing change.

Since children with AD/HD exhibit social difficulties with their peers, family, and teachers, have an acute awareness of their unpopularity, possess limited self-discipline, and are reluctant to face interpersonal demands, they often welcome being in a group with other children who have similar social difficulties. Throughout the sessions, the children's underlying motivation for their behavior or lack of it is brought to their attention through their play, role playing, and observed peer relations. The therapist also helps them identify their feelings about a particular situation or interaction, and how they choose to deal with it. In addition, the therapist elicits from the group members alternate and more constructive modes of expressing feelings and thoughts.

A clinical example of a session halfway through the twelve-week program includes a discussion of how a particular group of children dealt with their feelings in relation to peer or adults, and how gradual shifts in intra- and interpersonal relations began to develop. One child said, "I write it [his feelings] on a piece of paper and throw it in the garbage. I get rid of it." Another child stated, "I fantasize about having magical powers." The third child commented, "I get anxious. I want some help. But I bug someone else to show them how I feel." The fourth child bragged, "I tell everyone that I am smarter than them." The fifth child sheepishly put a paper bag on his head to cope with his feelings.

As is evident, various defenses were being used by this group of children to stay in control and to avoid feeling vulnerable and awkward. The therapist made the interpretation that when they have feelings toward another person, they either get rid of them, hide or deny them, turn to a fantasy world where magic is possible, make someone else feel how they feel, or tell everyone that they are smarter than the rest, when in fact their feelings are about anger, hurt, disappointment, or helplessness.

One child responded, "But if I show people that I am hurt or helpless, then they think I am a wimp and they will take advantage of me." This child was able to recognize the purpose of his defensiveness and the pain of being vulnerable.

As the end of the twelve-week program approached, further anxieties about the impending separation surfaced. One child confessed, "Friends are unreliable. They can leave you. I don't want to have friends." The therapist interpreted, "You must feel sad that we need to say good-bye. You seem to feel that I am abandoning you and that I don't want to continue our relationship. Rather than feeling sad about it ending, you believe that it is better not to have any friends so you won't ever have to miss them and experience their absence." At this point another group member shouted to the therapist, "I hate you. Leave this room." The therapist interpreted, "You hate me because you feel that I am abandoning you and I caused you to have feelings of pain." The child apologized and lamented, "I don't want the group to end. I really like it." This child's last comment demonstrated his improved ability to identify and verbalize his feelings, in addition to accepting the termination of the group meetings.

A mother of another child who was attending the group reported that her daughter cursed her out as usual and then immediately apologized, saying, "I am sorry, I must have hurt you by cussing you." The mother reported feeling surprised and pleased that her daughter understood the impact of her hostility. Prior to the group, the child had displayed limited ability to be empathic.

The above clinical example demonstrates the process in which AD/HD children are aided in developing well-adjusted behaviors. Through social skills training the children recognize both internal and external cues, enabling them to respond appropriately to their environment.

The feedback from the parents as well as the children suggested that there were marked improvements in the children's social behavior. However, a follow-up study was not conducted to determine if these improvements were long-lasting and generalized to other settings.

A recent study conducted by Pfiffner and McBurnett (1997) evaluated the residual effects of a social skills groups coupled with parent training. They found that a behavioral social skills training program significantly improved social interactions of AD/HD children. These gains were maintained in a 4-month follow-up study. This 8-week program consisted of using brief instruction, symbolic and in vivo modeling, role playing, and behavioral rehearsal techniques. In contrast to the social skills program example previously described, this study utilized a behavioral modification system. Treatment goals included acquisition and generalization of good sportmanship, accepting consequences, gaining assertiveness, ignoring provocation, learning problem-solving techniques, and recognizing and dealing with feelings. This model included the involvement of parents, who were taught to reward their child's use of newly learned social skills by use of positive reinforcements. The facilitation of the learned social skills was also carried out at school through daily report cards citing specific social behaviors. Reinforcement for targeted behaviors at school was then provided by the parents.

CONCLUSION

The significance of poor peer relationships among children with AD/HD urgently calls for further research clarifying the nature of their social functioning. Presently, social skills training for children with AD/HD must be considered experimental until more clinical evidence supports its effectiveness (Hinshaw 1992).

The literature suggests more directive and behavioral social skills interventions. The acquisition and generalization of interpersonal skills through social-cognitive and behavioral skills training is designed to enhance social competence and peer relations. However, a psychodynamic integrative approach both in the social skills training and parent's group provides a comprehensive understanding of unconscious behavior and feeling states. Persistent peer-relationship problems could cause tremendous psychic pain through adolescence and into adulthood. Therefore, not only do these children's behavioral problems need to be managed, but so do their intrapsychic wounds.

To be of maximum therapeutic benefit, clinicians, family members, and teachers need to be aware of the hardships encountered by children who suffer from AD/HD and to treat the disorder with a multifaceted intervention plan. Group settings provide exposure to multiple models, role playing, social reinforcement, and critical feedback. Training techniques within a group context target the child's social perception, knowledge of social rules, and peer group behavior. Although this training process has not yielded lasting benefits, any improvement of social status is a positive outcome.

REFERENCES

Alessandri, S. (1992). Attention, play, and social behavior in ADD preschoolers. *Journal of Abnormal Child Psychology* 20:289–302.

American Psychiatric Association. (1994). *Diagnositic Criteria from DSM-IV*. Washington, DC: American Psychiatric Association.

Barkley, R. (1990). *Attention-Deficit-Hyperactivity Disorder: A Handbook for Diagnosis and Treatment*. New York: Guilford.

Barkley, R., DuPaul, G., and McMurray, M. (1990). Comprehensive evaluation of attention-deficit disorder with and without hyperactivity as defined by research criteria. *Journal of Consulting Clinical Psychology* 28:873–881.

Campbell, S., and Paulauskas, S. (1979). Peer relations in hyperactive children. *Journal of Child Psychology and Psychiatry* 20:233–246.

Cantwell, D., and Baker, L. (1992). Attention-deficit disorder with and without hyperactivity: a review and comparison of matched groups. *Journal of the American Academy of Child and Adolescent Psychiatry* 31:432–438.

Carlson, C., Lahey, B., Frame, C., et al. (1987). Sociometric status of clinic-referred children with attention-deficit disorders with and without hyperactivity. *Journal of Abnormal Child Psychology* 15:537–547.

Clark, M., Cheyne, J., Cunningham, C., and Siegel, L. (1988). Dyadic peer interaction and task orientation in attention-deficit disorder. *Journal of Abnormal Child Psychology* 16:1–15.

Coie, J. D., Dodge, K. A., and Kupersmidt, J. (1990). Peer group behavior and social status. In *Peer Rejection in Childhood*, ed. S. R. Asher and J. D. Coie, pp. 17–59. New York: Cambridge University Press.

Edelbrock, C., and Costello, A. (1984). Empirical corroboration of the attention-deficit disorder. *Journal of American Academy of Child Psychiatry* 23:285–290.

Erhardt, D., and Hinshaw, P. (1994). Initial sociometric impression of attention-deficit hyperactivity disorder and comparison boys: predictions
from social behaviors and from nonbehavioral variables. *Journal of Consulting and Clinical Psychology* 62(4):833–842.

Erk, R. (1995). The conundrum of attention deficit disorder. *Journal of Mental Health Counseling* 17:131–145.

Grenell, M., Glass, C., and Katz, K. (1987). Hyperactive children and peer
interaction: knowledge and performance of social skills. *Journal of Abnormal Child Psychology* 15:1–13.

Gresham, F. (1983). Behavioral interventions in school psychology: issues in
psychometric adequacy and training. *School Psychology* 12:17–25.

Hartup, W. (1983). Peer relations. In *Handbook of Child Psychology*, vol. 4,
ed. E. M. Hetherington, pp. 103–198. New York: Wiley.

Hechtman, L., Weiss, G., and Perlman, T. (1980). Hyperactives as young
adults. *Canadian Journal of Psychiatry* 25:478–482.

Hinshaw, S. (1992). Interventions for social competence and social skill.
Attention-Deficit Hyperactivity Disorder (4):539–549.

Hinshaw, S., and Melnick, S. (1995). Peer relations in boys with attention-
deficit hyperactivity disorder with and without comorbid aggression.
Development and Psychopathology 7:627–647.

Hinshaw, S., Zupan, B., Simmel, C., et al. (1997). Peer status in boys with
and without attention-deficit hyperactivity disorder: predictions from
overt and covert antisocial behavior, social isolation, and authoritative
parenting beliefs. *Child Development* 68(5):880–896.

King, C., and Young, R. (1982). Attention-deficit with and without hyperactivity. *American Journal of Disabled Children* 142:153–155.

Lahey, B., Schaughency, E., Strauss, C., and Frame, C. (1984). Are attention-
deficit disordered with and without hyperactivity similar or dissimilar
disorders? *Journal of American Academy of Child Psychiatry* 23:302–309.

Landau, S., and Milich, R. (1988). Social communication patterns of attention-
deficit disordered boys. *Journal of Abnormal Child Psychology* 16:69–81.

Melnick, S., and Hinshaw, S. (1996). What they want they get: the social
goals of boys with AD/HD and comparison boys. *Journal of Abnormal
Child Psychology* 24(2):169–185.

Milich, R., and Landau, S. (1989). The role of social status variables in differentiating subgroups of hyperactive children. In *Attention Deficit Disorder*, vol. 4, ed. L. M. Bloomingdale and J. M. Swanson, pp. 1–16. Oxford, UK: Pergamon.

Pelham, W., Atkins, M., and Murphy, H. (1981). *Attention-deficit disorder with and without hyperactivity.* Paper presented at the annual meeting of the American Psychological Association, Los Angeles, CA.

Pelham, W., and Bender, M. (1982). Peer relations in hyperactive children: description and treatment. In *Advances in Learning and Behavioral Disabilities,* vol. 1, ed I. Gadow and I. Bialer, pp. 365–439. Greenwich, CT: JAI Press.

Pfiffner, L., and McBurnett, K. (1997). Social skills training with parent generalization treatment effects for children with attention deficit disorder. *Journal of Consulting and Clinical Psychology* 65(5):749–757.

Szatmari, P., Offord, D., and Boyle, M. (1989). Ontario Child Health Study: prevalence of attention deficit disorder with hyperactivity. *Journal of Child Psychology and Psychiatry* 30:219–230.

Weiss, G., Hechtman, L., and Perlman, T. (1978). Hyperactives as young adults: school, employer, and self-rating scales obtained during ten year follow-up evaluation. *American Journal of Orthopsychiatry* 48:438–445.

Whalen, C., and Henker, B. (1985). The social worlds of hyperactive children. *Clinical Psychology Review* 5:1–32.

——— (1992). The social profile of attention-deficit hyperactivity disorder: five fundamental facets. *Child and Adolescent Psychiatric Clinics of North America* 1:395–410.

Whalen, C., Henker, B., Collins, B., et al. (1979). Peer interaction in a structured communication task comparison of normal and hyperactive boys and methylphenidate (Ritalin) and placebo effects. *Child Development* 50:338–401.

Wheeler, J., and Carlson, C. (1994). The social functioning of children with ADD with hyperactivity and ADD without hyperactivity: a comparison of their peer relations and social deficits. *Journal of Emotional and Behavioral Disorders* 2:2–12.

PART IV

Treating Comorbid Learning Disability Symptoms in AD/HD Children and Adolescents

INTRODUCTION TO PART IV

It has been estimated that as many as 50 percent of all learning disabled children and adolescents have AD/HD. As staggering as that figure appears, some feel it is a low estimate of this comorbidity. That is why it is important not only to assess learning problems in children with AD/HD, but to consider these learning problems in treating both the child and his/her parents. This section addresses this important area.

In Chapter 14, Joseph Palombo, L.C.S.W., and Anne Hatcher Berenberg, Ph.D., while focusing on a specific type of learning disability, present a very effective model they developed from the field of self psychology that can be applied to working with the parents of AD/HD children and adolescents. In Chapter 15, Bonnie S. Mark-Goldstein, Ph.D., and Deborah Berger-Reiss Psy.D., look at the importance of working with parents of AD/HD children and adolescents with comorbid learning and emotional problems from a different perspective, as they address how such a child impacts on the parents' own relationship as well as on the whole family. In Chapter 16, Judith Kushnet, M.F.C.C., presents practical applications for working therapeutically with a child presenting with AD/HD symptoms, comorbid learning disabilities, and attendant emotional problems. In Chapter 17, Dana Levin Shrager, Psy.D., continues the theme of working with AD/HD children and adolescents who have comorbid learning and emotional problems, this time from the perspective of educational therapy.

14

Working with Parents of Children with Nonverbal Learning Disabilities: A Conceptual and Intervention Model

Joseph Palombo and
Anne Hatcher Berenberg

The success of work with parents of children with learning disabilities is generally dependent on two factors: the establishment of a sound alliance with the parents, and a discerning understanding of the nature of the child's deficits. Interventions must be tailored to the particular symptom constellation the child displays, those caused by the primary neurocognitive deficit as well as those caused by the consequences the deficits have for the child's developing sense of self. In the case of children with nonverbal learning disabilities (NLD), the primary deficits may be in the visual-spatial, conceptual, affective, or social areas. The sequelae of these deficits often manifest as distortions in the child's development and personality. Emotional and behavioral problems are commonly found. Emotional problems may include pervasive anxieties, depression, obsessive-compulsive rituals, and extensive fears. Characteristic behaviors often are oppositional or negativistic traits, lack of motivation, social isolation, poor school performance, and generalized relationship difficulties. If the parents are to be helped in minimizing the negative effects of the child's primary and secondary deficits, they must have strategies that address each of the child's symptoms. Parents who can respond in positive ways will enhance the child's functioning, permitting him or her to mature optimally while also compensating for his or her deficits.

We begin this chapter with a brief review of the profile of children with NLD. We then outline a conceptual framework that is useful in understanding the interplay between the parents and the child with NLD, and briefly discuss the relational problems that emerge between parents and children with these problems. We also define the concept of complementary function, which is central to the development of intervention strategies. The central focus of this chapter is the interventions we have found to be helpful to parents in dealing with the difficult task of parenting children with nonverbal learning disabilities.

By way of clarification, we differentiate work with parents whose child has a learning disability from family therapy. Theories of family therapy conceptualize the interactions between family members differently from the ways in which we conceptualize work with parents. Family therapy may or may not serve the same goals as the techniques we suggest for our families. Our goal with parents whose child has NLD is to provide the necessary support to facilitate their difficult task. This goal may be accomplished whether or not both parents are seen, whether or not the child is in treatment, and whether or not the parents themselves are in individual, couples, or family treatment. (We use the word *parents* in the generic sense of caregivers. We recognize that many people aside from the custodial parents are often involved in raising a child.)

THE CONCEPTUAL FRAMEWORK

Phenomenological Description of the Child with NLD

In previous papers we have detailed the profile of children with NLD (Palombo 1995, Palombo and Berenberg 1997), which we summarize here. These features are not a comprehensive picture of the syndrome, and children do not have every feature mentioned. Each child may be said to have his or her own topography of deficits and symptoms. There is a considerable range in types, combinations, and severity of deficits and symptoms. Some children may have severe deficits in some areas and be unimpaired in others. Each configuration of deficits produces its own set of presenting problems. What follows, therefore, is a composite profile of children with NLD, whose deficits and symptom presentation are in the moderate to severe range. This profile is culled from a review of the literature, and from our and our colleagues' clinical experiences.

From a developmental perspective, early on parents notice that the child with NLD is different from their other children, but they cannot pinpoint what it is about the child they feel to be different. They find themselves frustrated in their efforts to understand the child. They seem unable to decode the child's cues. Because they find the child to be socially unresponsive, they feel placed in the position of constantly having to correct, limit, or punish the child. They are puzzled when the child in turn responds with resentment or fury at what the child experiences as unfair treatment; the family feels controlled by the child in all its activities while the child feels victimized. Parents often feel guilty, blaming themselves for what they believe to be their failure in properly parenting the child. Their frustration may initiate a cycle in which they feel rejected by the child and in turn distance themselves emotionally from the child. Not all parents respond this way; some are intuitively able to read the child's messages. These parents are the only ones who can communicate effectively with the child. When the parents' intuition fails, difficulties proliferate as the child's demands increase and the parents' ability to cope diminishes. The full-fledged syndrome manifests itself at age 7 or 8. Then the parents are often desperate and turn to therapists for help.

By latency age, a pattern of strengths and weaknesses emerges that defines the NLD syndrome. The children's capacities for verbal expression are remarkably well developed, while their proficiency in nonverbal communication is impaired. The patterns of strengths and deficits manifest in a variety of ways. In academic areas, the children generally have poor handwriting and deficient skills in arithmetic. Although they are good readers, their reading comprehension is not on a par with their verbal skills. As they move up to higher grades, complex material becomes much harder for them to grasp, and concepts are harder for them to understand. In addition, they cannot organize a narrative to pick out the main points from supporting details, the relevant from irrelevant. In school they also have problems with attention, dealing with novel materials, and adjusting to new situations. But since the children's verbal skills are relatively well developed, adults respond to them as though they are capable of functioning at much higher levels.

The area of affective communication is problematic for children with NLD. In the *receptive area* of nonverbal communication, they appear unable to decode prosodic signs or vocal intonations correctly; some have difficulty reading facial expressions. Others are unable to decode the emotional message conveyed by people's faces or bodily gestures. In the *expressive area*, some do not use vocal intonations. They speak either in a flat monotone or with a singsong voice. Parents find it difficult to read their moods from his or her facial expressions. They find it hard to tell whether the child is happy or unhappy. Also, since the children's bodily gestures are often not congruent with the context, they seem wooden and constricted. In the *processing area*, some children may have problems decoding affective states; they respond to affect-laden situations with anxiety, withdrawal, or sadness. Some have problems modulating or regulating certain affects; they lose control and have temper tantrums. Their problems with regulation sometimes lead them to respond to situations with generalized excitement that is unfocused and lacking in content. These responses make them appear to lack compassion or empathy for others, so that they appear not to have the same feelings about events and people as their peers. These impressions may be erroneous, since some of these children are very sensitive and responsive to those who understand their difficulties.

Their functioning in social situations is often problematic. In interaction with others, many children find it difficult to decode social cues. The difficulties they have reading other people's body language, facial expressions, and vocal intonations make them appear odd and inept in social situations. Their eye contact (gaze) seems unnatural and they seldom make solid eye contact. When they listen to others, reading between the lines, making inferences, or understanding the double meaning of others' expressions is often beyond them. Since they lack the capacity to appreciate humor, and since they interpret colloquialisms or metaphorical expressions concretely, they do not know when they are being teased and misinterpret what they are told. These difficulties are often aggravated when they are confronted with situations in which they have to process multiple inputs simultaneously.

These impairments in social functioning often lead to a generalized discomfort in those interacting with them—a discomfort whose source is often difficult to pinpoint. For example, they will start conversations with strangers as though they were old friends, asking personal questions too quickly, appearing not to respect the privacy that we presume others to need. They will also share personal facts too quickly, giving intimate details to strangers. To strangers, the mixture of overt friendliness and inappropriate boundaries makes the children appear both interesting and odd. Often adults will overlook the strangeness and respond to the friendly overtures rather than to the mode of interaction. The children then appear to be socially well related. However, complicating the interaction are such features as the difficulties some children have with the physical aspects of social boundaries. The deficits in their sense of the body in space do not allow them to respect the accepted culturally determined social distances. They stand too close or touch people inappropriately, failing to maintain the distance dictated by the context and by their relationship to the person they are addressing. With peers, their play can be disruptive; they are unable to negotiate social exchanges.

In addition, coexisting with these features, some of the children suffer from other symptoms that may mask or aggravate their distress. Their level of anxiety is often very high. They may display signs of depression, obsessive-compulsive symptoms, or attentional problems. It is important that such psychiatric and/or emotional problems, which may overlap with the NLD, be diagnosed independently of the NLD.

The Relational Context

Each child is part of a human context that constitutes the community in which he or she lives. Parents transmit to the child the social/cultural norms and expectations of their community. Children's psychological well-being—their psychological existence—is dependent on their assimilation into that context in a manner that permits them to maintain a healthy sense of self-cohesion. The relationship between the parents and the child may be characterized in multiple ways. At times parents provide comfort and understanding; at times they provide experiences that are joyous or filled with sadness. At other times they are the source of information or of the tools to achieve desired ends. There is no catalogue that can adequately list the range of parent–child interactions. However, the ways in which we conceptualize the child's interactions with his or her parents determine how we think about the problems that arise between them. In the case of children with learning disabilities, where the interaction is made all the more complex, understanding the association between the child's competencies and deficits and the parents' responses is critical to finding effective interventions that parents can use to alleviate the child's distress and facilitate their parenting task.

Children with NLD tend to require two sets of psychological functions from parents. Both sets of functions serve to complement the child's immature or deficient sense of self. On the one hand, in the NLD areas parents become mediators or translators who help the child understand and cope with events around him or her. On the other hand, parents provide the necessary emotional nurturance and support for the child to progress developmentally. Much empathy is required for them to accurately identify the child's emotional needs and supply the selfobject functions or auxiliary ego functions from which the child can benefit.

With regard to the first set of functions, the parents' complementary responses fill in the child's specific neurocognitive deficits. Since these deficits are neither visible nor easily identifiable, parents are often left to rely on their intuition as to what the child lacks in order to complement the child's functioning. For example, while most parents can translate their child's nonverbal communications, in the case of children with NLD this task is extraordinarily difficult. Since the child cannot provide unambiguous feedback, the parents are often in the dark about what the child is communicating or whether the child is understanding their communications. They may respond intuitively, empathically translating what the child is saying. But often they are left with uncertainty as to whether their responses are correct. Unless they learn a "language" or a vocabulary through which to speak with the child, the dialogue is derailed. If they have other children, the parents will recognize the differences in their child. They may find themselves catering to this child's needs and responding differently to him or her than to their other children. Also, they will often feel that if they do not respond, they may cause the child serious distress. What often occurs is that through their intercession they are filling in the areas in which the child cannot perform. They may then feel guilty about their involvement with the child, thinking that they may be spoiling the child. But at some level they realize that if they fail to respond to the child's demands, the child suffers.

In many ways we can think of the central problem of children with NLD as a nonverbal dyslexia (Badian 1986, 1992), that is, the children suffer from an inability to use, decode, and/or process nonverbal signs. Since as infants, all children initially communicate exclusively through the use of nonverbal signs, they are totally dependent on others' abilities to understand these communications. Later, when they develop the capacity to communicate verbally and translate their experiences into linguistic signs that are comprehensible to others, the dialogue between them and their parents becomes more constructive. Communication becomes possible when the participants in this dialogue share the same signs and meanings about similar experiences. Eventually, the verbal and nonverbal dialogue with parents permits children to construe a coherent set of meanings out of their experiences.

However, most often such a dialogue cannot be established with children with NLD. The children's limited capacities in the nonverbal receptive and expressive capacities—their inability to understand parents' nonverbal communications—lead them to make erroneous assumptions about what is being communicated. They misunderstand or are misunderstood by others. The inability to integrate the meanings of other people's facial expressions, vocal intonations, gestures, and other nonverbal communications causes them to miss the significance of many of the affective messages these channels convey.

There is no simple answer to the question of whether we can say that these children "distort" what they perceive. It is clear that the children often do not fully grasp or observe many of the cues that people convey. Consequently, their responses are based on incomplete information. Because it is incomplete, it is often erroneous. At the same time, the children usually carry a conviction that their perceptions are correct and that they are justified in their responses. They are unaware that unsuccessful responses are due to their own deficits and not to obstacles placed in their path by others. In addition, evidence from neuropsychological testing suggests that sometimes there are actual distortions in visual-spatial perception. Often children are able to correct their misperceptions in the testing situation when provided with verbal instructions, but it is unclear whether they are able to so in everyday life.

In summary, a complex interrelationship exists between the child's primary neurocognitive deficits and the emotional sequelae of these deficits, and often the source of each is indistinguishable. While diagnostic testing can identify the neurocognitive deficits in early latency, at earlier ages a diagnosis may be difficult to establish. Since parenting issues often are the presenting problems, separating what the parent contributes and what the child contributes to the interaction is even more problematic. Later in this chapter we address some of these issues with a view to laying the groundwork for the types of strategies we can offer parents to assist them in their task. However, before we can discuss specific intervention we must lay the conceptual groundwork by defining the construct of *complementarity of function*. We propose that parents can enhance a child's functioning by providing the child with the missing neurocognitive functions. By augmenting the child's capacities, parents can strengthen the child's vulnerable sense of self, giving the child the opportunity to mature and develop compensatory structures that will replace the complementary functions the parents provide.

Three concepts are helpful in considering the issues of the interactions between the child with NLD and his or her parents: goodness of fit, selfobject functions, and attunement. While each of these concepts has its origins in a different theoretical paradigm, we believe they can be integrated provided we keep in mind that each paradigm approaches the task of data collection from a different viewpoint. Chess and Thomas (1986), in their use of the concept of goodness of fit, view the child from an objective, descriptive, interpersonal perspective. Kohut (1971), in his use of the concept of selfobject functions, takes an introspective perspective, where the child's experience is of central concern. Stern's (1985) concept of attunement focuses on the observer's capacity to resonate with the child's experiences. We suggest that the broader concept of complementarity encompasses all three of these concepts. Each can be considered to be a constituent component of the broader construct, but the construct adds to these components the specific dimension of the cognitive functions that the parent performs for the child.

Chess and Thomas (1986) characterize the relationship between parent and infant, when successful, as that of goodness of fit. Each partner in the dyad brings attributes that either help the dyad to mesh into a smoothly functioning unit or impede the caregiving process. Chess and Thomas focus on the particular ways in which the child's temperament contributes to the functioning of the dyad. The type of fit between a child's and a parent's temperament either enhances or interferes with a child's healthy development. A good fit can mitigate the temperamental factors that make a child difficult to care for; a poor fit can result in serious parent–infant negative interactions.

We can extend this analysis to the relationship between parents and children with learning disabilities, particularly children with NLD. In the latter case, the impact of the child's neurocognitive endowment on the interaction is at issue. The goodness of fit is dependent in part on a parent's ability to decode the child's nonverbal communication in the absence of clear cues as to what the child is trying to say. From the point of view of the child with NLD, the parents' ability to read his or her nonverbal signs is vital to the child's healthy development. Some parents are better at reading these signs than others. They are better able to understand the few nonverbal signals the child sends without having to rely on verbal signs. However, for parents who themselves have deficits in the areas of nonverbal communication, the situation is full of pitfalls. They are seriously handicapped in their efforts at making a "good fit" with their child. As parents, they are unable to send or receive nonverbal signals clearly. Since the child is equally impaired, the dialogue becomes disrupted and negative interactions become dominant. Whether or not the parent has an NLD, the parent or the child may interpret the failure in communication as an unwillingness on the part of the other to communicate or understand. The stage is then set for the child to respond negatively. As a consequence, some children become oppositional, while other children become intensely anxious and withdraw, feeling defeated. These patterns endure not only to become self-defeating but also as entrenched themes that carry over in other relationships.

At times the verbal channels become available once the child starts to talk. Parents of children with NLD then find themselves becoming increasingly reliant on this mode of communication for clarifying what the child is conveying. The extent to which parents form a good fit or a poor fit with their child is therefore dependent not only on the temperamental factors Chess and Thomas (1986) stress, but also on the capacity of the partners in the dyad to talk with each other.

Related to the concept of fit is that of selfobject functions. Kohut (1971, 1977, 1981) sees some relational experiences as selfobject experiences. For him, selfobject functions comprise the psychological functions people provide to significant others. These functions are essential for a child to sustain the sense of self-cohesion and integration. Kohut draws an analogy between the need for selfobject functions and the human need for an environment that includes oxygen in order to survive. Without oxygen, people would suffocate. The awareness of the need for the function is most urgently felt when a person is deprived of the function. It is then that the means to sustain a sense of well-being ceases to exist. At other times, when the function is available, it is taken for granted.

In contrast to the concept of goodness of fit, the concept of selfobject provides a narrower definition of the specific responses a child requires from parents. These are responses that are critical to the child's psychological well-being. Selfobject functions such as the need to be lovingly admired or sheltered and protected from overstimulation are essential to the attainment of a healthy sense of self-esteem. Consequently, for the child with NLD, the parents' ability to perform these functions is an indispensable ingredient of the context the child requires to develop a healthy sense of self. When parents are unavailable to perform the requisite selfobject functions for the child, or the child cannot make use of the selfobject functions that parents do offer, the failures in the dialogue that ensue impair the development of the child's sense of self. These failures interfere with the child's bonding and attachment to the parents. Even if the parents achieve a measure of communication, this measure is often insufficient to bridge the distance created by the child's self deficits. For example, the fact that some children with NLD cannot recognize facial expressions or vocal intonations prevents them from experiencing the feelings associated with peering into a nursing mother's eyes and sustaining the joy that comes from that interaction. They cannot experience the soothing that comes from having a parent talk to them in soothing tones and rhythms, since the nuances of vocal intonations are misperceived. The result is that the child finds it difficult to experience the parents' mirroring or soothing selfobject functions. The child fails to develop the psychological functions that are essential to the development of a cohesive sense of self. The primary neurocognitive deficits may then produce a secondary set of emotional problems in the form of self-esteem problems or narcissistic vulnerabilities.

Stern (1985) modifies Kohut's concept of empathy, suggesting that attunement to the child's internal states is an essential part of the communicative link between child and parent. Attunement occurs through the parents' ability to resonate with the child's feeling states. From an evolutionary perspective, affects are retained by the organism because of their survival value in eliciting a response from the parent. The infant's cry serves as a sign to the parent and is a signal to which the parent responds. The communicative dimension of affective states does not lie necessarily in any intention on the part of the infant to make a statement that is to be understood by the parent. Rather the statement is "read" by the responsive parent who imbues the sign with a set of meanings. Attunement by the parent consists of the interpretation of these states as calls for some form of intervention. The consistency of the response constitutes invariant patterns that, when combined with the infant's experience, form a set of action patterns or sensorimotor patterns that define the relationship between child and parent. Such patterns may later be transformed into what Piaget called schemas, and what Stern (1985) calls representations of interactions generalized (RIGs). For Stern the innate givens that form the emergent and core senses of self commingle with affective states and with the parents' responses to lead to the structuralization of self experience. Demos (1988), similarly to Tomkins (1987), suggests that these co-assemblies of sensorimotor experiences—affect arousal states and interactive responses—are experienced by the infant as continuous with the self, or, we might say, they constitute selfobject experiences. When the child experiences a failure in attunement, it may be due to a parent's limitations or to the child's difficulties in making a connection with a parent who is willing and capable of responding. Whichever the source of the disruption, the developmental process leads to a breach in the link the child makes between his or her affect states and parenting responses.

The neurocognitive difficulties from which children with NLD suffer are often compounded by neuroaffective deficits, which make the parents' efforts at attunement even more demanding. Some children appear unable to express or read other people's feelings or get in touch with their own affect states. For these children the world of emotion is difficult to decode. Their difficulties with the expression of emotions leads them either to overcontrol their feelings or to give vent to them as unregulated outbursts. Their capacity to be attuned to others' emotions is seriously limited. Conversely parents find it difficult to empathize or become attuned to the child's emotional states. These difficulties result in interferences with the relationship between the child and the parents. Parents may end up feeling that their lives are controlled by the child because the child requires them to be constantly available, or they may find themselves in entrenched battles around every interaction with the child. In the latter case, the storms that occur seem to center around the child's attributing how he or she feels to the parents' failure to adequately understand his or her emotional needs.

To summarize, the concepts of fit, selfobject, and attunement describe the conditions that establish an atmosphere in which, and a communicative link through which, the child can mature. Depending on their own temperaments, parents attune themselves and resonate with the inner states of their infant; they organize themselves to complement the infant's psychic needs and become translators of his or her nonverbal messages. In a variety of areas, their psychic structure compensates for those the child is too immature to perform. The harmony created from birth through these efforts provides a hospitable environment in which the infant can thrive. It includes an active, though unconscious, molding of the parent to the infant. Thus, parent and child harmoniously adapt to each other, creating an interaction in which each partner responsively cues the other so that no disruption need occur. When successful, this interaction has the appearance of a joyous engagement in which maternal bliss is accompanied by the infant's smile. These conditions permit certain processes to occur within the child. The product of these processes is psychic structure.

However, as we have seen, the child's NLD often compromises these processes. The conditions necessary for the establishment of a complementary relationship between parent and child are not optimal. Two further features of NLD present obstacles to the establishment of a dependable fit: the child's impaired capacity for fluid reasoning, and the child's difficulties in dealing with novel situations. Both of these at times interact with one another to make the nurturing task dreadfully difficult. Some children with NLD have great difficulty flexibly modifying learned patterns so as to make them applicable to new situations. Their good rote memory allows them to remember what they have learned from prior experiences. However, what has been learned is applied inflexibly and mechanically; the particular context is not taken into account. If a rule of conduct is applied, it is often one that is inapplicable to this particular situation, leading to a defeat in the goal the child was trying to attain. As a result the child appears unable to problem solve. When confronted with the frustration of failure, the child cannot shift sets or be flexible in finding different ways of attacking the problem. Instead, the child vents his or her anger at the others, whom he experiences as unhelpful or unavailable when needed. The parents themselves are at a loss as to how best to intervene when their every effort is met with inflexible responses.

The Reciprocal Contributions to Failures in the Dialogue

The lesson we learn from these observations of children with NLD is that these children are not just passive recipients of parental empathy or attunement. They are also active interpreters of the context in which the empathy is made available, is withheld, or is unavailable. This means that there is no predictable correlation between a parent's empathy and the child's integration of the experience of the moment. The impression that the very presence of an empathic parent guarantees the child's utilization of the selfobject functions offered is erroneous. The activity of the recipient of the attunement, his or her ability to understanding the interaction, is just as critical as the provider's capacity to respond empathically. The child's endowment as well as prior experiences shape his/her perceptions. Both endowment and prior experience script (Tomkins 1987) how the child interprets the events to which he/she is exposed. That is, they lay down patterns of interaction that guide the child's future responses. In some sense the child molds the relationship with the parents and is molded by the parents' responses.

Furthermore, the child with NLD is often engulfed by anxiety. His or her history has demonstrated that the world is not a friendly place. Failures are much more common than successes in interactions with others. The child fears approaching others or often inappropriately approaches others. The interactions become one-sided with the child making efforts at reaching out only to find that the responses he or she had anticipated are not forthcoming. This result is not always because of others' insensitivity to the child. Often, strangers and parents find themselves wishing to make a connection with the child. They try to empathize with the child's inner state, but find themselves confronted with almost insurmountable difficulties in truly understanding these internal states. In spite of their best efforts, the child may experience these adults as unable or unwilling to be supportive.

Complementarity

We have seen that the elements in the formation of a complementary relation include the goodness or poorness of fit between parent and child, the capacity of parents to provide and the ability of the child to utilize selfobject functions, and the sensitivity of the parents in becoming attuned to the child's experiences as well as the child's communicative competencies in conveying those experiences to others. In addition, the parents function as auxiliary egos in the sense of performing for the child functions that the child cannot perform for him- or herself. We can now define a *complementary relationship* as the relationship that is formed between a child with a deficit and an "other" who provides functions, whether social, psychological, or practical, that the child cannot perform for him- or herself. A complementarity exists between each child and the context in which the child is raised. Complementarity extends beyond the nurturing functions performed by parents. It includes a continuity with others as sign users with whom communication occurs. It includes the use of others to help achieve a goal. A *complementary function* is a function performed by another person who fills in an affective, cognitive, social, or functional deficit. The person performing the function augments the competencies of the person requiring the function (Palombo 1987, 1991, 1993a,b). As a partner in the process, the child's capacity to utilize what others offer sets a limit to the success with which the dyad will function and to the extent to which the child's distress will be relieved.

If the parents can assist the child in dealing with maturational tasks the child confronts, the child will experience the context as benign and will be able to function at a cohesive level. For many children the positive interdependence that develops with others safeguards the child's sense of self-cohesion and enhances the potential for maturation. If the parents and others cannot complement the child's deficits, the child may be defeated in his or her effort at dealing successfully with the maturational tasks. He or she will fail to integrate the meanings of those experiences.

However, difficult dilemmas confront all parents regardless of their capacity to complement their child. On the one hand, if a parent devotes him- or herself to complementing a child's deficits, a complex relationship evolves. The child may become extremely dependent on the parent, making it impossible for the parent to distinguish what the child can and cannot do. A parent who is exquisitely sensitive

404   Joseph Palombo and Anne Hatcher Berenberg

and responsive to the child's distress may find that the child has become totally dependent on him or her. The parent intuitively reads the child's messages and soon finds him- or herself being the only one able to communicate effectively with the child. A symbiotic tie may then evolve. As placement in day care or preschool becomes necessary, the child may display severe separation anxiety. These parents may then be accused of fostering the child's dependence or not permitting the child to become autonomous. Their motives in responding to the child as they do are brought into question, and their confidence in their parenting is shaken. It is important to recognize that the parents' responses often are motivated by the child's survival needs and not necessarily by their unconscious needs to maintain the child's helpless state. This dependence is further complicated by the anxiety and uncertainty the parent feels about how to proceed. On the other hand, if the parent is unable to complement the function or refrains from responding, the child either fails or his or her coping capacities are taxed maximally. The child develops serious behavioral problems, and either withdraws, feeling defeated by the environment, or simply fragments. The parents are then experienced as unempathic, negligent, or uncaring (Fairchild and Keith 1981, Ohrenstein 1979). This is not to say that all behavior problems result from dilemmas such as these, the same outcome may be reached by other paths.

Most parents cannot avoid these problems of complementarity. Often they will either provide functions for the child or get into power struggles by insisting the child perform tasks, not realizing that the child is often unable to perform those tasks. At times, parents will vacillate between two extremes. Understanding the dynamics that drive these interactions and the nature of the child's deficits at the earliest possible stages of development is essential to avoid these dilemmas. Since that is not possible before the child is 3 or 4 years old, clinical judgment must be exercised as to how best to proceed in those early years. Our clinical experience leads us to recommend that the better alternative is to allow the symbiosis between parent and child to form, reserving attempts to resolve the dependence for a later time when the nature of the deficits are clearly identified and the child has matured sufficiently to cope with the challenges the environment presents. Ultimately, the goal for any parent who provides complementary functions for his or her child is to permit the child to develop compensatory functions that will take over the functions the parents provides.

THE THERAPEUTIC PROCESS

We conceive of work with parents of children with NLD as a partnership between the therapist and the parents in which the goals are as follows: to give parents the necessary support to feel that they are not alone in dealing with their difficult child, to provide them with information that will allow them to understand the reasons behind their child's behaviors, and to supply them with a set of specific strategies to use when confronted with difficult behaviors. The aim of these goals is to create conditions that permit parents to form complementary relationships with their child, enhance the child's capacity to form compensatory structures, and ultimately increase the child's capacity to cope with his or her environment. Parents are encouraged to cultivate positive feelings for their child and maximize the child's strengths.

In many instances, parents come for assistance having had prior consultations or testing that led to their experiencing the interpreted result as blaming them for their child's problems. If the disabilities were not diagnosed correctly, the impression could have been conveyed that the child's behaviors are the result of the family dynamics or inadvertent trauma to which the child was exposed. As a result, many parents approach the new evaluation with suspicion and defensiveness. They come prepared for criticism, ready to resist suggestions for testing, viewing the process either as unnecessary or as endangering because it would expose their own vulnerabilities. Some parents are so guilt ridden to begin with that they anticipate the worst from the diagnostician. At times they may feel they have contributed to the child's problems because they suspect they themselves have similar problems. This chapter does not discuss the complex problems entailed in trying to help parents who themselves may be suspected of having (NLD).

The approach we find most helpful is one of respectful compassion for the plight of each parent. Children with disabilities are difficult to raise. Conveying to parents an attitude of concern for their child best characterizes the basis for the emerging alliance. Treating them as one would a colleague or a close friend who asks for counsel can allow the parents to feel that they are not going to be considered to be part of the problem; rather, their help will be solicited in finding better ways of coping with their child. Before they can begin to appreciate the positive aspects and strengths the child possesses, they may need to express the full weight of the sadness they feel at the disruption that having such a child creates. They need some preparation for the fact that even though help is now at hand, the chronicity of the child's disorder ensures that problems will arise at every turn. They continue to face the constant frustration of never being able to anticipate precisely when a problem will arise. Often it occurs when they least expect it. Crises may develop at the least opportune moment or when the family should be joyously celebrating an event. Their energies are often drained by the effort it takes to stabilize situations or avoid emergencies. As the child grows, the nature of the difficulties changes. Each developmental step is accompanied by a plethora of new challenges. Although these declarations may sound overly pessimistic, their effect is to convey a deep understanding of what parents confront, thus forming a bond of empathy with their distress. This bond serves as a model for the empathy they will later be able to feel for their distressed child and for the bond they will form with him or her.

Sometimes the downward cycle of disappointment and despair has taken such a toll that considerable work is necessary to help parents identify and respond to their child's positive qualities. Often, because of the pervasiveness of the child's problems they have been totally preoccupied with managing as best they can, focusing entirely on the child's weaknesses. For them to come to the point where they can value once more the child's identity and can nurture his or her strengths requires a change in perspective and in the way they view their child. Once that occurs, they can then begin the process of building a positive relationship. When the cycle is broken and the disruptions diminish, parents can then express their love of, and devotion to, their child. The child's qualities that at one time were seen as irritants can now be appreciated for their adaptive qualities. A child's perseverance, or wonderful memory for facts, or love of music, which may at one time have been used defensively by the child to keep people at a distance, now can be put to good service in achieving desirable goals.

Educational Focus

Parents are entitled to the best explanation available of their child's problem. To the extent possible, it is desirable to give the parents general advice on the management of the child and on ways to provide the child with positive experiences (Garber 1988, Rourke 1995, Vigilante 1983). When parents are given an understanding of the nature of the child's deficits and the ways in which these deficits impact the child's life, they often experience considerable relief at finally having answers to their questions. They begin to make connections between situations and the child's deficits. Often they seek to educate themselves about the disorder. If they feel comfortable in joining a group of parents of children with the same problems, they may find support in learning that they are not alone in their struggles with this kind of child. Sharing their experiences and learning from others can alleviate their anxieties and dispel their confusions. It can also help them learn different strategies for dealing with some of the child's difficult behaviors.

Providing parents with information about their child's deficits also involves the larger task of reframing their understanding of their child's behaviors. Parents come with many different views as to why their child behaves as he or she does. Some parents have tried to deal with their child using the same child-rearing methods they use with their other children only to find that these do not work. They responded with frustration and confusion. Their expectations were that their child was endowed no differently from their other children. They felt caught in treating one child differently, fearing that this would be interpreted by their other children as favoritism. For these parents it is important to convey that their child is different from their other children and requires special management because of his or her impairment. The specifics of the deficits can be interpreted with examples from the results of the testing as well as by giving them materials to read about the disorder.

Other parents who are caught up in the vicious cycle of oppositional behavior may believe that their child is responding as he or she does for lack of adequate socialization or out of simple meanness. For these parents, reframing the child's difficulties involves a slow and systematic demonstration of the ways in which the child's impairment leads to failures in communication, which the child has interpreted as lack of caring. Changing this type of interaction presents one of the more challenging tasks in work with parents.

Intervention Strategies for Parents

Every situation is different and therefore requires individualized strategies. These strategies must be tuned to the child's particular topography of deficits and strengths, to the temperament and personality of the parents, and to the history of their interaction. Some parents prefer addressing specific incidents and learning what went wrong so they can tailor their responses to the understanding they acquire. Other parents focus on relationship problems, wishing to facilitate social interchanges for their child. Still others expect the therapist to provide specific interventions that will relieve problem situations. Clinicians often find themselves using a combination of approaches. Since each approach has its own validity and is applicable to different aspects of the child's deficits, we will suggest a set of strategies we have found helpful, giving examples of their application to different situations.

It is important to help parents realize the scope of their child's difficulties. When hearing about learning disabilities, most people think of dyslexia, which is a focal disability that affects only a sector of the child's life. Other sectors such as playing with friends or relationships with parents may be unaffected by the disability. In striking contrast, nonverbal learning disabilities permeate every aspect of the child's life, from the time the child gets up in the morning until bedtime. For example, as the child tries to judge how much toothpaste to put on the toothbrush, visual-spatial problems interfere with the task. Problems intrude in the classroom where he or she may struggle with math or the nuances of fiction reading comprehension. At recess the child may be confused by the experience of twenty-odd moving bodies rapidly giving off multiple social cues. At the dinner table, negotiating the crosscurrents of family signals presents its own challenges. Every step in the developmental path presents new challenges for the child as he or she displays different behaviors and variations on old themes.

Once parents can see how pervasively nonverbal learning disabilities affect their child's life, they can be helped to focus on the particulars of their own child's experience. It is usually productive to examine their child's everyday life with an eye to the demands made upon the child for nonverbal competencies. Much as the parents of a physically challenged child need to assess the environment to see the obstacles to their child's functioning, so too must the parents of a child with NLD identify the impediments in their child's world. Parents can then introduce appropriate modifications. They can ask themselves questions such as, What is entailed in this child's walk to school? Older siblings may have easily managed the task at this age, but is it realistic to expect that this child can manage it on his or her own? On written work, does the child always get mixed up when there are too many math problems on a page? When school is over, is there a large group of neighborhood children with whom the child must cope, or is the child enrolled in a loosely run after-school program that overtaxes the child's meager social resources? Is he or she expected to manage playing with more than one child at a time on play dates? Even when limited to playing with one friend, does he or she need some planned activities and adult input to keep things running smoothly? Such a careful inventory helps to define what the stress points are for this particular child in this particular family. This enables the therapist and parents to find starting points for specific intervention.

As parents talk about the difficulties and challenges their child presents, it sometimes becomes apparent that over the years their patience has worn thin. They may have become irritated by the child's inability to modify his or her behaviors in spite of numerous attempts at getting the child to alter the dysfunctional patterns. When difficult situations are reviewed to see what goes wrong, they can be reinterpreted. The contributions of the child's deficits to the interaction can be highlighted in a way that has not been apparent to the parents before. Then the problems can be seen as arising from a failure in communication rather than being solely attributable to a willful child who is defiant.

It is essential to nurture the positives in the parents' relationship to and interactions with their child. This occurs on two different levels. As one thinks about the child's difficulties, it is always important to help the parents remember that there are other aspects of the child that they value and cherish. These provide the foundation for building the child's self-esteem. Parents may admire their child's capacities for verbal expression. They may take pleasure in the child's theater performances where he or she has learned to gesture appropriately or use proper vocal expression to give emphasis to a set of feelings. Even some things about the child that are irritating, such as the child's perseveration, may contain within them the seeds of something positive, such as perseverance.

A further consideration is that in any set of interventions with the child, it is important to build on success. The child needs to know what he or she is doing right. For children with NLD, it is particularly important to verbalize an appreciation of their gains, no matter how minor, in order to solidify them. When the child finally looks the neighbor in the eye while saying "Hello," the child needs to know what a difference that has made. Empty praise, such as the mindless "That's great!" in response to every drawing the child makes, is not useful because it cheapens real praise and because it is not specific enough to foster strengths or accomplishments. It is only confusing. Commenting on the use of different colors or the added detail in the drawing, however, nurtures the child's growth. Genuine positive responses keep the child moving forward. And as the parents notice what is going right, they also can begin to feel better about their own parenting.

In offering specific interventions for parents, we keep two goals in mind: to increase the child's coping capacities, and to enhance the child's self-esteem. An awareness of the issues facing this child in this family situation guides the therapist and parents as to where to begin. Some strategies are more useful for some children than for others. The order in which they are introduced varies from child to child. The therapist tailors the interventions in accordance with what is required by the problematic situation. And while the therapist provides information to parents, he or she is also mindful of the parallel process through which similar interventions are used by the therapists with the parents themselves to help model the strategies being discussed. Bringing the parallel process to the parents' awareness often helps them integrate the intervention.

The interventions that follow should not be thought of as discrete techniques to apply to children or situations without regard to the total context. Many of these interventions might be applied simultaneously or in combination with others. Of greater importance than the interventions as strategies is the mind set from which they stem. Parents who get immersed in their child's modes of functioning will find themselves using these techniques flexibly and creatively. Their sense of oneness with their child will lead to the establishment of the sense of complementarity.

Teaching the Child about Nonverbal Communication

The nonverbal domain in human communication involves the ability to decode others' nonverbal messages, to use nonverbal signals to convey messages to others, and to process the meanings associated with each component of the nonverbal domain. Among the most common components of this domain are facial expressions, gestures, gaze (eye-to-eye contact), body posture, vocal intonation, tactile communication (the use of touch), and proximics (the awareness of the appropriate social distance to use in different social contexts). Most children do not require formal instruction in the use of these modalities; they appear to absorb them through observation of others. However, children with NLD have deficits in one or more of these components or in the capacity to encode, decode, or process messages in this domain. Nowicki and Duke (1992) use the term *dyssemia* to characterize the difficulties children generally have in the use of this channel of communication. They believe that it is necessary to instruct all children more formally in its use. We believe that for the children with whom we are concerned, such instruction is critical for them to compensate for their deficits. This instruction should be undertaken much as one were to teach the child a foreign language.

It requires breaking down tasks and actively demonstrating to the child what is involved.

Parents then should consider the demands on the child to read nonverbal social cues. They can be helped in this process by asking themselves questions such as: How do people in our family communicate? Are there frequently given signals the child can be taught to recognize? Can family members modify their nonverbal communication by pairing their nonverbal signs with words the child can understand? Is the child regularly exposed to situations that demand problem-solving abilities or flexibility in thinking skills that may be over his or her head? Such questions heighten the parents' awareness of their own modes of nonverbal communication as well as the child's deficits in communicating.

Once parents have formed a solid picture in their minds of the problematic areas, the task of remediation can begin. The means through which this remediation can be given is complex. Demonstration alone cannot accomplish the task. What is required is the use of verbal mediation, that is, the use of words to translate for the child what is being taught. Language is an area of strength for children with NLD. While they may start out having articulation problems, they soon demonstrate verbal skills beyond their years. Nonverbal messages must be both demonstrated and translated into verbal forms so as to enable them to negotiate situations successfully. The task for parents is to develop the means through which to patiently instruct the child, for example, to look the person in the eyes when speaking to him or her, to notice whether the person is smiling or frowning, to listen to the tone of voice. At first the child will be puzzled and bewildered, not knowing what to look for, but eventually a sensitization process leads to the acquisition of a rudimentary vocabulary upon which the child and parent can enlarge.

Case Illustration

Jane, age 12, has had chronic problems acquiring and retaining friends. She either overwhelms new friends, pushing them away, or is so inappropriate in groups that others shy away from contact with her. In one of her sessions with her therapist, she brought a series of pictures from her birthday party to which she had managed to attract a few friends. One of the pictures had Jane holding on to the shoulder of one of the other girls, having pulled her toward her to have their picture taken. The friend looked clearly uncomfortable, forcing herself to smile for the camera. The therapist first praised Jane for her success in attracting the friends to the party, then gently pointed out the girl's discomfort in the picture. Jane respond by saying that the girl was smiling. The therapist noted that it looked like a forced smile. Jane said, "How did you know that? My teacher said the same thing!" The therapist then made a face that should have appeared as a forced smile and contrasted it with a genuine smile. Jane detected no difference. They then both went to a mirror and started making faces. It was clear that the various expressions were indistinguishable for Jane. Finally the therapist brought out a Polaroid camera asking Jane to pretend she was smiling and to make a genuine smile. Pictures were taken of both. She examined them carefully, beginning to notice some of the differences. The point was to teach Jane about a domain of communication of which she had no awareness. Pointing it out helped introduce the concept and illustrate for her an area of weakness.

When the therapist later met with Jane's parents, she went over the incident, which they quickly recognized since they too had reacted the same way to the picture. The therapist explained what she had done, conveying to them the need for Jane to be tutored to learn about different facial expressions. The visual cues must be pointed out and reinforced so as to help Jane decode them and make them part of her vocabulary.

Using Verbal Mediation

In the prior section we introduced the concept of verbal mediation as an important tool to help children compensate for their nonverbal deficits. We elaborate on this concept with parents so as to help them avoid feeling defeated when they begin using this approach and find it is not successful even after repeated efforts. While the idea of using an alternative channel of communication—one in which the children appear to be quite fluent—seems commonsensical, in reality the process by which the child learns is much more complex. We can draw an analogy with the difficulties that children who make letter reversals have when they beginning writing. At first it seems easy to think that by simply pointing out the error to the child, he or she will be able to correct the reversal. However, the fact that the child's neurological immaturity does not permit him or her to see the letter correctly may escape the inexperienced adult. A parent might simply think that the child was inattentive or simply made an error. In reality the child does not see the letter as others see it. Simply pointing out the correct form of the letter does not lead the child to learn the proper configuration.

This phenomenon is quite similar to the one we encounter with children with NLD. If they do not perceive as others do, it is not because they are inattentive or unmotivated but rather because their brains process that kind of information differently. Consequently, pointing out visual cues verbally does not necessarily lead the child to perceive those cues as others do. The child is made aware that something is wrong, but cannot at first fathom what it is that is wrong. Verbal explanations, given with empathy and understanding rather than with criticism, begin to help the child narrow the range of stimuli to which to attend and process. The child can learn to vocalize, rehearsing verbally, what he or she has been taught so as to reinforce the procedure. What often occurs is that the child begins to notice the visual cues but does not use the information attached to those cues in an integrated fashion. By having the verbal explanation paired with the nonverbal activity, the child learns to associate the words with the cue. For example, simply telling a child to look directly at the person with whom he or she is talking is insufficient. The explanation must be accompanied by a demonstration of what the child must do. At first the child will look at the person to whom he is speaking in the eyes, but the stare is penetrating and expressionless. Further explanations and demonstrations can make the child aware of the content of the communication and the appropriate feeling that should accompany this content. Eventually, it is possible that the meanings we attach to these modes of expression will also be learned so that the verbal explanations given the child will lead to a deeper understanding and a better integration of those signals.

Case Illustration

John, age 10, had another boy over to play. He was having a wonderful time making up rhymes using the other boy's name. John's mother could see that the other boy was becoming progressively more uncomfortable. Since she did not want to embarrass her son by chastising him in front of his friend, she resorted to signaling him to stop the teasing by raising her eyebrows or shaking her head. But these signals went unheeded. She became increasingly distressed by what she experienced as John ignoring her or defying her and continuing to tease his friend. She thought she was escalating by raising her finger, indicating clearly that he should stop, all to no avail. Now she got angry, raising her voice. She told John that since he was being rude he should go to his room and think about his poor behavior. Bewildered by his mother's response, he cried out that she was being mean for no reason. By this time the situation had deteriorated to the point the friend asked to go home. John's mother felt defeated; once again John had ruined a chance to develop a friendship.

As the therapist reviewed the incident with John and his mother, John maintained that his friend was having fun and enjoyed the teasing, "He was smiling, Mom. He must have liked it!" Obviously John had misread his friend's facial expression, misinterpreting the grimace of discomfort for a grin. From his perspective, his mother's anger came out of the blue; he felt he had no warning. For her part, John's mother did not realize that her attempts to spare him embarrassment through her nonverbal signals were totally lost on him. She learned that nonverbal signals must be accompanied with clear verbal comments if John is to understand her communications.

Preparing the Child for New Situations

Entering a new situation requires children to change their mind sets or frames of reference so as to contextualize themselves within the new environment. The shift in attitude that such recontextualization requires is most difficult for children with NLD. It is unclear whether this difficulty is due to the anxiety new situations create for them or to their inability to process the visual information with which they feel bombarded in a new environment or both. What is clear is that the child needs help in assimilating even the most pleasurable elements of new situations. Structuring the child's day, making it as predictable as possible, can help the child anticipate what is to come well in advance of the change. However, there are always events that are not part of the child's daily routine with which parents have to contend. Going to a new place in town, visiting relatives that had not been seen in while, starting in a new school, going on vacation—each of these is fraught with anxieties that lead to defensive responses by the child. Counteracting these anxieties requires patience and special strategies that are tailored to each child. Parents should be reminded that they often take for granted changes that for them and their other children present no problems. Some children can use verbal mediation alone, but as we have seen most children require more. What the child requires is anticipatory rehearsal of the events he or she is about to encounter. Optimally what should occur is a full dress rehearsal of the event. A child will feel most comfortable only if he or she can actually visit the setting prior to the event itself with a parent with whom a complementary relationship exists.

Knowing that the child needs to be prepared provides parents with an opportunity to teach the child to deal with his or her anticipatory anxiety. Some NLD children have not made the connection between the butterflies in their stomach and the fact that it is a signal that they are anxious. By making the connection, parents can not only help the child read his or her body signals but also begin to interpret the meanings these signal have. The child is then ready to struggle with the feeling, finding ways to accommodate to the situation.

Case Illustrations

Robert, age 8, was to begin a soccer program at the local park. Knowing his difficulties with new situations, his parents, at the therapist's direction, were proactive and anticipated the problems Robert might encounter. They first walked to the park with Robert several times, helping him identify landmarks on the way so that later he could orient himself through them. Once at the park, they helped him become familiar with the field, locating the goals, the sidelines, the center line, and other essential markers. To further compensate for his confusion about left and right hand, they discussed his wearing a sweatband on his left wrist. They helped him practice putting on his shin guards, and discussed with him the possibility that he might feel what he called "that jumpy feeling" in his stomach. They told him that meant that he was nervous and excited about doing something new and he could use it as a signal to remember what they had practiced. In addition, the parents met with the coach before the first practice session to inform him of Robert's enthusiasm about playing but also to alert him of his difficulties with directionality and his need to have verbal instructions to supplement any demonstration of physical activities. They also let the coach know that they did not expect the coach to turn Robert into a star player. These strategies were instrumental in making the experience a successful one for Robert.

The parents of Keith, age 10, were very upset as they reported that they had been unsuccessful in convincing him to come for a reevaluation appointment with his therapist. They tried reassuring him, thinking that he simply was anxious, but were unsuccessful in doing so. In fact, the more they talked with him about it the more upset he got. Finally he offered a compromise that he would come on condition that he would not have to talk to the therapist. He was due to see the therapist later that day. They seemed willing to accept that compromise, although they felt the session would end up being unproductive. Keith had seen the therapist a year ago and had enjoyed the evaluation. At the time the therapist determined that Keith was not ready for psychotherapy; instead the therapist suggested maintaining ongoing contact with the parents and recommended a reevaluation at a later point. Keith's mother called the therapist, quite distraught, asking for advice.

Upon further exploration of the incident, she revealed that she had told Keith that same morning about the session without prior preparation. Given his severe problems with novel situations and changes in routine, it was not surprising that he responded as he did. From his perspective the plan for the session came out of the blue. It was disorienting and unsettling for him to conceive of his day being different from his usual routine. While he was able to remember the therapist, he could probably not imagine what was entailed in deviating from his schedule. All he probably heard was that he had to do something unfamiliar, which generated a great deal of anxiety. His expectation was that he would end up feeling disrupted. When reminded of this particular problem of Keith's, the mother felt guilty at having created the situation and at having felt so angry at him for his refusal. Her own anxiety about his keeping the appointment had clouded her usual empathy for him. We agreed that it was best to postpone the session. Next time, he would be prepared ahead of time, the routine for the day when he was to come would be rehearsed with him, he would be reminded of what he did at the prior session when he came, and his cooperation would be enlisted. The parents were also able to discuss with Keith the understanding that his reaction was motivated by his anxiety rather than coming simply from his stubbornness or negativism.

Reinforcing Thinking about Part–Whole Relationships

When children with NLD are asked to report an incident in which they have been involved, their narrative of the incident is disjointed, fragmented, and often unintelligible. It is difficult for the listener to get a sense of what occurred, even from the child's own perspective. The sequence in which events occurred is unclear, the significant elements are not well highlighted, important details are left out, and the child's involvement is obscure. What appears to have gone wrong in the child's recital is not only that the sense of the sequence is disrupted but also that the relationship of the significant elements to other elements in the story are not clearly delineated. The foreground components are meshed with background components so that no gestalt appears. Part of the difficulty appears related to the child's inability to see the whole and relate the elements to each other.

The strategy parents can use to help correct for this difficulty is much like the one tutors use in teaching a child to outline an essay; we call it weaving a narrative. A good story has a beginning, a middle, and an end, which spell the sequence in which events occur. It also has a protagonist, who is the hero of the story; it has a theme or plot around which the elements are woven; it specifies the time and setting in which the action occurred; and, finally, its elements are organized into a coherent account. To deal with the deficit in seeing part–whole relationships the child must learn to tell a good story. One place where parents can begin with this task is by drawing the analogy between a story and a school essay, which the child has been taught to write at school. The parents should patiently ask about the main point of the story. This process could be reinforced by writing down what the child says so as to provide a different channel for the integration of the material. Next, they can ask about the other events and, even though the child may not be able to give them sequentially, they can be written down to be reordered at a later point. Finally, once they have gained a sufficient understanding of what occurred, the parents should reward the child with their approval for the effort he or she has put into the process, praising the child for helping them understand what had upset him or her. Other strategies involve role playing with the child the scene of the occurrence. This can be done either directly or through the use of dolls or hand puppets. The child may be able to concretely express what he or she could not relate verbally.

Once the child learns to tell his story in a coherent fashion, the next task is to help him or her modifying the dysfunctional patterns by rewriting the narrative of the problematic interactions. The child can then conceive of different outcomes from those to which he or she has become accustomed. Part of the child's inability to respond differently is due to the rigidity in the way he or she thinks about others' responses. To the NLD child, there appears to be no way to react differently from the way the child had previously responded. But once the child has been able to clearly understand the problematic interactions, the child can then be guided through a series of steps in which he or she will change the plot of the narrative so that a different outcome can be ensured. The characters in the story can change from being all-powerful tormentors to becoming insecure children who scapegoat to assert control over situations. The child with NLD can then imagine a different response and outcome from the one that previously occurred.

Case Illustration

Matthew, age 10, came home at least once a week with a jumbled set of complaints about kids being mean to him. The only clear communications his parents could get from him were "He keeps teasing me!" "He laughed at me!" "He chased me!" and "He hit me!" Clearly he was having trouble with his peers. Neither he nor his parents had any idea why. Matthew's parents and his therapist began to help him use an outline for his tales of woe similar to the outlines he was learning to use in school to write stories. First, Matthew was asked to set the scene: where was he, who else was there, what were they doing before the painful part of the incident began. Next, Matthew was asked to recount the first thing the other child said or did. Then, what was Matthew's response: what did he say, how did he say it, how did he move. Then, how did the other child respond to him, and so forth. At first he found it very difficult and frustrating to structure himself as requested. He insisted that the process was not helping him since he could not see the long-term benefits. After several months of friendly coaching, he got the idea of setting the stage before describing what occurred. Knowing that his parents were interested in talking with him about these incidents also helped him to become more alert to the events as they took place. In the early months, when Matthew had no idea how to describe the nonverbal aspects of the interaction, the therapist encouraged the parents to act out different tones of voice, facial expressions, or gestures. Matthew began to pick the ones that best matched the way his peer had looked or sounded. Finally, Matthew's accounts began to approach a coherent narrative. The parents, through their genuine interest, encouraged his efforts. They found that by clearly restating his story as they understood it, he could focus more on the essentials.

When Matthew could finally tell a reasonably coherent story of what was happening to him, he took a crucial step in problem solving. He was able to identify the source of the problem. In one oft-repeated scenario, his classmate Tim would come to Matthew's locker and call him a "dweeb." Matthew would feel provoked and insist he wasn't a dweeb. Tim would laugh at his discomfort and would call other kids to join in the teasing. Matthew's frustration would mount.

Tim would shout, "Dweeb, dweeb, you can't catch me!" and run down the hall. Matthew would feel compelled to chase him. The chase would end in a relatively secluded spot away from teachers where Tim would hit him.

Even after the pattern was identified, Matthew could see no alternatives to his actions. The next challenge was to get Matthew to consider the possibility that there might be other ways to respond. He came up with and rejected the idea of telling the teacher because it would bring about more teasing. Matthew's interest was captured, however, by an idea put forth by his therapist: the real problem was how to keep Tim from having so much power over Matthew. Tim was "making" Matthew chase him. How could Matthew take away that power? Matthew was able to be curious about how he could keep Tim from having that power. Although he had repeatedly rejected doing nothing as "wimpy," now he decided to experiment with choosing not to chase Tim. He came back from the next incident grinning. He had avoided chasing Tim. Tim, who expected the usual pattern, kept lying in wait for Matthew until he ended up being late for class. Matthew could see that by making an active decision not to allow himself to be goaded into following Tim he had rewritten the narrative. Later, Matthew would entertain the notion that he could similarly make an active choice to respond to name-calling by looking steadily at the other child but not getting drawn into arguing defensively. Practicing this new behavior with his parents before trying it out with other kids helped him to use it in peer situations. Matthew was getting the idea that he could change the course of the stories of peer incidents by trying out alternate actions.

Enhancing Problem-Solving Capacities

Children with NLD have problems flexibly applying what they learned in different contexts to new situations. The result is that they appear to perseveratively butt their heads against a wall when confronted with situations that they had not previously encountered or that are even slightly different from ones they had previously successfully negotiated. They seem incapable of getting around the barriers they perceive to be in their way, even when a simple shift in strategies would lead to a resolution of the situation. What seems to happen is that once they seize upon a rule derived from a previous situation, they generalize from that rule indiscriminately, applying it to all situations that bear any similarity to the original one. The sources of their inflexibility are probably multiple; what is relevant here is their inability to problem solve. Discussions of problems end up being circular. Suggestions and alternatives are met with resistance or discouragement that they would not work. The children feel a sense of hopelessness about their lives that leads them to not even try a different approach. It is as though they are convinced that people will generally be unresponsive to them no matter how much of an effort they made or that the world is simply not a friendly place that would welcome their attempt at being successful. Parents become disheartened by their failures to negotiate resolutions to situations. Helping the child develop patterns through which problems may be resolved, and resolutions achieved, is central to dealing with this issue.

One approach is to systematically begin by teaching the child about negotiation. This technique should be introduced around some fun activity that makes the process enjoyable. At times, some children can engage in strategy games that offer opportunities for negotiation. These games can become a model from which the child can learn, applying similar tactics to life situations. An important point to convey to the child is that negotiations can be structured so that they become "win/win" situations, rather than there having to be a winner and loser. Both sides can be seen to gain from a successful negotiation; one side need not humiliate the other by claiming victory. Some parents who have taught the technique to their child come to feel at first that they have created a monster. The child insists on applying the approach to every situation no matter how inappropriate it may be from the parents' point of view. Parents should be helped not to despair, as they have encountered another aspect of the child's deficit—the inability to contextualize his or her responses (see below). The beginning that parents make by having a child learn to negotiate may eventually be extended to broader problem-solving strategies that enlarge the child's repertoire of coping mechanisms.

Case Illustration

Kevin, age 12½, was mercilessly teased by his classmates. They found endless ways to torment him: they held the gym door closed so he could not get in, they took his hat and tossed it around so that he could not get it back, they falsely accused him of cruelty to pets, and so on. Kevin's invariable response was to scream in protest, hoping teachers would hear and come to his rescue, which at times in the past they had done. However, Kevin had also taken to screaming out in the middle of class when kids had taken his pencils, or snatched his books, or even simply laughed in his face. The teachers had not appreciated the ensuing disruptions. They had asked Kevin to come talk to them privately at the end of class so they could correct the situation. In spite of numerous conversations with teachers about finding alternate ways of dealing with these occurrences, Kevin persisted in using the same pattern. He in turn was convinced that the teachers were against him, and were unwilling to protect him or side with him. The parents reported similar responses from Kevin around sharing the television with his sister, choosing activities on family vacations, or involving him in any task that required his cooperation to attain a goal. His parents felt that he insisted on having his way, rigidly sticking to old patterns and not compromising.

What became clear during these discussions was that Kevin's rigid thinking style did not permit him to see that there are different ways of dealing with situations and that unless he could modify his approach he would end up frustrated. The task for these parents was to offer several alternate ways of solving the problem from which he can choose. Although there would be times when he would be unable to make a shift, the notion that there is more than one way to manage a problem situation is central to his learning new patterns. An opening occurred when Kevin reported to his tutor an incident that occurred in one of the science labs when he was once more provoked by another child. Kevin responded by throwing a book at the boy who provoked him. The teacher got furious and marched him to the principal's office to be severely reprimanded. For his part, he was furious; he felt he was treated unfairly, especially since nothing was done to the boy who had instigated the disturbance.

In trying to debrief him around this incident, Kevin's tutor patiently listened to what had happened. She had been through similar incidents many times and knew that unless she listened to his side of it she would get nowhere with helping him with his responses. She had also talked to the teacher and heard the concerns the teacher had about the possible disastrous effects of a book flying across the room with lab equipment and lit Bunsen burners on top of counters. The teacher feared for the safety of the class and the school.

Rather than address Kevin's indignation, the tutor talked with him about his inability to appreciate the fear he had induced in the teacher, and the concern the teacher felt for the safety of the class. She asked if he noticed her expression as being more than just anger at him for what he had done. Slowly it dawned on Kevin that what he had done was dangerous. It had never occurred to him that the teacher would be frightened by his action. He then felt guilty and contrite that he had acted so impulsively and expressed a desire to apologize to the teacher for his thoughtless behavior. The tutor then rehearsed with Kevin a strategy through which he would negotiate with the teacher as to how further incidents should be handled. The tutor knew that a model United Nations session was being held at school in which Kevin was a participant to discuss how nations negotiate with each other. She drew a parallel between Kevin and the teacher and other children, and different countries. Kevin, who was excellent in geography, not because he could visually locate regions on the map but because of his astonishing memory for facts, and had recently won a geography contest, loved the idea. He at first playfully imagined himself having nuclear weapons to wipe out the enemy. But then he was able to draw back to find more peaceful approaches to problem solving. Together they drew up a scenario in which he would have a "summit meeting" with his teacher to discuss his plight. The pride with which Kevin was able to engage in this process led his parents to take up the idea and generalize the practice to other situations.

Identifying Feelings in Self and Others

The area of feelings requires special attention. Frequently, children with NLD have difficulties with feelings. Many of these children find it hard to read others' feelings, to express their own feelings, or to understand the common meanings attached to some feelings. At times, the problems take the form of understanding or expressing feelings, except when they reach a significant level of intensity. It is as though their feeling "volume knobs" are either turned down or fully on, so that they either have little awareness of subtle feelings states or attend to intense feelings. At times, the children have problems regulating their feelings. They are given to serious outbursts or cannot calm down once they become excited. Consequently, there are two distinct areas in which parents can assist these children with their feelings: helping them learn to identify feeling states in themselves and others, and instructing them in ways to regulate their frustrations and affect states.

The display of feelings is a highly culture-bound activity guided by rules children learn at an early age. These display rules are also largely gender determined; what is proper for a girl may not be proper for a boy, and vice versa. However, before a child can learn display rules, he or she must first be able to experience and identify the feelings. Later, through attunement to others, the child can learn to read how others feel. The task for children with NLD is, first, to identify and be in touch with their inner feelings, and then to develop the capacity to identify others' feelings. This task is not just a cognitive task, for it involves the capacity to process the meaning associated with emotions generally.

We spoke earlier of the child who had difficulty identifying whether or not her friend was displaying a genuine smile. The cognitive component of the task involves simply recognizing the facial features that are indicative of a smile. Beyond that is the meaning associated with that display and the message the display conveys to the recipient of the smile. This latter task involves a capacity to be attuned to the other person's feeling state, to resonate with that state, recognizing the feeling in oneself and translating it as a friendly, receptive gesture. Some NLD children may be able to perform the cognitive component of the task but not have a clue as to how to process the signal. Others may be able to process the signal but not be able to give expression to the affective message they wish to convey. Understanding the nature of the child's problem in this area is therefore critical to the introduction of an intervention.

Generally, we approach parents by asking that they test out whether the child appears to have a range of feelings. They can ask themselves whether they notice the child is appropriately displaying feeling of joy, sadness, anger, or fear, or whether the child's responses are undifferentiated and indistinguishable from one another. If it can be established that the child's responses are difficult to differentiate, then we can next move on to distinguishing whether the child has difficulty in reception, expression, or processing elements. The strategy is to ask the child to stop and listen to him- or herself. It may sound artificial at first to require a child to stop in the middle of a social transaction and listen to the feelings. But once the initial embarrassment is overcome, the technique becomes automatic and gets smoothly integrated into the repertoire of day-to-day transactions. Eventually the child incorporates the strategy into his or her life.

The task for children who appear not to experience any feelings is much more difficult than it is for those children who give indications of the presence of feelings but have an impairment in their communication. We have seen parents of children with severe NLD struggle to teach their children about feelings. Some of them have done so through children's books, movies, music, or dance. The medium chosen was usually one the child enjoyed. At first children with good memories could identify the feeling by rote. Once that occurred the parents moved on to help identify similar feelings within the child. It is a moving experience to hear a parent report his or her success in getting a child to say "I am sad!" or "I feel happy!" in an appropriate context.

Activities are available to help children learn to express or recognize feelings. Activities such as art therapy, dance or movement therapy, and theater can be very useful in this regard. We also find that occupational therapy, especially if instituted at an early age, can be especially beneficial for the children's coordination or other motor problems, thus helping to build self-esteem.

The issue of the regulation of feelings in children with NLD is one that often looms large in parents' minds. They often refer to what we have come to identify as "affect meltdowns." Children dissolve in tears, have tantrums that last for prolonged periods of time, lash out impulsively and unexpectedly at siblings or adults, and seem generally unable to contain their frustrations. What seems characteristic of these children is that these outbursts are not always predictable, so that parents are often unprepared for their appearance. This makes it almost impossible to anticipate their emergence or to institute measures to prevent their occurrence. In addition to the problems of dealing with these explosions is the child's inability or unwillingness to process what happened once the eruption has subsided.

The counterpart of this phenomenon is the children's response to other people's feelings. Parents report that their child will appear either not to pay attention to their requests unless the volume of their voices are raised to the level of a scream, or they will be accused of screaming when they speak in their usual tone of voice. The children's perception of how others regulate their own feelings appears distorted.

In discussing these issues with parents, therapists must first try to determine whether the failures in regulation might be attributable to the child being depressed, or having attention deficit/hyperactivity disorder (AD/HD), or being overloaded with anxiety. If these are complicating factors that coexist with the NLD, it is possible that a regimen of medication might alleviate some of the problems. However, if the child does not have these conditions or if the medications are ineffective in containing the outburst, then the parents need help in becoming the regulators for the child.

It is probably correct to say that there are no good ways for parents to contain a child's emotional storms, there are only responses that are less destructive than others. When parents try to control the child who is out of control, verbal means are least effective. Generally the child is too upset to hear what is being said, much less benefit from the words. Soothing words may be effective if the child can discriminate between different vocal intonations, but if he or she cannot, then the balm does heal the wound or minimize the pain. Physically restraining a child, when done improperly, can be hazardous because it sets a pattern in which the child experiences the adult as more powerful but not necessarily as providing safety or empathy. Some children can experience this type of restraint as abusive. However, when a child is in the midst of a meltdown, the child must be protected from doing harm to him- or herself or to others. The child may need to be physically removed from the situation and isolated in a protective environment. Isolating the child has its own limitations in that it distances the child from those who should be available as nurturing selfobjects. Remaining in the presence of the child may attenuate that feeling.

Parents often find themselves running out of options and lapsing into helplessness under these conditions. The child, seeing that the adult are themselves helpless, becomes even more anxious and escalates to higher levels of despair. It is that helplessness that parents must avoid if the family is not to be robbed of all sense of rationality. The parents must remain sufficiently calm to weather the storm and be available to put the pieces of their disintegrated child back together again.

The strategy in helping a child become more regulated is to institute some form of time-outs. The time-outs we recommend are not meant to be a consequence for the child's behavior but rather a time to "chill out" until calm is restored[1]. The time-out technique is widely used by parents who often find it difficult to implement. In part this is because the definition of what constitutes a time-out may be unreasonable; in part it is because absolute consistency in implementation is the key to its success, something that parents often find difficult to do. The time to use this technique is not when the child is in the midst of a meltdown; rather, it should be introduced when the child is beginning to get worked up but is still sufficiently calm to be able to benefit. At its first introduction, the child is asked to stop, pay attention to what is being said, and sit quietly for 10 to 15 seconds. For a child who has difficulty with self-control this appears as a monumental task. Parents must be sensitive enough to request only what they are certain will succeed. They will build upon success, not upon the child's failure to use the technique. The lesson the child learns is that he or she can indeed contain the feelings for a brief period of time. As the child is successful in controlling outbursts, parents

---

1. We are grateful to our colleague Dr. Karen Pierce for making this distinction for us and providing us with the concept.

can reinforce that success by acknowledging the child's efforts and praising the child's growing self-control. Parents are then challenged to take on bigger incidents, but the technique should only be used if there is some assurance of success; otherwise, a negative pattern sets in and both parents and child will be discouraged and feel defeated.

Case Illustration

Jason, age 10, had severe NLD. He was an only child given to terrible tantrums. He would fall apart most often at home, but in many instances the tantrums would occur in extended family situations, in public places, and at school. The family felt controlled by their child because they could not face the embarrassment he would cause them whenever they went out of the house. Added to their humiliation was the criticism that teachers and close family member directed at them, attributing Jason's "misbehaviors" to the parents' indulgence of him. They could barely share with the therapist that in their efforts to control the boy they felt they were abusive to him. Whenever they tried to intervene in his tantrums he would become assaultive. An escalating cycle would evolve in which he would be out of control, and pursue his mother around the house challenging her to control him. When the father was present, he would physically remove the boy and lock him in his room. However, Jason would start throwing everything he could lay his hands on out the window and threaten to jump out himself.

While Jason's behavior might appear to be intentional and manipulative, this is only partly true. Behind the theatrics was a boy who truly feared his impulsivity and rage. Jason was placed on an antidepressant that significantly diminished the tantrums. The parents were amazed at the transformation produced by the medication. They became convinced that the behavior was more neurologically driven than the product of their mismanagement. However, as undesirable side effects appeared, they had to discontinue the medication. They were then able to mobilize themselves to obtain counseling for the boy and be less reactive to his eruptions. At that point it became possible to introduce time-outs to begin to help him acquire some of the internal controls he did not have.

Debriefing the Child to Encourage Compensations

The interventions we have discussed so far place the parents in positions in which they are complementing the child's deficits. But at the same time it is important that they encourage the child to be less reliant on these complementary functions by learning to compensate. For each child there exists a set of strengths that come into service when this process begins. It is often difficult to predict the specific ways in which a child will use these strength for purposes of compensation. Through debriefing the child about incidents, both positive and negative, the child is encouraged to process occurrences and learn through the debriefing.

The last case illustration lends support to the strategy of attempting to process what happened with the child once calm has been restored. Many parents find that it takes a great deal of effort to engage a child in the aftermath of an outburst. The child is either unresponsive or adamantly opposed to any discussion. It is important to remember under these circumstances that the child probably thinks the parents intend to punish or reprimand him or her for what occurred. Furthermore, the children's awareness of their deficits lead them to experience facing these issues as blows to their self-esteem. It is humiliating to a child to realize that there are interferences in his or her capacities to deal with complex events that are beyond his or her control. The matter, therefore, should be approached sensitively while the child's resistances to discussing what occurred are overcome. If possible, a dispassionate problem-solving attitude would help establish a working relationship with the child so that the child feels the parents are his or her allies. The debriefing also serves the purpose of having the parents work through and manage their own frustrations at the problems the child has created.

An important aspect of these debriefings is that they provide the means through which parents help the child learn from the troublesome incidents. First, parents must understand that the fact that they have gone over a series of incidents many times does not necessarily mean that the child will avoid such incidents in the future. The manner in which children with NLD learn from life events is unlike that of other children. Even if the child is helped to deal with the feelings that result from the episode, the conceptual task of drawing a set of rules of conduct that will guide future behaviors remains complex. The child may be able to indicate that he or she has abstracted a rule but still be mystified as to when the rule should be applied. Unable to see the bigger picture, the child may rigidly take an element from a previous discussion with the parents and misapply it to a context that appears to him or her to be appropriate, only to find the consequence to be no better than in prior instances. The child may then bitterly complain that he or she did indeed do what was agreed to in the discussions. Since none of the strategies we are offering can be applied singly or piecemeal, parents must resort to complementing the child's deficits by bringing in other aspects the child misses. The important point to remember is to help the child draw a simple lesson from what occurred and to build on what the child has learned from past instances of similar occurrences. Contextualizing the child's role by pointing to elements of the situation the child has overlooked may help the child enhance his or her ability to apply a rule appropriately. Having the child learn to take responsibility for his or her contribution can be a major achievement toward the goal of modifying his or her behavior. Debriefing the child after he or she successfully handled all or part of a problematic situations, and verbalizing what actions the child took, helps to solidify his or her gains and bolster the child's self-esteem.

Case Illustration

Robert, age 8, refused to get ready for bed by himself, saying he was scared. His parents felt it was ridiculous for an 8-year-old to be afraid of being upstairs by himself, attributing his stalling to manipulation and disobedience. He was supposed to start getting ready for bed by 8:00, take a shower, put his dirty clothes in the hamper, brush his teeth, and get in bed by 8:30. Things never went smoothly. In a detailed discussion with the therapist of the steps Robert had to take, his parents figured out some of the major pitfalls in their plan for Robert. They realized that Robert was confused about how to regulate the water temperature in the shower. He could never remember which was the hot and which the cold faucet. He could not keep in mind which direction to turn the faucet to get more or less water flowing. A strategy was developed with his father to help him through the process. First, they marked the hot water faucet with red nail polish. Then Robert learned to say "Lefty loosey, righty tighty." This helped remind him that screwing and unscrewing bottle caps was similar to turning on and off faucet handles. Step by step, Robert learned to master what for him was the intricate task of running his own shower, compensating by using his good rote memory. What was a simple matter for other family members required detailed instruction for Robert. This type of debriefing after encountering a problem became a pattern between the parents and Robert. They learned that rather than get upset and critical of him, they needed to go over the crises to discover the sources of the difficulties. The family's interactions became much more pleasant subsequently.

Managing the Anxiety Generated by NLD

It is often impossible to appreciate the level of the child's anxiety from the child's outward appearance. In our experience, most children with NLD live with chronic fears that pervade their lives. They take those feelings for granted, not realizing that most people do not feel the same way. The children often overtly display their fears in circumstances that appear reasonable to parents. A grandparent's illness or death, an unexpected traumatic separation, or a change in housing arrangements may suddenly bring on overt signs of severe anxiety. However, less overt may be the severe night fears, apprehensions about thunderstorms, fears that a parent will die, somatic complaints, or nightmares. It is easy for a child to associate his or her emerging anxiety state with an external triggering event. However, our observations reveal that the triggering circumstances provide the child with a rationale for the overt expression of feelings that were there to begin with. It is as though the child has been given an opportunity to express the mysterious and unexplainable feelings that had accompanied him or her for years. The child will then tenaciously cling to the triggering event as explaining the presence of the fears. The events give a concrete focus around which the child can organize the vague and chaotic feelings with which he or she was buffeted.

Adults will then often respond by trying to help the child work through the presumed cause but find that no amount of reassurance or discussion is effective. For children with NLD, the world is a dangerous place as they have repeatedly found from their experiences. From early childhood, their efforts at negotiating circumstances around them led to failures or disastrous results. Their perceptions are that parents did not respond in predictable ways. Their judgments were never accurate enough for them to feel assured that undesirable consequences would not follow. It is as though they became conditioned to failure in relationships. Consequently vigilance and watchfulness were substituted for spontaneity and carefreeness.

This understanding of the sources of the child's anxiety allows an appreciation of what it would take to calm the child's fears. Fundamentally, what appears to motivate this pervasive anxiety are the repeated experiences of failure to transact interactions with others and in the world. The child lives with a conviction that the world is an unfriendly or even dangerous place. To undo this conviction, the parents must work at replacing it with a view of the world as, on the whole, a benevolent, predictable place. The message to the child is that it is possible to discriminate between those whom one can trust and those from whom one must shy away. The message is also that by using areas of strength the child can find successes and satisfactions that are growth producing.

At times medication might diminish the extent of the anxiety. The relief the medication provides can permit the child to use more cognitive strategies for dealing with the anxiety. It is helpful for a child to learn to label bodily cues as related to anxiety states. The recognition of the somatic equivalents can then alert the child to situations that magnify the anxiety and signal that it is time to use the strategies he or she has learned for dealing with that situation. Eventually an antidote to the anxiety is found in the growing confidence a child feels in negotiating the world successfully. Through the efforts of parents who at first provide complementary function, and who as the child matures help enhance compensatory strategies, the child can eventually find the self-assurance that will pull him or her through the difficulties that lie ahead.

Case Illustration

Homework is often a source of much anxiety for children with NLD. For Maria, age 7, basic math concepts were very difficult to grasp. As her parents helped her understand simple addition concepts, they used concrete manipulatives to assist her in integrating what she learned. But after she finally grasped that 3 + 2 = 5, she would balk at writing the answers down on her homework sheet. She would start crying, sometimes escalating into full-scale tantrums. After the parents discussed the problem with their therapist, they realized that for Maria the task of grasping the concepts themselves was fraught with much anxiety; it required a major effort on her part to accomplish that task. By the time the further demand was made that she write down what she had grasped, Maria felt overloaded and exhausted. Handwriting itself was a task that she dreaded since it required great effort on her part and the task appeared overwhelming. The parents were encouraged to talk with the teacher regarding the priorities to be given to each part of the task. They agreed that if learning the concepts was the goal, then Maria could dictate the answer for her parents to write down. If it was the graphomotor task of writing and aligning numbers that was important, then Maria would be allowed to use a calculator and concentrate on the writing task. Much to everyone's relief this simple solution led to an enormous reduction in the power struggles over homework and an increase in Maria's successes in mastering math concepts. In some small way Maria learned that the teacher was on her side and could be approached as a person available to help. She also learned not to fear having to deal with problems, because once they are broken down the anxiety associated with them became manageable.

Case Illustration

Dennis, age 11½, has been in once a week individual therapy for two years. His parents became quite knowledgeable about his problems and were very adept at developing strategies to avoid serious disruptions. One day they came to his session with him to discuss some school issues. In the course of the session his mother noted that she was anxious about turning in a school form giving permission for

Dennis to go on an out-of-town trip with members of his class. They had discussed it together but she felt unresolved as to whether it was best for him to go. Dennis immediately protested that he really very much wanted to be part of this trip. As she talked about the pros and cons of going, his mother, who is very attuned to his problems, stated that part of the trip involved going to an amusement park. He had never been to one and she feared that it would be totally disorienting, overstimulating, and ultimately upsetting to him. She wanted to at least rehearse how he would manage in order to anticipate any problems. She hoped that he could learn to avoid situations he could not handle.

Dennis immediately started complaining that she must really not want him to go. When mother responded that she wanted him to be able to go and enjoy himself, he retorted that she then must be wanting *him* to decide not to go! His anxiety kept escalating, his voice got louder, he gestured wildly, writhing in his chair. It became evident to the therapist that Dennis's anxiety about the trip had now been displaced onto the fear that he would not be able to go. The therapist felt that it would be impossible to process the anxiety associated with the trip until Dennis was reassured that he would be going, and only then would he be able to sit still long enough to think about what he would face when he got there. The therapist interpreted his understanding to the parents, who agreed, and who then told Dennis they would allow him to go. Dennis insisted that they sign the form right then and there, which they did. But even then Dennis was too anxious and overstimulated to be able to listen, and the rehearsal of what he should anticipate had to be postponed to another session. In this example, Dennis's anticipatory anxiety was itself a barrier to processing the events he was to face later. Only after some days had passed and he had become used to the idea that he would indeed be going on the trip were his parents able to process with him what he was to face on the trip.

Encouraging the Development of a Sense of Humor

In spite of their excellent verbal skills, children with NLD have difficulties understanding humor. They take humorous remarks concretely and cannot appreciate the lightness that comes from levity or joking. Teasing is interpreted as aggression rather than as tenderness or a reaching out for closeness. Yet humor is a remarkable facilitator of human interaction. It can serve as a vehicle to bring to a child's attention mannerisms that interfere with communication; it can help overcome the narcissistic injury a child might feel from learning about a deficit or it can convey feelings that a child might otherwise miss. We ordinarily do not think of humor as something that is deliberately taught to a child. But since children with NLD do not seem to have that natural capacity, a studied approach to instruct them in the art of wit is indicated. For the child, the lesson to learn is that there is a place for joy and fun in this world.

Case Illustration

When Eric's parents met with their child's therapist they reported a novel development. The child had developed a quirky sense of humor that delighted them and his teachers at school. Situations that were previously fraught with anger or anxiety seemed not to affect him as intensely. He could joke about them, even making fun of some of his idiosyncrasies. Adults and peers were responding to him much more positively than they had done previously. The parents were curious as to how the therapist had accomplished that.

Eager to help the parents with a new strategy, the therapist described how he had begun by making some outlandish remark related to the activities in which they would engage. Eric, age 12, was at first totally bewildered by the therapist's remarks. The therapist would point out that Eric had not noticed the therapist's smile, which indicated he was joking. After many repetitions of this interaction, Eric began to peer into the therapist's face to decode an expression that indicated a smile. Eventually, he responded with funny comments of his own, and both would laugh. The enjoyment they both derived from these exchanges were indicative of the bond that existed between them. Eric felt comfortable, accepted, and strengthened. His first attempts at humor in other settings were not successful. As he talked about them, it was evident that what was funny to him was not to others. Fortunately, others began to appreciate his efforts and joined him in laughter. The parents were encouraged to use that approach to defuse tense situations. Eric's father, who himself may have had a problem similar to his son, had a distinctive sense of humor that fit in with his son's. He felt that they could enjoy each other's sense of the comical, bonding together around their common wit.

Teaching Social Skills

As we mentioned before, the manifestations of children's NLD have been called a social dyslexia. Nowicki and Duke (1992) give the name dyssemia to the range of difficulties children have in reading social cues. They regard the domain of nonverbal communication a "language" in the sense that the domain has its own vocabulary, grammar, and pragmatics. All children should be taught this language much like we teach a foreign language. We spoke earlier of the value of teaching children with NLD strategies to understand nonverbal communications. But social interactions involve more than just the ability to read or understand social cues. There is a "pragmatics" dimension that parallels the pragmatics in verbal language usage that must also be learned. We might distinguish this area by identifying it as that of social functioning in contrast to the area of social interactions. Social skills then are the competencies required to become assimilated into a social milieu. The inability to read or understand social cues leads the child to appear inept in social situations. Unable to function smoothly, the child withdraws, becomes socially isolated, or acts in a manner that appears perplexing to his or her peers. In contrast, we are proposing that the elements in successful social functioning involve a variety of qualities that our culture values—appearing cultured, gracious, sophisticated, or urbane, and having what is called savoir faire. For the child with NLD, these qualities seem as difficult to acquire as calculus is for a first grader. Yet that does not mean that this area should be written off. Keeping in mind that simply pointing out the correct behavior is not helpful to the child, the strategy to learning some of these qualities is systematic modeling and identification. The process of socialization often occurs silently as the child observes adults' behaviors, learning what is proper and what is not. For children with NLD this process not only must be made explicit but also must be rehearsed, reinforced, and rewarded until the behaviors become habitual. The child may never achieve the kind of naturalness of other children without this problem, but they can achieve a good approximation.

Case Illustration

Ten-year-old Tiffany's family had dinner with her grandparents every month. While the grandparents cared very much about the children, they were becoming estranged from Tiffany because they felt she was insolent and rude. They faulted their daughter-in-law for not raising her properly. When the grandparents made an effort to talk to Tiffany at the table, she looked bored, made no eye contact, did not respond to their questions, and gave little indication of even listening to what they were saying. When she did talk to them, she usually looked at her plate, her voice seemed expressionless, and what she said was difficult to follow. Tiffany's experience of these visits was that her grandparents were nagging her.

As her parents discussed this situation with the therapist, they realized that the poor eye contact and lack of appropriate expressiveness were symptoms of her recently identified NLD. They had come to overlook these traits, attributing them to Tiffany's personality. For their part, they knew that she was listening because she retained information and later gave evidence that she was quite aware of what went on. After alerting the grandparents to Tiffany's problems, they went about actively teaching her some of the social skills she needed in order to act appropriately in social settings. They instructed her to periodically look at the eyes of the person to whom she is speaking or who is speaking to her, even though that felt uncomfortable to her. At first when she complied, her efforts seemed mechanical and unnatural, but after a period of time she developed a style that fit her overall demeanor, eventually finding pleasure in her grandparents' positive responses to her. However, one of her parents would often have to sit next to her to remind and signal her as to what she needed to do. It became the responsibility of that parent, who had a very positive relationship with her, to extend the teaching to other areas, facilitating for Tiffany her interactions with others.

WHAT IS IN STORE FOR MY CHILD?

Parents often raise concerns for their child's future. They want to know whether the condition will handicap their child permanently. Except in cases of extreme deficits, the answers to these questions should be framed in the most optimistic light. Children's capacities for adaptation, for compensation, and for maturation must be emphasized. The younger the child at the point of diagnosis and the more aggressive the interventions, the more optimistic the outcome. We have seen many children who at a young age appear so vulnerable or disadvantaged by their deficits that there seemed little hope that they could become well-functioning adults. While systematic follow-up research remains to be done in this area, our clinical experience leads us to take a hopeful attitude.

There appear to be nodal points in the course of maturation that offer opportunities for forward leaps to occur. It is unclear whether these leaps occur because of neurological maturation, or because a greater integration occurs when the child attains the stage of formal operational thought, or for some other reason. One nodal point appears at around age 17, when the adolescent is a junior in high school. At that point the motivation to achieve academically drives some adolescents forward, and successes bring with them greater self-confidence and a different perspective on social relationships. For others, a similar point is reached late in the sophomore year or junior year in college. A sudden flowering of the personality appears to occur. The awkwardness diminishes, the young adult becomes more self-directed toward a goal, a career choice is made, all the elements of the personality appear to join together to make for personal success. Others are really late bloomers; these are children whose parents truly despair that they will never make it. Yet at around the ages of 27 or 28, a transformation occurs. New possibilities open up for the young adult. If the parents have not totally given up and if they have not alienated the young man or woman by taking a "tough-love" approach, the child may become open to being supported to find his or her way to a constructive path. What is paramount is that the parents make every effort to maintain a positive relationship with their child. No matter how alienating the child's behavior may be, if the bond is maintained, hope is kept alive and the child will eventually respond. That is the message we try to convey to the parents of these children.

ACKNOWLEDGMENTS

We would like to acknowledge the considerable assistance we received from our colleagues in thinking through many aspects of this chapter, particularly the members of the Nonverbal Disabilities Study Group, which includes Meryl Lipton, Pearl Rieger, Karen Pierce, and Warren Rosen.

REFERENCES

Badian, N. A. (1986). Nonverbal disorders of learning: the reverse of dyslexia? *Annals of Dyslexia* 36:253–269.

——— (1992). Nonverbal learning disability, school behavior and dyslexia. *Annals of Dyslexia* 42:159–178.

Chess, S., and Thomas, A. (1986). *Temperament in Clinical Practice*. New York: Guilford.

Demos, E. V. (1988). Affect and the development of the self: a new frontier. In *Frontiers in Self Psychology: Progress in Self Psychology*, vol. 3, ed. A. Goldberg, pp. 27–54. Hillsdale, NJ: Analytic Press.

Fairchild, M., and Keith, C. (1981). Issues of autonomy in the psychotherapy of children with learning problems. *Clinical Social Work Journal* 9(2):134–142.

Garber, B. (1988). The emotional implications of learning disabilities: a theoretical integration. In *The Annual of Psychoanalysis*, vol. 16, pp. 111–128. Madison, CT: International Universities Press.

Kohut, H. (1971). *The Analysis of the Self*. New York: International Universities Press.

——— (1977). *The Restoration of the Self*. New York: International Universities Press.

——— (1981). *How Does Analysis Cure?* Chicago: University of Chicago Press.

Nowicki, S., and Duke, M. P. (1992). *Helping the Child Who Doesn't Fit In: Deciphering the Hidden Dimensions of Social Rejection*. Atlanta: Peachtree.

Ohrenstein, D. F. (1979). Parent counseling. In *A Handbook for Specific Learning Disabilities*, ed. W. C. Adamson and K. K. Adamson, pp. 237–254. New York: Gardner.

Palombo, J. (1987). Selfobject transferences in the treatment of borderline neurocognitively impaired children. In *The Borderline Patient: Emerging Concepts in Diagnosis, Psychodynamics and Treatment*, vol. 1, ed. J. S. Grotstein, M. Solomon, and J. A. Lang, pp. 317–346. Hillsdale, NJ: Analytic Press.

——— (1991). Neurocognitive differences, self cohesion, and incoherent self narratives. *Child and Adolescent Social Work Journal* 8(6):449–472.

——— (1993a). Neurocognitive differences, developmental distortions, and incoherent narratives. *Psychoanalytic Inquiry* 3(1):63–84.

——— (1993b). Learning disabilities in children: developmental, diagnostic and treatment considerations. In *Proceedings: National Academies of Practice, Fourth National Health Policy Forum, Healthy Children 2000: Obstacles and Opportunities*. Washington, DC: National Academics of Practice.

——— (1995). Psychodynamic and relational problems of children with nonverbal learning disabilities. In *The Handbook of Infant, Child, and Adolescent Psychotherapy, Vol. 1: A Guide to Diagnosis and Treatment*, ed. B. S. Mark and J. A. Incorvaia, pp. 147–178. Northvale, NJ: Jason Aronson.

Palombo, J., and Berenberg, A. H. (1997). Psychotherapy for children with nonverbal learning disabilities. In *The Handbook of Infant, Child, and Adolescent Psychotherapy, Vol. 2: New Directions in Integrative Treatment*, ed. B. S. Mark and J. A. Incorvaia, pp. 25–67. Northvale, NJ: Jason Aronson.

Rourke, B. P. (1995). Appendix: treatment program for the child with NLD. In *Syndrome of Nonverbal Learning Disabilities: Neurodevelopmental Manifestations*, pp. 497–508. New York: Guilford.

Stern, D. N. (1985). *The Interpersonal World of the Infant*. New York: Basic Books.

Tomkins, S. S. (1987). Script theory. In *The Emergence of Personality*, ed. J. Aronogg, A. I. Rabin, and R. A. Zucker, pp. 147–216. New York: Springer.

Vigilante, F. W. (1983). *Working with Families of Learning Disabled Children*. Washington, DC: Child Welfare League of America.

15

From Apologists to Advocates: Treating the Parents of Children with Attention Deficit Disorder, Hyperactivity, and Other Learning Difficulties

Bonnie S. Mark-Goldstein
and Deborah Berger-Reiss

Parents face a multitude of issues when raising a child with learning differences, attention deficit disorder (ADD), or hyperactivity (AD/HD). While therapy typically focuses on addressing the needs of the child, parental therapy is vital to the success of any treatment program, both to help parents resolve their own feelings and to equip them to meet the needs of their child in family and social environments. This chapter addresses the issues that may arise in parent therapy, the role of the therapist in parent and couples treatment, and the multifaceted transference and countertransference feelings that may arise for the therapist when working with parents. The case study that is presented underlines the range of issues parents and families face prior to hearing a diagnosis, the role the therapist plays in facilitating the parents' understanding of their child's difficulties, the process of rebuilding the marriage and the functional family structure, and the treatment of siblings. The case study also demonstrates the need for the couple to become advocates for their children in the home, in school, and in the community, while simultaneously developing, implementing, and refining goals for the child. Issues including the development of specialized parenting skills, concerns of relatives and friends, and securing resources for parental assistance in coping with the inevitable social and educational challenges for the child and family are also addressed.

The good-enough parent, to paraphrase D. W. Winnicott (1958, 1965), is less than ideal—adequate to the task, but not perfect. In the case of families with children who have learning differences, hyperactivity, attention deficit disorder, or other related conditions, the parents and the child all experience feelings of inadequacy, frustration, self-doubt, and self-recrimination. Like a stone thrown into placid waters, the birth of a learning disabled child distorts family life and creates ripples that pass through all aspects of the child's and parents' lives. This was true for Ginger and Ben and their son Michael:

Ginger hadn't slept well in seven years. Since her son's birth, her life had become a constant roller-coaster ride. From his infancy through early childhood, Michael never slept well or through the night. Ginger chased him throughout the day, trying to prevent calamities, mop up spills, undo his destruction, and, more than anything, get him to sit still for a minute so she could get something done.

Relatives said he was "all boy," and subtly rebuked her for her lack of control over him. "What he needs is some good, old-fashioned discipline," they all advised. Her husband, Ben, agreed. He thought it was his wife's fault that Michael was destructive, inappropriate with adults, and impossible to control.

When Ben returned from work each day, the house was a mess and dinner was not ready. As a result, he began to doubt his wife's ability as a mother. His own upbringing and social/parental models had illustrated that a mother is efficient and organized in running a house and in raising a well-behaved child. Thus, the converse ineffectiveness and helplessness of his wife in their home and in controlling their son's misbehavior were a source of embarrassment for him within his family and circle of friends. When Ginger attempted to share her frustration with her husband, the discussion usually terminated in an argument as Ben reproached her for what clearly appeared to be her inadequacies in raising a child.

He loved his son; however, he could feel the emotional distance growing between them. In his basement workshop, Ben would quickly tire of trying to teach Michael how to work with tools because Michael would not stop whirling around on the stool.

Ginger was so exhausted all the time from dealing with Michael that she had no time and energy left for her increasingly angry and distant husband. By the time Michael was 6 years old, they had begun to talk about divorce. Ginger felt like a failure on all fronts and was depressed and felt hopeless.

It was not until Michael entered first grade that his teacher suggested Michael be tested. He was promptly diagnosed with attention deficit/hyperactivity disorder (AD/HD), and only then did the tide begin to turn. As the diagnostician explained the symptoms and behaviors of a typical AD/HD child, Ginger and Ben began to awaken from their nightmare.

This is a typical account of family life before a diagnosis. Families rupture, couples divorce, and children are unnecessarily punished and stigmatized for a condition they cannot help. By the time the family seeks help, the damage can be profound, but it can be reversed. Treatment helped Ginger to stop blaming herself, and therapy focused on assisting the parents to understand and become educated about their son's special needs, to look at the effects on the marriage and family, and to prepare to be actively involved and supportive. Michael was medicated, and, to an extent, the medication helped; but above all, the understanding that Michael's condition was no one's fault and that their bright little boy could be helped gave the whole family hope.

When parents enter the therapy setting for the first time, the baggage they are carrying is heavy. The years of agony and marital stress, coupled with the frustration of neither understanding what is wrong with their child nor being able to help, is deeply compelling. The therapist must begin by letting the parents weave their narrative and offering them empathy. Yet, it is crucial for the therapist to expeditiously commence the parents' education about their child's problems. Consequently, the therapist must be well versed in the range of differential diagnoses.

Children who have been diagnosed as attention deficit disordered, learning disabled, or hyperactive may have unique, marked differences in their personality functioning from infancy. Primary characteristics may include hyperactivity, impulsivity, distractibility, and excitability. Afflicted children may also demonstrate a short attention span, concentration problems, clumsy motor movements, inability to do fine motor tasks, restlessness, high levels of frustration, memory and speech impairment, overreaction to stimulation, and rapid and unpredictable mood swings. Children with attention deficit disorder also often experience difficulty in making friends, and they spend a disproportionate amount of time alone or with younger children. A common result is low self-esteem and depression. Others develop antisocial and maladaptive attention-getting behaviors; the emotional immaturity of the child is commonly reported. These children may also lack ambition and the ability to maintain any goals because they are so often frustrated in their attempts to achieve even the simplest, most immediate goals.

Symptoms generally arise at school, especially when the child must maintain extended focus upon what may be perceived as dull and repetitive tasks. Impulsive behavior and responding without waiting for (complete) instructions result in careless errors and other negative consequences such as unnecessary risk taking. This irresponsibility, immaturity, laziness, or rudeness is usually defined as a pattern of rapid, inaccurate responses to tasks (Brown and Quay 1977). These impulsive actions have also been attributed to poor sustained inhibition of responding (Gordon 1979), an impaired adherence to regulatory or inhibitory commands that control behavior in social contexts (Kendall and Wilcox 1980), or a poor delay of gratification (Rapport et al. 1986).

Hyperactivity is defined as a display of an excessive amount of motor activity, fidgeting, sleep disturbances, and inappropriate gross bodily movements, implying a failure to regulate activity levels to tasks or settings. A key trait in attention deficit disordered and hyperactive children is the inability to follow rules and instructions (Barkley 1981, Kendall and Braswell 1984).

In the last decade there has been an increase in the amount of research done on attention deficit disorder, hyperactivity, and learning disabilities, expanding our understanding of the behavioral deficiencies and excesses of these two disorders. Knowledge of the development of personality and the emotional characteristics of these children, however, remains limited (Barkley 1981). Therefore, while the therapist may facilitate parental understanding of their child's difficulties, it is imperative that the therapist focus on the individual characteristics of the child and the impact on the family.

The therapist can allay the parents' guilt over the genetic factor in having a child with special needs by describing the possible causes and thus reassuring them that the disorder is not the result of anything they could have controlled. Therapists may explore with the parents how they may have unwittingly exacerbated the condition before the diagnosis through a reenactment of their own family dynamics or by counteraction to a difficult child. It is of utmost importance to reverse the process of self-recrimination and end the parents' rebuking of one another as soon as therapy begins.

Next, the therapist must begin the arduous process of helping the couple develop and shape their parenting skills to the needs of their child and family. Patience, limit setting, problem solving, establishing realistic expectations of the child, creating goals and objectives, mood management, self-esteem building, flexibility, and positive reinforcement are concrete skills that must be acquired in the sessions. When the parents stand united in their position with their child, they become exponentially more effective. Also essential to the process is referring parents to the many books available that describe in detail these issues so that they better understand the process.

Concomitantly, the therapist must begin the intricate, painstaking work of addressing the marriage. All children inevitably take their toll on even the best marriage, and with the birth of a child with special needs the impact is far greater. In the case of Ginger and Ben, there was sleep deprivation, which wrought havoc on their marriage, and the daily exhaustion fatiguing and testing their mental health. The amount of attention Michael required left Ginger with little time or energy for her husband. Finally, the resentment, blame, and estrangement persistently challenged the marriage.

To rebuild intimacy and trust in the marriage, the relationship often must be overhauled from the very foundations. Helping a couple remember their initial attraction and reasons for marrying may be stimulated by asking them to tell the story of their romance from the first meeting through their wedding day. These memories, once jogged, create the impetus to work on the marriage.

As the therapist helps the couple come to terms with the inevitable impact of their special-needs child upon the marriage, and as the years of censure and recrimination come to an end, the couple should focus on the marriage itself. Carving out the time required for putting the marriage in the forefront, letting go of the past, and creating goals toward healing are integral components of the treatment plan. Furthermore, since time is a precious commodity and most of it must be poured into the needs of their child, help from a sympathetic family member, another parent who will take turns on Saturday night child care, or an educated baby-sitter is essential.

Not only does the marriage suffer from neglect in the families of the child with special needs, the siblings do as well. In addition to the inevitable lack of time parents have for them, unreasonable demands for patience, understanding, and maturity are often placed upon these children. Mahler and colleagues (1975) suggest that the process of separation and successful development necessitates the parents' attunement to their child's feelings, and ability to respond in a manner appropriate to the child's age. When there is a child in the home with special needs, time, energy, and individualized attention and attunement to the siblings is often difficult. Making the effort to reserve some special time for the other children and recognizing that siblings also need attention is essential. This might be achieved through the divide-and-conquer technique, in which each parent or helper takes turns focusing on the needs of one child. Involving each child in individual activities, such as tutoring or sports, sanctions the opportunity for spending individual time with the children. Organization, availability of resources, and awareness of the children's needs are vital to addressing and managing the needs of the siblings.

Charles Cunningham (1990) suggests that even in the most functional families, coping with an ADD or AD/HD child erodes family functioning skills. It is therefore vital to create a framework within which to rebuild and support a healthy family structure by combining the education of family members (parents, siblings, and extended family) with a family program designed to effectively change the reputation of the person with ADD and/or other special needs within the family dynamic (Hallowell and Ratey 1994). Reworking the reputation necessitates breaking the negative process within the home and diminishing blame. Moreover, encouraging siblings to express their own frustrations enables them to receive help from their parents and to create solutions to the difficulties they encounter with their learning disabled or attention deficit disordered sibling.

The increased understanding of how to manage their child's and family's situation, in tandem with the investment in the marriage, puts the couple on track, ready to face the daunting challenges of effacing the damage to their child's self-esteem and tending to his educational and social needs.

> Michael had few friends. Because of his behavior, it was difficult to forge much of a connection with other children. Parents of Michael's playmates described him as intense, a daredevil, or "in your face." Michael was frustrated because he was very affectionate and always asked to play with other children, yet Ginger's invitations to children were often turned down by their mothers, who usually claimed their children already had plans. Often Michael would find out that he had not been invited to a neighbor or kindergarten friend's birthday party, producing tears and tirades. Although his medication partially remedied his behavior, his negative reputation continued to perpetuate itself.
>
> Ginger and Ben learned to identify the behaviors that contributed to their son's social isolation in order to aid Michael in developing more appropriate social skills. A part of each therapy session was directed at assisting the parents to design and implement solutions to Michael's obstacles. Gradually, the parents shifted from their position as victims of their child's undiagnosed behaviors to acting as advocates for their son's needs.

They discussed Michael's condition with their families and close friends in order to educate them and correct the misconceptions that had been rampant throughout Michael's seven-year life. Family visits and outings had become well planned and defined, and were often limited to shorter periods of time. A typical Super Bowl Sunday at Michael's grandparents' home was reduced to a halftime visit or a meal afterward. This plan offered Michael a smaller and more manageable challenge at which he could succeed, and minimized everyone's frustration. As Michael achieved his behavioral goals, the time was increased in small increments.

Michael's extended family and friends generally were empathetic and increasingly accommodating toward the family, and slowly the family began to breathe a collective sigh of relief. Michael's self-esteem improved with each success, and family and friends were more patient when he blew it. Both the family and the couple continued to heal, yet the most formidable obstacle, ironically, was school. Michael attended a private, Lutheran school. In kindergarten, Michael fortunately had a teacher who recognized that Michael needed testing.

Not all children are so lucky, and not all parents are willing or able to follow through. Thousands of children with learning difficulties, attention deficit disorder, and hyperactivity regularly slip through the cracks of the education system because teachers do not recognize the symptoms, or when they do, the parents are resistant or lack the resources to follow through. These children, of course, become labeled as inattentive, unruly, and discipline problems. The longer they go undiagnosed and untreated, the more the stigma persists and the behavioral problems mushroom. Many studies over the past few years have consistently found that a stunning percentage (75 to 80 percent) of teen and adult criminals are undiagnosed as learning disabled. We are only now recognizing that a high proportion of this group may also be AD/HD.

In Bruno Bettelheim's book *Surviving, and Other Essays* (1979) he points out that to remedy a learning issue we have to find the anxiety behind it, try to understand this anxiety, then work to remove it. "When emotional disturbance exists in a small child but his par-

ents are unable or unwilling to recognize it, the disturbance goes unheeded until the child reaches school. There he is singled out, not
because the teacher always recognizes the presence of emotional disturbance, but because of academic malfunctioning" (p. 143).

Armed with Michael's testing report at the end of kindergarten,
Ginger and Ben made an appointment with the principal, the
school's resource specialist, and the first-grade teacher. By now,
their feelings of frustration, shame, and victimization had meta-
morphosed into a desire to protect their child from unaware, ill-
equipped adults. The school staff had been asked to read the report before the meeting, and at the meeting the parents candidly
asked if the school was capable of meeting the needs of their child
and if it was equipped with a plan.

The principal suggested meetings with the parents, the teacher,
and a resource specialist on a biweekly basis to refine and improve
the plan. The resource specialist would observe Michael in the
classroom and offer suggestions to the teacher. The teacher would
implement these suggestions, reduce the work load (as per the test
results), seat Michael in the front row so he could pay better attention, and send daily homework notes and weekly behavior
tracking charts to the parents. This sounded acceptable to Ginger
and Ben. Yet as all parents of special needs children quickly learn,
there are no simple solutions. Each child is unique and so must
be the plan. Despite everyone's good intentions and effort, things
did not always go smoothly, and virtually constant effort was required by each team member. There were twenty-one other children in the classroom who also needed attention. The teacher grew
frustrated, and could not always tend to Michael or spare the
additional time and attention he required. Ginger and Ben needed
to formulate a more flexible plan of action, adjusted to their child's
particular needs.

It is within the domain of the therapist to help such parents ar-
rive at the knowledge that they always, to a certain degree, must
advocate continually for their children by becoming well educated,
learning about options in the community, being creative in their
solutions, and reaching out to other parents who share similar expe-

riences. Kennedy and colleagues (1993) offer a series of guidelines that specifically outline and illustrate methods concerned parents may use in advocating for their learning disabled child. Helping parents explore these options and encouraging them join a support group in their community established for parents of children with special needs is an effective way of reducing the parents' sense of isolation and of sharing solutions with others in the some position.

Multifaceted transference and countertransference issues arise when working with parents around their child's and family's issues. Winnicott (1953) describes the need for consistent and frequent reexamination of the therapist's own issues, particularly when a therapeutic impasse arises. Impasses can develop when the therapist sees parents resisting or not implementing changes necessary for the benefit of the child or family, such as setting structure, providing consistency in the home, establishing firm boundaries and consequences, or not following through in advocating for the child. Since parent treatment often has a component of offering direction, suggestions, and essential interventions, the therapist's countertransferential response of frustration or anger may arise if the parents have difficulties implementing changes.

The organization of the dysfunctional family system exists in part to protect parents or other family members from facing their own pathology. Therefore, when a therapeutic impasse occurs, it is necessary to look at the multifaceted reasons that interfered with change in order to help make a breakthrough in therapy (Mark 1998). Suggestions to parents can elicit resistance in many covert and overt forms. Since the therapist serves both as an observer and as a participant in the dynamics of the family, the therapist's ability to attune to what is not being said, or looking for the missing pieces, is essential. Christopher Bollas (1987) describes this as the "unthought known." The therapist's awareness of his/her own countertransference can positively affect the course of treatment and facilitate overcoming impasses.

In the treatment of families whose children have learning differences, attention deficit disorder, or other related issues, the parents' own feelings of inadequacy may be quite pronounced. Parents may perceive the therapist as the expert and transferentially become dependent on treatment for nurturing, support, direction, and affirmation of their parenting abilities. Therefore, treatment becomes a model of delicate balance. Providing direction, education, and insight is fundamental; however, there is a potential counterproductivity to positioning the therapist in the role of all-knowing expert, as it can perpetuate the parents' dependency, insecurity, and helplessness. The therapist must recognize this and help the parents to develop their own abilities individually and within the family. It is all too easy for the therapist to assume the role of the specialist or the "rescuing" parent. Countertransferentially, the therapist may also desire to caretake. While this may feel empowering to the therapist, these feelings serve the therapist's needs and can interfere with the parents' developing their own skills. Moreover, the parents' yearning to be taken care of themselves must be addressed so that parents can begin to develop a supportive network in order to get their own needs met through family, friends, or other parents facing similar issues with their children.

Working with parents can be particularly challenging because of the potential difficulties that may arise due to the overlaps with the therapist's own childhood experiences, parenting experiences, and child-rearing values. Understanding these issues is essential to effectively working in parent treatment. According to an old proverb, it is not your burden, but rather how you carry it, that counts. Ultimately, the goal of treatment is for the parents to join together as advocates who help their child carry the burden of learning differences. Winnicott describes a secure relationship between parent and child as the framework that provides both the parent and a child with a sense of organization of boundaries, limits, and structure. In so doing, the marriage and family begin the healing process together.

REFERENCES

Barkley, R. (1981). *Hyperactive Children: A Handbook for Diagnosis and Treatment*. New York: Guilford.

Bettelheim, B. (1979). *Surviving, and Other Essays*. New York: Knopf.

Bollas, C. (1987). *The Shadow of the Object: Psychoanalysis of the Unthought Known*. New York: Columbia University Press.

Brown, R. T., and Quay, L. C. (1977). Reflection impulsivity of normal behavior and behavior-disordered children. *Journal of Abnormal Child Psychology* 5:457–462.

Cunningham, C. E. (1990). A family system approach to parent training. In *Attention Deficit Hyperactive Disorder: A Handbook for Diagnosis*, ed. R. Barkley, pp. 437–446. New York: Guilford.

Gordon, M. (1979). The assessment of impulsivity and mediating behaviors in hyperactive and non-hyperactive children. *Journal of Abnormal Child Psychology* 7:317–326.

Hallowell, E., and Ratey, J. (1994). *Driven to Distraction*. New York: Random House.

Kendall, P. C., and Braswell, L. (1984). *Cognitive-Behavioral Therapy for Impulsive Children*. New York: Guilford.

Kendall, P. C., and Wilcox, L. E. (1980). Cognitive-behavioral treatment for impulsivity: concrete versus conceptual training in non-self-controlled problem children. *Journal of Consulting and Clinical Psychology* 48:80–91.

Kennedy, P., Terdal, L., and Fussetti, L. (1993). *The Hyperactive Child Book*. New York: St. Martin's Press.

Mahler, M., Pine, F., and Bergman, A. (1975). *The Psychological Birth of the Human Infant*. New York: Basic Books.

Mark, B. (1998). Parenting pitfalls in couples therapy. *California Therapist* 8:2.

Rapport, M. D., Tucker, S. B., Dupaul, G. J., et al. (1986). Hyperactivity and frustration: the influence of control over and size of rewards in delaying gratification. *Journal of Abnormal Child Psychology* 14:191–204.

Winnicott, D. W. (1953). *Symptom Tolerance in Paediatrics*. London: Tavistock.

———— (1958). *Collected Papers: Through Paediatrics to Psycho-Analysis*. London: Tavistock.

———— (1965). *The Maturational Processes and the Facilitating Environment*. New York: International Universities Press.

16

Psychoeducational Therapy: A Case Study of Evolving Educational and Psychological Needs from Latency to Early Adolescence

Judith Kushnet

Educational therapy is a term that has been used variably over the years in an attempt to define remedial educational work with children exhibiting learning difficulties. It entails the work of closing a statistically significant difference between cognitive ability and performance. Recently the term has encompassed tutoring (assisting with day-to-day homework), study and organizational skills, time management, and the remediation of specific learning disabilities. All this work is offered to a child in a nurturing, supportive therapeutic environment. For many children this modality is effective. For many others it is not enough. Children who demonstrate attention deficits and/or learning disabilities often come to therapy with coexisting emotional problems that have become layered and interwoven into the fabric of their development.

Frequently the school experience for these children is anywhere from unpleasant to traumatic, and symptomatology can be subtle or blatant to the observer. The development of self-esteem can be thwarted by the child's continual unsuccessful efforts to perform at expected levels. Some children ostensibly find ways to compensate for cognitive and processing difficulties, delaying diagnosis of attentional, learning, and emotional problems. These children typically have had tutoring over a period of years and obtain moderate success in school, but are not actually working at their level of ability and are diagnosed only when unconscious compensatory measures begin to fail. This happens when higher order thinking becomes necessary, when the cognitive leap from concrete to abstract is essential to success in school. Success in the elementary grades might quickly turn to failure in middle school. The notion that kindergarten and first-grade performance are indicators of a child's later academic success has been held by therapists for decades. This baseline must be reassessed if more children are to have the tools to fulfill their potential.

Another profile is that of children who sink into emotional and behavioral patterns that quickly prompt adults' attention. Disorganization, avoidance of homework, procrastination, oppositional and/or defiant behavior, impulsivity, physical complaints, poor grades, and social/peer difficulty are flags that tend to be noticed more readily by parents and teachers. These are standard criteria for attention deficit disorder (ADD). Deviant behaviors are generally not confined to the school setting, making the family system more complicated and adding another "invisible" factor to the dynamic. This latter constellation usually brings a child into some form of treatment. In either case and in many variations, these children spend a good deal of emotional time and energy developing internal defenses in their efforts to achieve and maintain a self-image of being whole and undamaged.

In the last few years diagnosis of children with ADD has skyrocketed. Children are being referred for educational therapy for the comorbid learning symptoms associated with ADD. Coexisting features include, but are not limited to, fine and gross motor difficulty, sleep disturbances, difficulties with higher order cognitive functioning (time management, memory, sequencing, processing speed, expressive language), difficulties with academic subjects, and speech and hearing problems. Importantly, however, there often are coexisting emotional issues that remain untapped, making pure educational re-medial efforts minimally effective, or even futile. Emotional comorbid symptoms include moodiness, low frustration tolerance, perfection-ism, anxiety, low self-esteem, anger, depression, and defensiveness.

Because there is such a high comorbid link, accurate assessment and diagnosis is crucial. ADD is often misdiagnosed. Treatment must address the total picture.

Psychoeducational therapy is a modality that addresses how learn-ing is accomplished in an individual. The processes by which learn-ing occurs encompass perception, processing of information, and integration and expression of that information. Those with learning disabilities and/or attentional issues deal with information uniquely, and therefore need an approach that will help them not only to pro-cess and communicate with more ease but also to become aware of the differences and integrate this awareness into their emotional life and interaction with the world. Psychoeducational therapy utilizes interventions in both the psychological and the educational arenas to address emotional problems as well as educational and attentional needs (related and nonrelated) that have become intertwined with the individual's development and fulfillment of ability and potential. Children who have not responded to traditional psychotherapy, show-ing no signs of appreciable emotional growth or increased educational performance, can greatly benefit from this approach. Those who have experienced educational assistance but who continue to be plagued by emotional obstacles and inconsistent ability with school-related work can also greatly benefit. Approaching only one of these domains is usually not sufficient to facilitate true change; a transformation within the core of the child and in the child's relationships with oth-ers and with the environment is necessary.

The psychoeducational approach provides the therapist an addi-tional way and a new opening into the inner life of a child. Most of a child's time is spent at school and home. Relationships and day-to-day experiences in both of those systems provide the input for self-definition. The symptomatology of distress in these children appears in whatever way functioning is impaired: cognitively, educationally, socially, and emotionally. Accurate assessment of the types and se-verity of existing disabilities and associated social and emotional difficulties is crucial to effective treatment. The case study presented below highlights the use of psychoeducational therapy to determine diagnosis and treat a child who demonstrated many of the ADD "red flags," but did not have ADD.

Children come to therapy with various emotional layers. Differentiation of the educational and emotional factors determines the initial phases of treatment. For instance, if a child is not willing to deal with any representations of school (books or pencil and paper tasks) at the opening of treatment, and a moderate to severe auditory processing problem exists, the relationship could be established by using short verbal stimuli. In a flip-side scenario, a child may want to work only on educational tasks and be unwilling to talk freely or interact unless there is a structured task. For example, visual-spatial activities can facilitate the relationship while remedial work is accomplished. Anxiety and low frustration tolerance are often the first symptoms, but they are also the first to abate when problems in information processing are addressed in the therapy. This improvement alone can help address the emotional problems that stand in the way of paying attention and persistence in school tasks. Improvement in these areas may be reflected in improved grades, but this may take time.

Psychoeducational therapy is a marriage of psychology and education, both in application and in the therapist's training. There are many paths to explore in a psychoeducational model, and, like traditional therapies, the work can unfold in different ways. It is impossible to separate emotional life and educational life in children with learning disabilities.

CASE STUDY

Janie, age 9, came to the Reiss-Davis clinic at the beginning of third grade, with possible attentional, learning, and emotional issues. Janie's teacher had referred her for educational therapy. Her grades were poor and there were questions regarding the nature of her problems. At the time she was receiving three hours of resource room assistance per week in a private school setting. Father was employed in the entertainment industry. Mother had a part-time clerical job and spent as much time as possible volunteering at her daughter's school.

During the sixth month of her pregnancy with Janie, the mother suffered a stroke. She was hospitalized and underwent rehabilitation therapy. Janie was delivered without complication. It was not known if the mother's stroke had any adverse effect on Janie's cognitive development. Both parents described her infancy and toddlerhood as uneventful. She slept through the night within weeks and nursed for six months. Onset of talking and toilet training were reported as normal, and Janie began walking early, at 8 months. Mother stayed at home full-time with Janie and they participated in several mother and child relationship groups. Janie was an only child and seen by both parents as happy, well adjusted, and lovable.

Janie attended nursery school at age 2½. She remained at the same public school for kindergarten. Academic difficulties were beginning to surface at that time and it was advised that she repeat kindergarten. She did so, but in a private school, where she continued through fourth grade. She was first tested in the second grade. Findings included an above-average IQ and minor learning disabilities—notably a difficulty with staying on task and completing assignments. Father considered the results inconclusive and concurred with the teacher's recommendation for retesting.

Father described Janie as mature, popular, likable, and comfortable with adults. He maintained that though she could be demanding and strong willed at times, she was not a discipline problem. Her hobbies were sailing, art, biking, and swimming. He stated that she was aware of her low grades and difficulty keeping up with others at school, but did not believe that this emotionally affected her in any significant way.

During the initial interview and prior to retesting, Janie began to cry and said that school was frustrating. Math was difficult, and pronunciation, remembering words, and "how to say sentences correctly" were problems. Deviant verbalizations were noted. On the Wechsler Intelligence Scale for Children (WISC-III), Janie achieved a Full-Scale IQ of 109 (± 6), placing her in the average range of intelligence. Relatively low scores were seen on subtests of concentration, attention to task, tension/anxiety, motor skills, and planning. The question of attention deficit was raised, as it had been by her teacher. Janie exhibited some classic ADD symptomatology as well as many comorbid emotional symptoms. Areas of strength included verbal concept formation and awareness of environmental details. A hemispheric analysis showed that Janie would process information best using either the left hemisphere (logical, verbal, sequential, auditory) alone or the right hemisphere (visual/spatial, gestalt) alone. Tasks requiring an integration of both hemispheres prompted her performance levels to drop.

Reading, language, and mathematics were assessed. Foundation in phonics skills appeared to be weak, and Janie had difficulty naming letters and reversing letters in written work. In reading comprehension she tested at a mid–second grade level in oral reading, silent reading speed, and comprehension tasks. Passage meaning could elude Janie due to any mixture of poor phrasing, inability to decode words, vocabulary difficulty, and lack of attention to punctuation. Receptive language was weak, and written language suffered because of poor spelling, punctuation, and grammar. Math testing showed high computational errors and struggles with conceptual understanding. Janie was unable to attempt any multiplication or division. It was noted that low scores on orally presented arithmetic may have been related to a low verbal concentration ability, as seen on the WISC-III.

Though no formal personality testing was done, Janie was informally assessed as a passive, somewhat avoidant and needy child. There was some concern regarding the development of Polyanna-type defenses. Distractibility and impulsiveness were related by the diagnostician to personality issues rather than learning issues.

Janie was diagnosed with developmental reading disorder and developmental math disorder. She was referred for educational therapy, to focus primarily on specific strategies in expressive language, letter reversals, phonics, active reading, the use of punctuation and phrasing, written language composition and rules, and assistance with mathematics. A behavioral reward system was suggested to lessen impulsivity.

Janie was seen in educational therapy twice per week. After eighteen months the therapist left the clinic and Janie was transferred to me. At the time of transfer Janie was reported to have improved in her ability to work independently on school tasks while behaving appropriately in the classroom. Her grades improved in all academic areas and she had begun to volunteer in the classroom. Her self-esteem had risen with her performance, though no formal psychological interventions had been made.

Janie had just turned 11 and was about to enter fifth grade at a new school when we began our work together. She was an attractive, friendly, verbal child, who willingly came to sessions ready to work. She talked affectionately of her previous therapist, but appeared to make the transition easily. In the early stage of treatment it was clear that she perceived her therapy as a mission. She wanted better grades in order to win the love and approval of her father, whose expectations were high and unwavering. She behaved impulsively and was distractible and anxious, yet quite charming and sensitive.

Though eager and motivated, she was well versed in passively getting others to do her work for her. Frequently she put her pencil down and she became coy and expectant. While reading, Janie's anxiety escalated quickly. She became embarrassed about being seen in her struggle and frustration with words. Her low tolerance with the visual stimulus of words was equivalent to her emotional low tolerance of her feelings. She felt defective and seemed barely able to be in her own skin. Her response was to use some content in the reading to create a tangential monologue that served to distract her from the task at hand. Often, at the moment she reached her maximum tolerance, she would make a somatic complaint. Stomachaches, headaches, and dizziness were to be ongoing visitors in the sessions. On the surface this symptomatology looked like ADD. The subtleties of the relationship between the stimuli and the inattention, distractibility, and/or impulsivity were clues to the differential diagnosis. For Janie, severe anxiety, perfectionism, dysthymia, and family dysfunction added to her ADD. I began to delineate the start and end points of each task, and to interweave my participation (reading every other paragraph, spelling every other word). I also acknowledged her frustration so that she might learn to put a name to a specific feeling connected with a particular stimulus.

At this point my use of psychological interventions was passive and nondirective. Janie became very agitated if I attempted to directly talk about her apparent discomfort. Over time, her tolerance increased as she established trust with me (knowing she could meet my challenges and expectations) and trust in herself to apply new strategies to academic work. The most effective learning approaches included using visual cuing, and using Janie's acquired knowledge to assist in understanding and integrating new information. When she could associate either a concrete piece of information or an abstract idea with a familiar form, her attention increased and she was better able to learn.

When Janie began fifth grade, I worked with her parents in order to enlist their help in securing Janie's academic progress in the school environment. Arrangements were made at Janie's new school for approximately two hours of resource assistance per day in remedial reading and math. The grading structure was also modified in an effort to reflect Janie's true achievement and progress while taking the learning difficulties into account. Educational therapy continued twice per week as well.

Over an eighteen-month period, Janie was able to memorize the previously elusive multiplication tables, learn division, read without skipping lines, decode words, turn all homework in on time, and make research and report schedules for projects. Antonyms, synonyms, and metaphors were now used in written language, which was slowly becoming more organized and possessed more mature themes.

Test-taking skills remained poor and provided a good deal of anguish, since grades were the measure of her success. She could not accept her progress and appreciate the benefits of her efforts without her grades reflecting perfection.

A year and a half after beginning treatment Janie was retested at school. She had gained two years in both reading and math and one year in written language, with the highest scores in creative writing. She had also gained three years in visual motor skills and two age levels in auditory short-term memory. She was now at age-appropriate levels in these latter two areas.

With the evident academic progress, underlying emotional issues began to surface. She displayed a mixture of anxiety, motivation, pride in achievement, dependent behavior, frustration, anger, sadness, and sometimes apathy—all part of dysthymia. She began holding herself and rocking during sessions. The regressive behavior usually appeared with somatic complaints and did not, at this point, have a connection to an immediate educational task. She would sometimes come into my office and cry. She wanted to tell me about arguments with girlfriends, problems with teachers, or the pressure and expectation she felt from her father to get better grades. It was decided that a psychoeducational model would better assist Janie with emerging social/emotional problems while continuing the remediation of her learning disabilities.

Janie had opened the door to this new model herself, by trusting me to keep her confidences. She appeared excited but hesitant when I described the additional dimension our relationship would take on (talking about feelings as well as schooling). When I told her of the confidential nature of our sessions, she was relieved. In the next session she began an open dialogue about the never-ending quest for approval and love from her father.

When the transition was made to a psychoeducational model, objectives and goals for treatment were reassessed. The work would now focus on alleviating anxiety and depression and raising self-esteem while continuing remediation. This would now give me license to explore the factors that merged within Janie to form symptomatology that resembled ADD. In the early stages, when education was the focus, passive psychological intervention was used to remediate Janie's learning pattern. At this point the momentum of the remediation became the backdrop for more directive and impactful psychological intervention. Because my relationship with Janie now had a strong base that included an emotional attachment, I was able to address developmental and personality conflicts using the educational work as a resource and a tool—a tool that is not available in traditional psychotherapies.

At the outset of this stage of treatment I responded to Janie's emotional crises by listening and gathering more information about her perceptions of relationships with her mother, father, extended family, friends, and teachers. This was a significant activity in treatment because at the time of the intake little information had been offered by her parents about her development, her relationships with them, or their relationship with each other. The family dynamic was reported by them as virtually without trauma, except for the mother's stroke. Janie's problems, however, indicated that in fact there may have been more emotional disturbance within the family than was being revealed. At the same time, her father seemed distrustful of the therapeutic process and her mother was passive and worried about Janie's progress.

Janie experienced debilitating feelings of inadequacy and spent a good deal of time and energy searching for approval and avoiding abandonment, both in her relationship with her parents and in her relationship with me. She harbored a great need for both tenderness from a harsh, intimidating, and rigid father, and a firmer, guiding hand from her passive and ineffectual mother, from whom she could not separate. Janie was at first reluctant to verbalize any negative feelings toward either of her parents. Instead she manifested physical symptoms and sustained frequent bodily injuries. She was often sleepless and excessively worried about her performance at school. Crying jags were the inevitable sign that she was overwhelmed by her own feelings and her inability to identify and deal with those feelings. This kind of "flooding" was consistent with her learning patterns—she did not learn well with a multisensory approach in an academic setting and became overloaded easily.

Importantly for Janie, the top layer of these feelings was the shame of having them. That very shame made it hard for her to verbalize them. There was shame and depression around having learning disabilities (a condition that made her different from other kids), coupled with the shame and fear of not being able to meet her father's expectations and of venturing too far from her mother. (While many children have shame related to their parental figures, learning-disabled children have the additional shame related to their learning differences.) On top of all of this, Janie's learning differences demanded that she integrate information and learn about herself emotionally in a unique way. It is the intertwining of layers of shame and attendant feelings that can effectively be addressed by combining the educational and psychological domains in a purposeful, integrated way.

Unlike Janie, some children benefit from psychotherapy and educational therapy being conducted in separate arenas. While the emotional and educational difficulties are almost always enmeshed, some children need separate treatments in order to make sense of their inner world. For some children the combination is too confusing. They are not able to talk about feelings with the same person who is assisting them with cognitive tasks. Sometimes the emotional overlay does not interfere greatly with the ability to sustain attention and expanded educational learning. Janie, on the other hand, was full of feelings that interfered with learning and manifested in her body while trying to do cognitive exercises. For her, there was freedom and more space in which to resolve cognitive and emotional conflicts (that were occurring at the same time) with a combined approach.

Janie responded well when we read stories together and used them as springboards for uncovering her emotional traumas. I was able to ask her to investigate characters and their motivations, and I could use the resulting information as projective material. In this way I was bringing forth parts of Janie of which she was otherwise unaware. From there I could draw analogies to people and relationships in her own life. At the same time I could point out deeper abstract meanings and forms in the story and in her life. Eventually I broadened this technique to include writing original stories, and developing characters based on Janie's perceptions and observations. When Janie showed signs of resonating with a situation or feeling that came up during this exercise, emotional exploration was natural within the session, and Janie's anxiety significantly decreased. She was now verbalizing feelings that previously prevented her from working at her level of ability. When Janie had access to her feelings, she was not only able to express those feelings but she was also able to perform at a higher cognitive level. This phenomenon is at the heart of the psychoeducational approach with Janie.

Janie loved to draw and felt relatively confident about her talent and skill. Visual-spatial abilities were an area of strength for her, and drawing provided her with a bridge to her emotions because she felt less threatened while she was engaged in the activity. While her anxiety was reduced, she was able to address her dependent, regressive behavior. She was able to talk about her desire to be a baby so that she could be taken care of all the time, would be relieved of her responsibilities at school, and could gain positive attention from her father. Using this method, she was able to articulate her consistent fear of being punished.

Janie still had many somatic complaints and physical injuries (while playing sports). In the later stages of treatment, when she was able to discuss openly her fear of her father's rage and disappointment, her stomach problems began to alleviate. Though the injuries persisted and even escalated, Janie was beginning to perform at a higher level in her science and social studies tests. She clung to her resistance against making connections between her physical manifestations and her feelings toward her parents, though her tolerance for hearing me talk about these connections increased. At the beginning of the second year of treatment the balance had shifted significantly toward the psychotherapeutic. Structured educational tasks became less frequent and we were now dealing primarily with how Janie could conceptualize and integrate her emotional experiences.

She kept a journal of her feelings, which she shared with me regularly. I was able to open communication about her cognitive and emotional need for order (using one hemisphere or the other). Sorting out feelings from thoughts helped her to be calmer and more organized and integrated. One way she was able to recognize this phenomenon was through her love of the ocean. Once she accepted the idea that listening to a tape of the sounds of the sea could help relieve her anxiety and actually help her to sleep, I was able to introduce the concept of mind/body connection.

At this point we were finally able to address the connection between her rocking, stomachaches, and injuries as physical manifestations of her emotional distress. Our communication increased verbally without pencils, paper, or other props between us. Verbal concentration had been a weak point. Her ability to verbally conceptualize her thoughts and feelings, however, was a relative strength. She could conceptualize but not express. Janie was overwhelmed when she considered expressing negative, painful feelings. Her upset often would escalate to near hysteria—deep sobbing and fear. When she felt soothed and encouraged to talk through her tears, she could support herself rather than decompensate. When she did accomplish a succinct verbalization of her feelings, the experience of her thoughts, feelings, and body becoming congruent was remarkable. Feelings became "friends" in our work together, and Janie began to trust that her body and her feelings were talking to her all the time, even if she did not want to listen or simply could not hear.

Janie's ability to verbalize her feelings in a logical, sequential way was accompanied by a visceral awareness. Being able to express and feel her feelings at the same time gave her a sense of control and independence. Fear subsided as she experienced the distinction between a thought and a feeling in the same moment. As she developed a history of expressing anger and feelings of shame without punishment or retaliation, she could apply her budding inner security to her world at school. Attention increased, test anxiety lowered, she began to initiate academic tasks in session, she became more alert and able to self-correct, and she began to spontaneously ask for more information or help to expand her understanding of a specific concept. She demonstrated more responsibility for planning and following through with school projects, keeping her own calendar for her plans with her friends. She took great pride in her academic accomplishments, even when parental expectations were not met. She had begun to develop her own expectations.

As time progressed, similar feelings of victimization with her father were connected to her friendships and she began to uncover deeper awarenesses about her behavior in relation to others. She brought to session one day the very clear awareness that she thought she disliked another girl because she was "loud," but what she really disliked was her own loudness. Seven months before the end of my work with her, Janie was able to explore and talk about the anger she held for her mother, her long-time ally. After several experiences of expressing her anger and hurt to her father, she could acknowledge her unfulfilled need for her mother's protection from him. Previously she could not risk losing the measure of protection she received in an alliance of secrets and acquiescence. As Janie felt and demonstrated more independence from her father, she was able to risk separation from mother. Now 13 years old, Janie had enough self-esteem to embark on this developmental road.

Janie was retested at this point in the therapy. There was no intratest scatter on the WISC-III, as was seen in the previous testing. Consistency was apparent both within the subtests and in the overall test. Importantly, subtests tapping concentration, attention to task, and tension/anxiety were not lagging as they had been. Right brain functioning scores jumped into the high-average range. In the earlier testing both left and right hemispheres were at a par. Janie appeared now to show more strength in processing information in a visual-spatial or holistic way, though logical, sequential ability remained in the average range. The Bender-Gestalt Test of Visual Motor Integration indicated an improvement of approximately one and a half years in perceptual motor ability. Educational testing showed marked progress in decoding words, reading, receptive language, and writing ability.

Janie no longer showed a significant difference between ability and performance in reading, writing, or language. Arithmetic remained her weakest area, and remediation was a continuing need. The diagnosis was developmental arithmetic disorder, and, on Axis I, dysthymia. The additional diagnosis reflected the transition to a psychoeducational model and the findings within the treatment. Continued psychoeducational therapy was recommended.

Three months after this battery of tests, therapy with Janie was terminated when I left the clinic. I allowed most of that period for the termination process. Janie's attachment to me was strong. We had worked together for two and a half years. Terminating was difficult. Janie was able to clearly express her anger and sadness and, over time, talk about others lost in her life: grandparents who died, best friends who had moved away. Twice she brought music to help her match words with feelings. During this time many physical symptoms recurred and Janie filled sessions alternately with avoidance, denial, anger, hysteria, separation, and poignant sadness. She was increasingly able to tolerate hearing me talk about holding the pain of loss together with the good memories, her growth, and achievement. She was integrating losing me and internalizing me. In our final session we completed necklaces we had designed and made for one another. She was able to tell me in that last session that she still felt angry with me for leaving.

Janie transferred reluctantly to another therapist at the clinic to continue pyschoeducational therapy. Trusting another therapist seemed impossible to her. It only meant another inevitable good-bye. The update from the new therapist included Janie's recognition that she did not need me to be with her physically in order to maintain and further the work she had accomplished. She could use all she had learned and depend on herself more and more.

The prognosis for Janie is good. Interventions were achieved early and were successful in positively impacting her developmental course. In her case, psychoeducational work served as the bridge that helped Janie navigate information, both concrete and abstract. She gained the ability to focus on and structure her academic tasks, break things down into manageable pieces to circumvent cognitive multisensory flooding, and create building blocks toward a gestalt. Similarly, feelings flooded her. By identifying, separating, and expressing different feelings she was able to understand her experience in a totality. Janie had begun to feel in control of and responsible for her work and her feelings. With awareness, she could intervene or compensate consciously. Finding the individual pathways to transfer concepts to and from the emotional and educational realms remediated her attentional problems and gave her a foundation from which to build an independent sense of herself.

If it had been found that Janie did have ADD, the treatment would have differed. Though educational and emotional work may have been the same, other techniques and interventions would have been added. The family is an important piece in ADD treatment. Strong behavioral contracts and limit setting, including positive reinforcements and reasonable consequences, often help contain and provide parameters for the ADD child. Structured routines and activites both at home and at school are necessary. Frequent collaboration with teachers helps to provide consistency throughout the child's main environments. Preparation time before any transition of activity is also very important. Lastly, medication evaluation for Ritalin, Dexedrine, or Cylert may be indicated, and/or medication to address comorbid depression. If Janie had begun at the clinic in more recent years, newer, more advanced testing could have better determined whether or not her attentional difficulties were in fact ADD or stemmed from an emotional base.

The tapestry of psychotherapeutic and educational interventions is illustrated beautifully by the last essay Janie wrote for me. Technically, it showed her ability for developing a cohesive, mature theme, using appropriate paragraphing, vocabulary, reasonably correct grammar, structure, punctuation, capitalization, and the distinction between literal and figurative representations. The content of the writing encompassed hope, re-creating a new way of life and setting goals. She made herself the example in the last paragraph, sequencing a chain of experience: relying on and trusting herself leads to relaxing more, relaxing stops the fear of what might happen and helps to focus on what is really happening, pressure from everyone else stops, and without the pressure she feels better about her work and feeling better about her work makes her grades improve. The frame of the essay provided evidence of her educational growth and provided the structure to demonstrate a remarkable awareness and expression of her inner experience and emotional growth. The integration of remediation and psychological development are inextricably tied together in her words and the very meaning of those words. Janie's course of treatment exemplifies the psychoeducational model as a unique, viable, and effective psychotherapeutic approach for a growing population of children.

17

Psychological Factors That Impact the Educational Therapy Process with Children Who Have AD/HD and Learning Differences

Dana Levin Shrager

The main goal of educational therapy is to address a child's learning and attentional difficulties within a therapeutic relationship. To achieve this goal, attention to both the content and the process is crucial. Currently, academic content, teaching approaches, and compensatory strategies predominate the educational therapy literature. Of equal importance are process issues such as the therapeutic relationship and the psychological and emotional reactions of the client.

Before any learning can take place, the educational therapist first needs to establish and maintain a relationship with the client. The client needs to be open to taking in information from the educator. A number of psychological and attentional factors can interfere with the client's ability to learn from the therapist. Therefore, it is essential that the educational therapist address the inner emotional experience of the learner (Field et al. 1993). An educational therapist, who is trained in the field of education, needs to attend to the therapeutic aspect of the relationship, while being careful not to cross the line into psychotherapy. A psychoeducational therapist, however, is trained in the fields of both education and psychotherapy, and thus has the expertise and training to intervene fully in both areas.

POTENTIAL LEARNING SPACE

For a child to be in a position to learn, there is a critical psychological prerequisite. Children need to have available and open mental space in their minds. They have to be willing to let new information into their minds, and they need to be willing to take in the information from the therapist, or the teacher, or the book, as the case may be (Tufeld 1993).

To learn, children need space in their minds where they can think and hold onto ideas. According to psychoanalyst Wilfred Bion (1962a,b), thinking involves an ability to transform emotions and sensations into thoughts and ideas. Various dynamics can interfere with one's ability to make this transformation in a given moment. Interruptions may be caused by a lapse in attention as well as by a number of psychological factors, which will be addressed.

In addition to making mental connections in one's own mind, a client needs to be able to make a meaningful link or connection to the therapist (Bion 1959). Having an available space between two people in which the two can connect and communicate has been termed "transitional space" by the psychoanalyst and pediatrician Donald Winnicott (1971). It is important for the therapist to be attuned to the degree of openness in the potential learning space between the therapist and the client. Without this connection, the client cannot learn from the therapist.

It is normal for this potential space to vary in its degree of openness at different times, but it becomes a problem for learning if it is frequently closed. This potential space is not only a place for thinking, but also a place where imagination, creativity, curiosity, and learning happen. Thus, an important job for the educational therapist is to help the client keep this potential learning space open.

PSYCHOLOGICAL AND EMOTIONAL FACTORS

There are a number of psychological and emotional factors that can close down the potential learning space:

1. Fear of failure and low self-esteem.
2. Lack of structure and disorganization.
3. Difficulty tolerating states of "not knowing" and uncertainty.
4. Perfectionism and self-criticalness.
5. Projective identification—placing unwanted feelings onto the therapist.
6. Preoccupation with emotional and psychological problems.

All learners encounter some of these psychological barriers as an inevitable part of the learning process. The difference is the severity and the frequency. Many times therapeutic interventions can impact the way these factors interfere with learning. In other cases, however, the psychological issues may be so overwhelming that they need to be the main focus of attention for a period of time before the academic issues can be fully addressed.

Fear of Failure and Low Self-Esteem

By the time students with attention deficit/hyperactivity disorder (AD/HD) and learning differences (LD) see an educational therapist, most have experienced failures in school. Some of these individuals may view working with an educational therapist as another opportunity to fail and to feel inadequate. As a result, they may behave in oppositional and resistant ways. Because of their low self-esteem, they may not believe in themselves and may be afraid to take risks. These feelings and fears need to be interpreted and brought out into the open by the therapist.

Furthermore, an educational therapist can intervene with the following specific approach to the initial sessions and with carefully designed lesson plans. Such interventions can help increase the chance that the client's experience with educational therapy will be a successful one.

Initially, an educational therapist might engage a reluctant child by inviting him or her to join in a fun activity or game. Many children are more likely to begin to participate with an educational game than with an academic worksheet. Students with AD/HD, in particular, focus best when learning is as active and "hands on" as possible. A selection of activity choices could be offered to the child. The therapist should present choices that are within the child's ability and attention span, taking into account the child's developmental level and cognitive strengths and weaknesses.

In addition, the educational therapist can inquire about and observe the client's interests. High-interest activities and topics aid motivation and attention span. For example, reluctant readers are more willing to read with the educational therapist if the subject matter is interesting to them. Everyone has their own unique set of interests; some popular subjects include science experiments, sports, teenage magazines, current music, insects, and pets. Taking into account the client's abilities and interests can help create a positive experience. The rapport is also enhanced as the client experiences the therapist's interest in him or her.

It is also important that the therapist select educational material at an appropriate instructional level where the student can be successful. The time spent on any one activity should be within the student's attention span. Lesson plans can be designed to accomplish small, feasible steps at a time. During educational therapy, the client starts to build up a series of positive experiences. The therapist can acknowledge the individual's effort and progress along the way. The small and steady successes add up over time, and as the learning progresses clients start to believe in their ability to be effective and successful in the world.

The educational therapist strives to create a safe and trusting atmosphere where the client can feel safe to take risks and engage in the difficult process of learning. Whenever the therapist attends to this therapeutic environment, he or she is creating a space where learning is possible. As the trust grows in the relationship, clients generally begin to feel safe to reveal more thoughts and feelings about their learning process. The more the therapist is allowed into the clients' inner world, the more the therapist can help them understand and overcome their struggles.

Lack of Structure and Disorganization

Some individuals have trouble succeeding academically because they lack the necessary internal, cognitive structure. They may have difficulty organizing ideas that they are trying to take in as well as express. In addition, they may have trouble organizing their belongings and may also have difficulty with boundaries in relationships.

With schoolwork, these children may be very disorganized and unstructured in the way they keep their materials and approach assignments. These organizational problems are common among people with AD/HD and LD. These problems can interfere with their school success. To help such a student in educational therapy, first the therapist and student together need to develop an organizational plan for approaching the student's work. The plan needs to be one that the therapist thinks will be effective, and one that the students feel might fit for them. When students are a part of creating the new organizational systems, they are more likely to follow through with the systems. The plan can include specific techniques for organizing a school notebook, backpack, locker, desk, assignment sheet, calendar, and after-school time management. Because there are many areas to be organized, it is helpful to focus the therapy on one or two areas at a time. Most importantly, the organizational strategies being taught need to be simple and clear. Detailed, complicated organizational systems are generally not useful for people with AD/HD.

To teach a new organizational strategy, the educational therapist models the organization for the client. In essence, the therapist lends the client an aspect of his or her ego that is able to structure and organize. First, the therapist models and explains the organization, and then guides the client's practice. When this teaching method is used consistently, the child gradually internalizes the structure and will improve his or her ability to organize independently. Furthermore, meta-cognitive strategies for organizing ideas can be taught. Such skills include sequencing, categorizing, identifying main ideas, memory techniques, and problem-solving strategies. Therefore, when the educational therapist helps a client learn to structure and organize, an open mental space for learning is being created.

Learning to think and work in an organized, structured fashion does not come easily for some people with AD/HD. It is a skill, like many other skills, that needs to be learned over time. Thus, the student may need encouragement to stick with the new systems and to be patient because the systems will become more automatic for them to use over time. In addition, once the students try the new strategies, their feedback is essential for fine-tuning the systems so that the organizational plan will be tailored to their specific preferences and needs. Periodic follow-up lessons are also essential for the success of developing new organizational skills.

Some children with AD/HD and LD lack internal structure and tend to be chaotic and impulsive. They need containment to help them focus.

> Dennis, age 9, used to walk around my office and touch everything. He would want to open all the drawers and clearly needed limits to help him settle down. Dennis would try to work on several assignments simultaneously or would tell me a number of different stories all at once. Initially, he was chaotic and had poor boundaries. Dennis needed the containment and organization from me to help him focus and think. In particular, his chaotic approach to his homework interfered with his ability to complete his assignments. Dennis initially was unaware that he anxiously jumped back and forth between assignments, which was a disjointed and inefficient approach. He needed this behavior pointed out to him repeatedly so that he could change. He also needed to be taught how to use a homework assignment sheet, to have school supplies available at his desk, to prioritize the order in which he approached his work, and to have only one assignment on his desk at a time. Gradually, Dennis was able to internalize the structure that I provided for him in the office and over time was able to organize his homework time by himself. When Dennis could organize and structure more efficiently, he had more internal space and focus available for learning.

Difficulty Tolerating States of "Not Knowing" and Uncertainty

To be engaged in the learning process, children have to be able to tolerate a number of different psychological states of mind. To learn anything new, they first have to admit that there is something that they do not know and that the teacher knows something that they do not. They need to be able to tolerate the state of mind of "not knowing" (Beaumont 1993, Tufeld 1993). Presented with what they do not know, learners may feel inferior or anxious. These feelings can drive them toward learning or inhibit them (Ekstein 1969a). If the pain and frustration of these feelings is too unbearable, then thinking and learning will be impaired (Bion 1962a, Grinberg et al. 1977). This struggle is an integral and ongoing part of the learning process because children are constantly confronted with new information and ideas.

Often children with AD/HD have trouble getting through this period of not knowing because the waiting for mastery is difficult for them to tolerate. They tend to rush through their school assignments, to approach their work impulsively, and to want the learning to happen immediately. Thus, one important goal during educational therapy is to help them bear the wait so that they can work through the learning process.

Another important objective for educational therapy is to help children tolerate the anxiety, pain, and frustration of not knowing. When these feelings cannot be tolerated, learners engage in all kinds of other behaviors to avoid the feelings, including manic defenses (Beaumont 1993, Bion 1962a, Ekstein 1969a, Tufeld 1993). For example, clients may try to avoid doing work with the educational therapist by distracting and talking about other interests, or they may procrastinate starting assignments. Learners may omnipotently act like they know the information already. They may devalue the learning task and call it "stupid." All these defensive behaviors help evade confronting the pain of not knowing.

During the process of educational therapy, clients can be helped to work through their defensive behaviors and the pain of not knowing.

Jason, age 17, was having great difficulty studying for the Scholastic Achievement Test I (SAT I), a college entrance exam. While doing practice questions together, we began to recognize that every time Jason came to a question to which he did not immediately know the answer, he lost his focus and got distracted by other things in the room. He started paying attention to extraneous noises and would look around the room, but only when he did not know an answer. When the questions were easier for Jason, his mind was open and focused. His anxiety about not knowing interfered with his ability to think and concentrate. Jason's difficulty concentrating could mistakenly be attributed to AD/HD; however, his difficulty was due to psychological fear and anxiety.

Identifying these defensive symptoms was an important first step for Jason. He learned to use his distracting behaviors as a cue that he was encountering a difficult question. We then worked on his ability to talk to himself in an encouraging manner to help him bear the not knowing. He learned to say to himself, "I know that this test has some difficult questions; it's impossible to get all the questions right, but maybe if I concentrate, I can eliminate some of the choices and figure out the right answer." Once he talked to himself, he lowered his anxiety enough so that he opened up some space in his mind to think.

There are other ways to intervene to help clients learn to tolerate not knowing. The educational therapy work done with Nancy illustrates another important approach.

Nancy, age 15, could do very well with school assignments in which there was one right answer. If she needed to look up a specific fact in a textbook, she could do so with ease and confidence. However, if Nancy needed to give her own opinion or draw her own conclusions, she froze and would often avoid such assignments. When the right answer was not obvious to her, she became overly anxious and felt inadequate.

To intervene, Nancy and I worked on such assignments together. To help her learn, I used a teaching approach called "scaffolding," in which the teacher initially offers much guidance and structure and then gradually backs off the support as the student is ready. In Nancy's case, I first modeled for her and guided her through some of the questions, making some of the links for her. Gradually, Nancy began to do more of the assignment herself, even though she felt very insecure about her own ideas. She needed much encouragement and reassurance. Over time, after working together on many such assignments, Nancy began to expect to encounter her insecure and uncertain feelings while learning and gradually built up her mental muscle and ability to tolerate these difficult states of mind (S. Gooch, personal communication).

Perfectionism and Self-Criticalness

When children set perfectionistic and unobtainable educational goals, they increase their sense of failure. Their disappointment overshadows any progress made and takes the pleasure out of what they did achieve.

When Sarah, age 8, began educational therapy, she was doing poorly in her math class. Working very diligently, Sarah improved her math skills over time. However, she had difficulty feeling proud of her effort and progress because anything less than perfect was very upsetting to her. Sarah's perfectionism robbed her of taking pride in all that she did accomplish and learn.

It is important that students have realistic expectations of the learning process. Sarah would get frustrated if she did not completely understand and master new math concepts immediately. She would get so upset that she could not focus or try again. Generally, when children learn something new, they need to be presented with the information many times in different ways and need to practice it. Also, some things are learned fairly quickly and other things may take longer. Sarah needed to learn to give herself permission to take her time. However, to sit with the process of learning gradually over time means to sit with uncomfortable feelings of not knowing, inadequacy, and sometimes self-criticalness.

In particular, children with AD/HD tend to have an unrealistic expectation that learning new concepts in school should happen immediately. They may rush through their schoolwork impulsively or seek to know new material instantly and magically. Sometimes children with AD/HD seem like they might be rushing to finish their schoolwork before their concentration wanes. When they fall short of their quick expectations, they can become frustrated, self-critical, and discouraged. Tolerating the wait while one is mastering something over time can be challenging for these children. They also have difficulty picturing learning as a gradual process that unfolds over time. Thus, two important goals in educational therapy are to help clients tolerate the waiting and to teach them the specific, detailed steps and study strategies that they need in order to learn.

Often children are not aware of their unrealistic expectations and perfectionism.

> During one educational therapy session, Dennis was having a difficult time with his penmanship while he was doing an assignment. He was trying to form each letter exactly. Dennis kept erasing, rewriting, and grunting, but was unaware of his state of mind. I said to him, "It's a tough job trying to be so perfect," and then he smiled. I followed up with "You are really getting frustrated trying to make those letters so perfect." With my guidance, Dennis could identify that he had set out to do an impossible job because he could not focus simultaneously on forming exact letters and answering difficult questions. Then we discussed this problem, and he soon realized that he needed to choose one task to concentrate on at a time.

Letting go of one's perfectionism and unrealistic expectations is not easy because it also involves accepting one's own limitations. For many educational therapy clients it means coming to terms with their attention and learning problems, yet still seeing these struggles as just one part of their total self.

> Sarah took a long time in educational therapy to learn to accept herself as she is with her own unique set of strengths and weaknesses. Sarah was very self-critical and would get overwhelmed by

her perfectionistic expectations and her internal self-attacks for not measuring up. One focus in the therapy was to help her to formulate realistic expectations and to refrain from making judgments. The more Sarah could allow herself to be an imperfect human being, the more mental space she had for curiosity, interest, and learning.

Projective Identification—Placing Unwanted Feelings onto the Therapist

During the learning process, clients may experience feelings and frustrations that they find too unbearable to contain and think about. To defend against these feelings, clients may use projective identification, in which they unconsciously attempt to get rid of their unwanted feelings by mentally placing them onto the therapist (Bion 1962a, Klein 1946). While using this psychological defense, clients believe and act like their unbearable feelings are actually coming from the therapist (D. Garcia, personal communication). For example, if a client can no longer bear his or her own self-criticalness, he or she may put these feelings onto the therapist and then believe that the therapist is the one who is so critical of the client. Thus, the client may feel that the therapist is the critical one and the source of his or her pain, and then would want to stay away from the therapist.

At times therapists may sense these projected feelings and experience them as their own. It is important for therapists to pay attention to their feelings and then discern if the feelings belong to themselves or have been projected onto them by the client (Spillius 1988).

A clear example of this projective identification phenomenon happened during a particular educational therapy session with Nancy. She was acting like nothing I could do was right. She let me know that every teaching method I tried and every way I worded my message was of no help to her. Throughout the lesson she made noises of exasperation at me and blamed me for her difficulty with her assignment. I began to feel inadequate and frustrated. Then, I realized that these feeling belonged to Nancy. The way she treated me and the feelings she evoked in me served as a meaningful communication to me and helped me understand how she was feeling. Once I understood how she felt, I could interpret her feelings for her, which helped to make the feelings more bearable. Then she was able to calm down and had more space open for learning.

Another example of projective identification occurred during the treatment of Dennis. One session, while he was struggling to learn a new math concept, he asked me, "Are you a rookie?" We came to understand that in that moment Dennis was the one who felt like a rookie, a novice who did not know much about the new math he was attempting to learn. His feelings of inadequacy, not knowing, and self-judgment became so strong that he projected those feelings onto me and turned me into the rookie. Over time Dennis learned to identify his rookie feelings, which helped him bear the pain and frustration and enabled him to stay open to the learning process.

Preoccupation with Emotional and Psychological Problems

The potential space for learning and thinking is impaired when children are overwhelmed by their emotional and psychological problems. They may be outwardly aware that they are preoccupied, or they may not consciously realize that they are internally distracted. These problems interfere with one's ability to pay attention and focus, and one's internal preoccupation may even appear to look like AD/HD symptoms. If the psychological problems are pervasive, then these problems need to be the main focus of treatment by a psychotherapist before the academic subjects can be addressed directly.

In addition, when children have not sufficiently resolved the beginning tasks of psychosocial development, they are not well prepared to concentrate on the challenges of learning in school. Thus, for such children, an important focus of treatment is to help them achieve earlier developmental tasks such as the capacities to trust, be autonomous, and take initiative (Ekstein 1969b, Erikson 1963). These skills are important ingredients for learning readiness. If these skills are sufficiently underdeveloped, they need to be addressed in psychotherapy.

For clients with less consuming emotional and psychological problems, there are some interventions that the educational therapist can employ to help them free up some mental space for learning. One option is to allow some time at the beginning of each session for clients to talk about whatever is on their mind. Nancy would talk about feelings or problems that were bothering her. It felt like she needed to "unpack" whatever was on her mind before she had enough mental space to focus on academics. Another method is for students to use a "dreaming pad" (J. Dorman, personal communication). Whether in session or at home, students can keep a pad of paper beside them while they do their schoolwork. They can write down any intrusive, extraneous thoughts that distract them while they are working. These distracting thoughts are common among children with AD/HD. Using this method helps children temporarily set aside important thoughts but still have a record of the thoughts so that they can attend to them later. These strategies may help children temporarily set aside their emotional preoccupations in order to open up some space in the mind where learning can take place.

CONCLUSION

Educational therapists need to be aware of their clients' psychological states so that they can make necessary therapeutic interventions to help keep the clients' mental space open for learning. What educational therapists teach goes well beyond schoolwork. As therapists attend to their clients' internal experiences and feelings, they help them develop many essential ego functions such as an ability to observe oneself, to understand and tolerate one's feelings, to be self-accepting, to self-soothe, to plan, to organize, to problem solve, and to communicate. It is essential for the educational therapist to play this complex, dual role because the basic therapeutic interventions open up the space for the academic work to take place. It is also crucial that educational therapists, like all professionals, understand the limits of their training and know when to make a referral to a psychotherapist.

Although the major focus of educational therapy is on academic learning, the therapeutic relationship leaves a lasting and important imprint on the client. I have learned from my client Nancy, as well as from many others, that therapists can never be sure of all the ways in which they touch the lives of their clients.

> During Nancy's last session as she was terminating treatment, she let me know that I taught her something important that I had not realized. She said, "Out of all the things that you taught me, do you know what is the most important to me? I learned that you can have a relationship where two people can talk about whatever comes up between them. If there were any feelings or problems between us, we just talked about it. Whatever it was, we just dealt with it right away, and then there were no angry feelings left to build up between us."

Nancy described how clients can learn more than academics from an educational therapist. In the context of a close, therapeutic relationship, clients may learn how to build meaningful communication and trust with another person, which can translate to their other significant relationships.

REFERENCES

Beaumont, M. (1993). Reading between the lines: the child's fear of meaning. In *Emotions and Learning Reconsidered: International Perspectives*, ed. K. Field, E. Kaufman, and C. Saltzman, pp. 34–44. New York: Gardner.

Bion, W. R. (1959). Attacks on linking. In *Melanie Klein Today: Developments in Theory and Practice*, ed. E. B. Spillius, pp. 87–101. New York: Routledge.

———— (1962a). A theory of thinking. In *Melanie Klein Today: Developments in Theory and Practice*, ed. E. B. Spillius, pp. 178–186. New York: Routledge.

———— (1962b). *Learning from Experience*. New York: Basic Books.

Ekstein, R. (1969a). The boundary line between education and psychotherapy. In *From Learning for Love to Love of Learning*, ed. R. Ekstein and R. L. Motto, pp. 157–163. New York: Brunner/Mazel.

———— (1969b). The child, the teacher and learning. In *From Learning for*

Love to Love of Learning, ed. R. Ekstein and R. L. Motto, pp. 65–78. New York: Brunner/Mazel.

Erikson, E. H. (1963). *Childhood and Society*. New York: Norton.

Field, K., Kaufman, E., and Saltzman, C. (1993). *Emotions and Learning Reconsidered: International Perspectives*. New York: Gardner.

Grinberg, L., Sor, D., and Bianchedi, E. T. (1977). *Introduction to the Work of Bion*. New York: Jason Aronson.

Klein, M. (1946). Notes on some schizoid mechanisms. In *The Writings of Melanie Klein, Vol. 3: Envy and Gratitude and Other Works, 1946–1963*, pp. 1–24. New York: Dell, 1977.

Spillius, E. B. (1988). Projective identification introduction. In *Melanie Klein Today: Developments in Theory and Practice*, ed. E. B. Spillius, pp. 81–86. New York: Routledge.

Tufeld, M. S. (1993). *The effect of the manic defenses on learning and school achievement in children*. Doctoral Dissertation, California Graduate Institute.

Winnicott, D. W. (1971). *Playing and Reality*. New York: Routledge.

Future Trends in the Diagnosis and Treatment of AD/HD in Children and Adolescents

INTRODUCTION TO PART V

This book has presented an overview of the field of AD/HD in children and discussed a number of approaches to assessment and treatment of AD/HD and its most salient comorbid symptom complex—learning disabilities. The reader will now have a more comprehensive understanding and a more extensive perspective on current thought and practice in the field of AD/HD and on an integrated approach to working with AD/HD children, adolescents, and their families.

Chapter 18 focuses on things to come. Michael J. Goldberg, M.D. looks at where the field of AD/HD in children and adolescents may be heading as we enter the next century.

18

AD/HD—Approaching the Millennium: New Understanding, New Technologies, New Therapeutic Interventions

Michael J. Goldberg

As recently as the fifteenth edition of *Nelson's Textbook of Pediatrics* (Behrman 1996) attention deficit (hyperactivity) disorder (ADD, AD/HD) is still being characterized by

> poor ability to attend to a task, motoric overactivity, and impulsivity. These children are fidgety, have a difficult time remaining in their seats in school, are easily distracted, have difficulty awaiting their turn, impulsively blurt out answers to questions, have difficulty following instructions and sustaining attention, shift rapidly from one uncompleted activity to another, talk excessively, intrude on others, often seem not to listen to what is being said, lose items regularly, and often engage in physically dangerous activities without considering possible consequences. . . . It is difficult to distinguish adequately between AD/HD and conduct disorder, on the one hand, and between AD/HD and learning disabilities on the other. Restlessness, inattentiveness, distractibility, and vigilance deficits are commonly seen in conduct-disordered

children. In several studies, learning-disabled children could not be differentiated from children with AD/HD on the basis of attention or distractibility. Hyperactive behaviors often cannot be shown to be separate from aggressive and antisocial behaviors. [p. 91]

The confusion about an objective diagnosis and the differentiation of these patients has been a handicap affecting all studies and evaluations of these children. The subjective nature of symptoms and the characterizations of poor attention to task, impulsiveness, overactivity, fidgetiness, easy distractibility, short attention span, and learning disability have failed to give us objective criteria to differentiate and understand this complex disorder. In Chapter 1, Cantwell noted, consistent with the current statement from *Nelson's Textbook*, that ADD is a clinical diagnosis made on the basis of clinical observations, but there are no laboratory tests currently available that can be used to make a definitive diagnosis of ADD. This chapter presents some of the new tools and developments in the field of AD/HD. We are just beginning to formulate new insights and see new objective findings evolve, as we begin to understand this spectrum of disorders. Ideally this will lead to new and more appropriately directed pharmacological and other therapeutic modalities, along with a reevaluation of current medications and therapies.

ETIOLOGY

Etiology may be the key to an improved understanding of AD/HD and to the development of better therapeutic approaches. Over the years, neurologists, psychiatrists, psychologists, and other researchers have subjectively characterized this spectrum of disorders, but we have lacked the ability to look at a live human brain without significant complications. As new imaging tools are evolving, our understanding of the brain's anatomy, particularly as it pertains to various dysfunctional states, is improving exponentially. For the first time, we can look at the areas of the brain that are overactive, underactive, or normal, using quantifiable criteria. With the availability of such detailed information comes insight and understanding never before possible.

At a recent research symposium, Advances in Social Brain (Redondo Beach, California, 1997), researchers discussed some new insights about the brain based on new functioning and imaging information. The limbic system is now known to be important for learning, memory, emotion, and behavior. It also plays a major role in the processing, integration, and generalization of information. Imaging studies also suggest a ventromedial, prefrontal, corticolimbic-basal ganglia system interconnection with obsessive-compulsive disorder (OCD) patients. The implications are that areas of the brain function to capture the person's attention and direct appropriate responses to the most pressing needs of the moment, excluding less important competing responses. Dysfunction in these areas is likely playing a role in AD/HD and in some frontal lobe dementias. Serotonin may play a key role in determining whether dorsolateral or ventromedial portions dominate in the thalamic regions to which they both project. The prefrontal cortex is thought to be critical to the integration of multiple relations in working memory. Evidence confirms the important role of the frontal lobes in the neuropsychiatry of social behavior. The frontal lobes also have an important role in the integration of cognition and affect. Each new glimpse into areas of function helps us reevaluate our old ideas of brain function, dysfunction, and treatment.

There has been much conjecture that the mechanism of AD/HD involved the neurotransmitters, such as dopamine, serotonin, and others, but there was no way to measure these mechanisms directly. Any measurement of neurotransmitters or their metabolic products from peripheral blood is considered neither reliable nor reflective of what is going on in the brain.

Positron emission tomography (PET) scans began to provide insights into central nervous system (CNS) metabolism, and reports of altered patterns in AD/HD abound in the literature (Ernst et al. 1994, Matochik et al. 1994, Zametkin and Rapoport 1986). Unfortunately, these scans were considered too variable to show objective patterns defining overall dysfunctionor etiology. Newer single photon emission computed tomography (SPECT) scanners are beginning to live up to their promise of increased objectivity. More specifically, they are capable of documenting the blood flow and hence function in a child's or adult's brain. In the near future, functional magnetic resonance imaging (FMRI) may offer additional insights and data.

From a field dominated in the past by the concept of hyperactive ADD (AD/HD), we now routinely describe children as "hyper," "quiet," or a combination of the two ("mixed"). Recently the idea of executive function has entered into the differentiation of these children. Moreover, it is now acceptable to talk about adult AD/HD, a topic, along with quiet ADD in children, not widely discussed before. Through combined technetium (Tc99) (high resolution, quantifiable regional cerebral blood flow [rCBF]), Xenon 133 (lower resolution, but a highly quantifiable measure of rCBF), and NeuroSPECT (research in progress), we are looking at the first patterns allowing an objective distinction of these clinical disorders in adults and children. NeuroSPECT is a neuroimaging technique that, by allowing investigators to measure the blood flow in specific regions of the brain, defines precisely the relative function of those areas. With NeuroSPECT, blood flow is directly correlated to function (Costa et al. 1992, Ichise et al. 1992). Essentially, with hyper ADD, there is increased blood flow in the frontal lobes (Sieg et al. 1995) with an essentially normal blood flow in the rest of the brain; whereas with quiet ADD, there is decreased blood flow in the temporal lobes. Mixed ADD is exactly what it implies; there is increased flow in the frontal lobes, but decreased flow in the temporal lobes. In general, blood flow in the parietal and occipital lobes is within normal limits but there may be some areas of hypoperfusion (see Figures 18-1, 18-2, 18-3, 18-4). These findings have important implications for both causation and treatment.

While abnormalities of thyroid function have been reported in children with AD/HD (Matochik et al. 1996, Weiss et al. 1993), the general finding is that of no known pathophysiology. However, as stated above, it has been found that in mixed and quiet AD/HD children, there is reduced blood flow in the temporal lobe, including the hypothalamus, which in turn controls the pituitary gland. The pituitary gland directly affects the thyroid gland. This connection begins to explain the possible connection of enuresis in some children with AD/HD (Robson et al. 1997). Thus, as NeuroSPECT provides a pathologic/physiologic understanding of the brain, many observations unexplainable in the past not only may be understandable and explainable now, but also may help us comprehend the different populations of AD/HD.

While genetic causes of AD/HD have been postulated for years (Comings 1997), and may very well describe a model of altered dopamine/noradrenergic metabolism (i.e., the hyper ADD), an additional model would seem to be necessary to define the appearance of large numbers of quiet and mixed AD/HD children in recent years. While increased

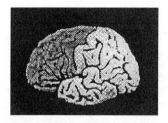

Figure 18–1.
Frontal lobe.

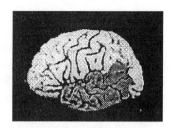

Figure 18–2.
Temporal lobe.

Figure 18–3.
Parietal lobe.

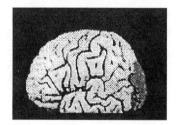

Figure 18–4.
Occipital lobe.

blood flow in the frontal lobe would be a possible genetically inherited dysfunction, decreased blood flow (seen with quiet AD/HD and mixed AD/HD) would seem explainable at this time only by an altered immune/autoimmune reaction or chronic viral processes. These hypotheses were discussed at recent research symposia—Advances in Social Brain, Redondo Beach, California, 1997, and the American Academy of Chronic Fatigue Syndrome (AACFS) meeting, San Francisco, 1996. If these findings hold up, then we need to consider different mechanisms and areas of dysfunction in these children, even though they are often grouped together as AD/HD. The interaction of various areas of the brain and limbic system and the resultant effects on attention, impulsivity, and various ADD symptoms increases the urgency to better understand the physiology of each patient and the goals of therapy. This emerging understanding will allow us to better evaluate the available treatments.

EPIDEMIOLOGY

Until recently, AD/HD has been thought to occur primarily in males. While past reports have quoted an incidence of 10 to 15 percent in boys (Baumgaertel et al. 1995, Wolraich et al. 1996), in discussions with researchers, school psychologists, and other professionals, numbers as high as 40 to 50 percent of children in many schools are being treated for AD/HD. As noted above, older models based on genetic neurotransmitter dysfunction, developmental disorders, and psychosocial family dysfunctions do not adequately explain the large increase of AD/HD in children (and adults) in recent years. Better recognition and understanding only explains a portion of this increased clinical incidence. However, with the findings of decreased blood flow using NeuroSPECT in mixed and quiet AD/HD emerges the likelihood of autoimmune and/or viral components explaining some if not much of this increased incidence. Moreover, consistent with many reports reflecting increases in autoimmune disorders and allergies (Levy and Bircher 1994) in children and adults, we may be looking at a genetic disposition (perhaps associated with higher IQ) for an altered neuroimmune state, creating an increase in cognitive dysfunction. There may also be a role for "slow" viruses and/or retroviruses and static encephalopathy.

While difficult to prove, there may be more than a coincidence in the changing patterns of cognitive dysfunction we are seeing. These may be reflective of issues related to the global environmental, immunological changes, and evolutionary changes. Denckla (1996) discusses concepts of intention, working memory, and executive function, creating a focus of dysfunction in theory, which was not found in the classic discussions of the inattentive hyperactive child. The classic hyperactive child was generally considered very bright and gifted, if he could only sit still and focus. The quiet or mixed AD/HD children often show lower IQ and cognitive abilities. This cognitive dysfunction is related to the findings of areas of decreased function on the NeuroSPECT for mixed and quiet ADD (Denckla 1996), not found characteristically with the hyper ADD. As newer research on AD/HD focus on different areas of dysfunction, it becomes more compelling to reevaluate the processes involved and the precise areas of dysfunction in the brain. With decreased perfusion on NeuroSPECT, these children may appear to have lower IQs, when in fact their potential may be equal to (or above) those of the hyper AD/HD child. Thus, new models are necessary to explain this disorder in both children and adults. In the past, one could often show first-degree relative connections (such as a parent's brother) with AD/HD. Now, one can find families with a mother and/or father having adult AD/HD or other neurocognitive dysfunction and one or two of their children also having AD/HD (often quiet/mixed type). I have found families where the mother or father had adult AD/HD or chronic fatigue immune dysfunction syndrome (CFIDS), an older child had AD/HD, and a younger child had autism or pervasive developmental disorder (PDD). None of these models fits those used twenty to twenty-five years ago. Before assuming all AD/HD is the same, perhaps it is time we reevaluate the etiologies, and, in turn, their epidemiological implications.

CLINICAL MANIFESTATIONS

The last twenty years have witnessed a significant increase in learning disorders and variations of AD/HD, now often discussed in terms of meta-cognitive dysfunction (Behrman 1992, Reeve and Brown 1985). A problem with the past treatment of AD/HD is that it addressed only family history, behavioral problems, and issues of conduct disorder; there was very little focus on medical history and/or medical/metabolic factors contributing to the patient's dysfunction. The focus was generally on separation anxiety issues or parenting factors. AD/HD was considered a behavioral, psychological disorder. Whereas Weinberg and colleagues (1997) and others have alluded to the difficulty of diagnosing AD/HD based on symptoms because of comorbid problems (behavioral disorders, depression, etc.), I would suggest that there is an even more serious concern—the need to define when AD/HD symptoms are reflective of an underlying physiologic disorder, perhaps immune or medically influenced, rather than just behavioral or developmental. Thus, it is important to inquire about allergies, colic, and sleep or eating difficulties. Moreover, when the brain is an altered immune/hypofunction state, it may not go into normal stage IV rapid eye movement (REM) sleep cycles; thus the patient will experience difficulty in forming memories and in other restorative functions. These children may seem "spacey," in a world of their own, rather than hyper and bouncing off the walls. As noted, many of these children are reported to have neurocognitive processing defects even when they are focused, a situation not routinely reported twenty years ago (Barkley et al. 1991, Barkley et al. 1992, Zamektin 1995). It is pertinent to note that Barkley and others describe a typical ADD/hyperactive child as having problems in sustaining his/her attention, while the consensus is that the nonhyperactives have difficulty focusing their attention.

Barkley (1995) noted that boys, who have been more often associated with typical hyper-ADD symptoms, have more behavioral disturbances than girls. In the early 1970s medical schools taught that if hyperactive children could be kept in their seats and if they were very bright, they would perform accordingly. But today we focus on lower IQ expectations in children with AD/HD (Faraone et al. 1993, Loge et al. 1990). It has been my experience that AD/HD children identified as ADD without hyperactivity may often have become so due to an immune dysregulatory disorder and secondary CNS dysfunction, which manifests itself as a lower IQ and lower overall abilities. Adults with this hypofunction have disorders of memory, and verbal, auditory, and learning retrieval malfunctions. Studies on these adults in the early 1990s showed IQ changes of over twenty to thirty points in those treated versus those untreated. In turn, the seemingly lower IQs in the ADD-H (without hyperactivity) subgroup may be a part of the children's CNS dysfunction, and not reflective of their true ability. Children who are found to be hyper do not appear to have the same compromised IQ. The difference reported between these subgroups and NeuroSPECT findings (research in progress) supports my hypotheses that ADD-H is most likely related to immune dysfunction and may in fact be one of the manifestations of what is mistakenly called CFIDS in children. While this dysfunction is best thought of as an autoimmune/immune dysregulatory phenomenon in adults, there continue to be arguments as to whether it is a true cognitive dysfunction/physiologic state or rather due to direct psychogenic factors. The argument in the adult literature concerning chronic fatigue syndrome (CFS)/CFIDS is similar to the ongoing battle over AD/HD, in that both conditions lack identifiable markers; thus, the need for research on imaging and controlled markers.

Barkley and colleagues (1990) reported on a comprehensive evaluation of the subtypes of ADD. A major goal of the study was to determine whether or not the hyperactive and nonhyperactive subgroups were distinct cognitive and psychiatric disorders. Results showed that ADD-H children had fewer problems with off-task behavior during a task than the ADD + H (with hyperactivity) group. The nonhyperactive group performed worse on the coding subtest of the Wechsler Intelligence Scale for Children, revised (WISC-R) and had greater problems on measures of retrieval of verbal information from memory. Both groups showed impairment of vigilance, but the ADD + H group committed twice as many impulsive errors. Barkley and colleagues note that sustained attention is more likely a function of the anterior prefrontal lobes and their rich connections with the limbic system, while focused attention is more likely a function of the posterior parietal temporal substrates. They also note that multiple differences were found between the two subtypes, including the finding that ADD + H children have considerably different patterns of psychiatric comorbidity from ADD-H children. This strongly suggests that these are not subtypes of a common shared attention disorder, but are different attention disturbances. The NeuroSPECT work (in progress) by Ismael Mena, Bruce Miller, and colleagues further suggests that there are different etiologies of dysfunction whose overlapping areas create the net effect of attention deficit disorder.

Barkley's studies on the differences in AD/HD types—quiet, mixed, and hyper—are clinically astute in light of the differences we have seen on NeuroSPECT. In a more recent article Barkley (1995) proposes a clinical difference between contingency-shaped sustained attention and goal-directed persistence, which may help explain the paradox that many children can sustain long-term interest in video games and other fun activities, but not on activities that are not fun—those without immediate reward and gratification. Fortunately, other researchers (Cantwell 1996, Hazell 1997) have also recognized that the subtypes of AD/HD are likely different in symptom complex, and that there are potentially different etiologies for quiet and hyper AD/HD. As Kong (1995) noted, the "etiological factors of preschool psychiatric disorders (such as AD/HD) include biological and psychosocial contribution" (p. 319). It is necessary to identify these different subtypes in terms of their etiologies in order to better pinpoint the appropriate therapy and management.

While the original discussions of hyper ADD assumed that it was outgrown by adolescence, the prevalence of AD/HD declines to about 35 percent in late adolescence and further diminishes through early adulthood (Raskin et al. 1985). However, for many affected adolescents the problems worsen amid the strenuous challenges of high school. Attention deficits, as reflective of disorganized CNS function, are either exacerbated or ameliorated by environmental and social factors. The symptoms of attention deficits in adolescence are thought to be more subtle than those of the elementary school child, and they are apt to be especially elusive when overt behavioral problems are not a part of the clinical findings. However, adolescents with attention deficits are especially susceptible to undue strain upon memory functions in school. Because of the inconsistency of their attentional patterns, these students are likely to register and consolidate nonsalient data in memory. For that reason, these children often have an excellent recall of trivia, and hence a highly developed episodic memory. Unfortunately, for those same reasons, they are apt to have difficulty determining and remembering what is relevant when reading a text or studying for an examination. Furthermore, the superficiality of their attention may result in information being stored or consolidated in a rather tenuous manner. The increased recognition of ongoing dysfunction into adolescence and adulthood warrants further understanding and evaluation of the changes in AD/HD patterns, etiology, and therapies. These studies need to be carried out in a carefully controlled manner or the results will just add to the confusion in the field.

As an example of the confusion in the research being done in this field, many articles (Boris and Mandel 1994, Breakey 1997, Shaywitz et al. 1994) argue the pros and cons for the effect or lack of effect of sugars, sweeteners, and foods on children's behavior. Some assert there are negative effects, others "conclusively" prove there are none. The study by Shaywitz et al. (1994) is often referred to as definitive proof that sugar has nothing to do with hyperactivity. However, this study suffered from at least two major flaws. First, while very meticulously designed, the authors failed to establish a baseline off sugar (i.e., no fruit, fruit drinks) for any of the children. Second, consistent with other such studies, there was no attempt to subclassify or define different subgroups. For many factors studied in this fashion, if one looks for statistical significance based

on the size of the subject group, one may very well be missing subgroups in which there would be a marked reaction to sugars or chemicals. It should be noted that sugar reaction is a problem that does not
affect all children with AD/HD, but to ignore it or other possible
factors is a disservice to these children and their parents.

Another example of the confusion surrounding AD/HD research
findings as outlined by Cantwell and others is the possible effect of environmental factors such as prenatal abnormalities, toxins, food additives,
vitamins, nutrients, and so on. The problem is that so far none of these
factors has received substantial empirical support. As mentioned previously, the reason for the confusion and lack of success or empirical support is that AD/HD, in encompassing such a heterogeneous mixture of
symptoms and etiologies, needs to be understood by using new tools, new
markers, and new tests to separate out these subgroups of children. In
studying AD/HD or any other heterogeneous group of children or patients without the ability to define subgroups, we may be missing important factors in both etiologies and treatment responses.

DIFFERENTIAL DIAGNOSIS

Laboratory studies and markers have been of very little help in
establishing a diagnosis of AD/HD. Various combinations of
psychoeducational and psychosocial test batteries have been assessed, with
often confusing results. Genetic studies that presume behavioral variants
and fail to use criteria to objectively differentiate AD/HD subgroups are
thus inherently flawed (Levy et al. 1997). Many reports in the literature
note the problems with psychometric testing and with the new continuous performance tests (CPTs), such as lack of specificity (Baren and
Swanson 1996). The diagnostic approach as outlined by Cantwell (see
Chapter 1) is probably still not sufficient, as it appears incapable of adequately differentiating developmental, behavioral, and medical/physi-
ological variables. Until recently, one has had to rely on behavioral history and other subjective clinical parameters. The problem is that they
are only guides, some more useful than others, but all are open to subjective variations and do not objectively or quantitatively define this disorder. Another important issue, as mentioned by Richters and colleagues
(1995) and others, is the absence of long-term evaluation, as is currently

done for the therapies being used. One can hypothesize that one of the reasons for this absence is that with AD/HD being a heterogeneous disorder in which patients are not subcategorized, some patients show short-term success but not long-term success, so long-term follow-ups are omitted.

Many doctors still continue to think of AD/HD as a mental disorder. Many articles have been written about the beneficial effect of stimulant medications (Matochik et al. 1994); they primarily look at the reduction of hyperactivity, and at diminishing or controlling disruptive and aggressive behaviors. However, if we do not develop and apply better measures for evaluation of the brain and cognitive function, we may never know if behavioral gains in the classroom (calmer, more focused) translate into long-term cognitive improvement. In fact, many long-term studies have shown these medications to be effective only if they are combined with other interventions. Other medical, nutritional, and supportive approaches combined with these interventions might be more successful in some subgroups.

In the past, the primary focus was on differentiating other behavioral or psychological disorders from AD/HD. As articles by Palmeri (1996) and others show, there is greater focus on neurologic evaluation of a cognitive impairment that is metabolic/physiologic in origin; thus the diagnosis of "unknown encephalopathy—static or progressive." There is now a focus on accompanying areas of dysfunction including auditory impairment, epilepsy (particularly petit mal), use of medication, and other drug usage or exposure. These changes reflect an urgent need to develop and apply diagnostic tools that allow greater objective differentiation of these patients. As Cantwell pointed out (see Chapter 1), the search for comorbid conditions may help identify subgroups that have different etiology. For example, it was found that conduct disorder and opposition defiant disorders were more prevalent in psychiatric samples, while learning disorders were more prevalent in pediatric samples. It has been my experience that many pediatric patients present with central nervous system dysfunction, cognitive dysfunction, and learning difficulties that are not consistent with the behavioral and psychological picture of AD/HD. The evolution of new neuroimaging techniques may be a large step in helping us develop and understand objective criteria for defining types of dysfunction and associated pathologies.

As noted previously, PET has demonstrated abnormalities, but these have not been consistent enough to facilitate an objective differential diagnosis. They are more akin to findings accompanying a specific diagnosis. NeuroSPECT, used far more in Europe than in the United States, may be a tool to facilitate an objective differential diagnosis. Using a combination of Xenon 133 (for sensitive quantification) and Tc99 (high resolution), we have been able to find consistent abnormalities that are different for each type of AD/HD (research in progress). Radiologists and neurologists have stated that we would likely have failed to pick up areas of increased blood flow in the frontal lobes (hyperfunction) were it not for the highly quantifiable Xenon 133 portion of the data.

As other researchers have begun to report NeuroSPECT abnormalities (Amen and Carmichael 1997, Heuser et al. 1994), although with differences of machine capability and technique, there should ultimately be consistent findings, particularly with the new combined Xenon 133 and Tc99 generation of scanners. We may finally begin to understand the CNS physiology of an AD/HD child. It is likely that immune and/or metabolic markers may evolve, further helping to differentiate some of these disorders. For example, many AD/HD children present with impaired social skills. It is believed that social skills are a right-hemisphere function, and it is interesting to note that our NeuroSPECT findings of quiet and mixed AD/HD generally show decreased flow in the right temporal lobe, consistent with impaired social skills.

This research may carry tremendous implications for therapy and behavioral approaches for AD/HD children. While preliminary NeuroSPECT work should show a theoretical logic for the use of a stimulant medication (as it acts as a vasoconstrictor) in the classic hyper ADD, one might need to reconsider this choice of agents, and/or the dosages employed if areas of decreased perfusion are found. In fact, Cantwell and Baker (1992) and Campbell and colleagues (1996) had described a subgroup of patients who showed cognitive toxicity when given stimulant medication. In light of our NeuroSPECT findings of decreased temporal blood flow in quiet and mixed AD/HD, restricting blood flow further through stimulant medication might cause a virtual shutdown of those areas of the brain and hence cognitive dysfunction. Fortunately, many psychiatrists have initiated the usage of selective serotonin reuptake inhibitors (SSRIs) in some of these children, based on symptomatology

(Barrickman et al. 1991, Connor and Steingard 1996, Findling 1996, Olvera et al. 1996). The decreased flow in the temporal lobes seen on NeuroSPECT implies a logical, physiological need for an SSRI-type medication (which helps reestablish normal function and flow), as well as other new medical approaches. There is mounting conjecture that this decreased blood flow seen on the NeuroSPECT (without abnormal MRIs or other known metabolic or neurologic syndrome) is due to a dysfunctional neuroimmune axis and/or subclinical viral infection. As longitudinal research continues, we may well find an additional link between the neurocognitive dysfunction appearing in these children and the increase in autoimmune disorders and neurocognitive dysfunction found in adults.

Using NeuroSPECT, this author and colleagues have found a striking overlap of temporal lobe hypoperfusion/hypofunction in young children with autism/PDD, children with AD/HD, and adolescents and adults with AD/HD and CFS/CFIDS. This overlap increases the likelihood that we are looking at a medical link between these groups. Thus, we need to reevaluate these disorders. Currently, I am working with a number of families in which one parent has AD/HD or CFS, an older child has AD/HD, and a younger child (or two) has autism/PDD. None of this was commonly found ten to twenty years ago, but it may be a major factor in the presentation of AD/HD and learning disorders now and in the future.

THE DIAGNOSTIC WORKUP FOR AD/HD AND POTENTIAL MEDICAL FACTORS

As cognitive processes receive increasing emphasis in learning-disabled children with and without hyperactive ADD, the battery of tests typically administered may include:

1. Intelligence tests

2. Tests of general learning abilities

3. Academic achievement tests

4. Diagnostic reading, math, and writing tests

5. Tests of perceptual and motor function

6. Assessment of speech and language skills

7. Informal assessment techniques, including a trial of diagnostic teaching and therapies

For further specifics, see Chapter 3.

I would also propose that children with AD/HD, particularly those without a pure, classic hyper pattern, warrant basic blood workup and medical evaluation;

1. Basic chemistries

   CBC, sed rate, chem panel, ferritin, thyroid screen

2. Immune markers (if history indicates)

   Immunoglobulin levels

   Current immune markers such as CD4, CD8, natural killer (NK) cells, and B cells.

   Future immune and metabolic markers as technologies evolve

   Viral screening/titers

3. Neuroimaging

   NeuroSPECT scan (ideally combined Xenon 133 and Tc99) with or without a PET scan, MRI, or computed tomography (CT)

   Functional MRI

4. Objective cognitive functional evaluations

   An evolving focus, which needs incorporation into clinical evaluations as they evolve

   Measures of cognitive testing, such as computerized batteries

As noted previously in this chapter, it is debatable whether most standardized tests are able to correlate specific neurological areas of function and dysfunction. While helpful in evaluating a given patient's dysfunction, they have never been considered definitive in identifying the neurological structures causing CNS dysfunction. The key to ultimately understanding the neurological structures of AD/HD and its subtypes in an objective manner is neuroimaging and the evolution of meta-bolic/immune markers to explain the physiological model of dysfunction.

THERAPY/PROGNOSIS

As discussed by Culbert and colleagues (1994) and others, while treatments for AD/HD vary, "successful treatment of AD/HD includes the fostering of normal development, as well as interventions directed at removing the problematic behaviors and treating associated problems." However, "longitudinal studies indicate that 60–70% of children who have AD/HD are still symptomatic into adulthood" (p. 6). This finding contradicts the accepted teaching of twenty years ago, that the majority of hyperactive/hyperkinetic children outgrew this problem with the start of puberty, adolescence, and neurologic maturation. As noted, over the last ten to fifteen years, it has become clear that many patients with AD/HD continue to suffer into later life, and that this persistence may or may not be associated with alcohol/drug addiction or ongoing psychosocial dysfunction.

While researchers debate the true incidence of dysfunction, and whether it was overlooked in teenagers and adults twenty years ago, there are now enough patients with different types of AD/HD so that the disorder cannot be overlooked or dismissed. In a 1990 study by Zametkin and colleagues, it was found that adults with AD/HD had lowered cerebral glucose metabolism in the premotor cortex and in the superior prefrontal cortex, which may be more consistent with the NeuroSPECT findings of the quiet ADD rather than the classical hyper AD/HD. Hallowell and Ratey (1994) found that in most samples of adults with no childhood evaluation or treatment, a substantially greater number of females were present. While unexplainable by past theories, many physicians have thought that women are much more susceptible to autoimmune diseases than men. If portions of AD/HD are immune or autoimmune in origin, that might explain an increased percentage of women in certain AD/HD populations, and the large increase in quiet AD/HD, which is probably immune related. We must develop tools to better define AD/HD and reevaluate modes of therapy based on different medical factors and etiologies. As illustrated in figures 18–5 and 18–6, and supported by ongoing clinical research, AD/HD dysfunction is a changeable phenomenon.

Wender (1995) and others report that medical training twenty to twenty-five years ago taught that AD/HD was typically outgrown by adolescence. Pharmacologists believed that while paradoxically a group of hyper children would respond to stimulant medications and slow down and be better able to focus and attend, one should never use such medications on adolescents and adults. Given the NeuroSPECT findings

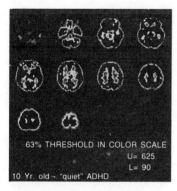

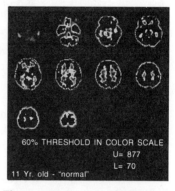

Figure 18–5. NeuroSPECT of a 10-year-old girl with quiet AD/HD.

Figure 18–6. NeuroSPECT of an 11-year-old girl; normal s/p (post) therapy.

(Campbell et al. 1996) that Ritalin and stimulant medications act as vasoconstrictors on the brain similar to cocaine (Wang et al. 1994), there is even more urgency to correctly diagnose AD/HD in adolescents and adults.

Many researchers have argued that AD/HD is an ill-defined constellation of behaviors without definable biologic etiology (Reid et al. 1994), and that most of the subjective scales currently in use are insufficient. Part of the problem is defining what is normal behavior and what is excessive. NeuroSPECT, advanced functional MRIs, and PET scans are critical tools in helping to objectify this nebulous diagnosis and invaluable in developing effective therapies and a positive long-term prognosis. These same tools will also be indispensable in our quest to overcome the problems of monitoring and evaluating therapy for these children. A recent article evaluating stimulant therapies illustrates the ongoing problems within the field (Efron et al. 1997). While the authors note the division of patients into AD/HD mixed type, AD/HD predominantly inattentive, and AD/HD predominantly hyperactive/impulsive, they do not break down their data by these subgroups, or further define these subgroups. Without attention to neuroimaging and new biological markers, patients can be misdiagnosed, jeopardizing their long-term therapy and prognosis.

Confusion remains about the specificity and sensitivity of the observation of symptoms in reports by parents, teachers, psychologists, and therapists. Normal psychological variants must be distinguished from physiological, medical patterns of dysfunction. Better therapeutic approaches, are needed, as are accurate prognostic indicators.

The ever-increasing number of children with AD/HD is rapidly overloading our mental health system. If a group of these children are medical in origin, and perhaps "correctable" by new approaches to therapy, then their need for long-term therapy might well be reduced, and existing resources better allocated to help the remaining children.

As this medical/pediatric group of AD/HD increases in number, the biologically different subgroups, their etiologies, and the medical and physiological dysfunction symptoms must be sorted out and understood. One cannot help but be impressed by the emergence of increased cognitive dysfunctional states in children and adults, the emergence of new chronic illnesses associated with memory and cognitive dysfunction such as CFS, and the potential connection to physiologic causes and biologic aspects of AD/HD symptoms. At a 1990 international conference on postviral fatigue syndrome (PVFS, the forerunner of CFIDS), Byron Hyde of Ottawa, Canada identified this syndrome as an overlooked epidemic in children. He said,

> It is evident we are not recognizing these children: they are there. They are there in large numbers. Depression, loss of energy, retardation of thought process, impairment of concentration, etc. These may be dyslexics, children that were getting good marks in grades six and seven, come down with a minor viral infection, and then become school problems. They sometimes get kicked out of school, sometimes sent off to psychologists. Parents do not believe these kids, the doctors definitely

do not. Impairment of memory, disorders of sleep, and the behavioral disorders are typical of the changes you see in children.

As Dr. Hyde noted, they become difficult kids and may eventually turn to drugs and even suicide. If their physiological dysfunction remains undetected and untreated, or treated incorrectly, it is unlikely that counseling or therapy alone will be very successful.

Therefore, we urgently need to reevaluate our definition of successful therapy and subsequent selection of therapeutic agents for these children. If applied and used constructively, the new technologies may give us a more objective understanding of what is occurring in a patient's CNS, and what the effects are of various medications and/or therapeutic modalities. These technologies stimulate optimism for the future. The ability to quantitate and differentiate patterns of dysfunction has the potential to objectify our understanding of AD/HD and other learning disorders. As educators and psychologists recognize these different disorders, the ability for them to develop specific, constructive therapeutic interventions for each type of dysfunction can begin to emerge. With a greater understanding of etiology comes the optimism that by being able to direct therapy at the cause rather than the effect, we may be much more successful pharmacologically and therapeutically. With an improved understanding of dysfunction will come better methods to improve the focus of our educational/rehabilitative efforts therapeutically, pharmacologically, and metabolically. If the causes are addressed rather than the effects or symptoms, the long-term prognosis should improve.

At the Advances in Social Brain Symposium in 1997, many top experts from the fields of neurology, neuroimmunology, and neurobiology discussed the brain in Alzheimer's disease and prefrontal temporal dementias in adults and autism/PDD in children. New insights were provided into the dysfunction of various areas of the brain, but there was little investigation or understanding of the cause of these dysfunctions. Subsequent discussions with other researchers and neurologists in this area have led me to the realization that up to now brain research has focused on identifying a problem and defining that problem, but the tools to investigate the cause of the problem were lacking. The best chance of success in treatment of any dysfunction requires focusing on the origin of the problem, not just on its consequences. It is my hope that we will see a rapid merging of the new knowledge and expertise discussed in this book, so that a more integrated effort may maximize a child's chance to learn and to succeed.

Medical research uses the scientific process with controlled studies. However, in a field predominated by subjective symptoms and the lack of consensus about objective or definite studies, what do controlled trials entail? What are we controlling? We must integrate new objective imaging and computerized profiles with clinical observation, evaluation, and test data, so that we may fully define what patient populations need what types of therapy. To be successful in this endeavor, we need an integrative approach combining various modalities (old and new) such as pharmaceutical (neurotropic agents, immune modulators), psychological, educational, and biological (metabolic, biofeedback, etc.) to most effectively address and treat the various aspects of AD/HD dysfunction.

ACKNOWLEDGMENTS

I thank for their help and contribution, my wife, Elyse Goldberg, without whom this work with these children would not have been possible, and Adam Zaffos, a future M.D.

REFERENCES

Amen, D. G., and Carmichael, B. D. (1997). High-resolution brain SPECT imaging in AD/HD. *Annals of Clinical Psychiatry* 2(9):81–86.

Baren, M., and Swanson, J. M. (1996). How *not* to diagnose AD/HD. *Contemporary Pediatrics* 13:53–64.

Barkley, R. A. (1995). Is there an attention deficit in AD/HD? *AD/HD Report* 3:1–4.

Barkley, R. A., and DuPaul, G. J. (1990). Comprehensive evaluation of attention deficit disorder with and without hyperactivity as defined by research criteria. *Journal of Consulting and Clinical Psychology* 58(6):775–789.

Barkley, R. A., DuPaul, G. J., and McMurray, M. B. (1991). Attention deficit disorder with and without hyperactivity: clinical response to three dose levels of methylphenidate. *Pediatrics* 87(4):519–531.

Barkley, R. A., Grodzinsky, G., and DuPaul, G. J. (1992). Frontal lobe functions in attention deficit disorder with and without hyperactivity: a review and research report. *Journal of Abnormal Child Psychology* 20(2):163–188.

Barrickman, L., Noyes, R., Kuperman, S., et al. (1991). Treatment of AD/HD with fluoxetine: a preliminary trial. *Journal of the American Academy of Child and Adolescent Psychiatry* 5(30):762–767.

Baumgaertel, A., Wolraich, M. L., and Dietrich, M. (1995). Comparison of diagnostic criteria for attention deficit disorders in a German elementary school sample. *Journal of the American Academy of Child and Adolescent Psychiatry* 34(5):629–638.

Behrman, R. E., ed. (1992). *Nelson Textbook of Pediatrics*, assoc. ed. R. M. Kliegman; senior eds. W. E. Nelson and V. C. Vaughan III, 14th ed. Philadelphia: Saunders.

——— (1996). *Nelson Textbook of Pediatrics*, assoc. ed. R. M. Kliegman; senior eds. W. E. Nelson and V. C. Vaughan III, 15th ed. Philadelphia: Saunders.

Benson, D. F. (1991). The role of frontal dysfunction in attention deficit hyperactivity disorder. *Journal of Child Neurology* 6(suppl):S9–12.

Boris, M., and Mandel, F. S. (1994). Foods and additives are common causes of the attention deficit hyperactive disorder in children. *Annals of Allergy* 72(suppl 5):462–468.

Breakey, J. (1997). The role of diet and behaviour in childhood. *Journal of Paediatric Child Health* 33(suppl 3):190–194.

Campbell, L., Malone, M. A., Kershner, J. R., et al. (1996). Methylphenidate slows right hemisphere processing in children with attention-deficit/hyperactivity disorder. *Journal of Child and Adolescent Psychopharmacology* 4(6):229–239.

Cantwell, D. P. (1996). Attention deficit disorder: a review of the past 10 years [see comments]. *Journal of the American Academy of Child and Adolescent Psychiatry* 35(8):978–987.

Cantwell, D. P., and Baker, L. (1992). Attention deficit disorder with and without hyperactivity: a review and comparison of matched groups. *Journal of the American Academy of Child and Adolescent Psychiatry* 31(3):432–438.

Comings, D. E. (1997). Genetic aspects of childhood behavioral disorders. *Child Psychiatry and Human Development* 27(3):139–150.

Connor, D. F., and Steingard, R. J. (1996). A clinical approach to the pharmacotherapy of aggression in children and adolescents. *Annals of the New York Academy of Sciences* 794:290–307.

Costa, D. C., Brostoff, J., and Ell, P. J. (1992). Brain stem hypoperfusion in patients with myalgic encephalomyelitis—chronic fatigue syndrome (abstr.). *European Journal of Nuclear Medicine* 19(8):733.

Culbert, T. P., Banez, G. A., and Reiff, M. I. (1994). Children who have attentional disorders: interventions. *Pediatrics in Review* 15:5–14.

Denckla, M. B. (1996). Biological correlates of learning and attention: What is relevant to learning disability and attention-deficit hyperactivity disorder? *Journal of Developmental and Behavioral Pediatrics* 17:114–119.

Efron, D., Jarman, F., and Barker, M. (1997). Side effects of methylphenidate and dexamphetamine in children with attention deficit hyperactivity disorder: a double-blind, crossover trial. *Pediatrics* 100:662–666.

Ernst, M., Zametkin, A. J., Matochik, J. A., et al. (1994). Effects of intravenous dextroamphetamine on brain metabolism in adults with attention-deficit hyperactivity disorder (AD/HD). Preliminary findings. *Psychopharmacology Bulletin* 2(30):219–225.

Faraone, S. V., Biederman, J., Lehman, B. K., et al. (1993). Intellectual performance and school failure in children with attention deficit hyperactivity disorder and in their siblings. *Journal of Abnormal Psychology* 4(102):616–623.

Findling, R. L. (1996). Open-label treatment of comorbid depression and attentional disorders with co-administration of serotonin reuptake inhibitors and psychostimulants in children, adolescents, and adults: a case series. *Journal of Child and Adolescent Psychopharmacology* 3(6):165–175.

Hallowell, E. M., and Ratey, J. J. (1994). *Driven to Distraction.* New York: Touchstone/Simon & Schuster.

Hazell, P. (1997). The overlap of attention deficit hyperactivity disorder with other common mental disorders. *Journal of Paediatric Child Health* 33:131–137.

Heuser, G., Mena, I., and Alamos, F. (1994). NeuroSPECT findings in patients exposed to neurotoxic chemicals. *Toxicology and Industrial Health* 4–5(10):561–571.

Hyde, B. (1990). First International Conference on Post Viral Fatigue Syndrome, Los Angeles, CA, February 18.

Ichise, M., Salit, I. E., Abbey, S. E., et al. (1992). Assessment of regional cerebral perfusion in 99 Tem-HMPAO SPECT in chronic fatigue syndrome. *Nuclear Medicine Communications* 13:767–772.

Kong, D. S. (1995). Psychiatric disorders in pre-schoolers. *Singapore Medical Journal* 36(3):318–321.

Levy, F., and Bircher, A. (1994). Allergic reactions of the respiratory tract. *Therapeutische Umschau* 51(1):24–30.

Levy, F., Hay, D. A., McStephen, M., et al. (1997). Attention-deficit hyperactivity disorder: a category or a continuum? Genetic analysis of a large-scale twin study. *Journal of the American Academy of Child and Adolescent Psychiatry* 36(6):737–744.

Loge, D. V., Staton, R. D., Beatty, W. W., et al. (1990). Performance of children with AD/HD on tests sensitive to frontal lobe dysfunction. *Journal of the American Academy of Child and Adolescent Psychiatry* 29(suppl 4):540–545.

Matochik, J. A., Liebenauer, L. L., King, A. C., et al. (1994). Cerebral glucose metabolism in adults with attention deficit hyperactivity disorder after chronic stimulant treatment. *American Journal of Psychiatry* 5(151):658–664.

Matochik, J. A., Zametkin, A. J., Cohen, R. M., et al. (1996). Abnormalities in sustained attention and anterior cingulate metabolism in subjects with resistance to thyroid hormone. *Brain Research* 723(1–2):23–28.

Olvera, R. L., Pliszka, S. R., Luh, J., and Tatum, R. (1996). An open trial of venlafaxine in the treatment of attention-deficit/hyperactivity disorder in children and adolescents. *Journal of Child and Adolescent Psychopharmacology* 4(6):241–250.

Palmeri, S. (1996). Attention-deficit hyperactivity disorder: sometimes a disorder, often a clinical tautology. *Journal of Developmental and Behavioral Pediatrics* 17:253–254.

Raskin, A., Altman, L., and Reating, N., eds. Workshop on attention deficit disorders. *Psychopharmacology Bulletin* 21:169.

Reeve, R. A., and Brown, A. L. (1985). Metacognition reconsidered: implications for intervention research. *Journal of Abnormal Child Psychology* 13(suppl 3):343–356.

Reid, R., and Maag, J. W. (1994). Attention deficit hyperactivity disorder as a disability category: a critique. *Exceptional Children* 60:198–214.

Richters, J. E., Arnold, L. E., Jensen, P. S., et al. (1995). NIMH collaborative multisite multimodal treatment study of children with AD/HD: I. Background and rationale. *Journal of the American Academy of Child and Adolescent Psychiatry* 34(8):987–1000.

Robson, W. L. M., Jackson, H. P., et al. (1997). Enuresis in children with attention-deficit hyperactivity disorder. *Southern Medical Journal* 90:503–505.

Shaywitz, B. A., Sullivan, C. M., Anderson, G. M., et al. (1994). Aspartame, behavior, and cognitive function in children with attention deficit disorder. *Pediatrics* 93:70–75.

Sieg, K. G., Gaffney, G. R., Preston, D. F., and Hellings, J. A. (1995). SPECT brain imaging abnormalities in attention deficit hyperactivity disorder. *Clinical Nuclear Medicine* 1(20):55–60.

Wang, G. J., Volkow, N. D., Fowler, J. S., et al. (1994). Methylphendiate decreases regional blood flow in normal human subjects. *Life Sciences* 9:143–146.

Weinberg, W. A., Harper, C. R., Schraufnagel, C. D., et al. (1997). Attention deficit hyperactivity disorder: a disease or a symptom complex? *Journal of Pediatrics* 130:6–9.

Weiss, R. E., Stein, M. A., Trommer, B., et al. (1993). Attention-deficit hyperactivity disorder and thyroid function. *Journal of Pediatrics* 123:539–545.

Wender, E. H. (1995). Attention-deficit hyperactivity disorders in adolescence. *Journal of Developmental and Behavioral Pediatrics* 16:192–195.

Wolraich, M. L., Hannah, J. N., Pinnock, T. Y., Baumgaertel, A., and Brown, J. (1996). Comparison of diagnostic criteria for attention-deficit hyperactivity disorder in a county-wide sample. *Journal of the American Academy of Child and Adolescent Psychiatry* 35(3):319–324.

Zametkin, A. J. (1995). Attention-deficit disorder. Born to be hyperactive? *Journal of the American Medical Association* 273:1871–1874.

Zametkin, A. J., Nordahl, T. E., and Gross, M., et al. (1990). Cerebral glucose metabolism in adults with hyperactivity of childhood onset. *New England Journal of Medicine* 323(20):1361–1366.

Zametkin, A. J., and Rapoport, J. L. (1986). The pathophysiology of attention deficit disorder with hyperactivity. *Advances in Clinical Child Physiology* 9:55.

Subject Index